ANTÆUS
JUBILEE EDITION
FICTION · POETRY · DOCUMENTS

ANTÆUS was founded in 1969 by Paul Bowles, and began publication a year later, edited by Daniel Halpern and published by Drue Heinz. Since 1970, it has established itself as one of the most successful and distinguished literary magazines in the world. In more than sixty issues it has published work by a wide range of internationally known writers and also, equally important, writers who are beginning to make their reputations. Contributors to *Antæus* have included W.H. Auden, Mario Vargas Llosa, Marguerite Duras, Joseph Brodsky, John Fowles, Czeslaw Milosz, Edna O'Brien, Richard Ford, Josef Škvorecký, V.S. Naipaul, Peter Matthiessen, Italo Calvino, Seamus Heaney, Joyce Carol Oates, Edmund White, Oliver Sacks, Stephen Spender and Raymond Carver. From time to time *Antæus* has produced special issues on a particular theme, and its literary interests have been wide – from Letters, Essays, Autobiography, Journals, Notebooks and Diaries to Poetry, Fiction, Nature Writing and studies of individual writers. These special issues are now being published in book form as Harvill Paperbacks and the following titles are available:

Antæus: Journals, Notebooks and Diaries (including Annie Dillard, M.F.K. Fisher, Mary Gordon, V.S. Naipaul, Edna O'Brien, Ursula Le Guin, Lawrence Durrell and Oliver Sacks)

Antæus: On Nature (including Italo Calvino, John Fowles, Jim Harrison, Edward Hoagland, Annie Dillard and Barry Lopez)

Antæus: Literature as Pleasure (including Richard Ford, Guy Davenport, Joyce Carol Oates, Gail Godwin, Charles Simic and Josef Škvorecký)

SELECTIONS FROM PAGE ONE

Never to lie is to have no lock to your door, you are never wholly alone.

—ELIZABETH BOWEN

The eye wants to sleep but the head is no mattress.

—HE OF THE ASSEMBLY

The dream of every honest cliché is to enter a great poem.

—CHARLES SIMIC

Eating is touch carried to the bitter end. —SAMUEL BUTLER II

What would be left of our tragedies if a literate insect were to present us his? —E. M. CIORAN

The ant sets an example to us all, but it is not a good one.

—MAX BEERBOHM

Fiction is obliged to stick to possibilities. Truth isn't. —MARK TWAIN

To sing the blues you have to live it, I can sing about my mule being stolen, so I don't have no way of actually getting my vegetables to the market, because that actually happened to me, but I can't sing about a bomb dropping on my house, they can do that in Europe, and that would be their blues. —BIG BILL BROONZY

The commonest ivory tower is that of the average man, the state of passivity towards experience. —W. H. AUDEN

I took a speed reading course and read *War and Peace* in twenty minutes. It involves Russia. —WOODY ALLEN

The hunting dogs are playing in the courtyard, but the hare will not escape them, no matter how fast it may be flying already through the woods. —FRANZ KAFKA

(Continued on page 428)

ANTÆUS

JUBILEE EDITION

FICTION · POETRY · DOCUMENTS

Edited by Daniel Halpern

Harvill
An Imprint of HarperCollins*Publishers*

Publisher
DRUE HEINZ
Founding Editor
PAUL BOWLES
Managing Editor
LEE ANN CHEARNEYI
Promotion Manager
BRUCE SHERWIN
Advertising Manager
LEE SMITH
Assistant Editors
JULIETTE GUILBERT
CATHY JEWELL
THOMAS KRADER
Contributing Editors

ANDREAS BROWN	STANLEY KUNITZ
JOHN FOWLES	W.S. MERWIN
DONALD HALL	EDOUARD ROTI
JOHN HAWKES	MARK STRAND

First published in the USA in 1990
by The Ecco Press, New York
First published in Great Britain in 1991
by Harvill
an imprint of HarperCollins Publishers,
77/85 Fulham Palace Road,
Hammersmith,
London W6 8JB

9 8 7 6 5 4 3 2 1

Copyright © *Antæus* 1990

BRITISH LIBRARY CATALOGUING IN PUBLICATION DATA

A record of the CIP data is available from the British Library

ISBN 0-00-272037-X

Printed and bound in Great Britain by
HarperCollins Book Manufacturing, Glasgow

CONTENTS

FICTION

JOHN ASHBERY

Just Wednesday

So it likes light and likes
to be teased out about it—please
don't take me literally. That winter light
should be upon us soon in all its splendor—
I can see it now—and the likes of the haves
shall mingle with the have-nots, to some point
this time, we all hope, and the pride encoded
in the selection process that made us what we are,
that made our great religions fit us,
will be deployed, a maplike fan so you can
actually sit down

and find us where we came from. True, some
at first claimed they recognized it and later
admitted they didn't, as though the slow rise
of history were just some tune. That didn't prevent others
from really finishing the job, and in the process
turning up points of gold that are we say these
things we shall have, now. And the jolly
carpentered tune merely played along with all that
as an obbligato, but on a day
took up residence in its own strength.
A weary sense of triumph ensued but it was the reality
of creation. There were no two ways.

And so one emerged scalded with the apprehension of this,
that this was what it was like. You gave me a penny, I
gave you two copies of the same word that were to fit
you like rubber ears. It is my fault if in the dust
of the sensation something got knowingly underscored, defaced,
a shame to all the nation?
After all, it suited when you set out dressed

in plum and Mama was to meet us at the midpoint
of the journey but she got taken away and an old
dressmaker's dummy draped in soiled lace was substituted
for the intricate knowledge at this juncture.
The grass grew looser but closer together,
the flowers husky and fierce as trees. On the spiffy
ground no wagers were taken and a few minutes'
absence is the bee's knees. It behooves

you to depart if the moon is cowled.
That homeless blanket you gave up—
you should have sent them both years ago. A few
cronies still gather there where the shore
was explained and now the waves
explain it with renewed mastery and suds. Almost
time for the watchman to tell it to the lamplighter
and I'll be switched, after all these years.

MARVIN BELL

He Had a Good Year

while he was going blind. Autumnal light
gave to ordinary things the turning
beauty of leaves, rich with their losing.
A shade of yellow, that once stood opaque
in the rainbow of each glitzy morning,
now became translucent, as if the sun
broke against his own window. As for white,
it was now too much of everything,
as the flat deprivations of the color black
moved farther away: echoes of a surface
unseen and misremembered. I must tell you
how he managed as the lights went slowly out
to look inside the top glow of each object
and make in his mind a spectrum of inner
texture, of an essence isolate from the
nervous trembling of things struck by light.
"Ah, if God were only half the man he is,"
he said, "he would see things this way."

EAVAN BOLAND

On the Gift of The Birds of America
by John James Audubon

What you have given me is, of course, elegy:
the red-shouldered hawk in among these
scattering partridges,
flustered at

such a descent, and the broad-winged one
poised on the branch of a pignut, and the pine
siskin and the wren are
an inference

we follow in the plummet of the tern
which appears to be, from one angle anyway,
impossibly fragile and
if we imagine

the franchise of light these camphor-colored
wings opened out once with and are at
such a loss for now, then
surely this

is the nature and effect of elegy:
the celebration of an element which absence
has revealed: it is
our earthliness

we love as we look at them, which we fear
to lose, which we need this rephrasing
of the air, of the ocean
to remind us of

that evening late in May when the Clare hills
were ghostly with white hawthorn and
two swans flew over us.
I can still hear

the musical insistence of their wings as
they came in past the treetops, near the lake.
And we looked up,
rooted to the spot.

JANE COOPER

Bloodroot

Reading your words
to find they are
just your words . . .

Waking:
what is this heaviness? only
a matter of money, or closure. Oh yes, the lease,
the rent is going up.

During the war
how I shouted at my mother:
It's only a thing! A thing got broken, suppose
some friend had been killed!

Reading your words.
Remembering how we were friends
in, say, 1974.

Fifteen years ago now, and the whole body
changes, every living cell,
in seven years, and seven years,

and now this one:
fragile as bloodroot,

releasing its unhurried freshness,
half earth, half air.

NUALA NÍ DHOMHNAILL

TRANSLATED FROM THE IRISH BY PAUL MULDOON

Nude

The long and short
of it is I'd far rather see you nude—
your silk shirt
and natty

tie, the brolly under your oxter
in case of a rainy day,
the three-piece seersucker
suit that's so incredibly trendy,

your snazzy loafers
and, la-di-da,
a pair of gloves
made from the skin of a doe,

then, to top it all, a crombie hat
set at a rak-
ish angle—none of these adds
up to more than the icing on the cake.

For, unbeknownst to the rest
of the world, behind the outward
show lies a body unsurpassed
for beauty, without so much as a wart

or blemish, but the brill-
iant slink of a wild animal, a dream-
cat, say, on the prowl,
leaving murder and mayhem

in its wake. Your broad, sinewy
shoulders and your flank
smooth as the snow
on a snowbank.

Your back, your slender waist,
and, of course,
the root that is the very seat
of pleasure, the pleasure-source.

Your skin so dark, my beloved,
and soft
as silk with a hint of velvet
in its weft,

smelling as it does of meadowsweet
or watermead
that has the power, or so it's said,
to drive men and women mad.

For that reason alone, if for no other,
when you come with me to the dance tonight
(though, as you know, I'd much prefer
to see you nude)

it would probably be best
for you to pull on your pants and vest
rather than send
half the women of Ireland totally round the bend.

DEBORAH DIGGES

London Zoo

Love takes liberties. So much gets by us,
as if the trick were learning not to want
   what doesn't want us. Here, for instance,
the animals seem happy. Even the sparrows
   stay. Children stop to feed them on the paths
between the cages. A bird swims underwater,
   stripes on the zebra and the zebra fish.
What we want, what we want is a lyric
   for forgetting, like the skill to fall
backward through the genes past wanting,

   past fear of falling, "faith," as if the tombs
of the muses were so many bombed-out
   houses the homeless set up camp inside,
careful to turn their backs at night
   on those ransacked rooms, careful to keep
their fires going where the little rain-soaked
   wallpaper flowers shine by the moon-dogged
moon *blessings on the hunter* and on
   the wanderer, his keepsake soul, though
the list of his extinctions approach his

   numbered wishes, though his child be a mooncalf,
though he spit on the angel whose likeness
   is a hanged man cut down some midnight
four centuries ago, and then by torchlight,
   opened in an alley, the hands severed
and set aside on which the pale hairs stand,
   as in love or terror of ascent,
the dead bright blood caught in a bowl of sand,
   and, freebased, distills the pigment for
the background's first spring or autumn cypresses.

ANNIE DILLARD

Light in the Open Air

pieced from The Nature of Light and Colour in the Open Air,
by nineteenth-century Dutch physicist M. Minnaert

Part One

Everything described in this book
is within your own powers of understanding and observation.

The Dark Inner Part.

The Bright Outer Part.

The Variability of the Colour of the Blue Sky:

> Try to imagine that you are looking at a painting
> and admire the evenness and the delicacy
> of the transitions.

The Blue Sky:

> What is the explanation of this curious phenomenon?

> What can be the cause of this wonderful blue?

> Compare the blue of the sky
> with the skies of Italy during your holiday.

The Colours of the Sun, Moon and Stars:

> It is difficult to judge the colour of the sun,
> owing to its dazzling brightness. Personally,
> however, I should say it is decidedly yellow. . . .

Be very cautious during these observations!
Do not overstrain your eyes!

Study the illumination. . . .

Compare the light. . . .

Compare the illumination. . . .

Compare the luminosity. . . .

Compare the light inside and outside a wood.

Intercept one of these images by a piece of paper.

Part Two

Above all study your surroundings intently.

Move your opera-glasses gently a little to the left,
then to the right, and back again to the left. . . .

> The Colour of Lakes.
>
> The Colour of Puddles along the Road.
>
> Strong Wind Rising, Grey Sky.

One more reason to keep our eyes open.

Which are the feeblest stars
perceptible by you?

Practice on cold evenings. . . .

How dark is this shadow?

Notice how much better you succeed with a little practice!

Estimate the strength of the ash-grey light
on a scale from 1 to 10. . . .

Watch the separate breakers along the shore. . . .

Imagine a pool of water in a hollow of the dunes:

> Be sure to carry out this experiment;
> it is as convincing as it is surprising!

Examine systematically the colours of the shadows!

Draw up a scale for the phosphorescence of the sea!

Everything is meant to be seen by you and done by you!

Always try to find the explanation.

This causes a very peculiar sensation,
difficult to describe.

STEPHEN DOBYNS

The Body's Hope

Whatever lifts the body up—muscles,
sinews, joints—whatever wrestles against
gravity itself—the raised step, the lifted arm—
these form the body's hope. But also hunger,

selfishness, desire, all that leads us
to put one foot in front of the other,
these too form the body's hope, whatever
combats that urge to lie down—greed,

anger, lust—these feelings keep us going,
while the imagination sketches pictures
of the desired future, how we will look
in that new hat, how we will feel

with a belly full of cherries: anything
that shoves us from this moment to the next,
motivation like a flight of stairs, and hope
like a push at the top, not dissatisfaction

but eagerness to plunge into the next second:
hope like a policeman urging the crowd along,
the travel agent with enticing descriptions
of where to go next, the tour guide director

with someplace specific to get to before dark.
You know those French châteaux where you stop
for a few hours on a summer afternoon,
how you are ushered through the ornate front doors,

shown the bed where Louis the Something slept,
the chairs where Madame de Maintenon sat,

then you are escorted to a door in the back,
and it is over and the peacocks cry their

abrasive cries and you return to your cars?
Life struggles to copy that French château,
while hope is the person leading you through
with promises of the splendor of the next room.

But the great bed looks fusty and hard,
and the chair is just a chair and on the way out
you pass tourists coming in and you want to tell them
not to bother, but hope has you by the arm.

Without hope we'd still be learning how to crawl,
while thinking, What's the point? We'd still
be staring into our first bowl of porridge
and fiddling with our spoons. Hope moves our feet.

It is the constant encourager, the enemy
of the stationary, the promiser of better moments.
In the next room waits a woman to curl our toes,
then a twelve-pound diamond, then the prize

to raise us higher than all the rest—oh, why
aren't we running faster?—hope: our dearest
enemy, slick-talking advance man for death itself,
and the back door beckons and the peacocks cry.

Desire

A woman in my class wrote that she is sick
of men wanting her body and when she reads
her poem out loud the other women all nod
and even some of the men lower their eyes

and look abashed as if ready to unscrew
their cocks and pound down their own dumb heads
with these innocent sausages of flesh, and none
would think of confessing his hunger

or admit how desire can ring like a constant
low note in the brain or grant how the sight
of a beautiful woman can make him groan
on those first spring days when the parkas

have been packed away and the bodies are staring
at the bodies and the eyes stare at the ground;
and there was a man I knew who even at ninety
swore that his desire had never diminished.

Is this simply the wish to procreate, the world
telling the cock to eat faster, while the cock
yearns for that moment when it forgets its loneliness
and the world flares up in an explosion of light?

Why have men been taught to feel ashamed
of their desire, as if each were a criminal
out on parole, a desperado with a long record
of muggings, rapes, such conduct as excludes

each one from all but the worst company,
and never to be trusted, no, never to be trusted?

Why must men pretend to be indifferent as if each
were a happy eunuch engaged in spiritual thoughts?

But it's the glances that I like, the quick ones,
the unguarded ones, like a hand snatching a pie
from a window ledge and the feet pounding away;
eyes fastening on a leg, a breast, the curve

of a buttock, as the pulse takes an extra thunk
and the cock, that toothless worm, stirs in its sleep,
and fat possibility swaggers into the world
like a big spender entering a bar. And sometimes

the woman glances back. Oh, to disappear
in a tangle of fabric and flesh as the cock
sniffs out its little cave, and the body hungers
for closure, for the completion of the circle,

as if each of us was born only half a body
and we spend our lives searching for the rest.
What good does it do to deny desire, to chain
the cock to the leg and scrawl a black X

across its bald head, to hold out a hand
for each passing woman to slap? Better
to be bad and unrepentant, better to celebrate
each difference, not to be cruel or gluttonous

or overbearing, but full of hope and self-forgiving.
The flesh yearns to converse with other flesh.
Each pore loves to linger over its particular story.
Let these seconds not be full of self-recrimination

and apology. What is desire but the wish for some
relief from the self, the prisoner let out
into a small square of sunlight with a single
red flower and a bird crossing the sky, to lean back

against the bricks with the legs outstretched,
to feel the sun warming the brow, before returning
to one's mortal cage, steel doors slamming
in the cell block, steel bolts sliding shut?

The Body's Curse

Sad to say there's more than one—loneliness
for example. What a devil. No one understands you,
no one wants to touch you, while the skin grows cold
and the mind has all the vigor of wet paper.

Yet I know people who are so distrustful
of the folks around them that when anyone gets
too close, they push them away. Get lost, they say.
Of course they are miserable, the poor babies,

but they think it is better to be tough from the start,
than to have some trickster turn on them later.
Loneliness for them is what's safest, although
no one is happy or likes getting up in the morning,

no one sings in the shower. And then there's pride:
that sense of self that says the self's first-rate.
But how hungry it gets, how malnourished, yet how
it poisons the world. I knew a fellow who received

a great gift and because someone he despised
was given an equal gift he destroyed his own.
His pride made each thing smaller than it was,
leaving him bitter, dissatisfied. And then

we have opinions, those conclusions which say
that what you don't know doesn't count: the ballot box
is closed, the votes are tallied and the decision
is reached that the world is flat or she loves you

not or that man's a fool. So even the smartest
grow ignorant and stumble through the twilight

like all the rest. And then ambition, that quest
to leave the road behind one packed with monuments

to one's own perfection, a statue in the park
to show the world one isn't the jerk one thinks
in those dark moments of the night. Or sexual hunger,
thirsting for ladies as a bowling ball thirsts for pins,

then casting them aside, the beauty forgotten
while still clasped in a postorgasmic embrace.
Greed, gluttony, sloth—but don't they all
go back to loneliness, that sense of a barrier

between oneself and others, as if they saw differently,
felt differently, as if one were a dog surrounded
by skeptical cats? And so a man develops pride,
ambition and all the rest, just to prove

that the awful place with which he has been blessed
is a blessing after all. He may *seem* miserable—
the loneliness gnawing him like a cancer—
but actually that pain is the pain of success,

and he makes his little smile that creaks
and walks on, while what he really wants
is to be held and stroked and be told: Poor thing.
Yet even were he to get it he would break it,

like someone giving him a ceramic plate,
he would hurl it to the sidewalk, hitch up
his pants and hobble away. What can be done?
Who can say what another man wants?

Ask the mouth, it says More. Ask the feet,
they say Faster. Try the hands, they say Mine.
Question the whole crazy and quarrelsome
conglomeration, and it says Touch me.

STEPHEN DUNN

A Secret Life

Why you need to have one
is not much more mysterious than
why you don't say what you think
at the birth of an ugly baby.
Or, you've just made love
and feel you'd rather have been
in a dark booth where your partner
was nodding, whispering yes, yes,
you're brilliant. The secret life
begins early, is kept alive
by all that's unpopular
in you, all that you know
a Baptist, say, or some other
accountant would object to.
It becomes what you'd most protect
if the government said you can protect
one thing, all else is ours.
When you write late at night
it's like a small fire
in a clearing, it's what
radiates and what can hurt
if you get too close to it.
It's why your silence is a kind of truth.
Even when you speak to your best friend,
the one who'll never betray you,
you always leave out one thing;
a secret life is that important.

CAROLYN FORCHÉ

The Recording Angel

I

Memory insists she stood there, neither able to go forward nor back,
and in that
Unanimous night, time slowed, in light pulsing through ash, light of
which the coat was made, light of their brick houses
In matter's choreography of light, time slowed, then reversed until
memory held her, neither able to go forward nor back
They were alone where once hundreds of thousands lived

Doves, or rather their wings heard above the roof and the linens
floating
Above a comic wedding in which corpses exchange vows. (A grand
funeral celebration. Everyone has died at once.)
Walking home always, always on this same blue road, cold through
the black and white trees
Unless the film were reversed, she wouldn't reach the house, as she
doesn't in her memory, or in her dream
Often she hears him calling out, half her name, his own, behind her
in a room until she turns
Standing forever, where often she hears him calling out

He is there, hidden in the blue winter fields and the burnt acreage of
summer
As if, in reflecting the ruins, the river were filming what their city
had been
And *had it not been for this* lines up behind *if it weren't for that*, until
the past is something of a regiment
Yet look back down the row of marching faces one sees one face
Before the shelling, these balconies were for geraniums and children
The slate roofs for morning

Market flowers in a jar, a string of tied garlic, and a voice moving
    off as if fearing itself
Under the lepered trees a white siren of light searches
Under the lepered trees a white siren of sun

II

A row of cabanas with white towels near restorative waters—this
    place, where once it was possible to be cured
A town of vacant summer houses
Mists burning the slightest lapse of sea
The child has gone to the window filled with desire, the glass light
    passing through its hand
There are tide tables by which the sea had been predictable, as were
    the heavens
As sickness chose from among us we grew fewer
There were jetty lights where there was no jetty
What the rain forests had been became our difficult breath

At the moment when the snow geese lifted, thousands at once after
    days of crying in the wetlands
At once they lifted in a single ascent, acres of wind in their
    wingbones
Wetlands of morning light in their lift
Moving as one over the continent, as a white front, one in their
    radiance, in their crying, a cloud of desire
The child plays with his dead telephone. The father blows a kiss.
    The child laughs
The fire of his few years is carried toward the child on a cake
The child can't help himself. Would each day be like this?
Hours on film yet only a moment of normal life

And the geese, rising and falling in the rain on a surf of black hands,
    sheets of rain and geese invisible or gone
Someone was supposed to have come
Waves turning black with the beach weed called dead men's hands
The sea strikes a bottle against a rock

III

The photographs were found at first by mistake in the drawer. After
    that I went to them often
She was standing on her toes in a silk *yukata*, her arms raised,
    wearing a girl's white socks and near her feet a vase of calla
    lilies
Otherwise she wore nothing
And in this one, her long hair is gathered into a white towel
Or tied back not to interfere
She had been wounded by so many men, abused by them
From behind in a silk *yukata*, then like this
One morning they were gone and I searched his belongings for them
    like a madwoman
In every direction, melted railyards, felled telegraph poles
For two months to find some trace of her
Footsteps on the floor above. More birds. It might have been less
    painful had it not been for the photographs
And beyond the paper walls, the red maple
Shirt in the wind of what the past meant
The fresh claw of a swastika on Rue Boulard
A man walking until he can no longer be seen
"Don't say I was there. Always say I was never there."

IV

The child asks about earth
The earth is a school. It is a waiting room, a foyer giving onto
    emptiness. It is for desires, small but beautifully done
The earth is wrapped in weather, and the weather in risen words
The child is awake, singing to himself, speaking in a language
    ending with the word *night*
Unaware of the sea entering, of the eternal dunes burying
Wooden matchsticks in a cup
The meaning of an object or its lack
Their preoccupation with suitcases and their contents
God returns to the world from within and the past
Is circular, like consequence
The earth tentative, blue: a fire wrapped in cold water

A sudden gust of yellow tickets, a cold blue rail and some boat lights
The barrier dunes, blue asters, the parabolic dunes, and wind
The children have returned to the beach, this time a boy and a girl
    hurrying toward then away from the water
He is wearing a red jacket and it is not important, the jacket
The child asks if fish have tongues. The other laughs, giving white
    tissues to the dog
A white sail tied over the bay's mouth muffles the sea
On the water's map, little x's: a cross-stitched sampler of cries for
    help
And yet every lost one has been seen, mornings in winter, and at
    night
When the fishermen have cast their nets one too many times
They surface, the lost, drawing great hillocks of breath
We on the shore no longer vanish when the beacon strokes us
The child's boat plies the water in imitation of boats
Years they sought her, whose crew left on the water a sad Welsh
    hymn
Voices from a ketch lit by candles
Days pass and nothing occurs, nights pass, nights, and life continues
    in its passing
We must try then to send a message ending with the word *night*

V

A river that later caught fire
A stone with its own list of names
Nothing that worked once can be tried again
That's what he told me. I didn't know
At night I found myself in a pasture of refuse
When the city vanished, they were carried on black mats from one
    place to another with no one to answer them
Vultures watching from the white trees
A portable safe found stuffed with charred paper
An incense burner fused to its black prayer
In the city's perfect emanation of light
We lost every alternate route
We were there, ill there, in the birthplace of humanity
In the last of the world's open cities, rain begins
The china cups are cleared from the chiming tables

A garden of black silk blooms
Forget the fish, the bottle, the bath towels stiffening on the grate
Sleeveless pajamas, skirts of fire and flowers
A girl's face turned toward a cup of water with no mouth
Hello child, hang your coat here. This is what she said after so many
    years. This was all she said

VI

It was an island wrapped in white fog, Angel Island, a wingless rock,
    a way station
Now it isn't possible to go farther, paper-thin and floating
Each small act of defiance a force
There would be blank winds in the debris and palm carnage in the
    half-life
Our faces are there
Mine bears the mark of your palm, yours the marks of gelignite
A bar of light touches the floor of a house long since torn down
Where the walls were, silence was
The playing cards you clipped to a window fan
To imitate the sound of helicopters all those nights
So as to return to the ruins of a wished-for life

Even the sign warning us away implied an obligation to go on
A bottle, a red bandana, a yellow bucket of bones behind the gate
We find a shovel near all of this
And as these were the final months, a radio

Their flesh like fallen snow
Leaf shadows burnt into a post
Burns of bamboo on bamboo canes
These ruins are to the future what the past is to us

VII

Someone has written FUCK with dogshit on the walls of Simone's
    atelier
A pall of exhaust over Paris
The woman with the shaved head seen twice in different
    arrondissements

Carolyn Forché / 35

And on Rue Victor Considérant, a boy with a white toy M-16
The days marched shouldering their little events
Tiny birds on the dining tables flew from spoon to bowl
As far as anyone knew, no one drowned
The hotel is no longer there
We were its final guests

A stone wall, white roses, birds and the whine of bright aerial
    antennas
Every window casement an empty portrait: radiant, formless,
    ancestral
In which he longs for her, whomever, her white bed
The remote possibility of another life
To look in the windows of that little place expecting someone
The two of us, the child, the two blue boats and the brown
The child comes into the room and leaves, comes and leaves

I loved her, he said, she was the woman of my life. Her blank eyes,
    her _____, this is what he loved
She sliced the photographs from their frames, chose what to bring
    with us, said
"Look what they've done to the windows! To my life."
You are a child, you think only of love, in whose other arms you
    will find refuge
The man walks on, blank and without veering. Where there are
    objects, he walks over rather than around them
The knife rises in her hand as she wipes her eyes
Comment vivre sans inconnu devant soi?
He departed with great pledges of love and went back to his life
    never to call her again

VIII

Dear L, I thought I knew what I was doing
On the island, a fuselage of wrecked plane, a wing in sharp
    vegetation
A radar dish filled with pumpkin plants
The blue wash of a cratered road
One thinks: The way back under cover of darkness

But as sickness chose from among us, we grew fewer
And so as not to appear in uniform he walked in his underwear
Through the village as if he were only strolling the asylum grounds

One morning slides aqua into the next, the night beach lit and tired
GRÈVE painted on the wall but what *grève?* Nothing to strike for here.
    Better pay? Better pay for what? Everybody in this no-name
    village is *chômeur*
It means they would carry your shit for you from your ass to the pit
    if they were paid
They plant flowers in cracker cans on the porch stair. They plant
    hibiscus in their wrecked cars
When you are talking about stupidity, only the military knows the
    meaning of the word *infinite*

Always he travels without maps as it is better to become lost than
    spend time thinking about the road
He drinks holy water, then pours some into a bottle in case he needs
    it again
Perhaps you have seen one of them?
A familiar man or woman, maimed, or a beggar who appears in
    several places at once
Why now and in such numbers?
If there are two doors, then only one gives onto normal life
Here, in this open field, that can never be a field again

IX

It isn't necessary to explain
The dead girl was thought to be with child, until it was discovered
    that her belly had already been cut open
And a man's head placed where the child would have been
The tanks dug ladders in the earth no one was able to climb
In every war someone puts a cigarette in the corpse's mouth
And the corpse
The corpse is never mentioned
In the hours before his empty body was found
It was this, this life that he longed for, this that he wrote of desiring,
Yet this life leaves out everything for which he lived

Carolyn Forché / 37

Hundreds of small clay heads discovered while planting coffee
A telescope through which it was possible to watch a fly crawling
    the neighbor's roof tiles
The last-minute journey to the border for no reason, the secret house
    where sports trophies were kept
That weren't sports trophies
Someone is trying to kill me, he said. He was always saying this.
Oranges turning to glass on the trees, a field strewn with them
In his knapsack a bar of soap, a towel the size of a dinner napkin
A map of the world he has not opened that will one day correspond
    to the world

In the spring, lilacs and mud roads, and later blossoming wind
Then the drone of beetles in high grass as if the grass were droning
He said a tongue doesn't have bones, he said tit for tat
Like a sack filled then emptied then filled
He was thin yes, but when he walked past it was not as if a human
    being had passed
And always he thought: This is it, the end of the world. God is
    coming
You were first in my thoughts, a chimera, first, then in the whisper
    of a sack's progress over the earth you were speaking:
We doubt we exist. We doubt with certain wisdom the world
Such pains as you took to convert a bedroom into a fire-base
Where an angry God, spilled blood itself, lives

                            X

Having taken these white rooms for a season, I imagine that it
    might be possible to recover
For an hour each afternoon I vow to sit in meditative expectancy
The light far on the rock promontory reaches Paris, where an old
    man's hand reaches out of the Seine, his wristwatch brilliant
    enough to catch the eye of a boat captain
There are times when the child seems not yet to have crossed into
    the world, despite having entered a body
Memory a wind passing through the blood trees within us
Someone was supposed to have come
He wrote: I tore open your letter and licked the envelope's seal for
    any lingering trace of you

In the worst of centuries, a merely difficult week, nothing, nothing,
    then from nothing, something
I noticed it today while walking to the pharmacy, where they were
    already selling woolen underwear
The market was closed. Monday. There were dead flowers for sale.
    Dead marigolds. Hydrangea. Peony.
Smoke rose in a perfect line from the roof
Then it wasn't possible to go farther
Everything seemed intentionally placed where it was, even the
    garbage bins
The children marched, holding their booklets
Peach leaves slipped earthward. Wind filled the souvenir shops
Doves painted white on the stopped wind
Making up a sort of game

Lamps in fog. Light fingering the canals.
And now, the defenselessness for which there is no cure
But it is a matter of shared history, or, as it were, we lived the same
    lie
Why lie? Why not life, as you intended?
I have the memory of a child in the southern slums, lifting the lid of
    an abandoned toilet
The child on my back, however was it kept from singing?
And falling back toward night
It was as if someone not alive were watching
Slowly, that is, over time, itself a barrier
And just then the doves rose and battered the wind
Where a notebook was kept once during a visit
*"This is my cap. This is my coat. Here's my shaving gear in its linen
    sack."*

JORIE GRAHAM

Detail from the Creation of Man

For three weeks I go down to the birdnest every day.
  The nest quick with twigs, grass,
woven in to make a stream, flame,
  flame with bits of dirt in it,
each filament a reference to what follows to what came
  before and disappearing now and feeding in.

  Even at the start, even before they hatched,
whatever there was to *know*
  was gone.
The mother was there, one yellow eye kicked up at me
  each time I lifted—barely—the hem of sage

  to see. Five eggs were there and then, one at a time,
three birds.
  Two eggs stayed there till the end of this story,
speckled with blue like this our earth
  seen from afar.
There was a fire I once saw
  which was below all thought like that

and left nothing undone. It was
  of gold mosaic tile and made a nest, too, partway down
its life—
  beginning at God's feet as hair—gold hair—
and traveling down becoming rivers, wheat fields, the hair
  of those that have to love, their love.
It flowed, burned, grew, until

darker of course, and near the end, it turned to
  blood and veins and promises, all systems

go—
   then at the very end it was, I guess, the lake
of Hell.
   But up near the top, somewhere between God's

hair and the serpentine gesture of Eve as she holds out
   the thing in her hand which is an open mouth,
or a mouth *opening*—discovering it
   opens—somewhere between or just after Eve it is
a road, dusty like the one behind our house,
   and leads to the knot which is this nest.

It burned at every stage,
   all gold-enameled tile and fire. Not the trace on it of an
idea, but gold, unreasoning, something like Time
   writ down in scrawl not meant to
clear,
   communicate.
Where Adam's being made his foot is fire

becoming mud, then, slowing further, flesh.
   The rivulets firm into toes, a heel, in-
step—
   then hair on him here and there
where the waters recede.
   For three weeks every day. Some days before the news,

some not. In case you don't know this,
   they're torturing five-year-olds in the kingdom of South Africa,
they're using their sexual parts to make a point.
   A woman testifies. She raises her right hand.
Next in line is the guy about the ozone.
   The butcher of Lyon. The Pope beatifies Anne Stein.
Let *x* equal perhaps. Let *y* be the

dizziness. There's this story
   where we continue, continue, fleshy and verbal over the globe,
talk talk, wondering what have we done—and this letter is to

confirm.
Once I lay down on the dirt and, holding up the fringe of sage,
   placed my face at the nest, breathing in,

the twigs and straw bits at my mouth. I lay there
   a long time. A bird the size of a quarter, very pink,
eyelids not opaque yet, breathed quickly at the height of my eyes
   —a breath, a breath, blue veins all over him,
him sleeping on the other eggs, her gone and watching me.
   I knew I should leave. I knew there was a scent

I left, terrible, perhaps sufficient cause for her to let
   them die—like a word that cannot be taken back,
so the ending cannot be undone—that scent.
   I stayed. Where in the fire is this, I thought.
What for, this tooth-sized piece of life too added
   on,

what for, looking around at all those
   woods. More under every bush. Pushing on into here.
Where the theater is empty. Where the lights are down.
   As if there were nowhere else to go. Pushed in. Has
nothing to do with love. Her sitting there some days like a

clock. *You must go in*, the Something says,
   pushing its thumbs in through,
making these protuberances extend—*Out, out you go*—right
   through the fabric, *in*—a madness from the other side—a

sweeping clean of some other terrain.
   In the picture I kept of Adam from the façade at Orvieto,
God has just called them and they are hiding.
   He sees them of course wherever they are, but that's not
important because now He's looking for them,

He's calling and looking. He's pointing.
   They're under three bushes that make a small shade.
They're folded up into their bodies, tight.
   As if they wanted no component parts.
As if they wanted to be themselves the nest, him with his hands

over his eyes, her with her hands

over her ears. A knot of flesh, they want to be
    the nest again, but they can't, they're the thing
in the nest now, the growing pushing thing, the
    image, too late.
Their hair falls over them but it is nothing.
    Their arms fold down over their selves,

tight:
    they hide; they are what waiting is.
When I went back there today the nest was there
    but torn and rained on, frayed. No trace of them.
A bundle of dead grass and straw. I took it up.
    I turned it for a feather, scent. Nothing. It crumbled in my

hand.
    But in the other panel, where He has just
made Adam—the moment of his making—
    Adam has not yet wakened into his madeness. His hands rest
one on the earth one on his thigh. His head is back.
    The hole in the cliff

takes its shape from him but he has no idea.
    The cliffs and bluffs arc across from the standing God
to the sleeping man as if they are
    the gesture itself which they contain—a pointing hand—You, you,
be now. A tree grows up out of man's mind. An angel grows
    out of God's stillness—the heat He gives off as it

cools. *You,* he points,
    and the finger reaches through space, and the cliffs bend, curl,
and the tree grips in, and the angel shuts his eyes, and the waters
    ripple into pattern—You, you there—and the angel shuts his eyes
as far as is possible, further, and the man, the man . . .

EAMON GRENNAN

Rights

FOR THE RUSSIAN POETS

He has every right to name her.

"The nimble muse of history," is
what the poet said, rolling his Russian
consonants and vowels around at us like
gravel, *gravitas*, like gravity, the solid
slow motion toward the core. She's
been to bed with him, both of them
out in the cold and tongue-tied, but oh
the oily motions of her quickened limbs
there in the dark, nothing between them
but, thin as air, the knifeblade and
—thinner than that—the flash of it
where their blind hips brush, barely,
and know one another for what they are.

He has earned her name, living at home
for years with her like that, her
bruised lips on his, his eyes wide open
to every wrinkle, nick, and imperfection
of age in her, the blackened orbs
of her eyelids, her cracked hands. She
is never the same as he remembers her:
a voice from childhood or a flicker of
cobbled light off water; the door
knocked open at two in the morning or
a letter from a friend in exile; silence
on the very edge of revelation. Or again
the raw igniting ice then fire of
vodka tongued and swallowed; the heartfelt

smell of morning—fresh bread, blue spruce,
snow in May—all the feints, glides, and fancy
handwork of that muse of his, who is nimble
as a dancer at the court of amazement, her
beautiful bleeding feet hardly touching the
double blade she bows and balances and spins on.

ROBERT HASS

Our Lady of the Snows

In white,
the unpainted statue of the young girl
on the side altar
made the quality of mercy seem scrupulous and calm.

When my mother was in a hospital drying out,
I would go in there,
light an aromatic candle
and bargain for us both,
or else I would stare into the day-moon of that face
and, if I concentrated, fly.

Come down! come down!
she'd call, because I was so high.

Though mostly when I think of myself
at that age, I am standing at my older brother's closet
studying the shirts,
convinced that I could be absolutely transformed
by something I could borrow.
And the days churned by,
navigable sorrow.

Happiness

Because yesterday morning from the steamy window
we saw a pair of red foxes across the creek
eating the last windfall apples in the rain;
they looked up at us with their green eyes
long enough to symbolize the wakefulness of living things
and then went back to eating;

and because this morning
when she went into the gazebo with her black pen and yellow pad
to coax an inquisitive soul
from what she thinks of as reluctant matter,
I drove into town to drink hot tea in the café
and write notes in a journal; mist rose from the bay
like the luminous and indefinite aspect of intention,
and a small flock of tundra swans
for the second winter in a row were feeding on new grass
in the soaked fields—they symbolize mystery, I suppose,
they are also called mute swans, are very white,
and their eyes are black—

and because the tea steamed in front of me,
and the notebook, turned to a new page,
was blank except for a faint blue idea of order,
I wrote: *happiness! it is December, very cold,*
we woke early this morning,
and lay in bed kissing,
our eyes squinched up like bats.

SEAMUS HEANEY

Glanmore Revisited

1. Scrabble

I. M. TOM DELANEY, ARCHAEOLOGIST

Bare flags. Pump water. Winter evening cold.
Our backs might never warm up but our faces
Burned from the hearth-blaze and the hot whiskeys.
It felt remembered even then, an old
Rightness half-imagined or foretold,
As green sticks hissed and spat into the ashes
And whatever rampaged out there couldn't reach us,
Firelit, shuttered, slated and stone-walled.

Year after year, our game of scrabble: love
Taken for granted like any other word
That was chanced on and allowed within the rules.
So "scrabble" let it be. Intransitive.
Meaning to scratch or rake at something hard.
It's us you hear, that scrape and clink of tools.

2. 1973

Our corrugated iron growled like thunder
When March came in; then as the year turned warmer
And invalids and bulbs came up from under,
I hibernated on behind the dormer,
Staring through shaken branches at the hill,
Dissociated, like an ailing farmer
Chloroformed against things seasonal
In a reek of cigarette smoke and dropped ash.

Lent came in next, also like a lion
Sinewy and wild for discipline,
A fasted will marauding through the body;
And I taunted him with scents of nicotine
As I lit one off another, and felt rash,
And stirred in the deep litter of the study.

3. Scene Shifts

The weekend after a good friend cut his name
Into the tree, our kids stripped off the bark—
The first time I was really angry at them.
I was flailing round the house like a man berserk
And maybe overdoing it, although
The business had moved me at the time;
It brought back those blood-brother scenes where two
Braves nick wrists and cross them for a sign.

Where it shone like bone exposed is healed up now
But, even so, there is another scene
Secluded in the ash tree's welted scar
In which old nurse sees old wound, then clasps brow
(Astonished at what all this starts to mean)
And tears surprise the verteran of the war.

4. *Lustral Sonnet*

Breaking and entering: from early on,
Words that thrilled me far more than they scared me—
And still did when I came into my own
Masquerade as man of property.
Even then my first impulse was never
To double-lock a door on the inside;
And fitted blinds and curtains drawn over
Seemed to boast that there were things to hide.

Then I broke re-entering here. And now I scare,
Remembering my commonsense instruction
To saw up the old bed frame, since the stair
Was much too narrow for it. A bad action
So Greek with consequence, so dangerous,
Only pure words and deeds secure the house.

ZBIGNIEW HERBERT

TRANSLATED FROM THE POLISH BY
JOHN AND BOGDANA CARPENTER

Elegy for the Departure of Pen, Ink and Lamp

1

Truly my betrayal is great and hard to forgive
for I do not even remember the day or hour
when I abandoned you friends of my childhood

first I humbly turn to you
pen with a wooden handle
covered with paint or brittle lacquer

in a Jewish shop
—steps creaking a bell at the glass door—
I chose you
in the color of laziness
and soon afterward you carried
on your body
the reveries of my teeth
traces of school torment

o silver nib
outlet of the critical mind
messenger of soothing knowledge
—that the globe is round
—that parallel lines never meet
in a box of the storekeeper
you were like a fish waiting for me
in a school of other fish
—I was astonished there were so many

completely mute objects
without owners—
then
mine forever
I put you respectfully in my mouth.
and for a long time felt on my tongue
a taste
of sorrel
and the moon

o ink
illustrious Mr. ink
of distinguished ancestry
highly born
like the sky at evening
for a long time drying
deliberate
and very patient
in wells we transformed you
into the Sargasso Sea
drowning in your wise depths
blotters hair secret oaths and flies
to block out the smell
of a gentle volcano
the call of the abyss

who remembers you today
dear companions
you left quietly
beyond the last cataract of time
who recalls you with gratitude
in the era of fatheaded ball-point pens
arrogant objects
without grace
name
or past

when I speak of you
I would like it to be
as if I were hanging an ex voto
on a shattered altar

2

light of my childhood
blessed lamp

sometimes in junk stores
I come upon
your disgraced body

and yet you were once
a bright allegory

a spirit stubbornly battling
with the demons of gnosis

wholly given to the eyes

in full sight
transparently simple

at the bottom of the fount
kerosene—elixir of primeval forests
slick snake of a wick
with a blazing head
the slender maiden's chimney
and silvery shield of tin
like Selene a full moon

your moods of a princess
beautiful and cruel

tantrums of a primadonna
not applauded enough

lo
a serene aria
summer's honey-light
above the flue of the chimney
a light braid of good weather

then all of a sudden
dark basses

a raid of crows and ravens
curses and maledictions
prophecy of extermination
fury of sooty smoke

like a great playwright you knew the surf of passions
and swamps of melancholy black towers of pride
glow of fires the rainbow the unleashed sea
effortlessly you could call into being from nothingness
landscapes a savage city repeated in water
at your sign
the mad prince the island and the balcony in Verona
obediently appeared

I was devoted to you
luminous initiation
instrument of knowledge
under the hammers of night

while my flat
second head projected on the ceiling
looked down filled with terror
as if from an angel's loge
at the theater of the world
all entangled
evil
cruel

I thought then
that before the deluge it was necessary
to save
one
thing
small
warm
faithful

so it endures further
with ourselves inside it as in a shell

3

I never believed in the spirit of history
an invented monster with a murderous look
dialectical beast on a leash led by slaughterers

nor in you—four horsemen of the apocalypse
Huns of progress galloping over earthly and heavenly steppes
destroying on the way everything worthy of respect old and
      defenseless

I spent years learning the simplistic cogwheels of history
a monotonous procession hopeless struggle
scoundrels at the head of confused crowds
against the handful of those who were honest courageous aware

I have very little left
not many
objects
or compassion

lightheartedly we leave the gardens of childhood gardens of things
shedding in flight manuscripts oil-lamps dignity pens
such is our illusory journey at the edge of nothingness

      pen with an ancient nib forgive my unfaithfulness
      and you inkwell—there are still so many good thoughts in
          you
      forgive me kerosene lamp—you are dying in my memory
          like a deserted campsite

      I paid for the betrayal
      but I did not know then
      you were leaving forever

      and that it will be
      dark

BRENDA HILLMAN

Dark Matter

It's good to stand at the head of the tram;
it seems like facing fate. Men and children
stand there mostly, next to the brochure rack
and the older women sit on cushions while
the blond, ski-sunburned guide points out
formations on our left: Red Dog Rock (sandstone
forehead furrowed like a basset hound's)
and KT-22, so mathematical. Below us, mixed
conifers, dazzling hurt granite from which
the basalt flowed, and with us the same confusion
as we rise; joy and terror have the same source.

At the top, families head up the rough trail
to mildly dirty patches of old snow. It's summer;
they want to touch it. Two red-haired boys
throw snowballs at their father. Some women
stand with their hands on their hips,
gazing eastward through infinite space.
Brewer's blackbirds land hysterically among
a mile of newly blossomed mule ears,
and on a cliff's face, a patch of ice shaped
like a sombrero; today, nature seems male.
More forevers and more forevers, and then—

I want to see everything but they say now
most of the universe is hidden;
they call what we can't see dark matter,
those particles straining unprovenly through
what is, sucking gravity from the edge
of galaxies. They're trying to find just one
speck of it . . . Why am I thrilled by the idea
that this hurried thing cannot be caught?

That this huge mountain's filled with it,
billions of it going through me every second.
That as I sit on this log, slightly drunk

from the high altitude, looking at sidalcea
in the sun, in awe of moraines, that
I'm being hit with it. Why love the thought
of being struck by a dark thing clean through.
That the little family throwing snow now
in their innocent ways are being penetrated
by an opposite, the main universe, a huge
allegorical black urgency—and we are nothing
but a rind of consciousness, a mild
excess, a little spare color, and not just us,
the thistles and the asters and the blackbirds . . .

Of course this happened at the start of time,
something had to pull away, and I've been trying
to love the missingness in the middle,
the caves of wounded magic; I've studied
the old terrors every day, the brightness
of the world, have loved the random causes,
have studied the kinds of pain in California
and have known the desire to make from pain
some words that would be beautiful and torn—
but now, I want this wholeness. Here,
the blackbirds swarm upward, and the chipmunk

with one-and-a-half brown stripes takes off
with a prize; the red-haired family hurries
toward the tram under the white ear
of the radar. The mountain seems to push up
through us, asking us to keep its hurt.
Today it seems possible to welcome
wounded matter; the ski-lift chairs,
which have lurched forward, being repaired
all afternoon, guard their incompleteness.
Each black, numbered frame pauses till its turn,
then offers its own darkness a ride.

JOHN HOLLANDER

Quatrains of Doubt and Death

With every breath I take, less of the sky
Lives; the same questions as I slowly die
    Gnaw on the world, that narrowed globe of light,
And eat away at the apple of my eye.

The darkening kettle strikes the blackened pot
In rage, but well before its iron is hot.
    You say my doubt slaps out thus at the world?
I know, I know. I know I know not what.

The figure of lean Questioning has wit
Only enough never to let him quit
    Fussing with every door—are there no locks
That any of his hundred keys will fit?

Doubt hops about as crickets do, in such
A manner as to keep in minimal touch
    With the hard ground in darkness. Is that stick
He carries a weapon? Or a sort of crutch?

(Doubt adds: "Crickets are not like me that much"—
Those fiddled cadenzas, sudden leaps and such
    Are all of the high grasshopping of Hope
In the bright air with which he keeps in touch.)

Drops have their plenitude in time of drought,
Doubt is the seed and wonder is the sprout.
    What comes green of all this clears the air
That is around us, that we are about.

The chill humanity of him who wrought
The sheer machine that severed *is* from *ought* . . .

Broken and rusted now, it's overgrown
With ghostly foliage of all he'd fought.

Not the pure *cogito*, nor yet the sum
Of infinite contingencies: the dumb
    Livestock of all our present moments drink
Deep from the shadowed trough of what's to come.

"She thinks": she and her thought are by design
Her property; "she is": by the same line
    Of reasoning, her being is her own.
But "therefore"—that's not part of her, but mine.

There is a last chance that our knowing takes
Before the brain, its sacred precinct, breaks:
    A final drawing in the raffle of breath,
A vacant lottery for pulled-up stakes.

Hope, in black tie, invites Mortality
To game away its final sovereign: see
    Bright reason squandered on the *rouge, impair.*
Les jeux sont faits. Click. Click. *Les jeux sont pris.*

The little foxes of desire may cry
Out for their bits of how and what and why.
    We are like hedgehogs of the heavy heart:
The one big thing we know is that we'll die.

RICHARD HOWARD

The Victor Vanquished

FOR TOM, 1989

At the going rate, your body gave you
—made you—too much pain for you to call it
yours. Oh, not the pain, the pain was all yours

and all you had; by the end you hugged it
closer than their anodyne substitutes:
pain was your one religion, pain was bliss.

But this body, where almost everything hurt
and what didn't hurt didn't work—*yours?* Never!
Like anybody's, it gave nothing up

that soap and water couldn't wash away.
Whose was it, then, this desecrated pond
where all fish die, where only scum persists?

Anybody's. Nobody's. Like a king
who keeps recognizing as "my people"
the rebels who have pulled him off the throne . . .

Your body not your body. What about
"your" friends? We want playmates we can own.
Could these be yours? Since every friendship

grows from some furtive apotheosis
of oneself, who were these dim intruders
presuming they inhabited your pain,

as if there could be room for them as well?
You would not have it—let them all go hang!
For two years, the body alone with its pain

suspended friendship like the rope that holds
a hanged man. All you wanted was to drop
this burden, even if it meant that you

would be the burden dropped. And "your" lovers?
What about love—was it like "your" disease,
an abnormal state of recognition

occurring in a normal man? Love is
not love until it is vulnerable—
then you were in it: up to here in love!

The verdict of their small-claims court: It takes
all kinds to make a sex. Had you made yours?
Everything is possible but not

everything is permitted: in love
you were a shadow pursuing shadows,
yet the habit of the chase enthralled you,

and you could not desist. You would make love
by listening, as women do. And by lying
still, alone, waiting. You did not wait long.

Life in general is, or ought to be,
as Crusoe said, one universal Act
of Solitude. You made it death as well.

DONALD JUSTICE

Body and Soul

1. Hotel

If there was something one of them held back,
It was too inadvertent or too small
To matter to the other, after all.

Afterwards they were quiet, and lay apart,
And heard the beating of the city's heart,
Meaning the sirens and the streetcries, meaning,
At dawn, the whispery great streetsweeper cleaning
The things of night up, almost silently.

And all was as it had been and would be.

2. Rain

Someone's umbrella, suddenly blowing free,
Escapes across the carhoods dangerously.
And you would follow—
                                    only to be lost
Somewhere along the avenues, long avenues
Toward evening pierced with rain; or in some mews
Whose cobbles once perhaps the young Hart Crane
Had washed with a golden urine mixed with rain.

3. Street Musician

A cold evening. The saxophonist shivers
Inside his doorway and ignores the givers
Dropping their change into his upturned hat.

High now or proud, he leans back out of that,
Raising his horn in some old bluesy riff
His fingers just do get through, being stiff—
Yet so sincere, so naked that it hurts.
Punk teens, in pink hairspikes and torn T-shirts,
Drift by; a horsecop towers above the cars;
And office lights wink on in place of stars.

Silence of cities suddenly and the snow
Turning to rain and back again to snow . . .

GALWAY KINNELL

Last Gods

She sits naked on a rock
a few yards out in the water.
He stands on the shore,
also naked, picking blueberries.
She calls. He turns. She opens
her legs showing him her great beauty,
and smiles, a bow of lips
seeming to tie together
the ends of the earth.
Splashing her image to bits,
he wades out and stands before her,
sunk to the anklebones in
leaf-mush and bottom-slime
—which he likes, mucus
is the intimacy of the visible world.
He puts a blueberry in its shirt
of mist into her mouth.
She swallows it. He puts in another.
She swallows it. Over the lake
two swallows whim, jink, juke,
and when one snatches
an insect, whirl up together
and exult. He is swollen
not with blood but *ichor*.
She takes him and sucks
him more swollen. He kneels,
opens the darker, vertical smile
connecting heaven and the underearth,
and with coarse tongue licks
her smoothest flesh more smooth
and wet. On top of the rock
they join. The hair

of their bodies startles up.
The coming already is coming.
A frog moans, somewhere
a crow screams. They cry
in the tongue of the last gods,
who refused to go
at the time of the driving-out,
chose death, and shuddered
in joy and shattered in pieces,
bequeathing their cries
to the human. Now in the lake
two faces float, looking up
at a great maternal pine whose branches
open out in all directions
explaining everything.

KARL KIRCHWEY

The Transformation of Light

August in the Alps of Vaud:
the rain is sudden and drives vertical.
I watch the storm gather over the mountains I know:
Grand Muveran, Petit Muveran, Dents de Morcle;

and watch the cloud closing its empty fist
as if the gneiss, in its plutonic weave,
were a napped cloth vastly caught in some outburst,
obliterating all for rage or love,

genealogy and profile lost, and then once more calm—
as it is sometimes with a family at supper,
though these are strangers who give me shelter from
the brief, irrational violence of weather.

He is something with the power authority,
distilling the cloudy water of the Rhône
into streetlights that zigzag up from the valley.
Like a knot in the throat I have passed the turbine

at a certain defile in the valley road
where the water drives into the flank of the hill,
is taxed in darkness and seethes from the louvered
gate to braid coldly onward over the gravel.

Noëmi has had her bath, his child of pleasure.
Her pup tent sags out back. She is seven.
Her gold curls gleam like pyrite in the later
dusk given to those who live in the mountains.

In one hand she holds a *tartine*, in the other
a cup of milk disturbed by the sweet obsidian
of blackberries from the forest. Then it is her
bedtime. Her mother is living in Lausanne.

All night she will hear the wrinkled bulk of the glacier
debride the land with its knives of aquamarine,
with its pistol-shots of torsion. It is speaking to her,
she thinks, saying, Child, when will you be grown,

when will you be adept at the transformation
of light, as your father is, and lost to me?
In the morning, mist will rise through each black chevron
of fir, and childhood lift off her insensibly.

CAROLYN KIZER

Marriage Song

with commentary

We begin with the osprey who cries, "Clang, clang!"
Which is the sound of the door of marriage slamming.
Our metaphor sits on a nest, surrounded
By blooming succulents; ospreys, like swans, mate once.
For form's sake they appear in public together;
Because she and her spouse play separate roles
They will forego connubial bliss if necessary
To save their feathered souls.

Complementary image: young, pale, scared,
Has menstruated once, sequestered in a cave,
Miss Chou Dynasty, under lock and key
Thus to preserve her sacred chastity,
Knows that some day her Prince will come.
But this occurs between stanzas two and three.
Thus far she is only a dream in his questing eye.
He doesn't come, he just breathes heavily.

The principal commentaries differ here:
Mao-fang believes the lady tossed from side to side
In bed with long long thoughts of separation.
A respected version claims that the aging bride
Dutifully tried to recruit the limberest dames
For her still-randy spouse, states earnestly
That she worried about the good ones getting away
—or so the followers of Confucius say.

But what, Students, was the intention of the Poem
Before the moral scholiasts worked it over?

The text obscure: was it maid or matron here?
Did not our Princess roll from side to side
Alone with long long thoughts of her absent lover,
Reluctant, yes, to pick out next year's successor
Yet feeling perhaps it was better to marry *and* burn
Than to stay yearning in that cave forever.

Now cry desire, shake silver tamborines
To cue the strings of gypsy violins
As the Fisher-Prince mates with his fluttering Bride.
O her chaste joy! She will hold him in her bosom
(suckle her spouse in dream), then toss and turn . . .
The girls glide out of reach like water-lilies
Slipping along the current of the stream.
Though Pound and Waley speak of zither and gong
In truth our modest heroine bursts into song:

"Alone, I become virginal again.
I know the cave, I learn the cave within.
And you, my Lord, are somewhere out of reach.
I hear your breathy sigh: the aging man
Tuning his lute in our remotest room.
Beside myself at last, I think and think
Of ospreys on their island, dark of wing,
Snow-breasted, and transfixed in abstract love."

PHILIP LEVINE

Soloing

My mother tells me she dreamed
of John Coltrane, a young Trane
playing his music with such joy
and contained energy and rage
she could not hold back her tears.
She sits awake now, her hands
crossed in her lap as the tears start
in her blind eyes. The TV set
behind her is gray, expressionless.
It is late, the neighbors quiet,
even the city—Los Angeles—quiet.
I have driven for hours down 99,
over the Grapevine into heaven
to be here. I place my left hand
on her shoulder, and she smiles.
What a world, a mother and son
finding solace in California
just where we were told it would
be, among the palm trees and all-
night supermarkets pushing orange
backlighted oranges at two A.M.
"He was alone," she says, and does
not say, just as I am, "soloing."
What a world, a great man half
her age comes to my mother
in sleep to give her the gift
of song, which—shaking the tears
away—she passes on to me, for now
I can hear the music of the world
in the silence and that word:
soloing. What a world—when I
arrived the great bowl of mountains

was hidden in a cloud of exhaust,
the sea spread out like a carpet
of oil, the roses I had brought
from Fresno browned on the seat
beside me, and I could have
turned back and lost the music.

Roberto

"Roberto," he would holler
in the white-hot face
of the steel we pressed.
"Roberto, call me Roberto
or call me nothing." No one
heard him until the power
was cut, the lights went
out, and we stood in
a curious peace descending
down our shoulders and arms
in the dark while his chant
went on, a song to no one,
a tune even now I can hear
when I close my eyes to
enter the past I still am.
Years later, I would shout
out my own name at the sea
which went on churning,
and once in a raging wind
full of snow and dread
I would cling to my name
as though it had become
all I had of me, alone
in the mountains, lost.
On Amsterdam Avenue people
tried not to look at me
as I sang out my anger
with the three syllables
of his name, "Roberto,"
seeing his face in my mind
beside me again, the dark
lips moving in the clash

of metal on metal, a man
finer and slimmer than I
in a black threadbare suit,
wool shirt buttoned at
the collar, erect, certain.
Don't forget this winter
of 1984 in Harlem, ever, I
shouted to myself. Don't
forget the faces cracked
with cold, the homeless kids
sleeping in the snow, don't
forget the bottle hurled
at you, and your only answer
hurled back, "Roberto,"
as a mysterious token,
an amulet to carry forever
into private and public hells.
My name has only the one
syllable, it silences easily
against wind, it comes
out as one long breath
meaning forgiveness. How
could I offer it back on
126th Street where the shards
of the vodka bottle jeweled
in the sun, that distant king
riding above in the perfect
blue sky that said nothing?

CAMPBELL McGRATH

Sunrise and Moonfall, Rosarito Beach

What I remember of Mexico
is how the glass apple of mescal glowed
and exploded like a globe of seeds
or something we couldn't pronounce
or know the secret name of, never,
and even when the *federales* shook us down for twenty bucks
as they must, to save face,
I couldn't lose the curve and rupture
of that sphere—half-full, hand-blown, imperfect
as our planet. Sure, everything is blowing open
now, all the freeways and skinheads, the music
invisibly blasting, radio waves invading the spines and craniums
of all this. San Diego, Tijuana, the Beach of Dead Dogs
where we slept in the cold, local kids incredulous
of Ed up early for no reason
driving golf balls out into the restlessly pounding surf.
Jesus, we're always hitting golf balls. It seems to be
some irreducible trait. There's Rob smashing the plaster icons,
all the bleeding martyrs and aqua pigs
and pink squinting Virgins the radiant chapel of candles
induced us to need. Jesus, let me ask,
please, before he decapitates you also with a wicked four-iron slice,
why are we always the ones on the beach
as dawn sucks the last drops from mescaline shards,
the ones who beat the sacred iguanas to death
as the sun comes right up
and the shadow-globe finally dances off stage,
the moon, I mean,
that other white world of men
driving golf balls to seas of dust and oblivion—
chrome-headed, flag-waving, violent, American.

Yellowknife

*A Cree elder told me how a man gone Windigo "had
been asking his own brother how it was in a nearby
beaver lodge . . . in the lodge! Because he saw his
brother as a fat beaver and he wanted to eat him."*

—HOWARD NORMAN,
*Where the Chill Came From:
Cree Windigo Tales and Journeys*

Late that day we stopped to help a family of Indians in a big red Chevy,
the first car in hours, out of gas by the side of the road. This far north,
Athabasca, Slave, and Swampy Cree Indians mix with Inuit or Eskimo,
the pure Mongolian features of the young daughter who smiles shyly and
plays peek-a-boo with Charlie while the father uses a length of hose as
a siphon, squatting on his heels, spitting out mouthfuls of gas until it
flows smoothly. Nobody says much, even Charlie doesn't talk. We stand
around slapping mosquitoes until the jerry can is full and he thanks us
and wanders back to his family, hidden in the backseat, smiling and
nodding stiffly, like dolls, as he jumps in and drives off into the dusk.
"It started right up," Charlie said. "They weren't out of gas at all."
According to the Cree, the Windigo roams this wilderness in disguise—
the Trails-End-at-Shivering Windigo, the Childhood Foxes Windigo,
the Echoing Moth Windigo—swimming glacial lakes in seconds, freezing the heart with hysterical exhalations, bringing famine, hunger, and
death. That night we crossed into the Northwest Territories and camped
along the Hay River where a wild waterfall fell a hundred feet into the
gorge. The air was filled with the torrent's crashing surge and sheets of
mist that left us unable to speak, just staring up the canyon of the Hay
River, winding off through scrubwood and muskeg wastes toward the
Great Slave Lake, nothing but wilderness for hundreds of miles, nothing
but desolation until Yellowknife, and nothing there but the Windigo,
though we didn't know it then. We climbed back up from the falls in

the glow of midnight sun. We ate hot dogs and Jiffy Pop in a hurry, fell asleep uneasily on ground gnarled with roots, the earth's fingers clutching our arms and legs, pulling us under, struggling to drag us down into the rocky soil.

This is something that happened on the Mackenzie Highway. One day two Americans were driving north when a young girl cried out to them for help. She stood next to a big red Chevy. When the Americans stopped to see what was wrong, the girl's family jumped out and captured them, and tied them with cords and thongs. The Americans saw nothing and yet her family was there—they had conjured themselves to look like trees! "Why have you tricked us like this?" the Americans asked. The little girl said: "We did not wish to. We also are captives." Then a strange voice spoke: "You are my prisoners." There was no one there, and yet something spoke to them—a voice like winter wind! Then the Americans understood—it was the Red Chevy Windigo! "I will take you to my home in Yellowknife. Get in." So they all got into the car, and the Red Chevy Windigo began to fly high above the ground. They flew over the swampy forest extending to the horizons. They flew over the home of the moose and the beaver and the lakes full of Arctic char. And they crossed the fearful Mackenzie River, past Fort Providence, along the Great Slave Lake, where the trees get small before fading off into tundra. They came to a city on the northern shore of the lake, a city with tall buildings and neon signs, with gas stations and heavy traffic and a McDonald's—like a suburb whose nearest neighbor was five hundred miles south. There were video games and four-wheel-drive vehicles! "This is my home," the Windigo said. "This is Yellowknife." In Yellowknife the Windigo left the Americans at the Motel 6. They ate Kentucky Fried Chicken and drank cold beer. In the evening the Americans drank whiskey at the Klondike Bar with gold miners and oil roughnecks. The streets of Yellowknife were filled with Eskimos and Indians who sat on the stairs of the city hall or the library, public buildings, so they couldn't be evicted, drunk or drinking white port, or staggered down the sidewalks, or tumbled into the gutter. The Americans stayed three days, drinking beer, depressed, watching TV cabled in from Detroit. They saw three shows with Dick Van Patten in one morning! Their Colonel Sanders piggy-banks came to life and danced in front of the screen! They cried out to the marten and the badger and the she-weasel, but no one came to release them. It happened that one day three ravens were passing by and saw the Americans and understood what had befallen them. The eldest raven said: "Look how piteously they cry out. They think they are tied down by fierce enemies, but the Windigo comes from within. Even in the barren lands he may make a place his own." Then the old raven's son said: "They don't understand that they are prisoners of their own hearts!" Then the ravens laughed and flew away. That was how it happened.

In the morning we broke camp for the last leg north. The Mackenzie was turgid, gray, compulsive, a timber wolf's river. The trees thinned and lichen-covered rocks poked up among wildflowers in the bogs and stagnant lakes. As we approached Yellowknife we somehow knew what to expect—the shadows of office buildings on the lake, blocks of prefab houses, the jingle of the player piano from Shakey's, the 7-Eleven.

To kill a Windigo you must melt its heart of ice. This far north it seemed unlikely.

The Windigo laughed as we pulled into the Motel 6, howled like the wind as we left three days later, and all the way back down the heart of the continent.

The Red Chevy Windigo has many names.

WILLIAM MATTHEWS

The Dream

A bare hill. Above it, the early evening sky, a flat,
blue-gray slate color like a planetarium ceiling
before the show's begun. Just over the hill and rising,
like a moon, the stuttering thwack of helicopter rotors

and then from behind the hill the machine itself
came straight up and stood in the air like a tossed
ball stopped at its zenith. It shone a beam of light
on me and a voice that seemed to travel through

the very beam intoned—that's the right word,
intoned—*We know where you are and we can find
you anytime. Don't write that poem. You know the one
we mean.* Then all was gone—the voice, the beam,

the helicopter and the dream. I'd lain down for a nap
that afternoon and slept through dusk. Outside the sky
was flat, blue-gray and slate. I'd no idea what poem
they meant. I lay swaddled in sweat five minutes

or an hour, I don't know. I made coffee and walked,
each muscle sprung like a trap, as far as the bridge
over the falls. I'd have said my mind was empty,
or thronged with dread, but now I understand

that in some way I also don't know how to say
I was composing with each trudge these words.
Until I steal from fear and silence what I'm not
supposed to say, these words will have to do.

JAMES MERRILL

Big Mirror Outdoors

Specter, inside with you where you belong!
Must the blond hibiscus be reminded
Of privileges tentatively won
From pay dirt? or our puppet selves grow pale

Here at their narrow lot's far end, beneath
Your glittering aplomb? Yes, yes, we know:
Artillery fern, chameleon, dinner guest,
Greens and blues, deck wreathed in fairy lights

Had begun, like us, to dodder and digress.
The realm of chance cried out for supervision.
One stroke and the casino stood corrected—
A halfway house. Now yours, inviolate

Heart, is the last word, the cool view we shrink
To couple with. Yet breeding likenesses
That don't need food or shelter has become
(Given the hapless millions lured into

Our networks) an undertaking not entirely
Vain. Ah, even when it's death you deal—!
Puss lays the feathered fool at Uli's feet.
Too weak this year to set his easel up,

He'll render it in charcoal. Alone, later,
You will reflect the lighted pool while slowly,
Darkly in the pool revolves a float
On which two baby blots of dew reflect

Glimmerings of you. So that, much as the plot
Was to make do without us, sun and rain,

Reds and blacks, terrestrial roulette,
Nature grows strong in you. Again last night

She put on all her costume jewelry
And rustled up to the table, challenging
The glacial croupier: Double or nothing!
Again dawn hot and airtight found you sweating

Out that horrifying, harmless dream.

W. S. MERWIN

The Day Itself

Harvard Phi Beta Kappa Poem, 1989

Now that you know
everything does it not come even so
with a breath of surprise the particular
awaited morning in summer
when the leaves that you walked under
since you saw them unfold out of nothing whether
you noticed that or not into

the world you know
have attained the exact weave of shadow
they were to have and the unrepeatable
length of that water which you call
the Charles the whole way to its end
has reached the bridge at last after descending and
gathering its own color through

all that you know
and is slipping under the arches now
while the leveled ground embraced by its famous
façades the ordinary place
where you were uncertain
late moonstruck cold angry able to imagine
you had it all to yourself to

use and to know
without thinking much about it as though
it were the real you suddenly shines before
you transformed into another
person it seems by the presence
of familiar faces all assembled at once
and a crowd of others you do

not really know
rippling in the shimmer of daylight row
upon row sending up a ceaseless leafy
shuffle of voices out of the
current that is rushing over
the field of common chairs one of them opened here
at the moment only for you

and you should know
who that is as the man some time ago
in Greece you remember is supposed to have
said and there was that other of
his countrymen about whom we
are certain of little who was sure already
without having met you that you

could get to know
you whoever that is if you were so
inclined which indeed you may not have been on
days of uncomfortable dawn
with recognitions bare of their
more proper perspectives and the phrase goes further
to suggest that perhaps you do

not in fact know
you in the first place but might have to go
looking for you when here you are after all
in the skin of the actual
day dressed and on time and you are
sure that you are in the right seat and behind your
own face now is the you that you

wanted to know
is it not and you feel that you have no
age at all but are the same you that you were
as long as you can remember
while every decision that you
made or thought you were making was conducting you
straight to this seat and to what you

would come to know
as today in the middle of which no
other you it seems is present furthermore
what influenced each of your
choices all of the accidents
as they are called and such chances as your parents'
meeting on their own before you

were here to know
where you were coming from those joys with no
histories those crimes painted out those journeys
without names the flawless courses
of all the stars the progression
of the elements were moving in unison
from what you had never seen to

what you now know
you were so long looking forward to no
wonder it floats before you appearing at
once inevitable and not
yet there so that you are unsure
that this time you are awake and will remember
it all assembled to show you

what you must know
by now about knowledge how it also
is a body of questions in apparent
suspension and no different
from the rest of the dream save that
we think we can grasp it and it tends to repeat
itself like the world we wake through

while as you know
it has its limits it belongs to no
one it cannot bring you love or keep you from
catching cold from tomorrow from
loss or waiting it can stand in
its own way so that however you stare you can
not see things about it that you

do in fact know
perfectly well the whole time and can so
loom that you cannot look past it which is more
important you have to acquire
it yourself but for that you need
gifts and words of others and places set aside
in large part for informing you

until you know
all this which of course may render you no
kinder or more generous since that is not
its function or at least not right
away and may not only make
you no wiser but make it sound wiser to mock
the notion of wisdom since you

have come to know
better and in some cases it can go
to your head and stay there yet we are all here
to speak well of it we treasure
something about it or we say
we do beyond the prospect of making money
and so on with it something you

certainly know
of it that has led to its being so
often compared to the light which you see all
around you at the moment full
of breath and beginnings how well
you know what that is and soon you will start to tell
us and we will listen to you

The Lost Camelia of the Bartrams

All day
the father said we rode
through swamps
seeing tupelo

cypress standing in deep water
and on higher ground palmettos
mingling with pine
deer

and turkeys moving under
the boughs
and we dined by a swamp on bread
and a pomegranate

with stands of canna near us
then poor timber for maybe a mile
of the lowland which
often the river

overflows to the great
loss of those who live there
we lost our way
and that was the day

we found that
tree with the beautiful
good fruit
nameless which I

found never again
it was then
already advanced autumn and the grass
exceeding tall

sand hills along the river
you see
only once whatever
you may say

winter
had passed maybe twelve
times over the wide
river lands

before the son
returned to those regions
when it was spring
and that same tree

was in perfect bloom while
bearing at that season its
woody apples he said
and the flowers

were of the first order for
beauty and fragrance
very large and white as snow
with a crown or

tassel of
radiant gold stamens
the lower petal cupped
around the others

until it allowed them to unfold
and the edges of all the petals
remaining waved or folded
each flower

set in the bosom of broad leaves
never
the son said did we find
that tree growing

wild anywhere else
so it was fortunate
that he gathered seed and cuttings
and took them

away to bring on
in gardens for
by the time he was fifty
it had vanished from

its own place altogether
only surviving here and there
as a cultivated
foreigner

Lunar Landscape

Nobody can tell you
anything new about
moonlight you have seen it
for yourself as many
times as necessary

nobody else ever saw
it as it appeared to you
you have heard all about it
but in the words of others
so that you fell asleep

it was photographed but
somewhere else and without
what was happening inside
its light and whenever it
was rhymed it disappeared

you cannot depend on
it use it for much send
it anywhere sell it
keep it for yourself bring
it back when it has left

and while it is lighting
the ocean like a name while
it is awake in the leaves
you do not need to look at it
to know it is not there

CZESLAW MILOSZ

TRANSLATED FROM THE POLISH BY
THE AUTHOR AND ROBERT HASS

Meaning

—When I die, I will see the lining of the world.
The other side, beyond bird, mountain, sunset.
The true meaning, ready to be decoded.
What never added up will add up,
What was incomprehensible will be comprehended.

—And if there is no lining to the world?
If a thrush on a branch is not a sign,
But just a thrush on the branch? If night and day
Make no sense following each other?
And on this earth there is nothing except this earth?

—Even if that is so, there will remain
A word wakened by lips that perish,
A tireless messenger who runs and runs
Through interstellar fields, the revolving galaxies,
And calls out, protests, screams.

At Yale

I

We were drinking vodka together, Brodsky, Venclova
With his beautiful Swedish girl, myself, Richard,
Near the Art Gallery, at the end of the century
Which woke up as if from a heavy slumber
And asked, in stupefaction: "What was that?
How could we? A conjunction of planets?
Or spots on the sun?"

                              —For History
Is no more comprehensible. Our species
Is not ruled by any reasonable law.
The boundaries of its nature are unknown.
It is not the same as I, you, a single human.

—Thus mankind returns to its beloved pastimes
During the break. Taste and touch
Are dear to it. Cookbooks,
Recipes for perfect sex, rules
For lowering cholesterol, methods
Of quickly losing weight—that's what it needs.
It is one (from brightly colored magazines) body
That every morning runs along the trails in parks,
Touches itself in a mirror, checks its weight.
Et ça bande et ça mouille—to put it briefly.
Are we that? Does it apply to us? Yes and no.

—For, visited by dictators' dreams,
Don't we soar above them who are light-headed
And unwilling to think of the punishment that awaits
All those who are too much in love with life?

—Not so light-headed after all, they worship
In their new temples, and mortality,
Having been overcome by the craft of artists,
Comforts them in the halls of museums.

—So the time came again for adoring art.
The names of gods are forgotten, instead, the masters
Soar in the clouds, Saint Van Gogh, Matisse,
Goya, Cézanne, Hieronymus Bosch,
Together with a cluster of the smaller ones, the acolytes.
And what would they say had they stepped down on earth,
Invoked in photographs, newspapers, on TV?
Where are those nights growing dense in the loneliness of the
    workshop,
Which protected, transformed the refugees from the world?

—All form—says Baudelaire—
Even the one created by man,
Is immortal. There was once an artist
Faithful and hardworking. His workshop,
Together with all he had painted, burned down;
He himself was executed. Nobody has heard of him.
Yet his paintings remain. On the other side of fire.

—Whenever we think of what fulfills itself
By making use of us, we are somewhat uneasy.
A form is accomplished, exists, though before it was not,
And we have nothing more to do with it. Others, generations,
Will choose what they want, accepting or destroying it.
And instead of us, who are real, they will need just names.

—But suppose all our internal dirt
And nuttiness and shame, a lot of shame,
Were not forgotten—would we prefer that?
They want to find in us their improved selves:
Instead of comic flaws, flaws monumentalized,
And secrets revealed, provided they are not too depressing.

"I have heard that Balzac (and who would not listen with respect to every anecdote, even the most insignificant, having to do with that genius?) one day found himself before a fine painting representing winter, a quite melancholy landscape, heavy with hoarfrost, with huts here and there, and sickly peasants. After having contemplated a small house from which meagre smoke ascended, he exclaimed: 'How beautiful it is! But what do they do in that hut? What do they think about, what are their worries? Did they have a good harvest? Certainly they have payments coming due?'

Let people laugh at M. de Balzac. I do not know who the painter was who had the honor of making the soul of the great novelist vibrate, speculate, and worry, but it seems to me that he gave us, with his adorable naïvete, an excellent lesson in criticism. I often will appraise a painting uniquely by the sum of ideas or reveries which it brings to my mind."

—BAUDELAIRE

III

Yale Center for British Art:
J.M.W. Turner: Châteaux de St. Michael,
Bonneville, Savoy, 1803

White clouds pass each other above the mountains.
And here a road in the sun, long shadows,
Low embankments, sort of a little bridge,
In a warm-brown color, the same as the tower
Of a château, which shoots up
On the dark right side, from behind the trees.
A second château far away, on the upland,
In a white blur, over a wooded slope
That descends towards the road and the hamlet in the valley
With its flock of sheep, poplars, the third
Château, or perhaps a romanesque church tower.
And most important: a peasant woman in a red
Skirt, a black bodice, a white
Blouse, carrying something (laundry to the stream?),

Czeslaw Milosz / 93

Hard to see her face—it is no more than a dot.
Yet she walked there, seen by the painter
And remained forever, only to make possible
The fulfillment of his own, revealed just to him,
Harmony in yellow, blue, and russet.

IV

Yale Center for British Art:
John Constable (1776–1837): The Young Waltonians–Stratford Mill,
ca. 1819–1825

To tell the truth, a rather miserable stream,
A little more abundant at the dam by the mill,
Enough to lure boys. Their angling tackle
Is quite sloppy. A branch, not a fishing rod,
In the hand of the one who stands. Others slouch
Staring at their floats. Over there, in a boat
The younger ones are playing. If only that water
Were blue, but the clouds of England,
As always ragged, announce rain
And this brief clearing is the color of lead.
This is supposed to be romantic, i.e. picturesque.
Yet not for them. We are free to guess
Their patched trousers, patched shirts
As well as their dream of escaping from the village.
But let it be, after all. We recognize the right
To change everything that is sadly real
Into a composition on canvas, which has for its subject
Air. Its changeability, sudden leaps,
Cloudy turmoils, a wandering ray.
No slightest promise of Eden. Who would like to live here?
Let us pay tribute to the painter, so faithful
To bad weather, who chose it, and remains with it.

V

Yale University Art Gallery:
Jean Baptiste Corot: Port in La Rochelle,
ca. 1851

His name is luminosity. Whatever he saw
Would bring to him, would humbly offer
Its interior without waves, its silence, its calm,
Like a river in the haze of an early morning,
Like a mother of pearl in a black shell.
So, too, this port, in an afternoon hour
With its slumbering sails, its heat,
Where we wandered perhaps, heavy with wine,
Unbuttoning our waistcoats, for him was airy.
It revealed radiance in the disguise of a moment.
These small figures are real till today:
Here are three women, another is riding
A donkey, a man is rolling a barrel,
Horses in their collars, patient. He, holding his palette,
Called out to them, summoned them, led them away
From the poor earth of toil and bitterness
Into this velvety province of goodness.

EUGENIO MONTALE

TRANSLATED FROM THE ITALIAN BY WILLIAM ARROWSMITH

Floodwaters

Frantic with love, I knelt
at the Castalian Spring
but no freshet reflected
my image.

I have never seen
the piranha's native waters, where swimmers
wash back ashore, bones picked clean.

And yet
other waters work with us,
for us, and on us, with an indifferent
monstrous effort of recuperation.
What once they gave,
the waters take back, aided by Time, their unseen
double. And the laving of this feeble, tumid tide
has preyed on us since we abandoned fins
to sprout these limbs of ours—a malformation,
a sad joke that has saddled us
with bad conscience and responsibility.

The seething junk which my window overlooks—
trash, crates, cars heaped up
in the courtyard below,
the slow, smoking flow that streams away
on its own account, ignoring our existence—
all this seemed final proof
that we are here for something, a trap, a goal.
It *seemed*, not *seems*. . . . Once
chestnuts exploded in the hot coals, tapers glowed

on the Christmas presents. Now the demon
of the waters no longer likes apprising us
that we, his spectators and accomplices,
are still ourselves.

In Silence

General strike today.
Deserted streets, no noise.
Only a transistor the other side of the wall:
somebody must have moved in a few days ago.
I wonder if production will fall.
This year even spring is late in producing.
They turned off the central heating in anticipation.
They noticed that the postal system wasn't working.
It's no disaster, this suspension of normal operations.
And inevitably a few gears aren't engaged.
Even the dead have started agitating.
They're part of the total silence too.
You're underground. No point arousing you,
you're always awake. Even today,
in the universal sleep.

PAUL MULDOON

The Briefcase

FOR SEAMUS HEANEY

I held the briefcase at arm's length from me;
the oxblood or liver
eelskin with which it was covered
had suddenly grown supple.

I'd been waiting in line for the crosstown
bus when an almighty cloudburst
left the sidewalk a raging torrent.

And though all it contained was the first
inkling of this poem, I knew I daren't
set the briefcase down
to slap my pockets for an obol—

for fear it might slink into a culvert
and strike out along the East River
for the sea. By which I mean the "open" sea.

Cauliflowers

*Plants that glow in the dark have been developed
through gene-splicing, in which light-producing bacteria
from the mouths of fish are introduced to cabbage,
carrots and potatoes.*

—NATIONAL ENQUIRER

More often than not he stops at the headrig to light
his pipe
and try to regain
his composure. The price of cauliflowers
has gone down
two weeks in a row on the Belfast market.

From here we can just make out
a platoon of Light
Infantry going down
the road to the accompaniment of a pipe
band. The sun glints on their silver-
buttoned jerkins.

My uncle, Patrick Regan,
has been leaning against the mudguard
of the lorry. He levers
open the bonnet and tinkers with a light
wrench at the hose pipe
that's always going down.

Then he himself goes down
to bleed oil into a jerry can.
My father slips the pipe
into his scorch-marked

breast pocket and again makes light
of the trepanned cauliflowers.

All this as I listened to lovers
repeatedly going down
on each other in the next room . . . "light
of my life" . . . in a motel in Oregon.
All this. Magritte's
pipe

and the pipe
bomb. White Annetts. Gillyflowers.
Margaret,
are you grieving? My father going down
the primrose path with Patrick Regan.
All gone out of the world of light.

All gone down
the original pipe. And the cauliflowers
in an unmarked pit, that were harvested by their own light.

ERIC PANKEY

In the Mode of Confession

If it is true that evil exists,
And that he knows it by reflection,
That he does not speculate, but knows
The workings of such a dark sweet hive,

Then every structure his hands have built
Is obstacle and every fabric
Stitched together remains disguise.
He manages to hide his crime.

Although in the mode of confession,
He does not ask for forgiveness.
He is unworthy, thus worthy of grace.
He asks for a practical miracle:

To relive the act, to undo the done.

LINDA PASTAN

Under the Resurrection Palm

If you eat the cabbage heart of a palm,
the tree will die. . . .

In Beaufort, South Carolina, Spanish moss
hangs from the live oaks, blurring
all distinctions,
turning the landscape into a room
so filled with cobwebs
that History becomes no more
than the moment that has just passed,
and the faces lifting
from the field to watch us
could be from an engraving
we know by heart already.

Our tour guide speaks of the War
as if there had been no other,
tells us how even the Yankees
spared this hospital town
where gravestones were lifted
from the ground like doors
from their hinges to rest
the wounded Confederate soldiers on.
Hamilton, Fripp, and Barnwell—
she knows their names, their houses,
which one married the other's sister.

She is as swollen with facts
as this moss which holds
twenty times its weight in water.
It is nearly silent here.

Behind the pillared porches nothing
seems to happen
except birth and death
and the barely perceptible seasons,
though sometimes drunk
on palmetto berries,
a mockingbird flies upside down.

How hard it is to believe
that the little heron
with its shy head,
the one that winters here,
is the same bird we will see
up north next summer
or that the sky which spreads
like watered silk
over this river town
is of a piece with the cold
sky at home.

Sculpture Garden

Between a bronze turtle
and a stone bird,
the wooden Adam and Eve,
carved with a chain saw
out of old telephone poles,
stand sap-stained
in this flowerless garden,
ringed with the years
of the trees they came from
transformations ago.

I wonder if they remember
their lost leaves or the voices
that flew swifter than starlings
from telephone pole to telephone pole,
those cruciform shapes
lining the hills of the country
like stations of the cross.
It is early November.
This silence
between fall and winter

will be brief as the pause
between movements of music
when we listen
with all our attention
but may not applaud.
I think of the voices lost
since last winter. Sometimes
loneliness is so palpable
it becomes a presence
of its own, a kind of company.

Eden is lost
each time a child slides
through the torn gates
of its mother's thighs.
But here in an invented garden
I find a bestiary waiting
to be named: a wire cobra;
a turtle patient as bronze;
the stone wings of a bird
about to fly.

ROBERT PINSKY

Hut

Nothing only
what it was—

Slates, burls, rims:

Their names like the circus
Lettering on a van: *Bros.* and *Movers*,
Symmetrical buds of
Meaning in the spurs and serifs
Of scarlet with gold outlines.

Transport and Salvage,
Moving and Storage.

The house by the truck yard:
Flag walk. Shake siding. The frontyard spruce
A hilt of shadows.

And out back in the wooded lot,
The hut of scrapwood and bedframes
Lashed with housewire by children,
Hitchknots of the plainsman
Or the plasterer shoring a ladder.

Cache of cigarettes, tongue
And groove, magazines,
Chocolate, books: *Moaning she guided*
His throbbing manhood and *Southwark Bridge*
Which is of iron
And London Bridge which is of stone.

Hobo cookery in tin cans.
Muffled coherence like dreams.

Printslugs,
Glass insulators, "Enemy Zeros."
Maimed mouth-harp and sashweight.
Trojans and Sheiks,

Esquire,
Beaverboard, Romex.
Each thing or name a river
With a silty bottom.
The source hidden, the mouth
Emptying in the ocean.

Hut as of driftwood,
Scavengers and Haulers,
Household and Commercial Removals.
Westphal's Auxiliator, *quim, poorhouse,*
Homasote,

The mighty forest of significance—
Possibly dreamed
By a man in Headlight overalls,
Even by the one we found
Sleeping there once
With his empty of Seven
Crown, not necessarily
By a god or goddess—
The embroidered letters
HEAD tapering each smaller and LIGHT
Each larger, like beams thrown
From the center—that snoring,
Historical heart.

STANLEY PLUMLY

Woman on Twenty-second Eating Berries

She's not angry exactly but all business,
eating them right off the tree, with confidence,
the kind that lets her spit out the bad ones
clear of the sidewalk into the street. It's
sunny, though who can tell what she's tasting,
rowan or one of the service-berries—
the animal at work, so everybody,
save the traffic, keeps a distance. She's picking
clean what the birds have left, and even,
in her hurry, a few dark leaves. In the air
the dusting of exhaust that still turns pennies
green, the way the cloudy surfaces
of things obscure their differences,
like the mock-orange or the apple-rose that
cracks the paving stone, rooted in the plaza.
No one will say your name, and when you come to
the door no one will know you, a parable
of the afterlife on earth. Poor grapes, poor crabs,
wild black cherry trees, on which some forty-six
or so species of birds have fed, some boy's dead
weight or the tragic summer lightning killing
the seed, how boyish now that hunger
to bring those branches down to scale,
to eat of that which otherwise was waste,
how natural this woman eating berries, how alone.

SUSAN PROSPERE

Peonies

Drifting on the downside of love, when all
must be retrieved, brought home again,
I see myself standing at the end
of the path in my childhood—the sky
above me darkening—& I am holding
a little pail & shovel,
frightened, I think, because it's later
than it should be, so I must whistle
softly with bravado to hear myself,
so far down the path I look
smaller than I ought to, while you looking out
on my room we made love in
are finding it even harder to fetch yourself,
so lost you look in this bower
you call "so brutally feminine,"
now that we are drawn apart on the other side
of ardor; thus it is I must take your hand
to lead you out past the fluted lamps,
past the scrolled cage suspended
from the ceiling—the artificial cardinal
on the red swing swinging, past the Sirens
bending over—their tendrilous locks flowing
over the ovolo moulding, their rosebud
mouths open, open, singing. . . . Then you & I
go hand in hand into the parlor
to the vase that holds a whole flock
of fluffed-up peonies, looking
as if they have walked to the edge of water
to dip their beaks in, their sickles
& saddle feathers spread wide
for bathing. Once a year, at least,
I must have them—too big, I'd say,

for beauty. If you could know me truly,
you could hide with me there
in the tangled vine at the end of the path,
two doors down from my grandmother's
house, where the hens fly loose
from the broody coop, their rose combs
quivering, & the rooster bobs
his crested head, a *miles gloriosus*
patrolling along the paling,
guardian of this grassy lot & the dark bordering
alley. Then out on the stoop come
the aging spinsters—glowering sibyls
who point us children toward the gates
of hell, promising us
we'll get there. Old maids, old maids,
can't get a husband, the neighborhood boys
call back, their voices rising
from the hollow, & though the day has barely
broken, the sisters cross the yard
to wring the necks of the waiting chickens,
their feathers ruffled
like these blossoms on the edge
of dying. Headless, they rise to go up
the porch steps & back down again,
their bodies remembering what their tiny brains
no longer tell them . . . & in the gathering
light, I throw down my bucket
& its hoard of eggs some stray hen laid,
filched from the shadows—one
with a window a baby chick pipped open—
lost forever; though later, to console me,
Mama & Aunt Gay will take me
down the block to Robinson's Drugstore
to drink floats with the workers
from the hosiery mill at the table
where John Scopes sat down to argue
for teaching the origin of man, & I'm
glad, I say, I came from a monkey,
so little *I've* seen of the floss & gold
of the angels they tell me

peer down on us from the heavens. I spend
my pennies on Atomic Fireballs & a glass ring,
its band expandable. Who, then, they ask,
laughing, will you marry? . . . *No one, no one,*
& in the late afternoon the chimes
from Bryan Hill drifting over the valley,
Mama will sit before the vanity
in the one upstairs bedroom,
the oscillating fan blowing, to take
off the face she "puts on" each morning,
the jar of vanishing cream open on the table,
while I, outside with the other children,
slip the skins off the scuppernongs
& place them in a petri dish,
shallow enough for feeling, & line up
sun-dried apricots & pasta swirling
in a bowl, taking each thing one by one,
blindfolded, believing, naming
the parts—eyeballs, ears,
the working brain—
willing ourselves to touch them,
even with our tongues, these human parts,
our hearts in our throats, our bodies
shivering, partly afraid, partly ecstatic.

YANNIS RITSOS

TRANSLATED FROM THE GREEK BY EDMUND KEELEY

The Diviner

Her hair always loose, like a paid mourner's
over some invisible dead body or over
her own dead body. "An evil gift," she says,
"to divine correctly." That net,
the dark one, from the bath, in front of her eyes
like her own hair—not simply
a death net, but worse, a net to be used for deception,
for murder or the unachievable. And again
the lovely spring hours arrive, the fragile hours—
a child thrusts his feet into that large basin,
plays with the soap,
and she, making two slits in her hair
with two fingernails, as though playing a lyre, looks
deeply through those openings,
divines correctly and correctly smiles.

1964–1965

Between Ionians and Dorians

Everyone acknowledged unambiguously that he was an important
and sensible hero,
and his actions showed it. A religiously tolerant lover of the good
and enemy
of all evil, even if it emerged from his own narrow circle (of course
assuming one can tell what is good and what evil).
                                                    Dorians and Ionians
laid exclusive claim to him. They pressed him in a thousand open
and secret ways.
He, as always, obstinate, just—all his effort given to unity.
He was nothing other than a Greek, he said, and only a Greek—
                                                    until in the end
he remained alone, with all his "unity," with all his "Greekness,"
suspect to both of them, equally hated, to the point that, agreeing in
their hatred,
the two stoned him to death one May morning at the Isthmus of
Corinth. And immediately
a battle began over who would appropriate his corpse.
                                                    A few years later,
the Dorians and Ionians dedicated their most splendid altars to him,
carving in the marble the brilliant words THE FIRST DORIAN in one
case
and THE FIRST IONIAN in the other—this for the man who was
nothing but a Greek only. And nobody ever ascertained
where his actual bones were laid—probably nowhere. The myth,
more reliable, relates
that a white eagle at the last minute snatched him up into the
clouds.
                        And when
a heavy winter comes to Attica and the Peloponnese, and the crops
are flooded,
and the river carries off lambs, stools, shoes, statues, then the two of
them

gaze up at the sky and, it is said, clearly make out the eagle and
      Him,
there where the black clouds rip apart and a golden ray of sunlight
      hangs free
—but (you'd think it their fate) even then they cannot come to their
      senses.

                                                    Leros, April 7, 1968

After the Treaty Between the Athenians and the Lacedaemonians Was Broken

AFTER THUCYDIDES

Corinth, Argos, Sparta, Athens, Sicyon, and other (how many?)
    smaller cities—
the Greeks have become a thousand fragments; the great treaty has
    been broken;
everyone is enraged with everyone else—new meetings, meetings and
    more meetings, conferences;
yesterday's friends and neighbors no longer greet each other in the
    street—
old grudges have come between them again; new alliances,
entirely opposite to earlier ones, are being sounded out, prepared.
    Deputations
arrive secretly at midnight; others leave. The statues of our heroes,
standing neglected in the city squares and gardens, are shat on by
    sparrows.
Group after group in the agora discuss our situation seriously,
exaltedly, passionately: Who gave them their orders? Who appointed
    them?
We, anyway, didn't choose them (Besides, how? And when? New
    bosses again? Who needs them?) April has arrived;
the small pepper trees on the sidewalks have turned green—a gentle
    green,
tender, childlike (moving to us) even if
rather dusty—the municipal service seems to be out of it,
no longer showing up in the afternoons to sprinkle the streets. But
    today,
on the portico surrounding the closed Council Chambers, the first
    swallow appeared unexpectedly,

and everybody shouted: "A swallow; look, a swallow; look, a
     swallow"—
everybody in unison, even the most violently opposed: "A swallow."
     And suddenly
everybody fell silent, feeling alone, detached from the others, as
     though free,
as though united in continuity, within a communal isolation. And
     then
they understood that their only freedom was their solitude, but that
     too
(though imperceptible) unprotected, vulnerable, a thousand times
     entrapped, alone.

                                                    April 4, 1968

Not Even Mythology

The day ends that way, with brilliant colors, so lovely, without
anything at all happening for us. The guards forgotten in the
    guardhouses.
A boat floats in the shallows, the light golden and rose, foreign;
the nets in the slime gather black fish, fat and oily,
reflecting the glimmer of twilight. And later, when the lamps were
    lit,
we went inside and again returned to Mythology, searching
for some deeper correlation, some distant, general allegory
to soothe the narrowness of the personal void. We found nothing.
The pomegranate seeds and Persephone seemed cheap to us
in view of the night approaching heavily and the total absence.

Leros, March 31, 1968

IRA SADOFF

1848

The starlings are black handkerchiefs on the lawn.
The protagonist coughing blood into them
at the Empire's last lawn party, before the railroad comes.

Grubby little chunks of coal, they nest on trees
and stones because they'll have them. I'm so drawn
to rainclouds, whole flocks cawing their dark

hallelujahs, I forgive the little boy
whose extended paws are bowls of sticky porridge.
Black-faced chimney sweep, hands of cobblestone, all the smoky

factories, little birds of Birmingham, make him cough.
So when a stranger takes pity, slides a pence from his silk pocket,
he takes it, to heart, the way the crow by the side of the road

takes apart the sinewy flank of venison.

DAVID ST. JOHN

Merlin

ITALO CALVINO (1923–1985)

It was like a cave of snow, no . . .
More like that temple of frosted, milk-veined marble
    I came upon one evening in Selinunte,
Athena's white owl flying suddenly out of its open eaves.
    I saw the walls lined with slender black-spined
        Texts, rolled codices, heavy leather-bound volumes
Of the mysteries. Ancient masks of beaten copper and tin,
    All ornamented with rare feathers, scattered jewels.
His table was filled with meditative beakers, bubbling
        Here and there like clocks; the soldierly
Rows of slim vials were labeled in several foreign hands.
    Stacks of parchments, cosmological recipes, nature's
Wild equivalencies. A globe's golden armature of the earth,
        Its movable bones ringing a core of empty
    Space. High above the chair, a hanging Oriental scroll,
Like the origami of a crane unfolded, the Universe inked
        So blue it seemed almost ebony in daylight,
The stars and their courses plotted along its shallow folds
    In a luminous silver paint. On an ivory pole,
        His chameleon robe, draped casually, hieroglyphics
Passing over it as across a movie screen, odd formulas
    Projected endlessly—its elaborate layers of
Embroidery depicting impossible mathematical equations;
        Stitched along the hem, the lyrics
Of every song one hears the nightingale sing, as dusk falls
    On summer evenings. All of our stories so much
        Of the world they must be spoken by

A voice that rests beyond it . . . his voice, its ideal melody,
        Its fragile elegance guiding our paper boats,
                    Our so slowly burning wings,
Toward any immanent imagination, our horizon's carved sunset,
            The last wisdoms of Avalon.

JAMES SEAY

Tiffany & Co.

FOR ELIZABETH SPENCER

Leafing through a friend's catalogue—
the Fall Selections 1987—
I linger on something the blue of a robin's egg
and wonder why I've never bought any of these *objets*,
never felt the specific fetish-force
of the commodity behind the revolution
of their brass doors or 800 number.
There's possibly history to explain:
we could go back, say, seventy years
to when my mother and JFK were born
and take a look around:
Freud's new Intro to Psychoanalysis on one hand,
Lenin entering the Winter Palace on the other,
but mainly there's the paradigmatic news
every winter day in Tyro, Mississippi,
of no indoor plumbing and a dead aunt's
five children extra to feed,
which lasted right on through my kindergarten
of visits to Granny's.
                    So why on Bolshaya Morskaya
would I go looking for Fabergé's old St. Petersburg shop
when where Lenin had breakfast
with smoldering Bolsheviks was just around the corner?
Well, maybe to have pissed into both the figurative
wind and a hole in the ground
is to be drawn to the abstract gloss
of privilege as though it might incorporate
and invite us to its private Mardi Gras—
such parades in life, for instance, as lunch
with the woman in Georgetown

whose every emblem was Camelot,
right down to sterling frame for the Presidential scrawl
on a scrap of teletype
thanking her for the intro to Ian Fleming
and 007.
But it didn't seem, on Bolshaya Morskaya, the same dream
of Fat Tuesday's carnival and masquerade.
I thought of old Fabergé, Russian to the bone and in Swiss exile
while Bolsheviks, quit with eating fable-cake,
were already breaking rank and bellying up
to the Tsar's bar, the monkey
of power settling on their backs,
jeweled eggs glittering in their words.
Power's not like Bond's regimental gin;
it wants to be stirred never shaken:
sooner or later there's the commissioned aria,
the room of shoes worn once or never,
cinema's kitten purr.
Or the threadbare velvet glove
on the stainless-steel hand
the cautious in any century recognize.
                                    She didn't smile—
my Intourist guide in Moscow—
but I meant it only as a joke
when I asked her if there was a tunnel
between the headquarters of the KGB
and the country's largest store of children's toys,
just across the street.
One imperial egg in the Kremlin nearby
still has as its surprise the miniature
Trans-Siberian Railway train.
Another opens to reveal Nicholas's yacht
scaled down in gold.
We have to imagine the cross-ties & rails, the constant steppes,
in all seasons, to the sea,
imagine the sea as well, and the globe
we want to shape and shape again.

CHARLES SIMIC

Paradise

In a neighborhood once called Hell's Kitchen
Where a beggar claimed to be playing Nero's fiddle
While the city burned in midsummer heat;
Where a lady barber who called herself Cleopatra
Wielded the scissors of fate over my head
Threatening to cut off my ears and nose;
Where a man and a woman went walking naked
In one of the dark side streets at dawn.

I must be dreaming, I told myself.
It was like meeting a couple of sphinxes.
I expected them to have wings, bodies of lions:
Him with his wildly tattooed chest;
Her with her huge, dangling breasts.

It happened so quickly, and so long ago!

You know that time just before the day breaks
When one yearns to lie down on cool sheets
In a room with shades drawn?
The hour when the beautiful suicides
Lying side by side in the morgue
Get up and walk out into the first light.

The curtains of cheap hotels flying out of windows
Like sea gulls, but everything else quiet . . .
Steam rising out of the subway gratings . . .
Bodies glistening with sweat . . .
Madness, and you might even say, paradise!

Le Beau Monde

A man got up to talk about Marcel Proust,
"The great French writer,"
From a soapbox famous for its speeches
About crooked bosses and the working poor.

I swear it (Tony Russo is my witness).
It was late one night, the crowd was thinning,
But then they all came back
To see what his mumbling was all about.

He looked like a dishwasher
From one of the dives on Avenue B.
He chewed his nails as he spoke.
He said this and that in what must've been French.

Everybody perked up, even the winos.
The tough guys stopped flexing their muscles.
It was like being in church
When the High Mass was said in Latin.

Nobody had a clue, but it made you feel good.
When it was over, he just walked away,
Long-legged and in a big hurry.
The rest of us taking our time to disperse.

GERALD STERN

A Song for Kenneth Burke

May 7–15, Iowa City, Iowa

I have in mind some dust; a sprite
called Burke shook down some apples once.
It was in Shadyside. I stood
on the same corner, the same tree
blossomed that spring. I loved the bees
going wild. I carved around the rotten
flesh and lifted them up; it was
a miniature world: the teacher was sleeping,
the wife was in her chair, the child
was squirming, there was a soldier screaming,
he was hunched over. What is it called
when the world is sliced apart? I lift
the Victorian age, I hold it by a stem,
I lift my childhood: there is the frog
in a mason jar, the glass is driven
into his body, it was an accident—
I think it was only three landings—there is
a woman named Liz, her mouth is full
of semen; I hold a tiny cat
in my arms—A diorama! A section!
A slice of life! Ah, shades of some school
or other, the girls are walking back
to their sewing machines, the miners are digging
by purple light.
                I stand by a tree
in the rear of my garden, it is surrounded
by lilacs, yet the blossoms are large
and lovely; I feel like a mother in awe
of her baby. How could those limbs be perfect
like that? How could those blossoms come

again and again? The whole tree is covered
with flowers. Poor Burke! When he finally gets here
there will be just a white rug, but that
is something too. I see him bend down—
the last time I saw him his legs were crooked—
and pick up a blossom. He holds it to his eye,
he blows on the edges. I heard he lived
in a cottage in west New Jersey, it is
ramshackle, no electricity,
a bottle of vodka on the sink,
the papers piled up, a stand of trees
outside the window, little hills
to soothe his spirit, a hand-dug pond—
with pickerel—a tiny sand beach,
with rushes, for Moses, so Moses can lie there
planning the future. My apples are yellow,
and hard and sweet; I eat them all day;
some are rotten, all are rotten
a little; I love a wrinkled skin,
I love the seeds. I pick some flowers—
it's early still—I'll put them in a vase—
with lilacs—I'll arrange them. This is
my month: tulips, lilacs, cherries—
and violets—under the apple—green
and purple and white; this is the month—
under our lake and near our river—
for plans, for visions; not September,
not December.
        Burke had a plan
to call things by their other name;
it was an exotic plan. He lived
near hills and water; that was in the blood,
that was in the mind; he lived
by moonlight—there is another race
among us; he was almost Li Po
for a minute; he pursued that face
for years, he stalked a soul, he cried
in Greek, he spoke to a shadow, he dropped
a stone in the pond; a part of him shivered,
it almost exploded; he spoke to the moon

with caution. Who is to say the moon
loved one of them less? How could you not
turn into a shadow? What would that fish
now eat? What if it nibbled on his hair?
What if it swam through his eye? Sustenance
is in the brain. How could Burke not
derive his knowledge from the talk
in drugstores—was the fish not brain food?
Didn't the pickerel swim in the mind?
Was there not a reversal? Didn't
the pickerel eat that meal? Was gray food
not what he ate? Did he not gobble
blood and nerves? Did he not dip
his nose into the skull, was he
not a fish of fury?
                                    Burke bends down
to pick up a porous stick, he sensed
the lightness, it shone in the moonlight, the holes
were there for the light to come through though water
took over sometimes and mud caked up
his exits—for him they were exits. He floats
his stick, it is another face;
a third; a fourth if you count the moon;
he should have put some feathers on
the forehead and scarred the cheeks. He runs
to the other side, the grasses scratch
his ankles, his slippers are soaked, he picks up
his stick; the water is black, the roots run
into his fingers. For just a minute
he thought of Thales—he could be Thales
explaining the world. Was he not Thales?
Did he not have one explanation—
and then another? If he had a glass
he'd lift it to the moon. Ah, vodka,
with ice. Vermouth. What if love
could be reduced? What are the words
in German and Hebrew? How did the Greeks
help lead him astray? How long did his Lucy
wait? What is the word for sorrow?
What is the word for live fish, for shadow?

MARK STRAND

The Continental College of Beauty

When the Continental College of Beauty opened its doors
We looked down hallways covered with old masters
And into rooms where naked figures lounged on marble floors.
And we were moved, but not enough to stay. We hurried on
Until we reached a courtyard overgrown with weeds.
This moved us, too, but in a moment we were nodding off.
The sun was coming up, a violet haze was lifting from the sea,
Coastal hills were turning red, and several people on the beach
Went up in flames. This was the start of something new.
The flames died down. The sun continued on its way.
And lakes inland, in the first light, flashed their scales,
And mountains cast a blue, cold shade on valley floors,
And distant towns awoke . . . this is what we'd waited for.
How quickly the great unfinished world came into view
When the Continental College of Beauty opened its doors.

Workshop Miracle

(a short opera)

Scene: A university classroom

PROF. SMITH:

Jones, did you write a poem today?

JONES:

I did.

PROF. SMITH:

You did? You, the least promising student in class, wrote a poem?
Only under my guidance could such a thing happen. Jones, will you
share your poem with us?

JONES:

I can't, sir. I haven't got it with me, and since I wrote it in free
verse, I can't remember it.

PROF. SMITH:

Can you tell us a little about it then?

JONES:

Only in rhyme, sir.

PROF. SMITH:

Well?

JONES:

It says that fields of autumn flowers will not end in frost,
which would be nice, but in a distant smear
of embers drifting everywhere, forever lost.

And farther down, it says much worse,
That those who were not friends on earth
will spend eternity together; the sheep
will ride the whale's great back in the silent deep,
the dog and the hare will swing side by side, year after year;
and then it says that we, no matter what we do,
will not be spared the rushing tides and heavy undertow
of dark. In every verse, one feels the slow
and fated burial of all we know. . . .

PROF. SMITH:

That will do, Jones. Clara, what do you think of Jones's work? Not
the rhymed paraphrase, of course, but what you take to be the real
thing?

CLARA:

May the Muses of Sicily fall to their knees! It is your work,
professor, that we should applaud. If a poem can be born in a place
like this, poetry will never die. Nor will it want to die, though I can
imagine it will be tempted from time to time.

PROF. SMITH:

Oh, Clara, as usual, you are right. Let's work together so poetry will
never die.

WHOLE CLASS:

Together, together, so poetry will never die. Together, together, etc.

The Couple

The scene is a midtown station.
   The time is 3 A.M.
Jane is alone on the platform,
   Humming a requiem.

She leans against the tiles.
   She rummages in her purse
For something to ease a headache
   That just keeps getting worse.

She went to a boring party,
   And left without her date.
Now she's alone on the platform,
   And the trains are running late.

The subway station is empty,
   Seedy, sinister, gray.
Enter a well-dressed man
   Slowly heading Jane's way.

The man comes up beside her:
   "Excuse me, my name is John.
I hope I haven't disturbed you.
   If I have, then I'll be gone.

"I had a dream last night
   That I would meet somebody new.
After twenty-four hours of waiting,
   I'm glad she turned out to be you."

Oh where are the winds of morning?
    Oh where is love at first sight?
A man comes out of nowhere.
    Maybe he's Mr. Right.

How does one find the answer,
    If one has waited so long?
A man comes out of nowhere,
    He's probably Mr. Wrong.

Jane imagines the future,
    And almost loses heart.
She sees herself as Europe
    And John as Bonaparte.

They walk to the end of the platform.
    They stumble down to the tracks.
They stand among the wrappers
    And empty cigarette packs.

The wind blows through the tunnel.
    They listen to the sound.
The way it growls and whistles
    Holds them both spellbound.

Jane stares into the dark:
    "It's a wonder sex can be good
When most of the time it comes down to
    Whether one shouldn't or should."

John looks down at his watch:
    "I couldn't agree with you more,
And often it raises the question—
    'What are you saving it for?' "

They kneel beside each other
    As if they were in a trance,
Then Jane lifts up her dress
    And John pulls down his pants.

Everyone knows what happens,
   Or what two people do
When one is on top of the other
   Making a great to-do.

The wind blows through the tunnel
   Trying to find the sky.
Jane is breathing her hardest,
   And John begins to sigh:

"I'm a Princeton professor.
   God knows what drove me to this.
I have a wife and family;
   I've known marital bliss.

"But things were turning humdrum,
   And I felt I was being false.
Every night in our bedroom
   I wished I were someplace else."

What is the weather outside?
   What is the weather within
That drives these two to excess
   And into the arms of sin?

They are the children of Eros.
   They move, but not too fast.
They want to extend their pleasure,
   They want the moment to last.

Too bad they cannot hear us.
   Too bad we can't advise.
Fate that brought them together
   Has yet another surprise.

Just as they reach the utmost
   Peak of their endeavor,
An empty downward local
   Separates them forever.

An empty downtown local
　Screams through the grimy air.
A couple dies in the subway;
　Couples die everywhere.

CHASE TWICHELL

Revenge

He was standing on the hotel balcony
when I awoke, watching the late afternoon

sluice down green-gold
over the fronds of the royal palms.

Palms in wind make a sound
like knives being sharpened,

languorous in my dispersing sleep,
slice-slicing against themselves.

He was watching the melon-colored light
run over the slow swells,

and the pleasure boats trailing
their long white creamy wakes,

their engines shuddering.
My waking thought was that

I was waking *inside a century*,
a cage bigger than our lives,

and that the freedom to roam around in it
was an illusion we both had, or an irony

we'd once abided by but had forgotten,
walking in the drifting dunes of light,

the snows of Perdido, snows of crushed coral,
on the edge of the trespassing sea.

The sheets were imprinted on my skin.
The cool air fingered each crease

and the fresh grass matting felt
pleasingly harsh and raw underfoot.

No one could see me
there in the palm shadows, naked

and dappled by the sun's warm camouflage.
The passing seconds were almost visible,

a faintly glamorous stream of light
that flowed over the moving boats,

brightened the frictional leaves.
He put his arm around my shoulders,

the smell of the day in his shirt,
so that his thumb not quite touched

my nipple, which shriveled,
and with the other hand slowly

unbuttoned and unzipped himself,
all the while watching the pleasure boats

glide past us trailing bits of broken mirror,
their engines pulsing steadily,

fueled by what's left of the future.

DEREK WALCOTT

Chapter XXXIX

I

The great headstones lifted like the keels of curraghs
from Ireland's groundswell and spray foamed on the walls
of the broken abbey. That far light was the lough's,

a salver held by a tonsured hill. The old well's
silence increased as gravel was crunched by pilgrims
following the monks' footpath. Silence was in flower.

It widened the furrows like a gap between hymns,
if that pause were protracted hour after hour
by century-ringed oaks, by a square Celtic cross

in wafers of snowdrops from the day webbed mortar
had cinched the stones to the whisk of a sorrel horse
grazing its station. In it, a paper aspen

rustled its missal. Its encircling power
lifted the midges in vertiginous Latin,
then slid a rook into the slit of a tower

like a card in the post. It waxed a blue tea van,
draped a booth with sweaters, then it crossed the dry road
to hear a brook talk the old language of Ireland.

There it filled a bucket and carried the clear load
for the sorrel to nuzzle with ruffling nostrils.
The weight of the place, its handle, its local name

for "wood-with-a-lake," or abbey with hooded hills,
rooted in the bucket's clang, echoed the old shame
of disenfranchisement. I had no oasis,

no clear language to drink from like a thirsty horse
or pilgrim lapping up soul-watering places;
the grass was brighter with envy and my remorse

was a clouding sun. The sorrel swaying its whisk,
the blue panes of sky in the ruin fitted a past
to which Glenn-da-Lough pointed with its obelisk,

as alder and aspen aged in an alphabet,
as the child-voiced brook recited today's lesson.
Now an elder clapped its leaves in approbation

until others swayed to the old self-possession
for which faith is known; but which faith, in a nation
split by a glottal scream, by a sparrow's chirrup,

where a prayer incised in a cross, a Celtic rune
could send the horse circling with empty stirrup
from a sniper's bolt? Here, from this abbey's ruin,

if the rook flew north with its funercal caw,
far from this baptismal font, this silver weir,
too high for inspection as it crossed the Border,

it would see a street that ends in wreaths of wire
while a hearse with drizzling lights waits for an order
in a wet accent, making the black boots move on

in scraping syllables, the gun on its shoulder
still splitting hairs, dividing a Shem from a Shaun,
an Ireland no wiser as it gets older.

Yet all its wiry hedgerows startle the spirit
of swallow-tailed bard or priest to a tinker's spoon
banging a saucepan; the fields those birds inherit

hold stones dreaming of violence. A wax-faced moon
mounted the green pulpit of Sugar Loaf Mountain
with its starched collar. Along a yew-guarded road,

a cloud hung from one branch in that orange hour,
like a shirt that was stained with poetry and with blood.
The wick of the cypress charred. Glenn-da-Lough's tower.

II

I leant on the mossed embankment just as if he
bloomed there every dusk with eyepatch and tilted hat,
rakish cane on one shoulder. Along the Liffey,

the mansards dimmed to one indigo silhouette,
then a stroke of light brushed the honey-haired river,
and, in black cloche hat and coat, she scurried faster

to the changing rose of a light. Anna Livia!
Muse of our age's Omeros, undimmed Master
and true tenor of the place! But I saw no gaunt,

cane-twirling flaneur. I blest myself in his voice,
and climbed up the wooden stairs to the restaurant
with its brass spigots, its glints, its beer-brightened noise,

and The Dead there in fringed shawls, as the wick-low shade
leapt high and rouged their cold cheeks with vermilion
round the pub piano, the airs Maud Plunkett played,

rowing her with felt hammer-strokes from my island
to one with bright doors and cobbles, and then his voice
led us all, as gently as Howth when it drizzles,

as fine as sun-drizzled Howth, its violet lees
of moss at low tide, where a dog barks "Howth! Howth!" at
the shawled waves, and the stone I rubbed in my pocket

from the Martello brought black-suited Ulysses
to the copper-bright strand, watching the mail-packet
butting past The Head, its wake glittering like keys.

CHARLES WRIGHT

Easter, 1989

March is the month of slow fire,
                                new grasses stung with rain,
Cold-shouldered, white-lipped.
Druidic crocus circles appear
Overnight, morose in their purple habits,
                                wet cowls
Glistening in the cut sun.

                        *   *   *

Instinct will end us.
The force that measles the peach tree
                                will divest and undo us.
The power that kicks on
                        the cells in the lilac bush
Will tumble us down and down.
Under the quince tree, purple cross points, and that's all right

For the time being,
                        the willow across the back fence
Menacing in its green caul.
When the full moon comes
                        gunning under the cloud's cassock
Later tonight, the stations
Will start to break forth like stars, their numbers flashing and then
    some.

Belief is a paltry thing
                        and will betray us, soul's load scotched
Against the invisible:
We are what we've always thought we were—
Peeling the membrane back,
                        amazed, like the jonquil's yellow head

Butting the nothingness—
                    in the wrong place, in the wrong body.

The definer of all things
                    cannot be spoken of.
It is not knowledge or truth.
We get no closer than next-to-it.
Beyond wisdom, beyond denial,
                    it asks us for nothing,
According to the Pseudo-Dionysius, which sounds good to me.

                    *   *   *

Nubbly with enzymes,
The hardwoods gurgle and boil in their leathery sheaths.
Flame flicks the peony's fuse.
Out of the caves of their locked beings,
                              candescent shapes
Roll the darkness aside as they rise to enter the real world.

ADAM ZAGAJEWSKI

TRANSLATED FROM THE POLISH BY
RENATA GORCZYNSKI AND BENJAMIN IVRY

At Midnight

We talked long at night, in the kitchen;
the oil lamp softly glowed,
and objects, encouraged by its gentleness,
emerged from the dark, revealing
their names: Table, Chair, Salt Cellar.

At midnight you said, Let's go
outside. Suddenly we saw the sky
and constellations burst, the stars of August.
The pale sheen of summer night trembled
over us, perpetual, unreined.

The world burned noiselessly, enveloped
by white fire in which hamlets slept,
parishes and haystacks smelling of mint
and of cloves. Trees and towers flamed,
water and air, wind and flames.

What is the silence of this night, since volcanoes
keep their eyes wide open, and the past
is omnipresent, threatening, lurks from its hiding place
the same as the moon or a juniper tree?
Your lips are cool, and cool will be the dawn,
like a towel thrown upon a feverish forehead.

R. Says

Literary rats—says R.—that's what we are.
We meet on lines at discount moviehouses;
At dusk, when thickly brocaded suns sink into green ponds,
we depart from libraries, enriched by readings of Kafka.
Enlightened rats in battle-dress jackets, in coats
of the pending army headed by a well-read despot;
we are the Secret Police of a poet who may come to power
on the outskirts of town. Rats with stipends, confidential
grant requests, caustic remarks, rats with bristled hair
and sharp, stiff whiskers.
Big cities, hot asphalt, and philanthropic ladies
know us well, but deserts, oceans, and jungles do not.
Benedictines of an atheist epoch, missionaries of easy despair,
we might just be a link in an evolution
whose address and sense are betrayed to no one.
We are paid in small, worthless gold coin: with
the bliss of a moment when the flame of metaphor
welds two hitherto free objects, when a hawk
alights, when a tax inspector makes the sign of the cross.

Presence

I was born in a city of wild cherries
and of hard-seeded sunflowers (halfway
between the West and East,
according to common belief). Globes covered by
verdigris kept careless vigil.

Can only nonpresence be perfect?
After all, presence is infested with the original
sin of existence: excess and savage
Oriental superbia. While beauty, like a fruit-paring
knife, makes do with a snip of plenitude.
Life accumulates in generations
as in a fishpond; it doesn't completely
vanish with the generation's disappearance
but turns dry and light. It reminds me of
an inattentive prayer, the chapped lips of a boy's first confession
while the wooden steps of the church booth
crack under his bended knees.
At night, autumn comes and possesses
the harvest: yellow, ripened for the flame.
I am sure there are at least four realities,
not just one, and all cross one another
like the Four Gospels.
I know I am alone and linked
with you, firmly, gladly, painfully.
I am aware that only mysteries are immortal.

WALTER ABISH

House on Fire

Lottery

Germany at its best. Full of promise. Ample, generous, agreeable. The divisive social categories, groupings, divisions, almost a thing of the benighted past. Money is king! Now, as never before. Now as never before? Not a new beginning, but an earth-shaking revitalization. And he, Franz, notwithstanding the gray of his age, willing and eager to reach for the compensatory rewards. Finally we have rediscovered our pride and can assert ourselves—able to participate not only in the society's industriousness or its dazzling consumer superabundance, but also in the forceful essence of its joyous spirit. What spirit? The spirit of life! Vigor! Zest! Anima! That's what. As the week before, and the week before, buying a dozen lottery tickets at the newsstand in the small oval park a stone's throw from the World War II monument, erected after much debate in 1973 in front of the former Piper Wacht Railroad Museum. We salute you, the mayor had said to much applause, echoing the words engraved in the marble base. As he owlishly stared at the tickets—Was he pondering the probability of a jackpot? It's going to happen—he had a failsafe system. It encapsulated all of history, at least the history he experienced. Thus, the number 4 was for the month, and 20, for the day, and 89 for the year, and 9,18, and 41 for the Battle of Kiev. Why those particular numbers? For Christ's sake—they're winning numbers! April 20, 1989, UNOHU's centennial. Not only battling the odds of something along the lines of one in a million but also acknowledging that embedded in the circuitry of each and every lottery administrator's brain was a tiny censor that relentlessly shredded all ideologically disputable numbers for the sake of the current democratic ideal . . . Anything, not to offend or stir up a furor! No matter! The round metallic kiosk, one of several dozen installed by the city to replace the battered green ones dating back to the fifties, was tightly shuttered and sealed by six each evening, the exterior coming to resemble an impregnable dome-shaped fortification. Although Franz had ample opportunity to purchase the tickets elsewhere, for some reason he was drawn to this particular neighborhood. Something in the air? Was it the inviting prosperity? Who lived here? Well you might ask? Everyday people? Just your young, relaxed, success-oriented execs and bankers, real estate investors, smugfaced art collector, friends of Axel Neurath-Klinge and Director Merkweise? Once in a while the news dealer, a disgruntled dour-faced disabled vet of Franz's age, was assisted by a younger woman. Daughter or relative? Possibly a second wife? In addition to the lottery tickets Franz bought the *Tagesblatt* and a pack of cheap cigars. Was it the occasion of UNOHU's coming centennial that prompted him to ask the news dealer if he had fought on the Eastern Front? The response, an immediate, furious no. Why the hostility? To ward off further inquiry? Or was it just a disinclination to converse? One of these days I am going to hit the jackpot, Franz asserted—just being amiable. I can feel it in my bones. In blank disbelief as the news dealer literally erupted, screaming, You smug condescending swine. Asking, Have you fought in the East? It's turds like you who destroy this society. Incredulously Franz watched the man drive himself into a frenzy—seeing tiny bubbles of spit form and burst as he ranted, Think you run things, eh? Shithead, all you do is rake it in. Franz raised his hand in a pacifying gesture. Listen . . . but as the man venomously continued his tirade, turning irate: I don't have to buy my tickets here. Encouraging the man to mimic his yet reasonable voice, That's it, going to strike it rich, are we? Put aside the past? Live it up in your shiny Mercedes? His exasperated Listen, I'm the chauffeur! had no effect. The man's gloating nasal laugh preceded the obscene pumping motion of one arm—A little nooky on the side, eh? Not willing to concede, Franz responded, If you think you . . . Think you're hot shit, don't you? the man shouted, triumphantly thumping the counter. I saw you ogling my woman. Franz was not quick enough to escape the flying glob of spit that landed on his sleeve. Enraged, he retaliated, sweeping a pile of newspapers and magazines off the counter—and then, exuberantly discharging his rage, I'll crumple your egg box, misfit. He was undaunted. You threatening me? I'll get you— like some mad apparition, emerging from a narrow side door, hopping on his one leg, the man was unhinged, the right trouser leg pinned to his upper thigh, crutches at the ready, one hand somehow able to clutch the empty wine bottle, which he hurled at Franz. It spiraled past Franz's head and shattered on the ground with a grenadelike effect, several pieces of glass hitting sharply against the polished lower rear door of the car. Franz, enraged, dashed to the car, fingers atremble as he set it in motion, jerkily backing away from the pavement in order to execute a U, then with the car pointed at the newsstand, accelerated on the broad gravel path, narrowly avoiding the news dealer, who, dropping his crutches, made a futile leap at the car. The car hit the kiosk a glancing blow that rocked the metal hut and scattered newspapers and magazines like so much confetti. As he sped away, Franz could see in the rearview mirror the newsstand listing like a sinking ship moments before it is about to go under, while the news dealer was still trying to raise himself up from the ground.

Back in the garage he examined the car. The damage was negligible. But it was only a matter of time before the police would be knocking at his door. What could he tell them? An hour later Uschi entered the garage and found him sitting in absolute darkness behind the wheel, smoking a cigarette.

Meditating?

Why bother to reply? He knew what he was going to do with the lottery jackpot. Piss on everyone. He even knew how he'd spend the first day, hour by hour. Head for the Porsche showroom. Select a 911 Carrera 4 or a 928 or the 944 S2. The 911 had a tire air-pressure monitoring device. Next, get himself a hotshot accountant, then . . .

Where Are We Now?

Tuesday. Calm. Aside from mention in the morning paper no sign of the police. Is anything the matter? Uschi wanted to know. Franz explained to Merkweise that the Mercedes needed an overhaul, and took the Audi. After dropping Merkweise off at Chemi Eins he drove to the institute by way of the park. No one about. He slowed down, peering in the direction of the shuttered newsstand—it was upright again, though badly dented—and saw the notice taped to the bunkerlike exterior. Under the circumstances he couldn't risk leaving the car to read it. He reached the institute just as Director Axel Neurath-Klinge was about to leave. It was poor timing. As always, Axel's imminent departure gave rise to a general inexplicable anxiety, a tension that hung in the air as the staff steeled themselves for what might yet occur. One could tell that Axel took an outlandish pleasure at their pained looks of concentration. They're all at his beck and call, Franz tried to explained to Uschi, who failed to comprehend the extent of Axel's authority and power. It's choreographed. A tableau. Director Axel Neurath-Klinge, taking all admiration, envy, even antagonism in stride, couldn't resist putting the staff to a test, teasing them one by one the way you might "lovingly" tease a dog until its resistance gave way and, hairs bristling, it would lunge forward trying to snap at the outstretched hand. The tension at the institute was in no small part due to the staff's disinclination to participate in this game. The turbulence that preceded Axel's departure receded only after the gray Mercedes had pulled away from the front steps and the faithful Guignola, who accompanied Axel to the front door and from there watched him drive away, briskly returned to her desk upstairs. By now everyone knew the procedure. The car stationed at the entrance with Manfred Schleif at the most five or six quick steps away, a watchful eye on the heavy metal front door, waiting for Axel to emerge. Franz had seen him jump into action. *Eins, zwei, drei!* The car door deferentially held open.

Manfred greeting Axel in a low voice—an acknowledgment that did not require a response. A flicker of the eyes sufficed. Manfred had his instructions. By now he could execute the maneuver in his sleep. *Eins, zwei, drei.* Open door, shut door. One was sustained by the familiar transitions. A rapid glance at the rearview mirror. Ignition, motion! As Guignola mounted the carpeted circular stairs returning to her office, the silence marked the receding turbulence of Axel's departure. Did someone mouth the word *Arschloch?* But how not to admire the manner in which Axel orchestrated these daily routine departures. Was Axel, like some tireless anthropologist, forever keeping them under scrutiny? Edel had as much as told Franz that to be employed at the institute was, in a sense, willy-nilly, to become committed to a style . . . a style reinforced by the elegant art nouveau building, the eclectic collection of paintings that Axel had begun to acquire for the foundation, and the carefully selected pieces of furniture on loan from the Merkweise estate . . . a Renaissance chest, two massive eighteenth-century tables, a Russian icon in Axel's office, a Roman bust of Alexander. As for the staff? They remained, so to speak, on approval—open to Axel's vituperative attacks. A week before, Franz had come upon Axel berating Edel in the latter's office, the door unaccountably wide open. I would like you to stop spreading rumors. Stop this insidious gossiping. If you have something to say, then out with it. Don't call attention to it by whispering.

White-faced, indignantly, but in a low voice so as not to be overheard, Edel attempted to defend himself: I never gossip. Never!

That's not the issue. When you whisper, you bring it to mind. When you whisper, everything you say becomes gossip.

What Is Baffling?

Axel Neurath-Klinge's frequent unannounced disappearances. His tendency to slip out of the institute, using the rear exit, probably with no one the wiser except for Guignola, his faithful-unto-death secretary. Her virginal smooth chalk-white face, etched with a permanent look of disapproval, sealed, inscrutable. Hours later Axel would suddenly reappear. Franz had seen Axel slip into the building using the basement emergency exit, which when opened triggered a shrill alarm. Only in this instant the alarm failed to go off. Afternoon, *Herr Direktor*, Franz greeted Axel, who seemed to stare through him without responding to his greeting. It was absurd. He had no reason to be apprehensive. Still. One reason Franz went to the institute so reluctantly—not wishing to come near Axel.

Why the emphasis on American painters? What with the present surge of local talent such as Vostell, Richter, Knoebel, Middendorf, Fetting, Baselitz, even Kiefer, wasn't it high time to dump the Americans? Certainly the critical interest in American art had waned, and the major collectors were dutifully divesting themselves of these American "heavies," dumping the Rauschenbergs, Indianas, and Lichtensteins, but Axel wasn't discouraged. For him the significance of American art remained undiminished—American art as the supreme paradigm for all things American, Axel confidently asserted: a vital commitment that showed no trace of a debilitating nineteenth-century memory. Did Axel really know what he was saying? Did it matter as long as Axel's excessively large budget requirements were being met by Johann Merkweise? But despite all the talk of artificially contrived prices and questionable money transactions, Axel continued to acquire whatever took his fancy. The triptych *House on Fire* was exchanged for, among other things, a sketch for a lamp by Rodchenko that had reached them via East Germany. Under Axel's enthusiastic supervision, the triptych was hung in the large reception hall on the ground floor; then, one month later, perhaps because it was considered too disconcerting, it was moved upstairs. It was too massive for any of the offices, and Axel, ruler in hand, traipsed all over the building in search of a suitable space, measuring every available wall, until he settled for the wall on the second-floor landing. It was less than ideal, but still the five-by-two-meter painting continued to receive the undivided attention of all visitors reaching the top of the stairs or emerging from the tiny elevator. What the hell? What does it mean? Baffled by the iconography, the row of lipsticks and the paper bag. Even though Americans lack all sense of propriety—what's the sense of enlarging something that is, let's face it, so void of meaning?

Franz, stepping out of the elevator, stopped to examine the painting if only to glean some information from it. What puzzled him was the seemingly arbitrary juxtaposition of everyday objects that—perhaps because they were enlarged—were made to appear menacing. On the left panel of the painting, resisting the force of gravity, were the contents of an upside-down brown paper bag, a crusty loaf of French bread, a bunch of green celery with a cluster of bananas to the right, beneath which one could see radishes, and the partially protruding grayish egg box that brought to mind a section of one of those World War II reinforced bunkers, a number of which, in varying stages of decay, can still be found here and there along the coast at sites once considered of strategic importance. Even the frustrated architect UNOHU designed a bunker in 1942. Whether it was ever built was another matter. However, it would seem unlikely that the American painter would have read anything else into the still-life composition. Or did he? The source of the mysterious reddish glow illuminating the luxuriant leafy parsley, which was a deeper green than that of the celery and resembled a giant elm seen from high above, might have been a vast conflagration.

The center panel was even more baffling, depicting a disconnected window frame, perhaps a kitchen window, its lower sash in a raised position (the frame and partially raised venetian blinds shielding the upper sash were painted a metallic blue-green), in front of which a red-hot ore bucket, the kind employed in a blast furnace, was held in place by the two distended corroded metal arms that inexplicably curved back through the partially opened window. The numeral 2 inscribed on the side of the red-hot bucket did not help clarify matters in the least.

The ten disproportionately large unfurled lipsticks in all shades of red in their shiny metal tubes, pointed or aimed at the central panel from the panel on the right, bore an all too marked resemblance to gun barrels, or might they be missiles? By focusing on the crumpled brown bag, a viewer could readily envision—such is the power of fantasy—the arid hills of a mountainous region, with the elongated loaf of French bread coming to resemble the elongated nose of a flying fortress in the air over, with that reddish glow, a devastated and burning city. However, Franz concluded that despite his German-sounding name, it was unlikely that Rosenquist could have had Germany in mind. More likely the triptych entitled *House on Fire*, was an attempt to introduce into the harmless everyday objects a more menacing element by the juxtaposition of bananas and parsley with the lethal ore bucket, to create a sense of uneasiness.

Observing him from the threshold of the conference room, Edel, with a look of tolerant or was it contemptuous amusement—as if there were something faintly ludicrous at the sight of Franz, of all people, trying to glean meaning out of this puzzling work of art—beckoned him to come over, I have something to show you, and led him by way of the large formal funerary conference room to an adjacent wood-paneled sitting room in which one eye-catching painting, a closely cropped view of a reclining female nude, immediately caught his attention. The painting excluded the head, neck, feet, hands of the nude, conferring artistically an indispensable anonymity, a peeper's view of the swell of her breasts partially covered by the bed sheet, to the compact belly, to the smooth thighs parted for what reason other than to display overtly, almost triumphantly, the abundance of riches in the curvature of the seductive line from the lower point of triangular bush (aha), tracing the vaginal fold down to the swelling buttocks. Dry-mouthed, Franz focused his attention on the startling explicitness, his eyes grazing, appraising, caressing the enticing flesh-colored topography of the pink inner thighs, the female torso laid bare, helplessly turning to Edel, What am I looking at? for what was presented so blatantly, in this context created an inner conflict. . . . The painting demanded an explanation? Edel, with a snicker, It's not porno, it's *The Origin of the World* by Courbet. Franz, baffled, However did it get here? Neurath-Klinge has his sources, said Edel. What's it worth? Franz asked, not taking his eyes off the painting. You need to take a course in art appreciation, Edel replied.

His Sunday

Trying to trace the source of his mild discomfort. His not unjustified unease. Suddenly, how to explain the house, this partly rebuilt more than two-hundred-year-old cottage, seemed confining. Passageway too narrow? No. Stairs too steep? No. What else could be the reason? Ceiling too low? No. Rooms too crowded? Was he burdened by the dark massive furniture? Burdened by gloom? With Hannelore and Dieter gone, there was all that additional space! The sounds are the unmistakable sounds of Sunday. Distant clanging church bells. Only a few cars on the road. Even the birds chirping at the window seem to accentuate this Sunday.

An inducement to relax? Do as one pleased. Running down a list of what he might do. Things suitable for a birthday? Go for a drive? Visit friends? Picnic somewhere in the mountains? Choices too numerous to count. Fishing? Unless of course, there was a compelling reason for Merkweise to require a chauffeur. No, this was his day. How to admit he dreaded celebrating it.

His Sunday. What can possibly be wrong with their present pastoral view? Everything. Your colleagues would give their right arm to live here, Uschi kept reminding him. Sure. Wasn't it like being in the country—that is, if one overlooked their proximity to the Merkweise garage? To the three cars in a polished state of readiness. Not to mention their annoying proximity to the main building. Never knowing when the next summons might come from Merkweise. A condition of his employment. Servitude, he called it. Acknowledged from the moment they had moved in. Although it was never spelled out in so many words. No need to, really.

Don't answer it, Uschi—knowing who it would be, urged whenever the phone rang late in the evening. Don't. It's after eleven. But how not to respond? What if it was an emergency? What if? If what? Nonsense. And then, on picking up the receiver, hearing Merkweise's impatient voice. A voice that took his presence, as much as his response totally for granted.

So where are we now? Not still in bed? Happy Birthday. Happy Birthday. April 20. The birthday as well of you know who. UNOHU! Indeed. As might be expected, the gravelly-voiced announcer on the radio made no mention of UNOHU. Maybe they were saving that piece of worthwhile information for the evening news. By now the motley crew of skinheads in their black leather outfits must have gathered at the Austrian border, waiting to cross the bridge into Braunau—pathetic. These current adherents of UNOHU. The more one thought of it, wasn't it a desecration of history? Happy Birthday! How many vets would celebrate Wolfi's birthday in the bars. But this time without him. For a split second, caught off guard, Franz actually attempted to return Uschi's beguiling smile. For a moment, that look of genuine, unconcealed pleasure on her face—dare one say happiness?—bypassed his defenses. Come, it said, trust me. Ah, that smile. There's nothing to fear. Framed in the wide-open window the Sunday landscape. Germany at its best. *Wouldn't you agree?* A readily available contentment. Yet wherever he turned his face, it (pleasure!) kept eluding him. He could, at the slightest urging, recall the setbacks, defeats. Missed opportunities. Instead of a chauffeur he could be one of the moguls. Let's face it, he didn't have the talent. Not sufficiently fast, slippery and smooth. The opportunists and careerists surfaced the day the war ended. As for his present garage buddies? Weren't Manfred and the other chauffeurs expectantly waiting for him to fade away? Sixty-two! Any day now! High time. At least transferred to a less taxing job. Not driving Director Merkweise and occupying the most desirable little house . . . Their smiles conveyed duplicity. Only a matter of time.

It's your day, Uschi reminded him. Your day!

Do what you like.

He placed his hand over his heart . . . concentrating.

The eye remains ever so selective. Despite the line of trees, one could glimpse the Merkweise house from their bedroom balcony. Scattered on the well-maintained sloping lawn the half-dozen brightly painted metal sculptures, all by contemporary Americans. All acquired for Merkweise by his loyal assistant Axel. Franz could see at least two of the sculptures, one an unnerving bright yellow, the other a multicolored geometric piece from the living room—no escape from the presence of Merkweise, was there? Can you really bring yourself to admire these people? his son, Dieter, had once asked. If by these people you refer to Director Merkweise or Axel, he had said with befitting dignity, then, my answer is yes. It is a mutual respect. I bet, said Dieter. Franz, ignoring the sarcasm: I am able to observe them from up close. And I will say this, unlike you everything they undertake to do is firmly rooted in reality. Dieter's disconcertingly shrill laughter had driven him from the room.

The thickly wooded property, as much as Merkweise had been able to purchase, insured a degree of privacy. Merkweise purchased land at double, even triple its value in order to keep people at bay. Though it may never have been put into words, Franz was given to understand that everything to the west of the garage was theirs. Really, the late-night phone calls from Merkweise were a small price to pay. Not only was their house near the garage sheltered from the road, they even had a private exit. Come and go as they pleased. Only the cook and Elli, the maid, a girl from the Teutoburger Wald, whose father had been in the same unit as he, sharing the servant's quarters above the garage, had an unobstructed view of their house. Once, on another Sunday, while the cook was at church, he had paid Elli a surprise visit. Claimed to be checking the windows. Her ready manner spelled out acquiescence. She acted as if it were his right. Not resisting as he unbuttoned her blouse, raised her skirt. He was carried away by the ease of his sexual conquest—yet, to his own mystification, kept postponing a return.

What else? In the hallway a framed black-and-white photo of a younger-looking version of himself along with his erstwhile pal Manfred in a dinghy, both with rod in hand, fishing on the Danube. Bliss, serenity. Manfred making eyes at Uschi. For Uschi, a pleasant recollection of an all too brief stay in Linz—UNOHU's favorite city, visiting Humboldtstrasse 31, where UNOHU had spent his happiest days. I just can't see Hitler as a boy, Uschi admitted. After being enlarged the photo had first hung in the dining room, then the vestibule, finally the bathroom. Now how did it come to hang in the hall? An unattainable, the out-of-reach freedom? Hannelore had been along. Pigtails. Sullen face. Always fussing, always gloomy, always too, too proper. And Dieter? Two years later he was in Frankfurt tipping over police cars and setting them ablaze. My son is a radical, Franz had confided to Johann Merkweise, who responded by briefly—one unforgettable moment—resting his hand on Franz's shoulder. One of my sons is a retard, a virtual cretin, Merkweise calmly replied, as if to balance the record. Two long-suffering fathers? They looked at each other—a moment of shared distress. I am the wrong father for him, explained Franz. Though he meant to say that Dieter was the wrong son.

How is one to accept the situation?
With a certain detachment?
With a certain tolerance?
With a certain degree of equanimity?
Now what?

He liked to relax in what had once been Dieter's room. Why? A few of Dieter's possessions still in evidence. But, somehow, each year they were reduced in number. He hadn't bothered to remove the poster of Che. He hadn't destroyed the Marxist literature. The offset pamphlets. He was no longer enraged by the sight of a letter bearing a Cuban stamp. Still, the mailman had strict instruction not to hand him any letters or packages, not even periodicals, mailed from Cuba. Without Uschi's knowledge, he bought several books on the Cuban revolution. On Castro's land reform. Even a large-scale map of Cuba . . . and by reading the letters from Dieter she kept secreted in the kitchen-table drawer he was able to follow Dieter's existence. He could take pride in the fact that by now he knew considerably more about Cuba than she did. Moreover, he knew his Dieter. How long would he last in Cuba? Before long, he'd have a falling-out with his so-called *compañeros*. He kept waiting for the letter in which Dieter would express a desire to return. A letter in which Dieter would renounce his Marxist outlook. It was bound to happen.

So where are we? At home? Is this your house?

Not still in bed, Franz?

Happy Birthday. I don't feel a year older, he told Uschi when he stepped into the kitchen.

Have you decided how you would like to spend the day?

Perhaps she shouldn't have inquired. He stopped in his tracks. I may go fishing. This said tentatively, probing, as though her response might influence his decision.

Framed in the open window, the Sunday landscape. Germany at its best! Sunday provides the rewards for hard work, integrity, honesty.

Wouldn't you agree?

Among the presents on the dining table, a book bearing the innocuous title *An Age of Fishes: The Development of the Most Successful Vertebrate*. Admittedly, he was fond of fishing . . . but where was one to fish with most of the streams and lakes polluted?

Spring or summer? How is one to accept the situation?

With tolerance. With a certain restraint. With equanimity. His visored chauffeur cap hung next to his dark blue uniform.

We could go for a drive, Uschi suggested.

Following breakfast, in Dieter's room, he pulled out his spiral notebook, writing in an untidy hand: *Achievements at sixty-two: A self-destructive daughter who suicides—plunging to the ground from the eighth floor, the better to draw attention to her unhappiness? A misshapen son who, after having been arrested on innumerable occasions for his so-called political activities, fled to Cuba. In a long letter to Uschi, Dieter attempted to explain his intentions: I have dedicated my life to the struggle for a better and a more just world.*

No one objected when Franz, using the tradesmen's entrance, let himself into the Merkweise house to pick up their retard, Atlas. He informed Elli that he was taking Atlas for a drive. No one ever inquired where he was taking Atlas. They couldn't care less. Least of all Merkweise or his wife. Atlas slid into the front seat of the station wagon, expectantly looking straight forward, waiting for the world to unfold.

Off we go, said Franz. As he drove in the direction of the river, he asked: Well, what shall we do? Atlas kept staring at the road ahead without any seeming recollection of ever having been along this particular road before. Everything he saw, he saw freshly, for the first time. How about a little fishing experience? For Atlas the word *fishing* carried an agreeable connotation. Nothing to cause anxiety.

Franz parked near the boathouse, and after a brief chat with the boathouse keeper, walked Atlas to the jetty where the rowboat was tied up. Awkwardly Atlas clambered into it headfirst.

What are we looking for? Franz asked as he started to row, heading for the middle of the broad river.

Atlas, across from him, gripping the gunwale, no sign of fear on his face, promptly responded: Fish.

That's it, agreed Franz. Though, by now, most people avoided the local fish. Only a few stubborn fishermen, like himself, unwilling to give up the sport, continued to fish in these polluted waters, hauling in flounder, catfish, pike and eel.

Atlas, always an amiable and attentive listener, was the recipient of his innermost thoughts. Everything that weighed on his mind. Uschi, Hannelore, Dieter, and Fehrn. Before you were born I used to come here. Just to get things straight in my mind. Just to establish who I was. After all, thought Franz, don't people speak to their pets? Whenever Atlas's attention strayed, Franz would ask: What are we doing?

The boat was old enough to have survived the war—it may, for all Franz knew, have ferried soldiers and refugees fleeing the Russians. . . . Atlas remained absorbed by everything he saw. Catching sight of a boat, no matter how distant, he'd wave. Once in a while, to his pleasure, someone in a passing boat would return his greeting. Thirsty? Atlas shook his head—though in his case the no could easily mean yes. Franz handed him the bottled water and watched him raise the bottle to his mouth, water spilling, as he drank. Franz kept rowing in the direction of the small river island. During the war the Americans had constructed a pontoon bridge across it. . . . A large bucket dredger was tied up near the opposite shore. Atlas stared at him expectantly as he stopped rowing to peer into the water, as if able to penetrate the murky depth and locate the fish with his X-ray eyes.

Franz made a low mewing sound—Mhhh-mhhh-mhhh. Magical incantations, to attract the fish. They hear everything. They are listening to us now.

Atlas, leaning over the gunwale, transfixed, his hand trailing in the water.

Do you know what day it is?

Atlas looked up, uncertain, the idiot's laugh at the ready.

April 20. My birthday.
Atlas laughed. But no sound, no movement.
April 20, my birthday and you know who else?

Drive

What does the clouded German chauffeur's brain think? Franz, with forced enthusiasm: It was a hard-fought game. As always the Trotters played spitefully. But our team . . .

So I hear, said Merkweise, not raising his head from the report on his lap.

Good turnout, remarked Franz. He spotted a deer in a clearing as they sped by. Merkweise grunted, to indicate that he did not wish to be disturbed. The traffic, as they set out, was unusually light. It was not going to be a particularly demanding day. After the visit to the plant under construction, they'd return in time for lunch. Franz, recalling the game, kept reverting to his discussion with Schultz. He caught himself humming the tune they had sung on the way back. The waitress, Betty, by now must be setting the tables for lunch. No resemblance whatever to his daughter. Filled with a spirit, laughter—everything Hannelore had lacked. Like an unwelcome apparition, the silver Porsche materialized in the rearview mirror, headlights blinking. Everything sparkled in the sun. The driver's broad, impassive face conveyed a displeasing challenge. Franz overtook a green van and then moving into the right lane made room for the Porsche, which zoomed past. For a split second, in passing, he and the driver exchanged glances. A moment of restraint. To his dismay, minutes later, after he spotted the sign indicating roadwork ahead, the Porsche, a 911 Carrera 4, came into view again. A roadworker, on the cement divider, was waving a red flag with an exaggerated flourish. The Monday traffic ahead was now reduced to a crawl. Only meters from the rear bumper of the Porsche, he could study alternately the driver's tightly compressed mouth in the Porsche's side mirror and in the Porsche's rear window the bald spot at the back of the man's head. The unblemished silver-painted body of the car sparkled in the sun. What he could not see of its cockpitlike interior was left to his imagination: the driver, to whom he had taken an instant dislike, most likely resting his hand on the stick shift and contemplating the snug interior as one might a coloring book, certain details, for instance the manicured fingernails, the tan trousers, the argyle socks, the brown Gucci loafers clamoring for his attention. Frankfurt license plate. A city notorious for its high percentage of sleaze, real estate crooks, stock market swindlers, profiteers . . . not to mention a variety of luxurious brothels that Merkweise and his sidekick Axel were in the habit of visiting. Just celebrating, Axel would say. Franz kept his eyes trained on the Porsche as they picked up speed. And you stay parked outside, Uschi said, showing disdain. Because Merkweise and his sidekick have to be driven to their entertainment, he explained, since they might not be in condition to drive home after they left the bordello. With his eyes glued to the Porsche, Franz missed seeing the head-on collision as a result of which one car was sent spinning out of control into the other lane; but so attuned was he to his boss, that he instantly registered, along with the fearfully high-pitched metallic screech, Merkweise's exclamation of surprise when he slammed on the brakes, stopping only a hair's distance from the now stationary Porsche's rear bumper—craning his neck to locate the source of the metallic crunching sound in time to see a van mount the highway divider, and after what seemed a second's indecision tip over, while from out of nowhere a heavy object, narrowly missing the windshield, landed with a resounding crash on their hood. In total disbelief Franz gazed through the suddenly dampened and misty windshield at the shapeless, lifeless mass that at first he failed to identify until it moved and he was able to distinguish a face, mouth agape, distorted in pain, the man's scream reaching him only after what seemed a long delay. He had barely time to collect his thoughts, before Merkweise, yelling at him to bring the first-aid kit, was out of the car. . . . The air was thick with smoke. To their right a man wearing a business suit and tie, cradling an injured arm as if it were an infant, was walking along the divider as if in a trance. By the time Franz had extracted the first-aid kit, Merkweise had slipped out of his jacket and propped it under the battered head of the man who had landed on their hood. By now several men were trying to extricate the injured driver of the van that lay smoldering on its side. Franz spotted the owner of the Porsche, a short ungainly man running hellbent for the emergency phone down the road with the awkwardness of someone unaccustomed to that activity. Don't just stand there, Merkweise snapped. Together they lowered the man who had landed on their hood to the ground. The hood, Franz noted sadly, was badly dented and bloodied. It took the highway police twenty minutes to get to the scene. Another fifteen for the ambulances. Merkweise, face smudged, irately tossed his soiled jacket on the seat next to Franz but after telling him to return to Chemi Eins, inquired in an unaccustomed friendly voice that put Franz on guard what he made of Manfred. Seeing Merkweise sizing him up, he pondered the question. He's reliable, he finally declared, though . . . Merkweise waited for him to continue. He may lack a certain . . . What? Franz groped for the word as Merkweise nodded encouragingly, but was it in agreement? Self-esteem? Or should he say, commitment?

Is anything the matter? Briefly they made eye contact in the rear-view mirror.

Someone claims to have seen him deliberately smash into a news-stand last Friday.

Looking startled, Franz asked, Is that what the newsstand dealer maintains?

No, Merkweise replied in a matter-of-fact voice, he's had a stroke. . . .

Is he dead?

I wouldn't know.

Manfred wouldn't go off his bat. . . . Franz shook his head. Not the Manfred I know. Unless . . .

Oh, he denies it, said Merkweise flatly.

You can't imagine my relief, he told Uschi, once we reached the exit and arrived at the secondary road. As we drove through Hüllbeck, I felt like waving to every pedestrian I saw. I kept hoping that Merkweise would want to stop. I could have used a drink. After he had, for the third time, described the mass pileup, did she mention having heard from Dieter, only this time the letter did not bear any stamps from Cuba. This time the letter was delivered by hand. Don't you see, he's back, she pointed out.

Four more years to retirement, Franz declared, was it to reassure himself? Then we'll head for the country.

But you don't care for the country, Uschi replied.

Sure I do.

Do you know what you really want?

I want what every German wants in his heart of hearts.

What's that?

Predictability!

Framed in the window, Germany at its best!

JORGE AMADO

TRANSLATED FROM THE PORTUGUESE BY GREGORY RABASSA

The Leather Strap

Adalgisa at the Street Door with the Five Wounds of Christ

Adalgisa's roar shook the foundations of the Avenida da Ave-Maria: "You get inside here right now, you fresh little brat! You slut!"

Manela scurried off, disappearing from her aunt's sight. When Adalgisa lifted her arm for the slap, she could no longer see Manela; she must have gone through the always wide-open door of Damiana's house—it even looked like a whorehouse with all that coming and going of people, in and out. In the morning Damiana prepared pots of dough for the cakes of cassava, corn, and sweet manioc that a sassy troop of black urchins would peddle in the afternoon from door to door to regular customers. A masterful sweets-maker, Sweet-Rice Damiana was famous—oh! Damiana's sweet rice, just thinking about it made your mouth water—not just in the Barbalho district; her clientele was spread out into all four corners of the city, and during the month of the festivals of St. John and St. Peter, the month of June, she couldn't fill all the orders for corn and coconut mush, tamales, and honey-corn cakes. A happy, hardworking house: comparing it to a brothel called for an excess of ill will, but Adalgisa wasn't one for halfway measures. Besides, she knew nothing about whorehouses, outside or in: if she chanced to pass a lady of the evening on the street, she would spit to the side to show her disgust and disapproval. She considered herself a lady, and not just any ordinary woman: ladies have principles, and they display them.

An expert in accented speech, she didn't lower her voice. She yelled so the neighbor woman would hear her:

"I swear by the Five Wounds of Christ that I'm going to put an end to that love affair if it's the last thing I do in my life. God will give me the strength to stand up to the lowlifes who are trying to put a young girl on the wrong road, the road to perdition. The Lord is with me, I'm not afraid of anything, nothing can touch me, nigger stuff doesn't get anywhere with me, I'm cut from different cloth, I don't mix with the commonality. I'll get the sin out of the girl if it costs me what health I've got left."

She was always complaining about her fragile health, because, in spite of her apparently healthy appearance, she was subject to recurring migraines, persistent headaches that would often last day and night, turning her mood sour, driving her out of her mind. She blamed acquaintances and relatives, the whole neighborhood, especially her niece and her husband, for the attacks that persecuted and plagued her. Dona Adalgisa Pérez Correia, of touted Spanish blood on her father's side and hidden African blood on her mother's: the nightmare, the terror of the street.

Adalgisa's Hips and the Rest of Her Body

It wasn't even a street. The Avenida da Ave-Maria was nothing but a blind alley, a cul-de-sac, to use Professor João Batista de Lima e Silva's pedantic expression. Still a bachelor at that time, in spite of being in his forties, the professor lived in the last little house in the area, the smallest. When he heard Adalgisa's ill-tempered echoes, he went to the window, lowered his reading glasses, and rested his eyes on his irritable neighbor's hips.

Irritable, but a knockout in looks: everything has its compensation. In the mediocre setting of the alley, bereft of lawns and gardens, trees and flowers, the greatest compensation was Adalgisa's behind, reaffirming the beauty of the universe. Fanny of a Venus, Aphrodite's behind, worthy of a painting by Goya, in the learned and corrupt meditation of the professor—he too exaggerated somewhat, as can be seen.

The rest wasn't to be sneezed at either, quite the contrary, the professor allowed, treating himself. Full, firm breasts, long legs, black braids encircling her oblong Spanish face, where her eyes burned furiously, dramatically. A pity that she had an aggressive expression: on the day Adalgisa lost her arrogant ways, mocking and disdainful, her air of superiority, and left the Five Wounds of Christ in peace and smiled without rancor, without affectation—oh! her beauty would conquer hearts, inspire poets' verses. During the late-night hours Professor João Batista would count syllables, rhyme stanzas, but his muses were others, not Adalgisa: innocent sweethearts from his adolescence in Sergipe.

On her paternal side, the Pérez y Pérezes, Adalgisa came on like a penitent in Holy Week processions in Seville, carrying the cross of Christ—she considered only that side, not wishing to know anything about the other, if there was another one. She took no pride in her Goya hips, and if she knew anything about Venus, it was that she was beautiful but didn't have any arms, and she'd never heard tell of Aphrodite.

The Junior Partner

The angry discourse of threats reached its height of rage when Adalgisa recognized, behind the wheel of the taxi parked by the entrance to the alley, Miro, the mangy dog, waving at her—cynical, cheeky, insolent, pauper! Noticing that she was being observed by the professor, a solid citizen, teacher, journalist, she nodded courteously, found herself obliged to explain the height of her bad manners:

"I'm bearing my cross, paying for my sins. That's what comes of raising other people's children: responsibility and mortification. That wretched girl is leaving me all skin and bones, ruining my health, driving me to my grave. Where have you ever seen anything like it, a girl barely seventeen. . . ."

"That's youth. . . ." The Professor tried to make excuses without knowing exactly what Manela's crime was, but he suspected it was catting around with her boyfriend: Could she have done so already? A girl of seventeen? The aunt was blind: she hadn't noticed that Manela was all woman, headstrong and wiggly, an appetizing body, ready for bed. Hadn't she been a candidate for Miss Something-or-Other? "You've got to be patient with young people. . . ."

"More than I've been? You don't know the half of it, Professor. If I were to tell you . . ."

If she still hasn't, she's wasting her time, drugstores sell the pill with no need for any prescription. Freed from the fear of pregnancy, the girls of today live it up, in a wild hurry, their tails on fire. They don't look at the example of Adalgisa, chaste and honorable.

As everyone was tired of hearing over and over, Adalgisa had no gentleman friends until she met Danilo, the first and the only one, who led her to the altar a virgin and pure. Virgin maybe, pure is more doubtful. There's no morality capable of passing unscathed through a year's engagement; a few daring things, minimal as they might be, always end up happening: a hand on the breast, a tool between the thighs. Danilo Correia, a modest but enterprising clerk in the registry of the Wilson Guimarães Vieira notary office, former soccer star, worthy opponent of the professor on the checker and backgammon boards, fortunate husband, exclusive master of those sumptuous hips and the rest of the body of Adalgisa, a chaste, virtuous woman—what a pity!

Professor João Batista de Lima e Silva was mistaken: he knew she was chaste, but he hadn't guessed her to be prudish. Danilo was at the very most a very junior partner—the one who really ruled Adalgisa's body, who laid out the limits in bed, was Christ Our Lord.

Historical Note

A solemn promise: In a little while we'll take up the burning and controversial theme of Adalgisa's prudishness again, the Catholic, puritanical bed, governed by her father confessor. Weekly control on Sundays in the confessional of the Church of Santana before the ten-o'clock Mass and Holy Communion. We will get to the Spartan personality of the Reverend Father José Antonio Hernández, Falangist, incorruptible, master of the fires of hell, a missionary in Brazil—*me cago en Dios*, what a painful, rotten mission!—inspector of Adalgisa's purity. At that time we will recount, with all the necessary details, the vicissitudes and bitter moments of the clerk Danilo Correia, the nonconforming victim.

First, however, the figure of Manela comes to the fore, barely glimpsed as she disappeared from her aunt's view into the wide-open door of fat Damiana's house. From Damiana's house there emerged the appetizing smell of spices mixed with coconut milk and grated lemon cooking in the oven: vanilla and clove, cinnamon, ginger, almonds and cashew nuts.

There are only doubts about Manela, brought on most of all by Professor João Batista's ponderings: Why does Adalgisa want to punish her? Can she still be a virgin or does she already know the taste of what's good? Was she or wasn't she elected Miss Something-or-Other? Something what? It's important to clear up such uncertainties as these, and others too, because a few pages back it had been announced that it was with the main object of freeing Manela from captivity that Oyá Yansã, the *iaba* who doesn't fear the dead and whose very cry lights up the craters of volcanoes on the summits of mountains, had come to the city of Bahia on a visitation, carrying her sack of thunder and lightning around her neck. So in the end, is it a question of Manela?

Manela, just as it's written, and not Manuela, as has already been asked when her name is read and is always asked when it's heard and thought a matter of misspelling or mispronunciation. A name inherited from an Italian ancestor, a memory kept in the family because the beauty of that first Manela had become legendary, a scandalous and fatal beauty. Two dashing and half-witted lieutenant colonels, in disrespect of edicts, had fought a duel over her; because of her a governor of the province had fallen in love and killed himself; because of her a priest on his way to the honors of a bishopric had committed a sacrilege, turned down the eminence, tossed his cassock aside, and gone to live with her.

In order to familiarize oneself with the extensive and lively chronicle of Manela Belini, for precise details of names and dates, titles and offices, a reading of the chapter in *Supplement to the History of the Province of Bahia*, by Professor Luís Henrique Dias Tavares, where the events mentioned here and others are exposed to the light of documentation, is recommended. The triumphs of the diva in the theater, singing operatic arias for ecstatic audiences; the deadly duel with swords when the honor of La Belini was bathed in blood—only a few drops, but sufficient—the rumors about the governor's suicide; the concubinage with the priest, which resulted in the Bahian family and the tradition of the name Manela: pleasant reading in spite of the title.

Luís Henrique Dias Tavares, historian, alter ego of the fiction writer Luís Henrique, Luís Henrique *tout court*, as his colleague and intimate friend João Batista de Lima e Silva would say. The fiction writer took advantage of the priest episode and created a charming picaresque novel out of it—it's hard to say who deserves greater praise, the historian or the novelist. It would be best to read both.

Eufrásio Belini do Espírito Santo, the descendant of the sacrilege, during rounds of beer and talk liked to retell the stories about his great-grandmother—a terrific Italian woman with her hair in the wind, a real hunk of a woman: the day he had a daughter he gave her the name Manela. He was a romantic and a reveler.

Manela's Procession

Manela wasn't out of the Procession of the Dead Lord on Good Friday in Seville. Her procession was that of Bomfim Thursday or, if you will, that of the Waters of Oxalá, the most important in Bahia, unique in all the world. She didn't come wrapped in compunction and penitence, covered with a black mantilla, reciting the litany to the sinister sound of rattles. "*Mea culpa! Mea culpa!*" Aunt Adalgisa repented, pounding her chest. Manela came wrapped in joy and merriment, dressed in the dazzling traditional white dress of a Bahia woman. On her head, balanced over her torso, she carried the jug of scented water for washing the church, went along dancing and singing carnival songs to the irresistible sound from the music truck.

That year, for the first time, Manela took her place among the Baianas. In order to walk in the procession—unbeknownst to her aunt, needless to say—she had played hooky from her English class at the vacation program of the Americans' Institute. She played hooky in a proper fashion, however, because the day before, the students had unanimously informed Bob Burnet, the teacher, of their decision not to come to class, in order to take part in the washing festival. Curious about Bahian customs, young Bob not only went along with the idea, but proposed keeping them company and did so with his well-known thoroughness: he sambaed ceaselessly under the burning January sun, bloating himself with beer. What you'd call a nice person.

Manela changed clothes at the house of another aunt, Gildete, in Tororó. When Dolores and Eufrásio died in an automobile accident—they were returning in the early hours of the morning from a wedding party in Feira de Santana; Eufrásio, behind the wheel, hadn't had time to get out of the way of the truck loaded with cases of beer—Adalgisa took charge of Manela and Gildete of Marieta, a year younger. In spite of being a widow and mother of three children, Gildete wanted to keep both of them. Adalgisa wouldn't allow it: the sister of Dolores, she was just as much an aunt as Eufrásio's sister. She took on her obligations, fulfilled her duty. God had not given her children, so she would dedicate herself to making a lady of Manela, a lady of principles, like herself.

She kept to herself what she thought of the fate awarded Marieta, relegated to an environment with customs she considered censurable—and she never lost an occasion to censure them. Gildete, widow of a shopkeeper at the market, a public school teacher, was not a lady, although a very good person and then some. To keep everything out in the open, it's worth making quick mention of the general opinion expressed by friends and acquaintances, all in agreement in considering that in the lottery of orphanhood Marieta had won the grand prize.

Manela had begun the merrymaking on the steps of the Church of the Conceição da Praia, the dwelling of Yemanjá. She'd come early in the morning in the company of Aunt Gildete, Marieta, and cousin

Violeta, and they mingled with dozens of Baianas waiting for the procession to form. What do you mean, "dozens"? There were hundreds of Baianas gathered on the steps of the church, all in the elegance of their white ritualistic costumes: the wide skirt, the starched petticoats, the smock of lace and embroidery, the low-heeled sandals. On their arms and necks they displayed silver *balangandã* bracelets and necklaces, jewelry and armbands with the colors of their saints. Pot, jug, or jar on the turbans atop their heads: scented water for their obligation. *Mães-do-santo* and *filhas-do-santo* from all Afro-Bahian nations—Nagô, Jeje, Ijexá, Angola, Congo—and from the halfbreed nation, with flirtation and merriment. Manela, the prettiest perhaps, was getting excited. Up on the trucks the *atabaque* drums were throbbing, calling the people together. Suddenly the music from a carnival truck exploded and the dance began.

From the Church of the Conceição da Praia, beside the Lacerda elevator, up to the Basilica of Bomfim, on the Sacred Hill, a distance that measured six miles, more or less, depending on how much devotion and how much cachaça. Thousands of people, the procession is a sea of people, it stretches on out of sight. Cars, trucks, carriages, donkeys festooned with flowers and sprigs, carrying full barrels on their backs: there mustn't be any lack of scented water. In the trucks lively groups, whole families, samba clubs, and *afoxé* groups. Musicians clutch their instruments: guitars, accordions, ukeleles, tambourines, *berimbaus de capoeira*. Popular singers and composers: Tião the Chauffeur, River Man, Chocolate, Paulinho Camafeu. The voice of Jerônimo, that of Moraes Moreira. Riding breeches, white jacket, dandified, kinky cotton hair, Batatinha, "Small Potatoes," smiles crossing the street. They shake his hand, shout his name, embrace him. A blonde—American, Italian, from São Paulo?—runs over, kisses him on his black and beautiful face.

Rich and poor mingle and rub elbows. In the mixed-blood city of Bahia all shades of color exist on the skins of the inhabitants: they go from black so dark it's blue to milk-white, the color of snow, and the infinite gamut of mulatto—they all show up. Who isn't a devotee of Our Lord of Bomfim, his countless miracles, who doesn't cling to Oxalá, the unfailing *ebós*?

The commanding general of the region, the admiral of the naval base, the brigadier of the air force, the president of the Assembly, the presiding judge of the Superior Court, the president of the Honorable Chamber of Aldermen, bankers, owners of cacao plantations, executives, senators, deputies. Some parade in black limousines; others, however—the governor, the mayor, the head of the tobacco industry, Mário Portugal—follow on foot along with the people. Also the mob of demagogues, candidates in the upcoming elections, covers the miles, butting in, distributing embraces, smiles, and pats on the back to possible electors.

The procession sways to the taste of the music from the trucks: religious hymns, prescribed songs, carnival sambas, *frevos*. The accompaniment grows along the way, the multitude increases in volume: people clamber down the hillsides, the São Joaquim market empties out, latecomers disembark from ferryboats and launches, arrive in sloops. When the head of the procession reaches the foot of the hill, a voice known and loved rises from the music truck of Dodô and Osmar—silence comes over everyone, the procession halts, Caetano Veloso entones the hymn to Our Lord of Bomfim.

The climb up the hillside begins to the sound of the drums, to the singing of the *afoxés:* it's the waters of Oxalá. The mass of people heads for the basilica, which is closed by a decision of the Curia. Previously, the whole church was washed, Oxalá was honored on the altar of Jesus; someday it will go back to being that way. The Baianas occupy the steps and entrance to the church, the washing begins, the obligation of the *candomblé* is fulfilled: *Exê-ê-babá!*

Arriving from Portugal during colonial times, in the mournful vow of a shipwrecked Portuguese, Our Lord of Bomfim, of the Good End; arriving from the coast of Africa during the time of the traffic in blacks, on the bloody back of a slave, Oxalá. They fly over the procession, come together in the breasts of the Baianas, plunge into the scented water and mingle—they are a single unique Brazilian divinity.

The Two Aunts

That Bomfim Thursday was decisive in Manela's life. Everything came together for the determination and the changes, the episodes and details. The procession, a happy time of singing and dancing; the ceremonious Baianas; the square on the hill, festooned with paper streamers, decorated with fronds of coconut palms; the washing of the steps of the basilica; the possessed women receiving the enchanted ones; the sacred ritual; lunch with her cousins at a table of love, eating and drinking, *dendê* oil running from her mouth down her chin, her hands licked, cold beer, *batidas* and the warmth of cachaça, cinnamon, and clove; prancing around the square with her sister, her cousin, and the boys; parties in family homes and the public dance in the street; the music trucks; the lighting of the footlights, the colored bulbs on the façade of the church; wandering in the midst of the crowd with Miro beside her, leading her by the hand. With a sense of lightness, Manela felt capable of taking off in flight, a free swallow in the euphoria of the festival.

In the morning, when she arrived at the Church of the Conceição da Praia, she was a poor, unhappy girl. Oppressed, without a will of her own, always on the defensive: timid, deceiving, disheartened, faking, submissive. Yes, Auntie. I heard, Auntie. I'm coming, Auntie. Well-behaved. She'd appeared at the procession because Gildete had demanded it, with an ultimatum of fearful threats:

"If you're not here bright and early, I'm coming to get you, and I'm a woman capable of swatting the face of that dame if she dares say you can't come with me. Where did you ever hear tell of such a thing? She thinks she's carrying the king in her belly, she's nothing but a stuck-up bitch, a shitlicker. I don't know how Danilo puts up with all that puke, it takes strong balls."

Hands on hips, on a war footing, she finished:

"I've got some accounts to settle with that meddler, she went around talking about me, calling me a street-rioter and voodooist. She'll pay me back someday."

Bighearted, cordial, loving, a piece of coconut sweet, Aunt Gildete held no rancor; the threatened revenge, the promised vengeance never went beyond words. But on the rare occasions when she became infuriated, lost her bearings, she would be transformed, turned upside down, capable of the worst absurdities.

Hadn't she, like a crazy woman, stormed wildly into the office of the secretary of education when the government attempted to cancel student lunches in the name of economy? "Calm down, my dear teacher!"—that was all the secretary said. He lost his composure, hastily left the room in fear of physical attack as he faced Gildete's robust, tall figure, ready for a fight, and the harsh words of accusation in the name of poor children—legs, do your duty. Panicky stenographers tried to restrain her, and Gildete pushed them away head-on; all determination, paying no attention to protests and prohibitions, she crossed through anterooms until she got to the sanctum sanctorum where the secretary of education was dictating. The picture came out in the newspapers illustrating the article about the plan to do away with school lunches, kept secret until then; the result was a wave of protests, the threat of a strike, and a demonstration. The measure was canceled, and Gildete escaped a negative report in her service file. Instead of a reprimand, praise, for the governor took advantage of what had happened to get rid of the secretary, whose political loyalty he doubted. As compensation, he attributed the authorship of the disastrous idea to him and threw him to the wolves.

Praise and a certain notoriety: in a speech in the State Assembly, Newton Macedo Campos, a combative opposition deputy, referred to the incident, praised Gildete to the sky, calling her an "ardent patriot and distinguished citizen, the noble defender of children, the leader of a self-sacrificing class of teachers." In addition they tried to coopt her for union leadership, but she refused: she enjoyed the praise but she hadn't been born to be a leader or a defender.

Manela turned her weakness into strength and obeyed, and early in the morning she struck out for Aunt Gildete's, taking advantage of the absence of Adalgisa, who had left along with Danilo for the seventh-day Mass for the wife of one of his fellow workers. She carried her English books and notebooks so they would think she was in class, figuring to be back for lunch. She would check her watch, leave the procession in time to pick up her dress and her books, catch the bus, all well timed. Trembling inside, astounded by her own audacity, she changed clothes, put on the petticoat and wide skirt, her breasts naked under the Baiana smock—oh, if Aunt Adalgisa could only have seen such a thing!

To say Manela wasn't sorry, that she was in love, was to say very little. When she took the road back home, poorly timed, she was a different Manela: the real Manela, the one who'd hidden herself after the death of her parents, had been extinguished in fear of punishment. The punishment of God, who, omnipresent, sees everything and makes note of everything for a settling of accounts on the day of the Last Judgment, and the punishment of Aunt Adalgisa, who was rearing and educating her. The aunt, watchful and nosy, when she saw or found out, would collect recompense for the lateness with shouting and the leather strap.

As the twig is bent, so grows the tree. Manela had turned thirteen when she came to live with her aunt and uncle, so she wasn't that young, and according to Adalgisa, her parents had brought her up very poorly. A teenager full of wiles and will, used to bad company, she consorted with rabble, was loose with her schoolmates at movie matinees, and in television studios took part in programs that were for children in name only; at festivals on the square, her parents had even taken her to *candomblé* temples, how irresponsible.

Adalgisa had put a rein on her, she'd laid down strict hours, she wouldn't let her set foot in the street, and as for festivals and movies,

Manela could go only if accompanied by her aunt and uncle. *Candomblé?* Not even to be mentioned: Adalgisa had a horror of it. A sacred horror: the adjective imposes itself. A short rein, a strong wrist were bringing Manela under control; Adalgisa would punish her without pain or pity. She was fulfilling her duty as adoptive mother—and one day, established in life, Manela would thank her.

MARGARET ATWOOD

My Life as a Bat

1. Reincarnation

In my previous life I was a bat.

If you find previous lives amusing or unlikely, you are not a serious person. Consider: A great many people believe in them, and if sanity is a general consensus about the content of reality, who are you to disagree?

Consider also: Previous lives have entered the world of commerce. Money can be made from them. *You were Cleopatra, you were a Flemish duke, you were a Druid priestess,* and money changes hands. If the stock market exists, so must previous lives.

In the previous-life market, there is not such a great demand for Peruvian ditch-diggers as there is for Cleopatra; or for Indian latrine-cleaners, or for 1952 housewives living in California split-levels. Similarly, not many of us choose to remember our lives as vultures, spiders or rodents, but some of us do. The fortunate few. Conventional wisdom has it that reincarnation as an animal is a punishment for past sins, but perhaps it is a reward instead. At least a resting place. An interlude of grace.

Bats have a few things to put up with, but they do not inflict. When they kill, they kill without mercy, but without hate. They are immune from the curse of pity. They never gloat.

2. Nightmares

I have recurring nightmares.

In one of them, I am clinging to the ceiling of a summer cottage while a red-faced man in white shorts and a white V-necked T-shirt jumps up and down, hitting at me with a tennis racquet. There are cedar rafters up here, and sticky flypapers attached with tacks, dangling like toxic seaweeds. I look down at the man's face, foreshortened and sweating, the eyes bulging and blue, the mouth emitting furious noise, rising up like a marine float, sinking again, rising as if on a swell of air.

The air itself is muggy, the sun is sinking; there will be a thunderstorm. A woman is shrieking, "My hair! My hair!" and someone else is calling, "Anthea! Bring the stepladder!" All I want is to get out through the hole in the screen, but that will take some concentration and it's hard in this din of voices, they interfere with my sonar. There is a smell of dirty bathmats—it's his breath, the breath that comes out from every pore, the breath of the monster. I will be lucky to get out of this alive.

In another nightmare I am winging my way—flittering, I suppose you'd call it—through the clean-washed demilight before dawn. This is a desert. The yuccas are in bloom, and I have been gorging myself on their juices and pollen. I'm heading to my home, to my home cave, where it will be cool during the burnout of day and there will be the sound of water trickling through limestone, coating the rock with a glistening hush, with the moistness of new mushrooms, and the other bats will chirp and rustle and doze until night unfurls again and makes the hot sky tender for us.

But when I reach the entrance to the cave, it is sealed over. It's blocked in. Who can have done this?

I vibrate my wings, sniffing blind as a dazzled moth over the hard surface. In a short time the sun will rise like a balloon on fire and I will be blasted with its glare, shriveled to a few small bones.

Whoever said that light was life and darkness nothing?

For some of us, the mythologies are different.

3. Vampire Films

I became aware of the nature of my previous life gradually, not only through dreams but through scraps of memory, through hints, through odd moments of recognition.

There was my preference for the subtleties of dawn and dusk, as opposed to the vulgar blaring hour of high noon. There was my déjà vu experience in the Carlsbad Caverns—surely I had been there before, long before, before they put in the pastel spotlights and the cute names for stalactites and the underground restaurant where you can combine claustrophobia and indigestion and then take the elevator to get back out.

There was also my dislike for headfuls of human hair, so like nets or the tendrils of poisonous jellyfish: I feared entanglements. No real bat would ever suck the blood of necks. The neck is too near the hair. Even the vampire bat will target a hairless extremity: by choice a toe, resembling as it does the teat of a cow.

Vampire films have always seemed ludicrous to me, for this reason but also for the idiocy of their bats—huge rubbery bats, with red Christmas-light eyes and fangs like a saber-toothed tiger's, flown in on strings, their puppet wings flapped sluggishly like those of an overweight and degenerate bird. I screamed at these filmic moments, but not with fear; rather with outraged laughter, at the insult to bats.

O Dracula, unlikely hero! O flying leukemia, in your cloak like a living umbrella, a membrane of black leather which you unwind from within yourself and lift like a stripteaser's fan as you bend with emaciated lust over the neck, flawless and bland, of whatever woman is longing for obliteration, here and now in her best negligée. Why was it given to you by whoever stole your soul to transform yourself into bat and wolf, and only those? Why not a vampire chipmunk, a duck, a gerbil? Why not a vampire turtle? Now that would be a plot.

4. The Bat as Deadly Weapon

During the Second World War they did experiments with bats. Thousands of bats were to be released over German cities, at the hour of noon. Each was to have a small incendiary device strapped onto it, with a timer. The bats would have headed for darkness, as is their habit. They would have crawled into holes in walls, or secreted themselves under the eaves of houses, relieved to have found safety. At a preordained moment they would have exploded, and the cities would have gone up in flames.

That was the plan. Death by flaming bat. The bats too would have died, of course. Acceptable megadeaths.

The cities went up in flames anyway, but not with the aid of bats. The atom bomb had been invented, and the fiery bat was no longer thought necessary.

If the bats had been used after all, would there have been a war memorial to them? It isn't likely.

If you ask a human being what makes his flesh creep more, a bat or a bomb, he will say the bat. It is difficult to experience loathing for something merely metal, however ominous. We save these sensations for those with skin and flesh: a skin, a flesh, unlike our own.

5. Beauty

Perhaps it isn't my life as a bat that was the interlude. Perhaps it is this life. Perhaps I have been sent into human form as if on a dangerous mission, to save and redeem my own folk. When I have gained a small success, or died in the attempt—for failure, in such a task and against such odds, is more likely—I will be born again, back into that other form, that other world where I more truly belong.

More and more, I think of this event with longing. The quickness of heartbeat, the vivid plunge into the nectars of crepuscular flowers, hovering in the infrared of night; the dank lazy half-sleep of daytime, with bodies rounded and soft as furred plums clustering around me, the mothers licking the tiny amazed faces of the newborn; the swift love of what will come next, the anticipations of the tongue and of the infurled, corrugated and scrolled nose, nose like a dead leaf, nose like a radiator grill, nose of a denizen of Pluto.

And in the evening, the supersonic hymn of praise to our Creator, the Creator of bats, who appears to us in the form of a bat and who gave us all things: water and the liquid stone of caves, the woody refuge of attics, petals and fruit and juicy insects, and the beauty of slippery wings and sharp white canines and shining eyes.

What do we pray for? We pray for food as all do, and for health and for the increase of our kind; and for deliverance from evil, which cannot be explained by us, which is hair-headed and walks in the night with a single white unseeing eye, and stinks of half-digested meat, and has two legs.

Goddess of caves and grottoes: bless your children.

RUSSELL BANKS

Xmas

FOR J.C.O.

He was a popular teacher of political science at the state university, was a man entering middle age in flight from the wreckage of two failed marriages. He refused to call them that, however—"failed," as if marriage were an experiment, a test of some giddy hypothesis he had cooked up in his youth. Gregory was sensitive to value-laden language. Besides, in each case, his commitment to the marriage had been total, absolute, without hedges, without a control. Gregory had loved both women.

He preferred to think of his marriages as "ended": to him they were distinct blocks in time that may as easily have been the best of times as the worst. Or why not simply the time of his life? For they had been that, too. Gregory Dodd was one of those men who in their mid-forties enjoy casting their past in a slightly elegiac light.

The important thing was that both marriages were ended now, that's all—the brief marriage of his adolescence and the fifteen-year marriage of his young manhood: over and done with and sufficiently behind him that he was able to begin anew, as it were, and he had done that, he believed, with Susan. (The elegiac view, even if somewhat premature, makes renewal possible.) So that, by falling in love with Susan, Gregory felt he had moved into a new block of time, one that was as endless-seeming as each of the others had been in the beginning, and he was thrilled again. And now, once more, it was Christmas Eve, and even though Gregory's own three nearly-grown children were in the home of their mother, his second ex-wife, he was nonetheless playing Santa Claus again, loading his car with presents for Susan and her three children, much younger than his, driving down on a snowy night from his house in New Hampshire to Susan's shabby flat just beyond Boston in Jamaica Plain, Handel's *Messiah* roaring from the radio and, at the chorus, full-throated Santa at the wheel singing gladly along: *Halleluiah, halleluiah, hal-la-loo-hoo-yah!*

In New Hampshire, the snow had been dry and had blown at the car from the darkness ahead in long white strings, and driving on the Interstate was easy. He kept the Audi at seventy all the way in to Charlestown. But here in the city, as he crossed the Fens from Kenmore Square to Huntington, taking the quicker back way across Boston's South End to Jamaica Plain, the snow was wet and fell in fat flakes that slickened and made driving difficult. It was the night before Christmas, and traffic was light; the nearly empty city streets and darkened brick buildings were beautiful to Gregory: they exuded a stoical melancholy that reminded him of an Edward Hopper painting, although he couldn't remember which one.

He had overspent, he knew, as usual, but what the hell, it would be worth it to see Susan's grateful delight when he brought into her living room and heaped under the tinsel-covered tree the dozens of carefully wrapped gifts he had carted all the way down from New Hampshire for her children. And for her, too—a lovely dark green velour robe, Braudel's *Civilization & Capitalism, 15th–18th Century*, all three volumes, an espresso machine he'd ordered in October from the Williams-Sonoma catalogue, and an antique cameo pin he had found in a boutique in Portsmouth. He would have to march up and down those narrow sour-smelling stairs from the car three times to unload it all.

Susan was ten years younger than Gregory, a photographer whose harshly documentary style was out of favor, especially in Boston, and who lived close to the same line of poverty that most of her subjects, blacks and hispanics in the projects and the worst sections of Roxbury, lived below. She viewed her poverty as the direct consequence and expression of her art; Gregory regarded it as a permanent form of bohemianism and a plight, which he tried to ameliorate with his bourgeois common sense and generosity. He balanced Susan's checkbook for her and for her birthday had bought her a dishwasher.

Near the Museum of Fine Arts, Gregory slowed and turned left off Huntington onto a pot-holed side street, following the taillights of the only other car in sight. The two vehicles moved past dark high buildings—alternating rows of warehouses and public housing from the fifties and sixties—where here and there a short string of Christmas lights or a solitary electric candle blinked from a window as if with sarcasm. The car ahead had slowed; the driver seemed to be looking for a number on one of the graffiti-splashed doorways. This was not so much a neighborhood as a zone of half-destroyed buildings located between construction sites, a no-man's-land still being fought over by opposing armies: people lived here, but not by choice, and only temporarily.

In the seventies Susan and her ex-husband, the father of her three daughters, had been active in the Weather Underground. Her radical past and marriage she regarded as a chapter in her life that had ended, although the momentum of that chapter had carried over long enough for her to have been five months pregnant with her third child before finally obtaining a divorce. By then her husband had gone underground altogether, and separating her life from his, she felt, had been like granting him his last wish. It had certainly been the best thing for the children. A year later, with two white women and a black man, he had tried to rob a Brinks truck in Framingham, and a guard had been shot and killed. Susan's ex-husband and one of the women had been captured the following day in upstate New York, and the rest, as she said, was history.

Gregory had tried to get Susan to tell him more about her life with her ex-husband: he was fascinated by it, slightly aroused in a sexual way that he did not understand, and he wanted either to chase his arousal into desire and satisfy it or else to exorcize it altogether. There were no pictures of the man in her apartment, and the children never spoke of him: it was as if he had died before they were born and their only parent was their mother.

Though the girls were little more than a year apart in age, the way Susan described it, she and their father had never actually cohabited: "Oh, God, it goes back to college, really, to Brandeis. But he was married to the Movement, from the start, like an organizer, sort of. He'd show up for a few days, and then he'd be gone for a month, sometimes longer," she said in her vague and elliptical way, which frustrated and sometimes annoyed Gregory.

Usually, when they talked about her marriage it was late at night in bed, after making love, over cigarettes and the last glass of wine from the second bottle. He didn't want to press her on the subject, to insist that she provide details, instances, dates and times and specific circumstances—although he surely did want to know them all—for fear that she would think he was unnaturally fixated on this closed chapter of her life. "It was like, every time we made love, I got pregnant. I couldn't take the pill, it made me sick and fluttery and all, and nothing worked. We didn't do it all that much," she said, and lightly laughed.

"Well, three times at least," Gregory said.

"At *least*," she said, and she punched him on the shoulder. "C'mon, Gregory, it's history."

"I know, I know. I'm only kidding you."

The vehicle ahead suddenly stopped, and Gregory hit the brakes, and the Audi slid and came to a stop a few feet behind it. Gregory reached over and turned down the radio, puzzled. The car ahead of him was a battered ten-year-old Chrysler with a huge flat trunk; the number plate was wired loosely to the rear bumper, and Gregory imagined fixing it with a pair of twenty-cent stovebolts.

The rear window of the Chrysler was covered with snow, and Gregory couldn't see inside. He cut left and pulled out to pass by, and just as he drew abreast of the other car, the driver moved out also, as if to make a U-turn in the middle of the street. Gregory jumped on his brakes and spun the wheel. The Chrysler drew quickly in front of him, the Audi swerved, and when its front bumper ticked the rear bumper of the other car, Gregory thought he heard the number plate clang.

Abruptly, the other car stopped, half-turned in the middle of the deserted street, blocking Gregory's passage. The driver stepped from the Chrysler and walked slowly toward Gregory. He was a black man, tall and wide, in a leather jacket and watch cap, scowling. A second black man got out of the Chrysler and came along behind. They were both middle-aged, his age, and seemed irritated but not threatening. A mistake, Gregory thought. He must not have known I was so close to him. Gregory pressed the button and lowered his window, to explain and even apologize for nearly colliding with the man's car and ruining Christmas for all of them.

He said, "I thought you were stopped—" and the larger of the two men simply said, "Yeah," and slammed his fist through the open window straight into Gregory's face. Then they turned and walked back to their car and got in. Gregory spat a piece of tooth, touched his lip with fingertips and came away with blood: he looked at the steering wheel and thought: I must have hit the wheel when I stopped; I must have broken my mouth by accident; something that I didn't know about must be what just happened.

The Chrysler pulled back onto the street and moved slowly away, its taillights shrinking in the snowy distance ahead, and Gregory began to tremble. Rage washed over him like a cold wave, and when he was covered, his entire body turned suddenly hot. He touched his lips again and found that they had swollen to nearly twice their normal size. His shirt was spattered with his blood, and when he groped through his mouth with his tongue he realized that a tooth had been broken and several others loosened by the blow.

The Chrysler was gone now, and Gregory was alone on the street, sitting in his car with all his presents for Susan and her children. What was he to do now? Where could he go, his face all bloody and swollen, his chest heaving, his hands clenched to the steering wheel as if he were being yanked violently from the car? He was utterly ridiculous to himself at that moment. He was a fool, a man whose life was unknown to him and out of control, a man whose past was lost to him and whose future was a deliberate, willed fantasy. He felt like an unattached speck of matter afloat in space, and all he wanted was to be in his own home with his own children and their mother, in his proper place, his life intact, all the parts connected and sequential.

He put the car into gear and drove slowly away, toward Susan's home, where she lived with her children. He knew that she would be alarmed when she saw him and then would comfort and take care of him. But they would not be the same together as they had been before and as he had planned, so that while he drove he had to fight against the new and terrible longing to turn back.

ANN BEATTIE

Name Day

Taking the puppy to Sherando Lake was a mistake. Jean was more interested in the dog—a collie mutt—than Frank. Amid the yellow, orange and red brocade of leaves glowing in the sunlight on the trees packed together on the hills across from the lake, there were still some green leaves, which now looked quite exotic.

Frank and Jean were taking a fall vacation. In September, much to his surprise, Jean had not re-enrolled at the University of Chicago. What had turned out to be a messy affair between Jean and her mathematics professor was over. Jean—who had not lived with Frank, even though she had initially moved to Chicago to be near him—had moved in with Frank only recently, in the summer, after the affair with the professor ended. Frank had explained then that he did not want to be her good friend and wise counselor; if she wanted to be with him, he wanted the past forgotten. In retaliation for the year in which she had divided her attention between the other man and him, Frank went to bed with one of the women who had been pursuing him, although he did not tell Jean about his retaliation. Lisa was a pretty woman in her mid-twenties who seemed to know how attractive she was, and how smart. It was clear to her that she was going to be rewarded for those things. When the rewards did not come fast enough, she bought herself strawberries out of season and silk camisoles. He was interested in her idea that small things could fill the gaps. When Jean made it clear that she wanted to come back to him, Frank in one day went from being one of Lisa's rewards to being her adversary. She would accept no explanations—and probably shouldn't have, because what he tried to tell her omitted mention of Jean and wasn't the truth. In his guilt and anger— he was angry at everyone, himself included—he surprised himself by hugging Lisa hard, after he said good-bye. The feel of that stayed with him. The camisole might as well have been a bulletproof vest, she was so rigid. Lately, it bothered him that he had treated her badly. He remembered the sound her high heels made, tapping on the concrete as she walked away. In a movie of their affair, that would have been the soundtrack. During the last week that he saw Lisa, he had gone to her birthday party. There had been a pot of water, on top of the empty cement planter on Lisa's balcony, with champagne corks dropped in. If she wanted to, Lisa could still see Frank on videotape, hands behind his back, drunkenly snapping at corks, trying to capture one as if he were bobbing for apples. That image of himself had come strongly to mind the evening before, when he and Jean arrived in Virginia to visit his brother and sister-in-law. He thought of it driving past apple orchards.

His brother had bought a bottle of wine to serve with dinner. His brother's wife, Pauly, had asked Frank to pull out the cork. She watched, as if a genie might rise out of the bottle. Though she had a wineglass at the table, hers was filled with Tropicana. His brother Jim drank the wine, and even said that he wished he had gotten two bottles.

Driving to the lake, Frank had said to Jean that they ought to buy some wine, and she had said that that might insult Jim and Pauly. "I hope he goes out and gets more, then," Frank said. "I don't want to sit around all night listening to her chatter without a drink in my hand." The liquor store was no doubt miles away. They were—or at least they felt they were—in the middle of nowhere. Out of that lack of connectedness, that emptiness, he had begun to remember Lisa, and the champagne party.

Jean was quite interested in playing with the dog. It had been patted and admired ever since they got to the park. Every two-year-old with droopy pants stopped to look, staring with wide-eyed wonder. Their mothers pulled them away. Some fathers picked them up, whining and kicking. Some parents clutched the children to them, whispering in their ears.

Jean had already said that she wished the puppy was theirs. He had said that since she was home all day, he wouldn't mind if she got a puppy and trained it. She looked at him, and there was an awkward silence. The issue of her dropping out of school had never really been discussed.

A boy about six or seven began to pat the dog's head. The dog was on a purple leash. It had a leather collar not much bigger than the bracelet on Jean's wrist. She held the leash, and the boy stroked its head.

"Come on," an older boy said, emerging from behind a tree. "Hurry up—I'm not going to wait for you."

The younger boy stayed in his crouch, whispering to the dog.

"Did you hear me?" the older boy said.

Jean smiled halfheartedly at the older boy, to let him know that she understood his frustration. "Yes. That's enough love for right now,"

Jean said, giving the leash a little tug. But the dog never broke eye contact with the boy, and the boy stayed the way he was. He put his forehead against the dog's.

No one paid attention to the older boy after that until he began to run. A breeze had begun to blow, which seemed strangely to coincide with the speed with which the running figure moved. They squinted. The little boy looked at Jean. He was obviously panic-stricken.

"Is he your brother?" Jean said, crouching to be more nearly the child's height. The puppy was licking the boy's ankle.

"Yes," the boy said, on the verge of tears.

"Are your parents here?" Jean said. Frank could tell that she meant to keep her voice calm. It was the same tone of voice she had used with him in July, when she questioned whether he really wanted her back.

"He's not going to come back," the little boy said. He rubbed his eyes, breathing through his mouth.

The dog was playing with something: an acorn it would choke on; a bottle cap. Frank bent down and pulled a piece of red plastic out of the dog's mouth. The dog looked up, wagging its tail. Frank started to throw the piece of plastic away, then realized that would just be tantalizing to the dog. He dropped it into his pocket.

"It'll be all right," Frank said to the boy. "We can find your mother and father."

"My mom's at work," the boy said. "He brought me on the bicycle, but I don't know how to ride it."

Jean put her arm around the boy's shoulder. She looked at Frank, and Frank looked off in the distance, where the boy had gone. It seemed impossible: there had been no indication that the boy would bolt; there had not even been a real argument.

"I'll call your mother," Frank said. The breeze came up again. It was a bright day. They were standing just off the path, in the shade. A building with a ladies' room and a men's room to one side, a bulletin board to the other. One large sign said that liquor was not allowed in the park. Another said that dogs were not allowed on the beach.

"My mother's at work," the boy said again. "He's not coming back, either. I know it."

"We'll find a forest ranger," Frank said, delighted that he had suddenly remembered the existence of forest rangers. It was a big park. Kids must get lost all the time. The puppy had begun to whine. Jean picked it up. "You stay with him," Frank said. He turned to consult the bulletin board more closely, to see if there was a map of the park. Facing away from them, he thought how strange it would be if he, too, ran. He had no impulse to do it—just the thought. He could imagine Jean's surprise. The boy's fear. He gnawed his bottom lip and wondered why he had such a thought.

From the map on the bulletin board, it was clear where he should go. It looked as if the station was about a mile up the road. He started toward his car in the parking lot. Jean called to him. Her voice was louder than it needed to be to stop him, and quite shrill. He turned and saw the older boy, on a blue metallic bicycle, facing Jean and the little boy. He couldn't hear what the boy was saying.

He began to walk back. In the breeze, and under the shadows of the trees, it was cold. He saw another piece of red plastic on the ground in front of him. When he bent and scooped it up, he saw that it was a shotgun shell. He tossed it back on the ground and took the other piece of plastic out of his breast pocket. He rubbed it between his thumb and first finger. It seemed to be the fin of a red plastic fish. That, or some part of something.

"Get on the bike, asshole," the older boy shouted, swooping his arm through the air. "Get on, or I'm going for good."

What was frightening was that the boy did not acknowledge either Jean's or Frank's presence. It was hard to tell what the younger boy thought: whether he kept his grip on Jean's sleeve because he was stunned that his brother had returned, or whether he was afraid.

"Did you hear me?" the boy on the bike said. "Dad's gonna kill us if we're late. I'm going to tell Dad you never listen to me. I'm not ever bringing you to the park again."

Though the words came out in a rush, Frank was relieved to hear them. They let him know that the older boy was frightened of something, too. Everything was complicated. The boys had a father who would be angry with them. That was what he told Jean when the little boy reluctantly let go of her sleeve and got on the bike. "Listen," he said. "That's the way kids are. You were an only child. You never had to deal with things like that. It looks like a big drama, but they're just brothers. They understand each other."

It was getting cold. Frank picked up the dog and clutched it to his chest. He had had a dog as a child: a spaniel named Daisy. He also had an older brother who had been a bully. He thought to himself that he was secretly glad that the tables had been turned: that now Jim had to worry about money, and lived in a place so flat and depressing that

Frank himself had never managed more than a day and a half's visit, because he would jump out of his skin.

In the car, the dog curled up on Jean's lap and panted itself to sleep. Frank looked at Jean. She was looking down at the dog, but Frank had the feeling that even if the dog weren't there, she might still be looking at her lap. She was worried about the boy. She also hadn't wanted to take the trip in the first place; he had twisted her arm about that. She *had* been an only child, so she was interested in what other families were like. He got her to come to Virginia by telling her that his brother was very down on his luck; he'd lost his job, and he needed a show of support. That was the true meaning of family solidarity. And Pauly was hypersensitive: she would think that Jean hadn't come because she disliked her. Subtly, he had convinced Jean that by her not coming the trip would be a failure. Of course, he admitted that he wanted her along because she made it easier. Jim wouldn't argue with him if Jean were there, because he was insecure and tried to impress people. Jean was protection. Without her, his brother would still be a bully—even if he overpowered Frank just with talk. Actually, Frank knew that it was not family solidarity that made him see his brother, but guilt. There had been no money for Jim to go to college, but when Frank's time came their grandfather had died and the land had been sold, and Frank went to Dartmouth. When Frank was in New Hampshire, Jim was stationed at Quantico. He was already married to Pauly.

Frank stopped for gas. He pumped his own, then went inside the store to pay. He asked directions and found out that there was a store that sold liquor three miles away. The woman who gave the directions had gray hair held back from her face by a headband with an ornamental turtle crawling up one side. Frank came out of the store smiling.

Jean was looking out the window. "Frank," she said, "were those boys in the store?"

"No," he said. "Nobody was in the store."

"Because that's his bike, isn't it?" she said, pointing.

In the distance, he saw what might have been a bicycle on its side, glinting in the sun.

"It probably is his bike," Frank said. "They probably stopped."

"But what would they stop for, over there?" she said.

He started the car without answering. As they got to the place where the bike lay on its side, he saw that there was an embankment. Below that, the hillside fell off steeply.

Ann Beattie / 185

"Come on," he said. "They're boys. Something came into their minds, and they stopped."

Frank accelerated. It was windy, and after a minute he asked Jean to put up her window. She rolled it up slowly. They were in a rental car: a small silver Chevy that didn't have enough power. He hoped that the ride to the liquor store wouldn't get hilly.

Jean didn't ask where they were going. Her sense of direction was bad, and he thought she might have assumed that they were on the road back to his brother's. When he pulled up alongside the little white clapboard building, though, she didn't seem surprised. She didn't say anything, or get out of the car. The dog was shuddering in its sleep. He pushed the door closed lightly, so he wouldn't awaken it.

The bottles were lined up on a wall to the right. There were cardboard signs with arrows pointing down above each shelf. "Champagne" was the first sign he saw. There were two kinds of domestic champagne. Next to that was the bourbon. He got a bottle of Jack Daniel's and two bottles of red wine and checked out. A pickup truck had pulled in while he was in the store. A man in a red and black plaid jacket got out. A black Lab moved into the driver's seat and watched its owner go into the store.

"Hey," Frank said, putting the bag between the seats, then patting Jean's leg. "I love you. Don't be such a sadface."

She looked up and smiled. Her cheeks were rosy from the sun. She looked pretty, and he did love her. On her lap, the dog's paws twitched. Frank held her hand as he drove, going back on the same road they had taken to the store. He hoped that the blue bicycle would be gone, but it was still there when they passed by, right where they had seen it before. He said nothing, and neither did Jean. As he rounded the curve, the bottles knocked together in the bag.

His brother's house was red brick, with slate-gray shutters across the front. One shutter had fallen, and was leaned up against the wall inside the front door, waiting to be repaired. Jim's foot hit the shutter by mistake, tipping it over, as he opened the door to let in Frank and Jean. Jean was carrying the puppy, who was awake by then—woozy but awake—and Frank held the bag from the liquor store.

"Enough nature out there for you?" Jim said. They had tried to get him to go to the park with them, but he wouldn't. Pauly had had an appointment at noon to get her hair done. The directions were simple, so they had gone alone—both happy to have a reason not to sit around the house all day.

Pauly was sitting in the recliner chair. She had gotten a permanent, and the curls were Shirley Temple tight. She didn't like the way it had turned out and, as Frank and Jean soon realized, had been sitting there crying when they came in. Pauly reached up with one hand when they came through the doorway, pushing the Kleenex deep in her pants pocket with the other.

"I missed you," Pauly said, nuzzling the dog's neck as Jean lowered it into her lap. "Mama missed her pretty puppy dog," Pauly said. "Come to Mama and sit right here."

By now the dog was very alert, eager for more attention.

"You were gone so long," Pauly said, baby-talking the dog. "You were gone so long that do you know what Mama did? Mama thought of a name for you. Mama's going to name you Sherando."

Pauly puckered her lips and smacked little kisses to the dog. The dog was rolling on its back. Pauly looked at Jean and Frank, smiling. "If you two hadn't of gone to the lake, this puppy might never have had a name," she said. "I forgot it was out there, we haven't been for so long, but it makes for a real interesting name."

Pauly began to rub the dog under its neck. "You tell me what went on there today," she said, looking at Jean. "That way, once a year I can tell him stories about his name day, because we don't exactly know on what day he was born."

Jim snorted. He was sitting at the card table in front of the living room window, piecing something together. Blue smoke twirled up from his cigarette. He lit them, but hadn't smoked one for almost three weeks. "What's so important about when he was born?" Jim said. He looked through the cigarette smoke at Frank. "We took him to the vet, and the vet said he was about four months old," he said.

"But honey—a thing like that matters to a woman," Pauly said.

"I didn't want the dog, because I thought it would just be something else she'd be sentimental about," Jim said. He did not say it to anyone in particular. Then he looked at Pauly. "Offer our guests some refreshments," he said.

"Oh, I'm sorry," Pauly said, getting up. "We've got coffee and Cokes and most things."

"Also this," Frank said, plunging his hand in the bag and pulling out the Jack Daniel's with great flourish. He held the bottle by the neck, high over his head.

The dog looked up at the bottle and froze, wagging its tail, as if the bottle were one of those magic sticks people throw that would go flying through the air.

Jim might have been thinking the same thing. Looking at the raised bottle, his face also froze. He thought that in a matter of seconds the window beside him was going to be broken glass. That cold air might as well be blowing through the house.

"Hey," Frank said, lowering his arm. "Hey: how about some glasses. We'll have ourselves a sipping party." His brother's frightened expression had registered. He didn't know why Jim was frightened, or what to do about it, so in a split second, he had decided just to ignore it.

What Jim had been doing, Jean saw, when she left Frank's side and walked closer to the card table, was assembling a Tyrannosaurus. It had been sent to him, he told her, by a buddy of his from the Marines, whose wife worked in some museum gift shop now. The buddy had it all wrong about when his birthday was, but still: it was the thought.

"It came at a good time," Jim said, stubbing out the cigarette.

"Yes, it did," Pauly said, coming back into the room. "It came at just the perfect time."

Thin wooden pieces were spread out on the card table. The middle section was complete. Most recently, Jim had been working on the tail. Pauly brushed the tail aside gently as she put the four glasses down on the card table.

Family solidarity, Jean thought. They were all going to have a drink and see what happened next. Already, that day, the dog had been named Sherando.

ROBERT COOVER

The Gambero Rosso

It has begun to snow. At first just a flake or two like a fleeting dispatch
sent from the world he has left behind, vanishing as quickly as glimpsed.
Then a steadier fall, gently swirling, touching down, lifting up, touching
down again, until the little square, or *campo*, outside the steamy window
of the Gambero Rosso is aglow with a dusting of the purest white. Like
a crisp clean sheet of paper, he thinks, and he is struck at the same time
by the poignancy of this metaphor from the old days. For paper is no
longer a debased surrogate for the stone tablets of old upon which one
hammered out imperishable truths, but rather a ceaseless flow, fluttering
through the printer like time itself, a medium for truth's restless fluidity,
as flesh is for the spirit, and endlessly recyclable. The old professor sits
there at the little *osteria* window, alone now with his reveries and musings, sipping the last of the fine *grappa* the landlord has offered him (he
has forgotten how lovely the people are here, *his* people after all, to the
extent he could be said to have any: how pleased he is to be among them
again!) and staring out on the softly settling snow, letting himself be
gradually submerged in a sweet melancholic languor. His erstwhile companions, perhaps sensing the onset of this pensive mood, have graciously
slipped away for the moment, the porter to guide the blind hotel proprietor back to prepare the professor's lodgings for the night and to move
the luggage up before returning for him here. Yes, blind as well as
maimed. Upon leaving the hotel to come here, the unfortunate creature
walked straight out the door and down the water-steps into the canal.
"Now look what you've done! You've gotten your feet all wet!" the
porter had scolded, pulling him out, and the hotel manager had whined:
"My feet are all wet!" Which for some reason had made the professor
laugh, made them all laugh. Then they'd come here together, the ancient traveler in the middle holding both of the hobbling locals up,
feeling quite jolly and youthful in spite of himself.

They'd met no one en route except for a poor deranged drunk,
shouting to himself in an empty *campo*, lamenting the hammerings he'd
taken and excoriating a no doubt imaginary untrue lover as though she

were present, a deplorable reminder that even here, in the noblest of settings, loathsome disorderly lives are possible, beauty being no proof against asininity. Virtue, he once wrote (the line is now in *Bartlett's*) in his pioneering transdisciplinary work, *The Transformation of the Beast*, a "lucid and powerful prose epic in the tradition of Augustine and Petrarch," as it was widely heralded, standing as a fortress against the false psychologism of the day (there was perhaps in this work a youthful fascination with beastliness rather than its transcendence, since successfully purged, but it remained to this day the most convincing composite image of the Genius-in-History), *is* sanity. Indeed it would have done the crazy man in the *campo* no harm, what with all his ravings about untamable beasts and savage natures untouched by kindness and unredeemable evil fates (or fairies; his slurred ramblings were ambiguous), to have read that book before falling victim to his own self-fulfilling prophecies: natures *do* remain just as they first appear if they are completely mad. However, the poor creature, storming up and down a bridge over and over as though in the forlorn hope, a hope repeatedly renewed even when repeatedly baffled, that it might one time translate him to greater heights—up into one of Tiepolo's sky-high parades perhaps, though nothing so fair was above him now—did succeed in startling the professor as they passed by with what amounted to a demented paraphrase of another of his famous sayings, this one from the book the world best knows him by, *The Wretch*, his first essay in unabashed autobiography, stark precursor to *Mamma*, his current work-in-progress. Originally little more than a film treatment, notes for a storyboard, as it were, *The Wretch* evolved into a program guide to the completed picture, sold in the lobbies, and from there into a comprehensive best-selling assault upon all the heretical modern and eventually postmodern (he was a man ahead of his time) denials of what in a famous coinage he called "I-ness," a masterpiece whose single message (other than learning not to be naughty and helping one's parents when they are sick and poor) was that each man makes himself and thus the world: *"Character counts!"* "Making makes the made mad!" is what the poor devil cried in his delirium, his voice eerily hollow as though coming from the other world. "Crackers! Curses! Listen to me and go back home!" Then he rushed to a church wall and beat his dark bony head against it, wailing forth his "Woe! Woe! Woe!" (*"Guai! Guai! Guai!"*—or maybe it was "Cry! Cry! Cry!") and eliciting from the beak-nosed porter in his role as the Plague Doctor the laconic remark: "That's what happens to people who get all their ideas on one side of their head, dottore: it tips their brains over."

He has been introduced here at the Gambero Rosso as *"un gran signore,"* and in truth has been treated as such by the beaming host, who seems to be chef, waiter, barkeep, and master of ceremonies all in one, as liberal with his wine as with his chatter, accepting their incongruous lot with that democratic grace and forbearance typical of the people of these islands, so leery of popes and kings alike, even joining them briefly for a plateful of stuffed pig's trotters and a Pinot Bianco from Collio, much recommended and indeed nothing amiss. On entering this simple inn with its yellow-painted walls and tattered football posters and plastic wine barrels, he had felt suddenly that he had been here before, not in this particular *osteria* of course, nothing so mawkishly improbable as that, but rather in all those village *osterie* of his childhood, all too long forgotten, of which this one now seemed the quintessence. What was it? A certain rancidity in the frying oil perhaps, the scrape of the cheap chairs on the wooden floors, the frayed napkins, a sharpness to the Parmesan on the tripe: whatever it was, he was overtaken by a sudden sorrow, and a sudden joy, as though life itself were reaching out for him in one last loving embrace, an embrace in which he feels himself still happily, if wistfully, enfolded.

Unable to sham an appetite which has utterly abandoned him in his weariness and excitement, the professor has nibbled at all the dishes for old times' sake yet eaten little, suffering, as it were, a mental indigestion of memories and anticipations churned up in the language by which he means to capture it all, the individual words springing up and flowering now in his head like golden coins on a magic tree, all atinkle with their manifest profundity and poetry. *Zin! zin! zin!* they go. I should be taking notes, he thinks. The blind hotel proprietor, likewise, complaining of a "grave indisposition of the gut, as it is called," said he could eat very little, settling in the end for a few modest portions of mullet *al pomodoro*, grilled cuttlefish, sea bass baked in salt, razor clams, and stuffed crabs, the house specialty, and finishing with sweetbreads and mushrooms, plus a simple *risotto* with sliced kidney *trifolato*, smoked eels, and prawns with chicken gizzards and *polenta*, all of it consumed noisily from beneath the grim visor of his *bauta* mask, pressed upon his plate like a pale severed head, his one black-gloved hand left free thereby to clutch his glass, from which he seemed not so much to drink the wine as to snort it.

The porter, contrarily, protesting that the night's exertions had aroused in him a most woeful discomfort in the stomach that closely resembled appetite, declared that he intended to consume at one sitting all that the liberality of the *dottore* had bestowed upon him, down to the last *quattrino*, speaking in the old way, and in demonstration of this proclamation, proceeded to consume monumental quantities of *tortellini* and *cannelloni*, *penne all'arrabbiata*, rich and tangy, spaghetti with salt pork and peppers, heaps of thick, chewy *gnocchi* made from cornmeal, a tender *pasticcio* layered with baked *radicchio* from Treviso, pickled spleen and cooked tendons (or *nervetti*, as they call them here, "little nerves," slick and translucent as hospital tubing), bowls of *risi e bisi* and sliced stuffed esophagus (the professor skipped this one), fennel rolled in cured beef, and breaded meatballs with eggplant *alla parmigiana*. His doctor unfortunately having put him on a strict regimen (and here the masked porter patted his overflowing hips plaintively), he was denied the pleasures of the fish course; but he was able, in all good conscience, to round off his evening's repast with a dish of calf's liver *alla veneziana;* wild hare in wine sauce with a homely garnishing of baby cocks, beef brains, pheasants, and veal marrow; a small suckling lamb smothered in kiwifruit, sage, and toasted almonds; and a kind of fricassee of partridges, rabbits, frogs, lizards, and dried paradise grapes, said to be another famous specialty of the house and particularly recommended for persons on stringent diets. "Ah, that was its own death!" he exclaimed on crunching up the last of the little birds. "I'm full as an egg!"

Of course there was an abundance of wine to be had with all this food, for as the porter put it: "You can't build a wall without mortar, professore!" True, true, and with the hearty generosity of the hotel manager in providing such a feast, even if he himself in his jet-lagged condition was able to enjoy so little of it, how could he refuse them all a few simple bottles, especially since in this respect at least he was able to join in the festivities. Indeed, it was the delicate whisper of a fizzy Cartizze from Valdobbiadene, the soft cheeky blush in a Pinot Grigio from the Veneto, the meaty brusqueness of a young Friulian Refosco, the tangy, faintly sour aroma of a spilled bottle of Venegazzù Riserva as it spread through the tablecloth stiffened with stains (not to mention the evaporation of his own reserve as the wines coursed through his age- and travel-stiffened limbs: good wine makes good blood, as they say here) that most pungently drew him back to the drama of his origins and left him now in this delicious metaphysical torpor, blessed as it were with purposeful idleness, at rest in the face of perfection—the very indolence in effect of Paradise itself, wherein self-knowledge is not pursued but intuitively received: Seek not and (a belch arises from some deep inner well like a kind of affirmation of the pneuma, and he welcomes it, clothing it in his spirit as it climbs toward the world, hugging it to his heart as he might a child, caressing it at the back of his throat as though to hone its eloquence, releasing it finally with a kind of tender exultation:)—*Wuurrrp!*—and ye shall find. . . .

"How's that, *Signore?* You've lost something?"

"Ah! No, I said, 'I feel fine!' Another round, my friend—while we wait!"

Though he shouldn't, of course. Thinking out loud like that, always worse when he's had a couple, but the magic of this moment and this place has him utterly entranced, and he wants to prolong the moment, to reach, if he can, the very dizzying heart of that enchantment. This, *this*, is what I have come back for, he thinks, sipping the pale *grappa* with its stalky aroma, its harsh green flavor, faintly reminiscent of winter pears and vanilla, his father's favorite drink. The old man brewed it himself, aging it under the stairs in an old oak barrel, black with antiquity, and every week Maestro Ciliegia, as they called him because of his notorious love for *grappa* and the cherrylike nose it conferred upon him (he can't remember his real name; it doesn't matter), would drop by with a little something for them, some fried pastry or a basket of figs or a few scraps of firewood, and his father would invite him in then for "a drop of Riserva," as he called it, dignifying it in that way, Maestro Ciliegia protesting all the way to the barrel. Then they would pull the broken-down table up to the cot and the rickety old chair up to the table, and commence a game of *bazzica* with cards as soft as empty pockets, or sometimes a chess match with little pegs and splinters only they knew how to identify, Maestro Ciliegia reminding his father each week that if he would only bring the table over to his workshop he would put a new leg on it, his father replying each week that the last time he visited that place he got pregnant, he would rather live with a ruined table than a ruined reputation. There would be more trips to the *grappa* barrel and sooner or later a piece would seem to move by itself on the chessboard or a card would magically turn up twice in one round, the joking would turn to insults, the words to pokes and punches, and soon the room would be a shambles, both men scratched and bruised, their ears and noses bit, their buttons torn off and their wigs scattered, and then from somewhere under all the rubble his father would say: "Another drop, Maestro Ciliegia?" "One more spot perhaps before I go."

The Gambero Rosso landlord, yawning, fills his glass once more. Is this a gift or has he just asked for it? In either event, he thanks him, feeling somewhat abashed. What is happening to him? It is as if the force of his reason and of a discipline which he has practiced since youth had suddenly abandoned him. In his time, it is true, he was young and raw; and, misled by his greenness and his admittedly peculiar identity crisis, he blundered in public. He lumbered about, he stumbled, he exposed himself, he offended against caution and tact. He has written about all this in *The Wretch*. But he renounced vagabondage and rebellion and idle amusements, and so, through discipline, has acquired that dignity which, as all the world insists, is the innate goad and craving of every moral being; it could even be said that his entire development has been a conscious undeviating progression away from the embarrassments of idleness and anarchy, not to mention a few indelicate pratfalls, and toward dignity. Indeed, he is one of the great living exemplars of this universal experience, this passage, as it were, from nature to civilization—from the raw to the cooked, as one young wag has put it—or, as he himself has described it in his current work-on-hard-disk in the chapter "The Voice in the Would-Pile": "from wood to will." And now, suddenly, that voice has returned to haunt him, as though to avenge its long confinement by reclaiming, as his own powers weaken, its mischievous autonomy. Nor is that the worst that has beset him. What is most alarming is that—pain, sorrow, and the door on top, as the porter might say: if it's not one thing, it's another—he is turning back to wood again. It's poking out now at his knees and elbows, he can see it, bleached and twisted and full of rot, maybe even a worm or two. He can also see the *osteria* landlord standing in front of him with his camel-hair coat over his arm and a long piece of paper. He stares up at him quizzically, lowering his sleeves and pant legs.

"You said something about paying, *Signore*, and to show you the door."

"Ah." His *grappa* is gone, though he doesn't remember drinking it. His stomach is not turning to wood, it feels like a soft collapsing bag, burbling indelicately now from under his napkin. "Of course." He stands, bumping the table, but luckily there's nothing on it left to spill. He'd rather sit for a while longer, it's quite peaceful here really, but he's too humiliated to admit it. "That's exactly what I said." But he can hardly say even that. "Said": he said "said," he heard that part himself, it's still ringing in his mind, but he is not sure about the rest. He is reminded, as he stands there weaving from side to side, of certain particularly odious faculty luncheons of the past. Yes, I could use a digestive walk, he thinks, hoping he is only thinking it. He reaches for the bill, but the landlord seems to be waving it about. He pauses, studying its movements, the patterns (he has always been particularly skillful at discerning patterns), then, with an abrupt lurch that sends his chair flying, snatches it: "Got you!" He laughs. But he can't read it. Must have the wrong glasses on. He asks the landlord to explain it to him. "Just the general principles," he says with a generous wave of his hand. It seems he is paying for all three suppers. The figure is astronomical. Of course all sums expressed in Italian lire are astronomical. You have to take off three or four zeros, he can't remember which. And his hotel bill will be credited, the landlord says. That's his understanding. The landlord removes the requisite banknotes from his wallet, which the professor seems to have given to him for this purpose. There is apparently just enough to cover the bill, which is a good thing because he left his traveler's checks back at the hotel. His good friends had not wanted to pay the bill for fear of implying he was not at liberty to have all he wanted to eat and drink, the landlord explains, handing the empty wallet back. It might have been an insult to a gentleman like himself. "I would not have minded the insult," the professor says grandly. He has one arm in a sleeve of the coat, but cannot find the other one. The other sleeve, that is. He knows where the arm is. "In fact, it would have given me—*bwrrpp! scusi!*—considerable pleasure." He has found the sleeve, but now he has lost the arm. This is because the first arm is in the wrong sleeve, or anyway that is the landlord's interpretation of the dilemma, an interpretation that proves functional if perhaps overly simple, for no sooner is it enunciated than both arms and both sleeves appear in their proper places. Whereupon a certain magic ensues: the professor finds himself, seemingly without transition, out in the snowy *campo*, all alone, bundled up in his coat and muffler, the Gambero Rosso behind him locked and dark, and such an immaculate silence all about that he can actually hear the snow falling upon other snow.

GUY DAVENPORT

August Blue

I

On the way to school, just past the bird market, there is one of the largest fig trees in Jerusalem. It was believed by some to be as old as the temple and to have a special blessing on it whereby its figs were fatter and sweeter than any others in the world, except, of course, those in the Garden of Eden. They were, in color, more blue than green. The milk that bled from its stems when you pulled one of its figs cured warts, the quinsy, and whooping cough.

Schoolboys could see this great fig tree. A red wall, however, kept them from helping themselves to the occasional fig, even though Roman law said that a traveler, or a child, could pick an apple, pear, or fig, for refreshment, without being guilty of theft, and the Torah was equally lenient and understanding of the hunger of travelers and boys.

On a fine morning in the month of Tishri, Daniel, Yaakov, and Yeshua, having inspected finches and quail in cages, and leapfrogged in the narrowest streets, shouted at by merchants, gave their usual longing looks at the fig tree.

—If only figs, Daniel said, knocked down like apples, and if we had a pole.

—But they don't, Yaakov said. And they wouldn't fall in the street, anyway.

They sighed, all three.

—Figs and dates smushed together with ewe milk, and roasted barley sprinkled on top, Yeshua said.

—Figs and honey, Daniel said.

—Figs just so, juicy and ripe, said Yaakov.

—What do you *say* to the donkeys? Daniel asked.

It was a game of Yeshua's to stop along the way to school and whisper into donkeys' ears, something quick and confidential, with a knowing smile. The donkeys never failed to quicken, lift their ears, and stare at him.

—Behold the grandfather of all jackrabbits! he would say out loud.

—I tell them something they think I don't know, Yeshua said. I spoke to the quail, too.

—Yeshua's *meshuggeh*.

—Want a fig? Yeshua said. One for each of you. Close your eyes and hold out your hands.

—You've got figs for recess?

—No, I got them off the tree back there.

Daniel looked at Yaakov, Yaakov at Daniel.

—So don't believe me, Yeshua said.

With a flourish of his hand he showed them a plump blue fig in his fingers. He gave it to Daniel. Another twirl and wiggle of fingers, and there was a fig for Yaakov.

—Holy Moses!

—Don't swear, Yeshua said. There's Zakkaiah looking up and down the street for us.

They ran to the school gate, herded in by their teacher, Zakkaiah, whose beard was combed and who smelled of licorice. They sat on cushions on a clean wooden floor, in a semicircle before Zakkaiah, who sat on a stool.

—*Alef*, Zakkaiah said.

—It's an ox, said Daniel.

—It comes first, a boy named Nathan said.

—So listen, said Zakkaiah.

He explained the derivation of *alef* from the old Phoenician alphabet, and talked about the versatility of a set of signs that could graph speech, contrasting it to the barbarous syllabaries of the Egyptians and the Assyrians.

—Greek is an even further advance. Their *alpha*, however, is not our *alef*. They have letters for their vowels, and use their *alpha* for one of them. Micah, what letter comes next?

—*Beth*.

—Yeshua! Zakkaiah said, are you chewing something?

—A fig.

—And what kind of manners is it to eat figs when we are learning the alphabet?

Nathan, who had just been slipped a fig by Yeshua, tucked it inside his blouse and looked innocent. Amos, who was also eating a fig passed back to him by Yeshua, swallowed his whole.

—And what is *beth*, Micah?

—But teacher, Yeshua said, we have not learned what is to be known about *alef*, and here we are hastening on to *beth*.

Zakkaiah's mouth fell open.

—So? he said. You want me to forget that you were having a late breakfast rather than paying attention to the lesson?

—Oh no, Teacher.

—I'm listening to what you have to say about *alef*, if you're quite through eating figs.

Yeshua worked his fingers in the air until there was a fig in them.

—Have a fig for yourself, O Teacher. And another. And yet another. They are from the great tree down the street, and are the juiciest and tastiest figs in all Jerusalem.

Zakkaiah stood with the three figs in his cupped hands, staring at Yeshua, speechless. He looked at the figs and he looked at Yeshua.

—My father sent them to you, O Teacher. They are good for the bowels, he says.

A silence.

—I will thank him when I see him, Zakkaiah said in a soft voice.

—*Alef*, Yeshua said. I will recite about *alef*.

There was an uneasiness in the class. Zakkaiah was obviously thinking several things at once.

—*Alef!* Yeshua said in a voice pitched bright. In the *alef* there's a *yud* up here, and a *yud* down there, with a line between. As with all boundaries, this line both joins and separates. The *yud* above is the Creator of the universe, of the earth, the sun, the moon, the planets, and the stars. The *yud* below is us, the people. The line between is the Torah, the prophets, the law. It is the eye for seeing what we can of the Creator. He is evident in his work, the world.

—You are reciting a commentary, Zakkaiah said, but whose?

—I'm making it up, Yeshua said. The Creator made us creators, too. Look at the spider knitting its web and at the bird building its nest. Every work has a maker.

—Is it the blessed Hillel your father has taught you?

—Who is Hillel? The alphabet is all pictures. You can look at them and see what they are: a house, a camel. The *alef* is a picture of the whole world. Cool water on dusty feet, that's a grand thing, and the smell of wood shavings and a crust dunked in wine, and honey, and dancing to the tabor and flute. These good things belong down here, but they come from up there. That's why there's a line between the top *yud* and the bottom *yud*. Everything has a fence, so we can know where it is. A house has rooms, a garden has a wall.

Zakkaiah sat on his stool, hard. He stuck the fingers of his left hand into his beard. His right hand held three figs.

—But the fun of the line between the *yud*s, Yeshua went on, is that it's a fence only if you look at it that way. It is really a road, and like all roads it goes both ways. You have to know which way you're going. Look at the anemones that make the fields red all of a sudden after the first rain of the wet season. The grand dresses at Solomon's court were not such a sight, and they were made with looms and needles, whereas the master of the universe made the anemones overnight, with a word. You can get near the line with much labor, or you can cross it with a step.

—I told you Yeshua's *meshuggeh*, Daniel whispered to Yaakov.

—Why don't you eat your figs, O Teacher? Yeshua asked. I have more.

II

On a blustery late afternoon in March 1842, Professor James Joseph Sylvester of the University of Virginia was walking along a brick path across the lawn in front of Jefferson's Rotunda. He had been brought from London to teach mathematics only the November before, and still wondered at these neoclassical buildings set in an American forest, and at the utilitarian rowhouse dormitories, at the black slaves who dressed the students and carried their books to class. He taught arithmetic and algebra from Lacroix's serviceable manual, trigonometry, geometry, the calculus differential and integral. Next term he was offering a course from Poisson's *Mechanics* and Laplace's *Mécanique céleste*.

He was a member of the Royal Society. At age twenty-seven he had distinguished himself with so brilliant a series of mathematical papers that he had been invited to come to Virginia. Jefferson's plan was to bring the best minds of Europe to dwell in his academic village, as he liked to call it. And now Jefferson was dead, leaving his faculty of European geologists, chemists, linguists, historians, and mathematicians to carry on his work of civilizing Virginia and her sister states.

Professor Sylvester's problem was one he had never before met. His students, all healthy, strapping young men from the richest of families, were illiterate. They knew nothing. He could scarcely understand a word they said. They came late to class, if at all, accompanied by their slaves. They talked with each other while Professor Sylvester lectured. The strangest thing about them was that they did not want to learn. Take Ballard. He was from Louisiana, some great plantation with hundreds of slaves. He was a handsome lad, beautifully dressed. Yet if called upon, he would say:

—I could answer that, Fesser, if I wanted to, but frankly I'm not minded to do so.

—Is this not insolence, Mr. Ballard?

—If you were a gentleman, Fesser, you'd know how to talk to one, now wouldn't you?

A roar of laughter.

He had gone to the faculty. They told him that the students had reduced Jefferson to tears, that they had shot three professors already, that he had best deal with them as patiently as he knew how. There was no support to be expected from Charlottesville, which was of the opinion that the faculty was composed of atheists, Catholics, Jews, Jesuits. A Hungarian professor had had to leave town in the dark of night.

They dueled, and fought with Bowie knives. They drank themselves into insensibility. They came to class drunk. When Sylvester tried to find out why this was allowed, he was reminded that the students were aristocrats.

—Mr. Ballard, will you rehearse Euclid's proofs for the Pythagorean theorem of the right triangle?

—Suck my dick.

He had had to ask what the words meant, and blushed. On the advice of a fellow professor he had bought a sword cane. One never knew. He was paid handsomely, but what worried him was that the papers he had been writing were harder and harder to finish. He was famous for averaging a mathematical paper a month. He knew that he had the reputation among his peers of having the most fertile genius of his generation. He was a Mozart of mathematics. He was finding it embarrassing to keep up his correspondence with the few men in Germany, France, and England who understood his work. These barbarian louts with their slaves and dueling pistols were making him sterile, and that tore at his soul more than their childish disrespect and leaden ignorance.

Why were they here, at a university, at least a university in name and intent? The French professor was slowly losing his mind, as none of his students had learned two words together of French. They gambled all night, knifed each other at dawn, drank until they puked.

And on this March afternoon Professor Sylvester found himself approaching the brothers Weeks, Bill and Al, or Mr. William and Mr. Alfred Weeks, gentlemen, as he must address them in class. They wore yellow and green frock coats, with flowery weskits. They were smoking long black cigars, and carried their top hats in their hands.

—You ain't a-going to speak to us, Jewboy?

Thus William, the elder of the brothers.

—Sir! said Sylvester.

—Yes, Fesser Jew Cockney, said Alfred. If you're going to teach rithmatic and that damn calc'lus shit to gentlemen, you ought to take off your hat to them when you meet us on the lawn, oughtn't he, Bill?

—Sir! said Sylvester.

—May be, said William Weeks, that if we pulled the fesser's Jew hat down over his Jew chin, he'd remember next time to speak to gentlemen.

Sylvester drew his sword from his cane with one graceful movement, and with another drove it into Alfred Weeks's chest.

Alfred screamed.

William ran.

Alfred fell backward, groaning:

—O Jesus! I have met my fatal doom!

Professor Sylvester coolly sheathed his sword, tapped it on the brick walk to assure that it was firmly fitted in his cane, turned on his heel, and walked away. He went to his rooms, packed a single suitcase, and walked to the posthouse to wait for a stage to Washington. This he boarded, when it came.

Alfred Weeks writhed on the brick walk, crying like a baby, calling for instant revenge. William came back with a doctor, who was mystified.

—Have you been bit by a m'skeeter, son? They ain't no wound. There's a little tear in your weskit, as I can see, and a kind of scratch here on your chest, like a pinprick.

—You mean I ain't killed dead?

Sylvester retrenched in New York City, where he practiced law. The mathematical papers began to be written again. He was called to the Johns Hopkins University, where he founded the first school of mathematics in the United States, where he arranged for the first woman to enter an American graduate school, where he argued with Charles Sanders Peirce, and where he introduced the Hebrew letters *shin* and *teth* into mathematical annotation.

Years later, the great Georg Cantor, remembering Sylvester, introduced the letter *alef* as a symbol of the transfinite.

III

As we descended westward, we saw the fen country on our right, almost all covered with water like a sea, the Michaelmas rains having been very great that year, they had sent down great floods of water from the upland countries, and those fens being, as may be very properly said, the sink of no less than thirteen counties; that is to say, that all the water, or most part of the water of thirteen counties falls into them.

The people of that place, which if they be born there they call the Breedlings, sometimes row from one spot to another, and sometimes wade.

In these fens are abundance of those admirable pieces of art called duckoys; that is to say, places so adapted for the harbor and shelter of wild fowl, and then furnished with decoy ducks, who are taught to allure and entice their kind to the places they belong to. It is incredible what quantities of wild fowl of all sorts they take in these duckoys every week during the season, duck, mallard, teal, and widgeon.

As these fens are covered with water, so I observed too that they generally at this latter part of the year appear also covered with fogs, so that when the downs and higher grounds of the adjacent country were gilded by the beams of the sun, the Isle of Ely looked as if wrapped up in blankets, and nothing to be seen, but now and then, the lanthorn or cupola of Ely Minster.

IV

Now the bike that was idling down the sheepwalk to the cove as sweet as the hum of a bee was a Brough, we saw, Willy and I. The rider of it lifted his goggles, which had stenciled a mask of clean flesh on the dust and ruddle of his face. A long face with shy blue eyes it was, and his light hair was blown back. He wore a Royal Air Force uniform and was, like, we judged, a private.

Willy asked if he was lost or had come a purpose, after naming the bike a Brough and the uniform RAF, showing that he knew both by sight.

—Right and right, the motorcyclist said.

He spoke Oxford.

—I'm here on purpose if I've found Tuke the painter's, though I shan't disturb him if he's busy. I wrote him last week.

—Aye, the penny postal, I remembered. He was interested in it.

—Name's Ross, the cyclist said.

—Sainsbury here, Willy said. My mate's Georgie Fouracre.

We all nodded, fashionable-like.

—Mr. Tuke, I said, is down yonder, in the cove, with Leo Marshall, painting of him in and out of a dory. If your postal named today, he'll be expecting you. We get the odd visitor from London, time to time, and some from up north and the continent.

So we rolled the motorbike down to Mr. Tuke and Leo. The canvas was on the easel, the dory on the strand, and Leo was drawing off worsted stockings, brown as a nut all over.

For all of his having the lines of a Dane, this airman Ross was uncommonly short. The crinkle of Mr. Tuke's eyes showed how pleased he was. His blue beret and moustache, his French blouse and sailor's breeks made one kind of contrast with the tight drab uniform Ross seemed to be bound in, with no give at all anywhere, and horse-blanket tough, and Leo's want of a stitch made another.

Ross was interested in the picture on the easel, which was the one that got named *Morning Splendour*, two of us in a dory and me on the strand as naked as the day I came into the world. It hangs in Baden-Powell House, in London, bought by the Boy Scouts. The color harmonies are the same as those of the more famous *August Blue* that's in the Tate.

This visit of Ross's was a summer morning in 1922. And a nice little watercolor came of it, of Ross undressing for a swim. Except that it isn't Ross.

What was it about him? He was at ease with us, as many are not, but he wasn't at ease with himself. Tuke got on with his painting. He posed Leo with a leg up on the dory.

—And your hand on your knee, just so. Turn a bit so that the light runs gold down your chest and left thigh.

He explained to Ross how he made quick watercolor studies, light being fugitive.

—There's nothing here, you know, but color. Light on a boy's back can be as mercurial as light on the sea.

Ross, it turned out as they talked, knew a lot about painters. He said that Augustus John is a crack draftsman but that of light and air he knows nothing.

Tuke smiled, and then he laughed, with his head back.

—These modernists. Ah, yes.

—And Wyndham Lewis paints a world that has neither air nor light.

—Do you know Lewis?

—I've met him. I dropped over his garden wall one evening. He was drawing in a back room. I introduced myself. It gave him quite a start. A childish trick on my part, but it amused him immensely. He fancies eccentricity.

He mentioned Eric Kennington, Rothenstein, Lamb. At one point Tuke gave him a very hard stare.

When Willy and I undressed, horsing around, as was our way, Ross paced as he talked with Tuke, holding his left wrist and wrenching it, as if he were screwing it off and on. He talked about Mantegna's bathing soldiers, which we had a print of in the studio, and a bathing place called Parson's Pleasure at Oxford. He was like a professor with a subject. One thing reminded him of another, and he thought out loud about it.

—Oh yes, well, Eakins in America. No one can get near him, Tuke said.

—Things return, Ross said. Here in the autumn of time you are recovering a spring which we have forgotten in our culture, a spring we know about in Greece and in the late Middle Ages.

Did Tuke know a man named Huizinga? A Dutchman.

—Meredith, Tuke said, has a lovely scene of boys bathing, in *Feverel.*

It was Leo, stretching between poses, who asked Ross why, if he was as educated as he sounded, he wasn't an officer.

—Cowardice, probably, Ross said.

—Leo didn't mean that in an untoward way, did you, Leo?

—Lord, no.

The sea had taken on a wonderful green brightness, a shuffling of silver, and the sky was glorious in its blue. Willy had swum out, dog-paddling. Tuke had removed his scarf. I was beginning to ponder what this visit of the little soldier Ross was all about. Tuke seemed to know things about him that we didn't, and to be keeping a secret. A confidence, perhaps I should say.

Willy did a devil dance on the sand, to get warm.

—We've often turned fair blue with cold for Mr. Tuke, he said.

In many of the pictures where we all appear to be toasty brown in fine sunlight we were actually freezing our ballocks off.

—Will you pose, Aircraftsman Ross? Tuke said abruptly. I covet your profile.

—I wonder, Ross said with a smile that was also a frown.

—We're a kind of *comitatus* here, Tuke said. Friends, all. The vicar, who likes to visit at tea, usually when the boys are still half undressed, has his doubts about the propriety of it all.

—Eats his doubts in muffins, Leo said, and drowns 'em in tea.

—He reads Housman, and Whitman.

—But brought back the Edward Carpenter we lent him without a word to say about it.

I liked the mischief in Ross's eyes as he listened to all this.

—We are hypocritical dogs, we English.

—Decent, Leo said, patting his tranklements.

—A naked English lad is as decent as a calf, Willy said. Though the best painting I've posed for is fully clothed with Mary Baskins in the apple orchard.

—For which, Tuke said, I hope to be remembered, if at all, that and *August Blue*.

—It is insufferably egotistical, Ross said, unbuttoning his tunic, to assume that one cannot possibly be understood by another, or for that matter by people at large, but there is that residuum of privacy at our center which we do despair of exposing to the world's mercy.

Tuke thought that over carefully, very interested, you could tell by the cock of his head.

—True, he said. We aren't quite ready to admit that we are all alike, all human. And in our sameness we are wonderfully different.

His tunic open on an Aertex vest, Ross sat to unwind his leggings and to pull off his glossy hobnailed boots.

—I'm wondering, he said, what I've come here to find. I'm forever, I think, looking for one thing or another. When I first saw your painting, Tuke, I recognized a fellow spirit, and life is not so long that we can afford to put off meeting one's kin.

He shed his trousers, which had a complexity of buttons and flaps.

Naked as Willy, Leo, and I, he seemed little more than a boy with a shock of hair and shy blue eyes. There was something wrong with his balls, as if they hadn't come down properly, or were stunted.

—Sit on the sand, Tuke said. I can do a crayon study fairly quickly.

—The sun feels good.

—Have you been drawn by any of these artists you've talked about?

—John. He did me in pencil. Kennington, pastel.

—Would it be a liberty, Leo said, as I had wanted to say, to pry into how a private in the RAF is so up on painters, sitting for them and all?

—There goes Leo again, Tuke said, drawing the thinnest possible line between good manners and intelligent curiosity.

—Oh, I don't mind, Ross grinned. The answer, Leo my fine fellow, is that I'm not Aircraftsman Ross 352087. The Brough is real, and the 352087 is real, and the uniform is real enough for the RAF. For the rest, I was born an impostor.

—Look straight ahead, and slightly up, Tuke said. I do hope the vicar doesn't turn up. He's well up on things, if you see what I mean.

—I don't, I said without thinking.

Tuke and Ross exchanged smiles.

—He would most probably recognize Private Ross.

—You're playing a teasing game with us, I said. Vicar, of all people! He didn't know Lord Gower when he was here with Frank or that French writer with the square face.

—Ross is different, Tuke said.

—Oh, I'm not afraid of the vicar, Ross said. I've got being an impostor down to an art. I've posed for a painter who didn't recognize me in the street the next day. The trick is to feel that you're nobody, and act accordingly.

—You've got to tell us, Leo said. You've gone too far not to.

—But, said Ross, there's really nothing to tell. I could tell you that my name is Chapman, which happens to be true, and you're none the wiser, are you? Things in this world are like that. A bloke whose name you know as Ross turns out to be named Chapman. It's worth Fanny Fuck All, as we say in barracks. Georgie Fouracre is Georgie Fouracre. You know who you are. You will beget strapping boys like yourself, and sit by your own fireside, you and your good wife.

—Mary Baskins, Leo said, more fool her.

—You lost your hopes with her by belching in church. Sounded like a bullfrog, and Vicar lost his place in Deuteronomy.

—But Vicar would recognize Chapman here, from the papers, from the pictures, from knowing him?

—I've said quite enough, Tuke said. I've got the profile. What about a bathe, what say?

Tuke was out of his clothes in the shake of a lamb's tail. Ross swam well, effortlessly. It was Willy who said later that he did everything with style, as if there was the one right way of doing a thing.

We had no towels, and were sitting and drying in the sun when there were steps down the path, and here was Vicar, shouting jovially, using a wholly unnecessary brolly as a cane, fanning himself with a cream panama.

—Oh! I say.

—You've seen us mother-naked before, Vicar, Leo said, giving Willy's ribs an elbow.

—Oh, I say! Of course, of course. A painter of lads must have lads to paint. If I'm intruding, I shall beat a prudent retreat, what what?

—Not at all, Tuke said. As a matter of fact, I have been making a watercolor study of a visitor, who came on that motorbike, and whom I'd like you to meet.

—I noticed the motorbike, yes. The etiquette of meeting a gentleman in a state of nature is an interesting one which our nannies rather passed over lightly.

Ross rose with an easy dignity and shook Vicar's hand.

—The Reverend Button Milford, Tuke said. Aircraftsman Ross. He has sat for John and is kind enough to like my work.

—Ever so pleased, I'm sure, said Vicar. Don't get dressed on my account. A classical education gives one a taste for the, ah, pastoral, don't you know.

Vicar dithered about, causing Leo to search the horizon for, as may be, a ship. And then asked:

—Were you, Ross, in this late, and one hopes last, terrible war? But of course you weren't: you're too young.

—I was indeed in the war, Ross said. And it is not the last.

MARY GORDON

Separation

The social worker said: "I think he needs a group experience."

Not looking at JoAnn, handing a piece of paper with a black design JoAnn saw later was the steeple of a church. Ascension Play School.

"It's no trip for you," the social worker said to JoAnn. "See that building there, behind the Episcopal church. They wrote to us, saying they're offering a scholarship to any child of ours who might benefit from a group experience."

Child of *ours?*
  Of *yours?*
  No one's but mine.

She put her hand over her mouth, to keep back something. Sickness? Bad words that would cause trouble later on? Words that would be put down in the file. She knew their ways. This Mrs. Pratt was not the first of them, she'd had a lot of them in towns over the years.

The game was shut your mouth.
  The game was shut your mouth and keep it shut.
  The game was shut your mouth and give them what they wanted.

Town after town. Arriving. Making your way to the county seat, the hall, the metal desks, the forms to be filled out, the bad lights with their buzzing noises, and the questions.

Name?

Her husband's. Not an out-of-wedlock child. Her son. Hers, but everything all right before the law. The husband, not abandoning, but driven off. Pushed out. No room for him, he knew it, and was sorry, but he knew. One day: "Well, I'll be shoving off."

"All right."

A night she stayed up, when the baby had the croup. Her husband saw her happiness. He saw how happy she was, after the steaming shower and the rush outside to the cold air, after all this, the easy, even breathing. And her humming. Song after song.

"Well, I'll be shoving off."

"All right."

Rubbing the boy's wet head with a dry towel. Wet from the steam she'd set up in the bathroom. His hair that smelled like bread. She put her lips to it, and breathed it in. His easy breath, the wet smell of his hair. And looked up at the father, at the husband, sorry for him, but it was nothing, he was right to leave, there wasn't any place for him.

Humming, his damp head and his easy breathing. Happy, happy. All I want.

He needs a group experience.

All I have ever wanted.

Her childhood: blocks of muteness. Of silence because what was there to say. Neglect, they called it. She was kept alive. Fed. Clothed. She saw now that could not have been so easy. The flow of meals, sweaters, jackets, in the summer short-sleeved shirts and shorts, a bathing suit, washed hair, injections that were law. She felt sorry for her mother, whom she barely could remember now. She had trouble calling up the faces of the past.

Her memory: the outline of a head, a black line surrounding nothing. The faces blank. Unharmful ghosts, but nothing, nothing to her. And of course no help.

It was why she didn't like the television. All the filled-in faces. She wanted, sometimes, to ask people about their memories. Do you remember people when you are away from them? The faces? At what point do they come alive?

Even her husband's face grown ghostly.

But she never said these things. She kept to herself. Smiling, quiet, clean. She and her son.

Never causing trouble.

Keeping things up.

Arriving on time for the social worker.

The clinic.

The dentist, who said it was all right if she sat on the chair and he sat on her lap to be examined. Otherwise he'll scream.

Fine, then, Mrs. Verbeck. Just keep it up. Keep him away from sugar snacks. Fresh fruit. Apples or carrot sticks. Water rather than soda or other sweetened drinks.

Yes, thank you. Yes.

You've done a good job. Not one cavity. You floss his teeth?

I will.

We'll show you how. Miss Havenick, the hygienist, will show you.

"Let's open our mouth, Billy."

Not yours. His.

And mine.

She wanted to phone the call-in radio and ask one of the doctors.

Are the faces of people empty to other people as they are to me?

Except his face. The one face I have always known.

At night while he slept she sat on a stool beside him just to learn his face. So that she never would forget.

An angry baby. Happy only in her arms.

He doesn't take to strangers. Thanks, no, I can manage. Thanks.

Did anyone look at her face? In the shadowy childhood, family of shadow, furniture the part of it that she remembered most. The green couch. The red chair.

Did anyone look at my face?

He needs a group experience.

But we are happiest alone.

But never say it. She knew what people thought. Children need other children. They believe that, everyone believes it.

Only I do not believe it.

Only he and I.

Happy, happy in the studio apartment, in the trailer, in the basement rented in the rotting house. Happy in the supermarket, laundromat, bank where we stand on line to cash the check from welfare. Singing, eating meals we love, the walks we take, bringing back leaves, pine cones. Puzzles we do in silence, cartoon shows we watch.

She wanted to say to them: "We're very happy."

She never said these things. She moved.

Five towns. Five different states.

He needs a group experience.

This time she thinks they may be right. Now he is four years old. Next year, no hope.

No hope. No hope.

All I have ever wanted.

On the first day of school, she dresses him. She didn't dare to buy new clothes for school. She puts on him the clothes that he has worn all summer. Black jeans with an elastic waist. An orange short-sleeved shirt with a design of a bear on the left breast pocket. White socks, his old red sneakers he is proud of. Velcro. He can do them himself.

The teacher says: "He's never had a group experience?"

"No, just with me."

"Maybe, then, for the first few days you can stay with him. For a little while. Until he adjusts to the group situation."

She sees the other mothers bought their boys and girls new clothes. And for themselves. She parks the car behind the church and waits till they have all gone in the little building, like a hut, built for the children. All the other mothers know each other. Like each other. And the children.

There is no one that we know.

The teacher is standing at the door. "Good morning Jessica, Kate, Michael, Daniel, Jason, Alison."
"And here comes Billy."

Children are playing on the swings and slides.
Children are playing in the sandbox.
Girls are pretending to cook at the toy stove, using toy pots and spoons and dishes.
Boys are in the corner making a house of large blocks, then shoving it down, building it, knocking it down, fighting, building.

Billy hides his face in her shoulder.
"I won't leave you."
"Maybe tomorrow," says the teacher. "After he gets more used to the group, you'll feel that you can leave after a while."

The teacher's pants are elastic-waisted, like the children's pants. She wears blue eye shadow, her fingernails are pink as shells. She is wearing sandals with thin straps. She is wearing stockings underneath the sandals. JoAnn wonders: Maybe they are socks that only look like stockings. Maybe they stop.

At night he says: "Don't take me back there."
"All right," she says. Later she says: "I made a mistake. We have to go."

The second day of school he will not look at anybody. When the teacher puts her hand on his shoulder to ask if he sees anything he might like to play with, he pushes her hand away and looks at her with rage. "No one said you could touch me." He hides his eyes. He grinds his eyes into his mother's shoulder blade.

She's proud that he can speak up for himself. But she is frightened. Now what will they do?

In the playground, he lets her push him on a swing. She lights a cigarette. The other mothers don't approve, although they try to smile. They tell her about their children, who had problems getting used to school.

"My oldest was like that. Till Christmas."

No one is like us. No one is like he is.

One morning he says he's tired. She tells him he doesn't have to go to school. She keeps him home for three days. Both of them are happy.

But the next day it's worse in school. Only one of the mothers smiles at her. She says: "You know, maybe Billy's finding the group too large. Maybe he could just come over to our house. Daniel's used to the group. If they made friends, maybe that would help Billy in the group."

"Thank you," JoAnn says. "But we're so busy."

The social worker says: "You're not working on this separation."

Everything has been reported. The social worker takes it as a bad sign that JoAnn refused the other mother's invitation. Which she knows about.

"If I were you," she says, ". . . or maybe some counseling. For both your sakes."

JoAnn is terrified. She tells the other mother she would like to come. The other mother writes her name and address down on a piece of paper torn from a pad in the shape of an apple with a bite out of it. It says "Debi—35 Ranch Road." And in parentheses "Dan's mom."

For this, she buys her son new clothes.

He never cries anymore. Nobody can make him do anything he doesn't want to. His eyes are bright green stones. No one can make him do anything. This makes her feel she has done right.

The morning that they are going to the house they take a bath together. They laugh, they soap each other's backs. Lately she sees him looking at her sex a second longer than he ought to, and his eyes get hard and angry when he sees she sees. She knows they will not bathe together much longer after this year. But this year. Yes.

Debi, the mother, has to look several places for an ashtray. JoAnn hasn't realized there are no ashtrays until she has already lit up. They are both embarrassed. Debi says, "Somehow most of the people I know quit." She goes through her cabinets and then finds one from a hotel in Canada. "We stole it on our honeymoon," she says, and laughs.

Billy knows his mother doesn't want him to play with Danny. She knows he knows. But she can feel his bones grow lively on her lap; she feels his body straining toward the other children. Danny and his sisters, Gillian and Lisa. And the toys. The house is full of toys. Trucks, cars, blocks, toy dinosaurs are scattered all over the wooden floors. But the house is so big it still looks neat with all the toys all over. The house is too big, too light. The house frightens JoAnn. She holds Billy tighter on her lap. He doesn't move although she knows he wants to. And she knows he must.

"Look at that truck," she says. "Should we go over and look at that truck?"

Debi jumps out of her chair, runs over to the children.

"Let's show Billy the truck. See Danny's truck, Billy?" She gets down on her knees. "Look how the back goes down like this."

JoAnn doesn't know whether or not to go down on her knees with Debi and the other children. She stands back. Billy looks up at her. His fingers itch to touch the truck. She sees it. She gives him a little push on the shoulders. "Go play," she says. She lights another cigarette and puts the match in the heart-shaped ashtray she has carried with her.

Billy isn't playing with the other children. He is playing alongside them. Danny and his sisters are pretending to make dinner out of clay. They don't talk to Billy; they don't invite him to play with them; they leave him alone, and he seems happy with the truck. She sees he has forgotten her. For him she is nowhere in the room.

Debi says, "Let's go into the kitchen and relax. They're fine without us."

JoAnn feels the house will spread out and the floor disappear. She will be standing alone in air. The house has no edges; the walls are not real walls. Who could be safe here?

In the kitchen in a row below the ceiling there are darker-painted leaves. She tells Debi she likes them.

"I did them myself. I'm kind of a crafts freak. Are you into crafts?"

JoAnn says she always wanted to do ceramics.

"I do ceramics Thursday nights," says Debi. She brings a cookie jar shaped like a bear to the table. "I made this last month," she says. "And while you're at it have one." She offers JoAnn the open jar. "I made them for the kids, but if you won't tell I won't."

The cookies frighten JoAnn. The raisins, and the walnuts and the oatmeal that will not dissolve against her tongue.

"If you want, there's room in our ceramics class on Thursdays. I think it's important to have your own interests, at least for me. Get away, do something that's not connected to the kids. Get away from them and let them get away from you."

JoAnn begins to cough. She feels she cannot breathe. The walls of the big room are thinning. She is alone in freezing air. Her ribs press against her thin lungs. Debi says: "You okay, JoAnn?"

"I smoke too much. This year, I'm really going to quit. I've said it before, but now, this year I'm really going to do it."

They hear a child scream. They run into the living room. Danny is crying.

"He hit me with the truck."

"Did you hit him with the truck?" JoAnn says. "Tell Danny you're sorry."

Billy looks at them all with his bright eyes. Except at her. He does not look at his mother. He knows she doesn't want him to apologize. He knows that she is glad he did it. He did it for her. She knows this.

"We've got to be going," says JoAnn, picking Billy up. He presses the truck to him. "Put the truck down," she says.

He doesn't look at anyone.

"Don't go," says Debi. "Really, they were doing great. All kids get into things like that. They were doing great for a long time."

"We've got to go," JoAnn says, looking in the pocket of her plaid wool jacket for the keys. "Billy, give Danny back his truck."

"Danny, can Billy borrow the truck till school tomorrow?" Debi asks.

JoAnn pulls the truck from her son's grip.

"Thanks, but he doesn't need it," she says, smiling, handing back the truck. "It isn't his."

The truck falls from her hand. It makes a hard sound on the wooden floor. Hearing the sound, Danny begins to cry again.

"Let's try it again," says Debi. "They were really doing great there for a while."

JoAnn smiles, holding Billy more tightly. "Sure thing," she says.

At night, while he sleeps and she sits on the stool beside his bed to watch, she thinks of him in the room with the other children. Him forgetting. She thinks of him pushing the truck back and forth on the floor beside the other children, thinks of the walls thinning out, and her thin lungs that cannot enclose the breath she needs to live.

Alone. Alone.

All I have ever wanted.

In the morning he says: "You should have let me take that truck."

She says: "Do you want to go back to that house?"

"I want the truck."

"Danny's a nice boy, isn't he?"

He says: "Are you going to leave me alone today?"

"I don't know," she says. "I'll see."

When they arrive, the teacher says: "I think Billy's ready for a regular day today. I think the time's come definitely."

She doesn't look at JoAnn when she says this. She takes Billy's jacket off and hangs it on his hook below his name. She does not let go of his hand. "Billy, I heard you played with Danny yesterday. That's so terrific. He brought in the truck today, for you to play with while you're here."

The teacher leads him into the class, closing the door behind her so JoAnn can't see them. So that he cannot look back.

She stands in the hall. Her hands are freezing. She pulls the fake fleece collar of her plaid coat around her ears. Her heart is solid and will not pump blood. She walks into the parking lot. She gets into her car and starts it. She does not know where she will get her air, how she will breathe. The engine stalls. She pumps the gas pedal and starts the car again.

And then she hears him. He is calling. He is running toward the car. She sees that he has put his coat on by himself. She sees him standing at the car door, opening it, getting in beside her.

She can breathe, the air is warm and helpful for her breathing. They are driving, singing. They are happy.

She says to him: "Let's pack up all our things. Let's find another place, a better place to live in."

Happy, singing.

He will leave me soon enough.

PETER HANDKE

TRANSLATED FROM THE GERMAN BY RALPH MANHEIM

The Companions

The train in the middle of the city, two steps from the department store, also seems like a toy. There isn't any station, the tracks it is standing on merge with a marketplace right after the last car, and this enhances the toylike impression. But the train is crowded, and more and more people—unlike streetcar passengers, loaded with baggage—come running and get in. Like certain international expresses, it is made up of sections of different trains. The locomotive is far ahead of the platform. The unusual length of the train, and still more the excitement and bewilderment of the passengers, who cannot be seasoned travelers, give it for a moment the air of a special train, reserved for a group of emigrants or pilgrims from all over the country.

It is still high noon; the noonday, springtime light shines most brilliantly on the rounded tops of the cars. A signal rings out—not a train whistle, more like the tooting of an ocean liner, so long-drawn-out that a child on the platform treats himself to a kind of radio play by rhythmically stopping and unstopping his ears. But, surprisingly at the departure of so long a train, few people have come to say good-bye, and hardly anyone is looking out the open windows. Consequently, the gambler has no need to twine his way through a crowd as he runs past the market stalls; he is able to head straight for the compartment, which is reached not through a corridor but directly from outside. The door is thrown open for him even before he gets there, and closes after him like that of a funicular cabin once it is loaded to capacity.

Yet a number of seats are still vacant after he has sat down. There are only three other persons, who, though thrown together at random, seem to acquiesce in the arrangement. With the gambler the group is complete. The woman at the window does not favor him with so much as a glance—her attention is concentrated on her aluminum suitcase, as though it were in danger; pencil in hand, the old man across from her is immersed in his notebook; and the soldier's back is turned, for he is standing at the door as though to guard it. True enough, some others try to get in: first a loudmouthed couple, who at the sight of the four fall silent and go away; then a priest in travel dress who, after a greeting all around with one foot already on the threshold, vanishes as though to resume his greetings in the next compartment. Only a child strong enough to open the door by himself pushes past the soldier, and his parents have to stick their heads in and order him out with the words: "Not there. Somewhere else." The child complies with a shrug.

The hubbub outside dies away. But the train doesn't move. There's plenty of time. The soldier sits down, pulls himself up again as though in expectation—not of an event but of a first word. It's the woman who turns quite casually to the others and says: "When my childhood was over I began to wander around. I left the house and went farther and farther away, until I didn't know where I was anymore. When they caught me in some small town or out in the country, I didn't know my name and address. I usually took the train, never one that was going very far, always a local; no matter where it was going, I never bought a return ticket. What did I do when I arrived there? They told me I just sat around in the waiting room at the last stop or on the loading platform, and sometimes at the edge of a field, in a gravel pit, or by the side of a brook, regardless of the season. People began to notice me because of the way I'd sit there for hours—before that, when I was wandering around, it seems I walked like someone who knew his way and was going somewhere. Men often stopped their cars and told me to get in, but none of them touched me, they never laid a finger on me; there was never any conversation, because my answer to everything was the same: I don't know. So they took me to the police. I couldn't be a tramp, that was out of the question; even the village constables came out from behind their partitions when they saw me, and all of a sudden they stopped talking dialect. I always had plenty of money on me. And that is what made them think I was crazy. Instead of sending me home, they took me to an institution. There I was exhibited to students in a lecture hall shaped like an amphitheater. The professor showed me off, not because I was sick but because it was me. Though I only answered his rehearsed questions with yes or no, he always shook my hand with both of his and held the door open for me when my act was done. The students were crazy about me, too. My wanderings can't have made me very happy, because often when they found me sitting there I'd be crying or even shouting for help—but my act must have opened the eyes of the onlookers to something they'd never known before. While the mental patients were performing, I'd be sitting in the cubicle waiting for my turn, and I'd hear the listeners coughing or laughing, but when I appeared, they'd all fall silent. They didn't feel sorry for me, they envied me. What they heard about me filled them with longing. If only, instead of moving in crowds through familiar streets, they could wander around like me in a dream and alone. My adventures made them long, not for other continents, but for the towns and villages nearby, which up until then had meant nothing to them. Thanks to me, the names took on a resonance and the places became possible destinations. Though I was standing there barelegged in an institutional gown, for them I was a heroine. And it's true that, though actually I wasn't so very well off, I was better off than those people, who thought they were well off. One of you was there too, as a visiting student. He only attended my demonstration because he thought I was the kind of person that moved him. He came because he respected me."

Something of hers falls on the floor. The soldier bends down. It is a fountain pen with a mother-of-pearl cap. As he turns it slowly in his hand, the light from outside seems to shine through the cap. A jolt runs through the train, and it pulls out under two trees, the one close to the track, the other by the side of the parallel road. Their branches have become intertwined so as to form an arch, though an irregular one, because the tree beside the track has been pruned to make room for the wires and the pylon, with the result that the arch has scorched or bare spots that make it look like the tusk of a mammoth. The clouds in the breach are diesel smoke mixed with soot, and the birds swerve to avoid them. The deserted platform glitters for a moment; on a high-rise tower the sign appears: HOTEL EUROPA.

At first the four in the compartment stop whatever they are doing. The gambler has a cigarette between his lips and his lighter in his hand. The soldier has a finger in his closed book. The old man, his pencil point at the ready but motionless, holds his notebook in such a way as to show the letters CUMBERLAND. Pocket mirror in hand, the young woman stops freshening her lipstick. Further speech seems unauthorized for the present. The silence adds to their contentment. Only the woman looks questioningly from one to the other; she is the only one of the four whose face is not turned toward the window. Outside, there has been a quick succession of short tunnels and viaducts. Then, though there has been no noticeable change in the vegetation or the shapes of the houses, the light seems different, perhaps because the view of the sky is less obstructed. The train, which for a time was running at high speed like a transcontinental express, has begun to stop as frequently as a streetcar. The track is no longer running parallel to the road; for a time it skirted fields and woods, but lately it has been running straight through a forest. Hardly anyone has been getting on, but crowds of passengers have been getting out at every stop and invariably forming processions that march off on identical roads, heading for village churches miles away, on identical hilltops. At one station—actually no more than a shelter in the woods—just one person gets off, and vanishes into the woods with his worker's briefcase. Convinced that this was their last fellow passenger, the woman—who also has turned toward the window by now—reaches for the door handle. The old man restrains her with a quick shake of his head. A far from empty train, coming in the opposite direction, stops on the other track, and a group of screaming schoolchildren comes trooping down the center aisle. As the train starts up again, the old man raises his surprisingly high voice in a chant, every word of which can be heard above the hubbub: "In the childhood of peoples, unknown countries came into existence beyond the mountains and the oceans. They had names, but nobody knew where they were. Only their direction was more or less certain. The sources of the Nile were south, the Caucasus east, the legendary Atlantis west, and Ultima Thule north. Then came trading ships and wars of conquest, then came history, and then—violently, by leaps and bounds—came the adulthood of the peoples and it exploded the legends of childhood geography. The sources of the Nile were muddied, the peaks of the Caucasus reduced from heavenly heights to their actual dimensions, and Ultima Thule dislodged from its place as the kingdom at the end of the world. No Atlantis will ever again rise out of the sea. But the names remained; in epics and songs they took on a fantastic power that gave life to the realm of legend. Since then Paradise as the source of the Tigris and Euphrates and the landing of Noah's ark on Mount Ararat after the flood have been all the more real, and the infant Moses in his basket will float for all time in the slowly flowing Nile. The name is the guest of reality. In much the same way, we in our childhood gave our few favorite places faraway names; that was how the brook at the edge of the cow pasture, where we roasted potatoes under a tree in the rain, came to be called Lethe or River of Forgetfulness, how a few spindly vines came to be transposed into the Amazonian jungle, how the cliff behind the house came to be a foothill of the Sierra Nevada, how the wild lilies on top of it took on Indian colors and the hole in the garden hedge became the entrance to our New World. We, too, are grown up now, and all the names from those days, without exception, are null and void. We, too, have a history, and what was then, in those days, cannot be retrieved by any changing of names. I don't believe that those days can be brought back, even if that brook had broadened into a river, even if those vines had turned into unbreakable lianas, even if a real Apache were standing on top of the cliff where the lilies used to be. But I still believe, in earnest and no longer in play, in the power of places. I believe in places, not the big ones but the small, unknown ones, in other countries as well as our own. I believe in those places without fame or name, best characterized perhaps by the fact that *nothing* is there, while all around there is *something*. I believe in the power of those places because nothing happens there *anymore* and nothing has happened there *yet*. I believe in the oases of emptiness, not removed from fullness but in the midst of it. I am certain that those places, even if not physically trodden, become fruitful time and again through our decision to set out and our feeling for the journey. I shall not be rejuvenated there. We shall not drink the water of life there. We shall not be healed there. We shall simply have been there. Over a stretch of rotten plank road, past a wilderness of rusty carpet frames, we shall have gone there. The grass there will have trembled as only grass can tremble, the wind will have blown as only the wind can blow, a procession of ants through the sand will have been a procession of ants, the raindrops in the dust will have taken on the incomparable form of raindrops in the dust. In that place, on the foundations of emptiness, we shall simply have seen the metamorphosis of things into what they are. Even on the way, merely because we are looking at it, a rigid blade of grass will have begun to sway, and conversely, in the presence of a tree, our innermost being will for the moment have taken on the form of that tree. I need those places and—hear now a word seldom used by an old man—I *long* for them. And what does my longing want? Only to be appeased."

In the course of his speech the weather has changed several times, alternating between sunshine and rain, high wind and calm, as in April. One river crossed by the train, hardly a trickle between gravel banks, is followed by another, a roaring, muddy flood, which is perhaps only the next meander of the first. As so often on branch lines, the stations are farther and farther apart. Once, the train has stopped in open country. The wind was so strong that from time to time the heavy car trembled. Withered leaves, pieces of bark, and branches crashed against the window. When at last the train started up again, the lines of raindrops in motion crossed those of waiting time.

Surprisingly for a place so far out in the country, there are many tracks at the station they arrive at. All end at a concrete barrier; with the exception of the rails on either side of the platform, which have been polished smooth, all are brown with rust. The station is in an artificial hollow; a steep stairway leads out of it. The soldier carrying the woman's suitcase, the four climb it together, more slowly than the few other people, all of whom are at home here. But even the newcomers are sure of the way. On leaving the ticket hall through a swinging door, they turn without hesitation in the direction indicated by the gambler, who has taken the lead. After crossing an area of bare ground and sparse, stubbly grass, suggesting an abandoned cattle pen or circus ground, they find themselves at the edge of a large forest. The trees in its dark depths seem at first sight to be covered with snow; in reality they are white birches. Here the four hesitate before crossing a kind of border, the dividing line between the yellowish clay of the open field and the black, undulating, springy peat soil. The peat bog and the forest rooted in it are also several feet higher than the field. Instead of a path cut through the earth wall there are several small wooden ladders, to one of which the gambler directs his followers with an easy gesture, showing that this is a man who gets his bearings without difficulty wherever he goes. He climbs up last, and once on top resumes leadership. Strolling through the woods—there is no underbrush between the birches—all four turn around in the direction of the station, toward which passengers are converging from all sides, all goose-stepping in single file, though there is plenty of room in the field. Seen through the white trees, the shacklike structure seems to be somewhere in the taiga.

The forest is bright with birch light. The trees stand in beds of moss, as a rule several in a circle, as though growing from a common root. As one passes, they revolve in a circle dance that soon makes one dizzy. Over a footpath that suddenly makes its appearance—white stones sprinkled over the black ground—the four emerge at length into a wide clearing, announced some time earlier by the substitution of berry bushes for moss and by the widening middle strip of grass in the path. By now the path has become so wide that the four are able to walk abreast. On the threshold of the clearing, each of the four, on his own impulse, pauses for a moment; the woman has taken the arm of the old man, who nods his assent. Now they are fanning out in different directions, as though no longer needing a leader.

The clearing is rather hilly, shaped like a moraine spit thrust into the peat bog, and so large that the herd of deer at the other end goes right on grazing though the arrival of the newcomers has been far from soundless. Only the stag has raised his light-brown head like a chieftain. For a moment, his widely scattered herd looks like a tribe of Indians. In the middle of the clearing there is a small lake, which at first seems artificial but then—with its islands of rushes and black muddy banks, marked with all manner of animal tracks—proves to be a bog pool. Only at one point, at the tip of the moraine, so to speak, can the pool be reached dry-shod over gravel outcrops; and here its water, instead of presenting an opaque, reflecting surface, is perfectly transparent. The bright pebbles at the bottom stand out all the more clearly thanks to the glassy streaks in the water of the spring which emerges underground from the moraine and can be followed as it twines its way through the gravel to the lake which it feeds. This is also the place for a hut built of weathered, light-gray boards, shot through with amber-yellow or reddish-brown trails of resin, and for a strangely curved uphill-and-downhill boat dock that juts out over the water like a roller coaster.

Here, one by one, they all gather. The woman, the old man, and the soldier look on as the gambler fishes an enormous bunch of keys out of his coat pocket, unlocks the padlock on the hut, throws the door wide open, unlocks the glass-and-metal compartment inside it, and, after turning a last key, drives out in a car that gets longer and longer: a camper. Birch branches—camouflage and ornament in one—slide off the top.

He pushes open the back door, sets up a folding table on the grass, and spreads a white tablecloth over it. The soldier hastens to help him and brings four chairs from inside the vehicle. But for the time being no one sits down. The old man vanishes purposefully through the trees, the gambler goes into his camper, and the woman, again with her silver suitcase, signals the soldier to follow her to the boat dock. Standing behind him with scissors and comb that she has taken out of her suitcase, she changes his hairstyle. Then with a quick gesture she bids him take off his uniform and, repeatedly stepping back to scrutinize not so much the soldier as her handiwork, dresses him in civilian clothes, likewise out of her suitcase. She keeps tugging and pulling and plucking at the soldier, who doesn't seem to mind; his transformation from a chubby-cheeked bumpkin to a smooth, ageless cosmopolitan, dressed for summer and ready for anything, seems perfectly natural; only his eyes, when he turns back toward the woman, are as grave as ever, behind the happily smiling woman, ever so pleased with herself, they see the old man, who has just stepped bareheaded out of the woods, his hat full of mushrooms. While the woman takes an awl—she has everything she needs in the suitcase—and makes an extra hole in the soldier's belt, the old man, sitting beside them on the bank, cleans his varicolored mushrooms.

By then the table has been set for all. The gambler in the camper also seems changed, not only because he is officiating at the stove in his shirtsleeves and wearing a flowered apron, but also because for cooking he has put on a pair of half-moon glasses. It is only when he suddenly looks over the edges that his glance seems as cold and dangerous as it used to. In the cramped galley he moves with the grace of a born cook—carefully wiping the glasses, putting the plates in the oven to warm, reaching for the bunches of herbs hanging from the ceiling—and shuffles in and out of the camper as though he had been running a restaurant for years.

Meanwhile, the woman and the soldier are at the table waiting. The old man is sitting on a mossy bank with his canvas-covered notebook, inscribing his columns as though in accompaniment or response to the kitchen sounds. Then he too sits motionless, though without expectation, his strikingly upright posture attributable solely to the place or the light; there is no wind, but his cape is puffed out. A bottle of wine is cooling in the spring at his feet.

Now all four are at the table and the meal is over. The glasses are still there, but only the old man is drinking wine; the gambler and the woman are smoking; the soldier has moved a short distance away; resting one heel on the knee of the other leg, he is twanging a Jew's harp rendered invisible by the hand he is holding over it—isolated chords with such long pauses between them that in the end we stop expecting a tune. As though in response to the music, the old man puts his wineglass down after every swallow, or waits with the glass in midair. Under his gaze the open back door of the camper turns into a cave, while the shingle roof of the boathouse becomes vaulted and shimmers like the scales of the fish that dart to the surface of the pool after scraps of food. Now the entire clearing has the aspect of a garden where time no longer matters. The only sounds to be heard are garden sounds, the fluttering of the table-cloth, the splashing of a fish, the brief whirring and chirping of a bird among the ferns at the edge of the forest. The clouds drift across a sky which becomes so high that space seems to form a palpable arch overhead. The blue between the clouds twists and turns and is reflected down below in the water, in the grass, and even in the dark bog soil.

The woman and the old man, who have taken their clothes off behind the camper, run down to the lake without a trace of embarrassment; the old man starts his run with a jump—like a child—and his way of running is equally childlike; the woman waits a moment, as though to give him a head start, and overtakes him at the brink of the water. The gambler and the soldier, each with a toothpick in his mouth, watch as the two swim out into the pond. The water is warm. The woman turns to the aged swimmer beside her and, speaking as though they were strolling down a path together, says: "I wish I could just stay here. Any other place I can think of would be too hot or too cold, too light or too dark, too quiet or too noisy, too crowded or too empty. I'm afraid of any new place and I hate all the old ones. In the places I know, dirt and ugliness are waiting for me; in the unknown ones, loneliness and bewilderment. I need this place. Yes, I know: it's only on the move that I feel completely at home. But then I need a place where I can spread out. Tell me of one woman who lives entirely out of suitcases, and I'll tell you about all the little things you can't help noticing the moment she arrives—a framed photograph here, a toothbrush there. I need my place, and that takes time. I wish I could stay here forever."

Her swimming companion dives under; when he comes up, he has the face of a wrinkled infant. He answers in a voice made deep by the water, which resounds over the surface of the lake: "That wish cannot be fulfilled. And if it could be, it would bring no fulfillment in the long run. Whenever in my life I have thought I arrived, at the summit, in the center, *there*, it has been clear to me that I couldn't stay. I can only pause for a little while; then I have to keep going until the day when it may be possible to be *there* somewhere else for a little while. Existence for me has never been more than a little while. There is no permanence in fulfillment, here or anywhere else. Places of fulfillment have hurt me more than any others; I have come to dread them. It's no good getting used to staying in one place; wherever it is, fulfillment can't last. It loses its magic before you know it, and so does the place. *It* is not here. We are not *there*. So let's get going. Away from here. Onward. It's time."

The garden has undergone a transformation while the swimmer was speaking. Though the light is unchanged, the lake has taken on a late-afternoon look. The spring has almost dried up and the water level has fallen, uncovering the usual junk—tires, metal rods, whole bicycles—along with bleached, barkless tree trunks. The skeleton of some animal appears in the underbrush at the edge of the forest, and elsewhere a collapsed shooting bench comes to light; prematurely fallen leaves are blown over the springtime lake, and those soot-gray spots in the hollows are deposits of old snow. The clouds grow longer and are joined together by vapor trails of the same color; the faded scrap of newspaper in the bushes shows a distinct date; and that importunate noise is the persistent blowing of horns on an expressway.

The clearing is deserted, the boathouse sealed. The swimmers have left no trace in the wind-ruffled lake. Only the mud bank reveals the prints of bare feet and of the camper's tires, vanishing in the gravel path as it mounts the moraine.

LARRY LEVIS

Black Freckles

1

At the moment I'm watching some guy on a bus. He's just sitting there, staring out—I can't tell if he's unhappy or anything—he's just staring out through the rain-streaked windows of the bus outside the Slavija.

At the moment I don't like him or dislike him, or know really why he caught my attention.

It is a late spring night and the windows of the bus are completely clear. He's looking at the marquee of the Slavija Theatre. It's a dirty marquee. Not because of the late-night porno film announced there. I mean the marquee itself is dirty. Even with no movies announced on it, even when it's blank, it's dirty. A dirty blank in the middle of downtown Belgrade. Why not? Why would anyone bother to wash a marquee? The letters are so big you couldn't miss them. You can read them clearly enough, even through the wet windows of a bus, even ten years ago when they were still in Cyrillic, you could read them, those ancient lovely characters that looked engraved, read them through the falling snow, through rain too. If anything, it's a little harder to see them in direct sunlight. But if the sun's out, if you're going to a matinee, you're usually going there to get away from something, from someone. And the darkness that swallows you there, that keeps you out of the exposure of light, that allows you to think things over carefully for a couple of hours, that's a dark that can save you: who cares what's playing?

At the moment I don't dislike this guy, but I don't like him either.

At the moment he's just sitting there, thinking about his girlfriend. He's wondering what she's doing at the moment. He thinks maybe she's doing the dishes even though she doesn't, in fact, wash them all that often. I mean she's not a fanatic about the dishes. So then he thinks how improbable it is that she's washing the dishes, although it is, in fact, not unlikely that she is. He has no reason to think otherwise. But in the next rush of his thought, he sees her screwing someone else on the kitchen table, a guy with dark hair, skinny and attractive in this very angular way. But then, no, looking out the window of the bus, he sees she's just throwing a stick for the dog to fetch. The dog goes crazy over this. He loves to fetch the stick, loves the stick falling, repeating itself, but landing in a slightly different place each time so that there's just enough variation to make it interesting but never so baffling that he loses the scent and has to bring back another stick, the wrong stick, one without her smell on it. The stick landing in snow. In dry grass. At twilight with the sound of crickets in a ravine. Gazing out at the marquee, he realizes that he has no reason to be suspicious of her. No reason at all. But he has to do no more than think this phrase to himself, this "no reason at all," and this time it's the blond mechanic who lives in her neighborhood, long hair, big shoulders. She's on top of him and going crazy. Her knees are getting a little bruised from the carpet but she doesn't feel it.

This is how the guy on the bus torments himself. Unfortunately a little arousal is mixed into the torment. But there is, after all, no reason to suspect her of anything. She's probably really doing the dishes at the moment. Or else they're just lying in the sink, the dog racing after the stick and the stick falling among the gravestones where they're walking. I can see them now: she has light brown hair and green eyes. The gray sweater looks good on her for some reason. The dog is black and white, collie mixed with whatever else was available. The gravestones are gray and pompous or else gray and modest. Above them the sky is cloudless.

No reason. No reason at all. Except she's there, he's here, waiting on the bus. Now he sees her slipping out of her dress, and this time it's me who's with her, or it's Rajko. Or maybe Dragan.

Who cares what's playing?

It's snowing. Well, it was snowing before it turned to rain. I mean, before the rain stopped and it became one of these unbearably clear, lissome, late-spring nights. But can a night be lissome? Isn't it the girl walking through graves who is lissome?

Okay, the night is comely, then.

The driver climbs onto the bus, looks around for a second, sees that no one is on it, or only this one guy, motionless at the window, a guy, the driver thinks, who is just one guy, and who is therefore equal to no one, a guy who somehow stands for no one, and now the doors close with their grand, worldly sighs. So tired, so indifferent to every guest, are the doors of buses. And the buses? They are the momentary prisons in which all the inmates daydream after their little gulags of work, or, for others, home is the gulag. At his window, he hasn't budged an inch. He's still looking really hard at the marquee of the Slavija as the bus hits second gear and begins to swing down Terazija, lurching slightly as it always does in that moment.

2

Now it's gone, he's gone, and Belgrade is beautiful in this moment when he's vanished from it, taking with him his face, that little windowpane through which you can see hell for a moment. Hell's always the same. It has that sallow face for a gate. Behind it, his girlfriend does not exist, for no one exists there, not really, not in fact, not there, where pleasure and pain are by now so mixed together, so quick to transform each other that you couldn't tell one sensation from the other. Hell, where he fetches the stick again, where it flies through the air, where he wags and trembles and cringes, where he sits like a sink full of shattered dishes, where she is stripped to the waist, where he raises the whip but no one's there when he turns to her. So he has to put the whip down and wait until he can get her image back again, bare shoulders, her arms above her head and hands tied, and . . .

Once, I admit it, he was an acquaintance of mine. In fact, I was getting to know him pretty well, and so were Rajko and Dragan.

I don't know what happened, exactly. But one night I realized that I was complimenting him even when there was no reason to do so. So were Rajko and Dragan. His silence made us all a little uneasy. And in order to speak at all, he seemed to need this approval from us; it was like a little fee he required. And then he would begin, he would really open up, and if speech could give off an odor, there was something in his talk, in its sadness, in its stale plumes. Like those cattails, unattended, in the lobbies of apartment buildings. But behind this sadness, after he spoke, there was only another sadness. You could see right through one layer of it, the layer he was finishing his tale of, to another but identical layer. And these layers, these rinds, these circles . . . they kept widening as he spoke. They pulled you into them somehow like those rides at fairs that depend on centrifugal force to hold you. What were they called? Tilt-A-Whirls? And although each layer would at first appear opaque, it would soon grow translucent in the motion of speech, then semitransparent. Blank marquee to dirty window. I could see right through it to his girlfriend washing dishes or playing with the dog, the stick falling, and the snow falling. Soon she would begin to undress. At first it was exciting. No one we knew had ever spoken this way. But after I had seen her there on the carpet, on the kitchen table, in the parked cars of strangers, on trains with everyone watching, something inside me began to turn away. I kept feeling that with each repetition—her breasts bare as she pulled the sweater over her head, the way her hips curved slightly as her panties were removed, each shallow, quickened, aroused breath, each moan: her mouth open and her eyelids half closed as she came, and came again, even with a complete stranger—the more I watched through his words the more I felt that a privacy was being stripped away, not from her, for it had nothing to do with her (if she even existed), or with screwing (which began to seem far more admirable than listening to it from afar), no, a privacy was being stripped from everything, even from me as I listened to him. It was as if someone had stripped Rajko's sister to the waist and begun to flay her in a boathouse, five yards from the public beach, and as if we were watching it and doing nothing about it. Or as if the Body Itself had a privacy that was somehow involved and violated. I remembered those photographs of dead villagers, spliced into a peculiar animation in a film, their bodies stripped of clothing and thrown into ditches to float forever, the way the pale nakedness shone a little, seemed to look back with the blank stare of flesh. You couldn't say what it meant, a stare like that, a stare that had no eyes.

It was like that and it was not like that.

If you suspect by now that this guy on the bus was, or had been, a variation of me, and of Dragan and Rajko too, that he merely displayed in public our fantasies and our anxieties, how they mixed together in our mutual, prolonged adolescence, at least the three of us kept our mouths shut about it.

In my case, I turned away from the teller and his story in the same motion. I walked out without saying a word, and never saw him again, until now.

But why? In the middle of Belgrade, which is to say, in the middle of the most perfect constellation of cynicism and disbelief, where had this sudden impulse come from? Was it some simple, innate decency from childhood that rose bobbing to the surface like a shoe on a boiling river at spring tide? Was it embarrassment? Was it some simple, adult fatigue?

But if it was simply good and decent to walk out, in that moment it felt embarrassing. For doesn't the sudden surfacing of the good, the decent, deprive one of that small portion of evil that is one's right at birth?

And isn't it more interesting to be Bad than to be Good? Dragan, Rajko, me: we were all nineteen or twenty then.

All right: once, it seemed more interesting to be Bad.

And what is left if in fact these notions of Good and Evil are by now as exhausted as his limited, finite, and gradually impotent fantasies? For if he persisted in them, wouldn't they lose their power to excite him, to arouse him? And through their repeated employment, wouldn't that young woman gradually become someone else, a girlfriend of no one at all? Wouldn't there be nothing left for the guy on the bus but cruelty? And finally, wouldn't it be only a whip in his hand and her naked body, her hands bound in leather and stretched above her head, with perhaps a sprig of baby's breath around them too or around her neck or hips, as an added insult; wouldn't this be all that could make it seem real to him?

Still, it did not surprise us to learn that he was arrested in a demonstration a year later, and immediately released. After all, this isn't Prague. Nor did it surprise us later to hear that he had married, that he had become the father of two sons, that he was living, and not unhappily, in Novi Beograd.

Why is it so difficult to be surprised in Belgrade?

Or to be Bad in Belgrade?

Or Good in Belgrade?

Are there other cities now where it has become just as hard to be surprised? Well, I'd have to say I doubt that.

In fact, I doubt that very much.

I doubt even my doubting of it, and my doubt remains, as I remain, in what remains of Belgrade.

3

Spliced into films that whirred and whispered in warm May classrooms, those photographs of dead villagers, naked in ditches . . . they were designed to teach us history. We were all ten or eleven and they were showing us a world that was over. History itself, they said then, was what we had been liberated from forever. What was hard to understand then seems simple now: They owned the Present. If you owned the Present, you owned also the Past. And you could delete or add to the Past as you wished. If something seemed wrong, out of place, you could erase it as you would a line in a sketch.

In Belgrade not much was erased. It was Stalin who loved to erase things, and so his absence now, that space, that air above his pedestal in Bucharest, is an erasure more glaring, more present than his bronze's turning to a dark effigy. That empty space reminds everyone of Stalin. My teachers, on the other hand, were too busy trying to recognize (and their squinting seemed less and less morbid as time went on), in those photographs of floating, naked bodies, a distant cousin, a landlord. And although none of the images was clear enough, the horror of the war had passed gradually, because it had to pass; once again, they were looking at old photographs in some family album they'd found in the attic. "And here, this looks like my uncle Milan," our teacher would say, pointing with a cue, "fastest runner in all of Kosovo." She had his fastest times, in Prĩstina and Skoplje, memorized; it seems they ran the 1,500 meters pretty slowly once.

Instead of teaching us anything, such films had, as a result, our turning away from the Past and also from the Present. For in the Present, Uncle Milan, lucky fellow, was allowed to run his fastest times, over and over. We waited patiently to see what might be left of the future—even now I refuse to capitalize the first letter of the word. For in the future the bell would ring, and we could go. But the future was taking its own sweet time. We'd put our cheeks on the wood of our desks and dream of recess, we would close our eyes and smell the chronic odor of watery Spanish rice from the school cafeteria. We'd look sideways, studying the folds in dresses, the ripples in shirts and pants. That ocean of clothing over which our eyes, at least, could sail for a while, sail and come to rest. To rest on . . . what? On a minute Milky Way, a tiny galaxy, a swarm of shockingly frank black freckles scattered over Ivana Kommadinja's pure white bony shoulders! In that second just after I knew I could not see her breasts beneath the blue cotton of her blouse, and sensed that her collarbone, so sharp and meager, could never arouse me, I saw the freckles clearly. How could I have missed them before? And why did they become so interesting in that moment? Why were the freckles so determinedly black, so irrevocably black, as if they had taken a vow to be so? And why was her skin so white? Black seeds on a field of snow? But that was too easy. No, they refused to look like anything else, and to compare them with anything else falsified them. That was the power of those freckles, their refusal to refer to anything else except themselves, to what they were in their singularity. Not only were they unlike everything else, they were adamant about being unlike everything else. They were adamant without lifting a finger. But how, I wondered, could shoulders be so different from other shoulders? Or freckles from other freckles? Ivanas from other Ivanas? How could people be so different from each other? Was there some purpose to it? Was there some joy to be taken in this, or in that insistence, never quite convincing, that all differences were, somehow, one? But wasn't it precisely the nature of differences to go on being indifferent to attempts to explain them, to make them the same? And after the idea of their unity had been spread thinly over the land in a light snow, wouldn't they just go on being different anyway? What was the point of all these seemingly endless variations if it was not to suggest, like a vast secret pouring itself into my ear, that there was no point in them, no point at all? That they just . . . were.

But I have spent all this time trying to explain a few freckles, and I still haven't explained them.

4

Let me put it another way: To become an adult, forget the variations. Narrow your focus.

Isn't this why the pornographic film gets to the point immediately, why all distracting freckles have been airbrushed from the film, or why makeup (including pussy blush, which they must have learned from watching baboons in the zoo) has been applied everywhere on the bodies. ADULTS ONLY: NO BLACK FRECKLES.

No eye to sail inward. No infinities.

And the marquees blank in wartime. On an Easter Sunday, the bough of the Luftwaffe threw its shade over Belgrade, as over some troubled sleeper in a park, and in three hours 25,000 died. Or put it another way: In three hours approximately . . . what? . . . seventeen and a half million inscrutable, purposeless variations were erased or distorted beyond recognition. In any event they were forgotten completely, forgotten abruptly even by those who possessed them, who were possessed by them: candor of freckles, birthmarks, silent moles. In Hitler's hatred of variations, of their pointlessness, Jews, Gypsies, Slavs—all were superfluous. But he couldn't forget, and so he made forgetting into a system.

A bomb is the literalization of forgetting. But in literalizing this, it has corrupted forever the act of remembering. Remembering now has a purpose: it is to oppose forgetting. Remembering has had to grow up and to behave like an adult. It has become, forgive me, *partisan*. And this is why, I think, I liked my teacher with her uncle Milan; her memory had retained its childhood. It was incorrigible. She had our childhoods too, however, and never gave them back.

Yes, so what I want to know is: Why were her freckles so black? No, why were they so frank about being black on such snow-white, bony shoulders? No, not *snow*-white, but something of porcelain and something of cloud, peppered with freckles.

What monument with a fountain was ever built in their honor?

Why do I remember them?

Why does nothing give me so much pleasure now as passing a dirty, blank marquee in the middle of downtown Belgrade?

Were audacity and restraint made one and at ease there, her shoulders rising and falling slightly as she breathed the chalky dust of the classroom, her head on the desk and her eyelids closed? The delicate swarm of freckles expanded a little each time she inhaled in that moment. An expanding, a widening moment. They became so . . . interesting as I watched them there. So purposeless. So unenlisted in any cause.

5

Confronted with a freckle, the world says, forget it. And it is tempting to consign it to some category, tempting to shrug and call it Beauty; to consign it, that is, to oblivion. For you may call it Beauty only if you feel a need to falsify it, and then you may write it on a blackboard. In short, only if you wish to forget it do you call it Beauty and therefore make a contribution to the planned forgetfulness of the world. For which you will be rewarded, in Los Angeles or Sofia, with the same bowl of watery Spanish rice.

And what is amazing is that you actually *do* this.

I too have done this, or something like it, thinking that I had to do it.

For see the bum in his quilts of cardboard in the shadow of that doorway? How motionless he is, and yet how near he comes if you watch him long enough from the unwashed, second-floor bay window of the high school. How close and motionless he always is to you, how he comes near without lifting a finger.

Eat your rice.

I'll eat mine if you eat yours.

6

As for me, at the moment I was just on my way to see a movie at the Slavija, something with Richard Gere and Kim Basinger perspiring a lot together, and lots of Uzis, even small artillery. It is called *Bez Milosti*, and in one scene Kim is moving in a slow, lissome trance to rock music on the dance floor of a crowded bar; she's perspiring so much that the fabric of her blouse is taut over her dark nipples, the dampness making them visible. She may as well be gift-wrapped; no freckles.

And then, well, I decided not to see it.

Or it seemed, somehow, that I had already seen it.

And that's when I saw him, sitting there on the bus, staring out at the rain coming down in sheets. He seemed to look right through me, and after a while, it seemed impossible that he did not see me on such a clear night, the moonlight filling the whole square until it brimmed with the visible. It's just like him to be so absorbed in his own thoughts, staring out the window without once noticing the wet snow sticking for a moment to the letters on the marquee of the Slavija.

And after the bus pulled out it seemed like a good idea, a good night, just to walk. It's funny about walking, walking without knowing why. I'm not ready to say I like it; that's too simple. But I don't dislike it either. Therefore I catch the rhythm of my stride, my strolling, the slight heel-and-toe scratch of my shoes like brushstrokes on a snare drum; I hear it through these two gatekeepers of mine: my yes, my no; my like, my dislike. And through them, I come and go at my leisure. I can walk for hours.

If I walk far enough, do I only imagine myself diminishing, getting smaller, and at the same time becoming wider, enlarging, finally populating entire streets until I am the crowd, their whole neighborhood, until I embody their wariness and slight malice, and their endless civility?

Well, of course I only imagine it. Who do you think I am, Yevtushenko? Besides, in the dusty park below the Zeleni Venac market, at the end of Lomina Street, there is an idiot howling because the drunk has taken away his toy again and is laughing at him. The idiot is tied to a green bench with a dog leash and is bare to the waist, having lost his shirt somewhere. But he never once realizes it is the drunk who takes his toy. Yet these two often stroll along together in the crowd, moving slower than the secretary of the Cuban Embassy in her leopard-print dress, slower than the girl who never looks up or to either side, who carries a book of Chopin's *Nocturnes*, its cover the shade of apricots, beneath the yellowing trees. To *be* them?

But the crowd, the crowd in abstract, that is irresistible, a falsification composed of so many complete strangers. If this crowd has a single mind, as it seems to have, what is admirable is the way that mind never cherishes any one thing, or loves it, to the exclusion of every other thing. The way it is a crowd without knowing that it is a crowd, that's what I like about it. Of course there are crowds everywhere now, and when you see them, brimming over curbstones like a perpetually rushing floodtide, an unsubsiding swirl of brown froth on a river's back, you think that maybe something is about to happen, or think that maybe something has just happened. And maybe it will; maybe it already has.

When did "maybe" begin to mean "no?"

In Warsaw it must be different. There, the crowds go out, already stricken with belief, and hungering for greater belief. Crowds of steelworkers, crowds that close down whole shipyards.

In Belgrade, every riot takes the form of a riot, and every riot reminds one of another riot, earlier, a riot in adolescence. A curious nostalgia sets in as one watches it with a crowd of other onlookers. Why is it so hard to be surprised in Belgrade? Why can one be arrested and thrown into jail for no reason and feel no surprise? And no surprise a day later, when one is released?

7

The crowds I have in mind are the ones that always appear to be shopping for something. But they're only window-shopping, not buying. A crowd staring into shop windows long into the evening does so to confirm, not the polonaise and the slim cavalry of belief, but only its own Disbelief. "*Je bi ga*," they mutter, and "No, thanks" replies their even gaze to the windows lit softly with goods on sale there. Even to the lowliest, most humble idea, the crowd says no: no to the idea that finds its fulfillment in a pair of perfectly copied Gucci loafers made by Srbijateks and on sale for 30,000 dinars, an idea in leather, in what passes for leather now. But something's wrong with the idea. It's not a Gucci loafer after all. In fact, the moment you slip it on, it looks ridiculous, and you look ridiculous. You look as if you were about to make a political statement about something obscure, some minor point, and have now forgotten what it was. And in a moment or so, you feel as if those shoes had somehow betrayed all that was left of you.

You slip them off, your socks damp with sweat, and the smell rises from them.

Let it rise, you tell yourself, let it rise to the nostrils of God. You aren't buying.

No; the mind of the crowd just window-shops, idly, and its daydreams, like those of any capitalist, flicker with images from travel posters of the topless beaches of Dubrovnik, or the long nude beach at Ulcinj that ends with a storm fence meaning Albania, the tourists sunbathing forever in such places, reading novels in German, English, French. Novels! the mind cries out, more novels!

But what can the mind be talking about? The streets here are lined with bookstores. There are thousands of novels, in every language. Too many to read. Far too many.

8

And even though you pause in silence, with everyone else, on the anniversary of the death of the Great Unifying Unmentioned One, pause for the full, required five minutes, irony slips into that vigil like a practiced thief. Irony begins to rise from it like dust from a wrecker's ball; it begins to ascend fitfully into your thought like termites flying (and I think they must fly) lazily from some rotting foundation of damp wood, from the memory of some guy in your adolescence who had two tattoos: one that said "Lenin," on his right wrist, and the other, on his left, stitched over again by a second needle and all but indecipherable, one that said "Stalin." In the last moment of that silence you realize that the economic system in which you live is founded on such images, damp wood, obliterated tattoos, and that the country is a sleigh gone out of control with a dark wood fast approaching; that you speak inside a vast, unfinished elegy that comprehends you from the moment of birth so no one hears you. How can it go on? Nevertheless, it does, and you do, and you do this with millions of others, and although it baffles you that it all continues after belief has been withdrawn from it like cash from a savings account, you don't remember squandering it at all.

When the mind of the crowd (a purely imaginary mind) cannot believe in anything, it begins to attach a great importance to whatever isn't belief. It begins to construct, slowly at first, then more rapidly and completely, a faith in Disbelief, and in the emblems of that Disbelief; it rejoices in the faded pallor of political billboards, in the young dog trying to hump the leg on Marx's statue as the face of Marx remains imperturbably the same, serene as a librarian's.

The mind of the crowd loves this dog.

And the other mind? The freckles on her white shoulders? I can remember them, yes, but *only* remember them. In a few, rare instances, I can also feel, or else strongly remember feeling, that kind of wonder or bewilderment that occurred when I first saw them in that classroom, but such intervals of recall have grown shorter, shorter—it lasted less than a second the last time it happened, about two years ago. And now I seem able only to remember it, or remember a feeling that has no name although wonder is certainly mixed into it, the kind of wonder that makes me suspect that, if I could feel the same as I did in that classroom each time I recalled those freckles, I would not be here. I would be dead, dead from the exhaustion of it, dead from some thoughtless gesture in which I hailed oblivion instead of a cab, or if I lived, eventually I would end up howling like the idiot in the park, but not forever. Even howling ends.

Freckles, in fact, are the reason I gave up painting, and night school at the university. For gradually I watched my paint change things regardless of my desires, black freckles on a white canvas becoming dots, larger or smaller ones, then minimalist dots, until the paint took over completely and the girl was obliterated by it. Adult paint. A way of forgetting.

I prefer to think I would have stopped breathing.

It's that little bit of wonder mixed up in it all, wonder that is neither good nor bad, and that is its problem, that it is neither, that it is a wonder or bewilderment that suggests that anything less than what it is in that moment is less than what is real, less than what the world requires of you if you should wish to see it, just once, as it is. The frank, triumphant, shockingly useless fact of it.

Sometimes you get a glimpse of it in passing. Sometimes an eyeful.

Useless fact that it was, it felt like being visited.

And what comes in its wake, in the wake of those freckles, is just this. This Disbelief. No more.

9

So: The mind of the crowd? Or a swarm of black freckles?

The first is easier, for the mind of the crowd falsifies itself ceaselessly in even a few words; add a few more, sketch in a street, a marquee, the tracks of a bus in swirling snow, and it takes on a life more or less its own: "In the wilderness of her newfound shame, she paused at the door," and so on.

But the other, the swarm of freckles, refuses finally to show itself at all in words, or is there within them, and there so matter-of-factly that it is concealed, camouflaged by the very thing meant to reveal it.

And so, among the things I must consign to oblivion, I add also this failure, this swarm of freckles; here, take them.

And my friend on the bus? But isn't it time to admit what is already clear enough, that he never existed, that along with his girlfriend, with Dragan and Rajko, he never existed? Still, I put him on the bus outside the Slavija for a reason: to get rid of him. Why would I need to get rid of someone who never existed? As a matter of fact, he took on a life without me, a life of his own. And it is just as well.

I suppose I should feel ashamed of him.

Why is it so hard to feel shame in Belgrade?

Disbelief is what I feel. Under the streetlamps, a young soldier is kissing his girl, slowly, languorously, openly beneath the sky. Disbelief is kindling to them; her lips are by now hot, dry, unwilling for it to end. Or would her lips be moist by now? I have forgotten.

My friend on the bus wanted to believe. But where could he worship? Between whose thighs is there an altar? And if there is, doesn't one lose faith when the whole village begins to take communion there? For fantasies attract villagers. In order to believe, he required her complete and purely imaginary betrayal, and his daydreams extracted from that world an ugly penance that the world never noticed. In this way he became untrue, untrue to this moment, this street, this Disbelief. To all that remains of freckles. And to this crowd, which has never quite become a congregation.

In its absence, you will hear only the drone of the Luftwaffe, Hitler's daydream, or the beginning of that absence in the sound of the militia clubbing Albanians in the streets of Priština.

In its absence, the scrape of a soldier's bootheel, his whistling, can echo a long way through the boulevards, and there is usually a declaration of martial law.

Which they are threatening, once again, to impose.

But they could not possibly impose it until sometime early next year, for in accordance with our constitution, the forms necessary require the signatures of eighty-seven government officials, and six of those needed to sign are dead, their offices vacant, the dust specks swirling in the sunlight there. Over the years, someone should have appointed replacements in their positions, but someone forgot to. And to amend the constitution, Parliament would have to meet twice, with a thirty-day interval between the meetings, and translators fluent in Slovenian would have to be appointed, as well as new representatives of the Albanian Moslem minority, and Parliament, anyway, is not in session now. But threatening to impose it, that is a different matter, and perfectly legal, and the absence of such a threat would seem a little curious, like those neglected offices, the dust specks swirling there forever, or like a sensation of cold in the groin suddenly which you cannot explain.

I tilt my head back for a second to feel the rain on my face, the filthy rain which cleanses me.

Maybe I got rid of something after all.

Come on, let's go to the movies.

WILLIAM MAXWELL

A Fable Begotten of an Echo of a Line of Verse by W. B. Yeats

Once upon a time there was an old man who made his living telling stories. In the middle of the afternoon he took his position on the steps of the monument to Unaging Intellect, in a somewhat out-of-the-way corner of the marketplace. And people who were not in a hurry would stop, and sometimes those who were in a hurry would hear a phrase that caught their attention, such as "in the moonlight" or "covered with blood," and would pause for a second and then be spellbound. It was generally agreed that he was better than some storytellers and not as good as others. And his wife would wait for him to come home, because what they had for supper depended on what he brought home in his pockets. She couldn't ask him to stop at this or that stall in the market-place and buy what they needed. Being old, he was forgetful and would bring part of what she needed but not all. Standing on the marble steps of the monument, with his voice pitched so that it would carry over the shoulders of those who made a ring around him, he never forgot and he never repeated himself. That is to say, if it was a familiar story he was telling, he added new embellishments, new twists, and again it would be something he had never told before and didn't himself know until the words came out of his mouth, so that he was as astonished as his listeners, but didn't show it. He wanted them to believe what was in fact true, that the stories didn't come from him but through him, were not memorized, and would never be told quite that same way again.

Forgetfulness is the shadow that lies across the path of all old men. The statesman delivering an oration from the steps of the Temple of Zeus at times hesitated because he didn't know what came next. And the storyteller's wife worried for fear that this would happen to him, and of course one day it did. Kneeling in front of the executioner's block, the innocent prince traveling incognito waited for the charioteer who was going to force his way through the crowd and save him from the axe, and nothing happened. That is to say, there was a pause that grew longer and longer until the listeners shifted their feet, and the storyteller took up in a different part of the story, and then suddenly swooped back to the prince and saved him, but leaving the audience with the impression that something was not right, that there was something they had not been told. There was. But could the storyteller simply have said at that point, "I don't remember what happened next"? They would have lost all faith in him and in his stories.

"I think you were just tired," his wife said when he told her what had happened. "It could happen to anybody." But in her heart she foresaw that it was going to happen again, and more seriously. "Once upon a time there was a younger son of the Prince of Syracuse who had one blue eye and one brown, and a charm of manner that made anyone who talked to him believe that—" This had to be left hanging because he who had always known everything about his characters, as God knows everything about human beings, didn't know, and tried to pretend that he meant this to be left hanging; but of course the listeners knew, and word got around that his memory was failing, his stories were not as good as they used to be, and fewer and fewer people stopped to listen to him, and those who did had to be content with fragments of stories, more interesting sometimes than the perfectly told stories had been, but unsatisfactory and incomplete.

Knowing that this was going to happen, his wife had been putting a little by to tide them over in their old age, and so they didn't starve. But he stayed home from the marketplace because it was an embarrassment to him that he couldn't tell stories anymore, and sometimes he sat in the sun and sometimes he followed his wife around and while she was digging a spider out of a corner of the ceiling he would say, "Once upon a time there was a girl of such beauty and delicacy of feeling that she could not possibly have been the child of the hardworking but obtuse couple who raised her from infancy, and although they seemed not to realize this, she had an air of expectancy that—" Here he stopped, unable to go on, and although his wife would have given anything to know what it was that the girl was expecting and if it really came about and how, she said nothing, because, poor man, his head was like a pot with a hole in it. Sometimes when her work was done she sat in the sun with him, in silence. They had been together for a very long time and did not always need to be saying something. But she would have liked it if he knew how much she did for him; instead, he seemed to take it for granted that when he was hungry there would be food, and when he was tired there was the bed, with clean sheets on it smelling of sunshine.

She realized that it was not in his nature to be aware of small, ordinary things of this kind—that his mind trafficked in wonders and surprises. And it was something that she lived with the beginnings of so many wonderful stories she could think about as she went about her work: The story of the flute player's daughter, who picked up his instrument one day and played—although she had never to his knowledge touched it before or been given any instruction in the fingering or in breathing across the hole—better than any flute player he had ever heard. When he asked her how she was able to do this, she said, "I don't know. It just came to me that I knew how to do it." And when he asked her to do it again she couldn't, and this troubled her so much that she became melancholy and—and what? The storyteller didn't know. The thread of invention had given way at that point. . . . The story of the African warrior who was turned into a black cat, who at night wanted to be outdoors so that he could search for the huge moon of Africa that he remembered—the only thing that he remembered—from before his transformation . . . The story of the old woman with a secret supply of hummingbirds . . . The story of the brother and sister who in some previous incarnation had been man and wife . . . With all these unfinished stories to occupy her mind, the storyteller's wife did not lack for things to think about. She wished that he could finish them for his sake, but she had come to prefer the fragments to the finished stories he used to tell. And in time she came to see that they couldn't be finished because they were so interesting there was no way for the story to go on.

The old man felt differently. I would like just once before I die, he said to himself often, to finish a story and see the look of thoughtfulness that a perfect story arouses in the faces of the people listening to me in the marketplace. Now, when he took his stand on the steps of the monument, the passersby hesitated, remembered that there was no use listening to him, because he always lost the thread of the story, and so passed on, saying to one another, "What wonderful tales he used to tell!"

Some vandal had chipped off the nose and two fingers of the statue to Unaging Intellect, and it had never been much admired, but he had told so many stories with the recognition that the monument was at his back that he had come to have an affection for it. What he had no way of knowing was that the monument had come to have an affection for him. What would otherwise have been an eternity of marble monumentality was made bearable by his once-upon-a-times. But why all these princes and talking parrots, these three wishes that land the guesser into a royal palace which is more marble, and uninhabitable, these babies switched in their cradle for no reason but to make a strange story, these wonders that are so much less wonderful than the things that are close to home? And because it is part of the storyteller's instinct to know what his audience wants to hear, one day when there was nobody around, the storyteller began: "Once upon a time there was an old man whose wits were slipping, and although he knew he didn't deserve it, he was well taken care of by his wife, who loved him. They had children but the children grew up and went away." Here the statue took on a look of attentiveness which the old man did not see because his back was turned to it. "The old couple had only each other, but that was a lot because with every year of their lives they had a greater sense of the unbreakable connection that held them. It was a miracle and they knew it, but they were afraid to talk about it lest something happen. Lest they be separated . . ." On and on the story went, with the monument rooted to its place by interest in what the old man was saying. Monuments do not have anyone who loves them. They exist in solitude and are always lonely, especially at night when there is no one around. The thought that human beings could undress and get into bed and sleep all night side by side was more beautiful than the monument could bear. The fact that she cooked for him because he was hungry and that his hunger was for what she cooked because it was cooked with love. That he was under the impression that, old and scatterbrained as he was, he was the one who took care of her and that she would not be safe without him . . . When the storyteller said, "From living together they had come to look alike," the monument said, "Oh, it's too much!" For there is no loneliness like the loneliness of Unaging Intellect.

STEVEN MILLHAUSER

Alice, Falling

Alice, falling, sees on the top shelf of the open cupboard a jar bearing the label RASPBERRY JAM, a yew-wood tea caddy with brass fastenings and a design of hand-painted plants and flowers on the lid, and a tin of lemon snaps: the dark-green top shows in the center an oval containing a colored head of Prince Albert. On the bottom shelf Alice sees a porcelain dessert plate with a gilt border and a center panel showing a young man in a tilted tricorne, red jacket, and white breeches, standing beside an oak tree; a bread knife with an ivory handle carved with a boy holding wheat in his arms; and a silver-plated cream jug with a garland of silver-plated leaves and berries encircling the base. So slowly is Alice falling that she has time to take in all the details, to note the pink thistles on the lid of the tea caddy and the yellow buttons on the red jacket of the man on the dessert plate, to observe the faint reflections of her face above and below the label on the jar of raspberry jam.

Alice does not know how long she has been falling, but when she looks up she has the sense of a great shaft of darkness stretching interminably upward. In the alien tunnel-world she tries to think of the bright upper world, where her sister sits on a bank, under a tree, reading a book without pictures or conversations, but as she falls deeper and deeper it becomes harder for her thoughts to reach so high, as if each thought were a heavy rope that has to be hurled upward in the act of falling. And gradually, as she falls, a change comes about: the mysterious shaft or vertical tunnel through which she is falling begins to seem familiar to her, with its cupboards, its shelves, its lamplit bumps and hollows, while the upper world grows shadowy and strange; and as she falls she has to remind herself that somewhere far above, suddenly the air is blinding blue, white-and-yellow daisies grow in a green field, on a sloping bank her sister sits reading in sun-checked shade.

The dark walls of the shaft are faintly illuminated by globed oil lamps attached at irregular intervals to wrought-iron wall brackets: each bracket has the shape of an elongated S-curve turned sideways, and on the apex of the outermost curve sits a brass mermaid holding up a cylindrical chased-brass base with a brass adjustment knob; on the cylinder rests the globe of glass, topped by a slender glass stem. The light from the lamps permits Alice to observe the objects that abound on the walls. In addition to the cupboards with their shelves, she passes maps and pictures hung on pegs, including a black-and-white engraving of Scotland showing all the counties outlined in red, and a painting of a lion leaping onto the back of a horse: the horse's head is twisted backward, its teeth are bared, the flared nostrils are wide as teacups, and dark-red streaks of blood course along the shiny brown sides; a pair of oak bookshelves holding *Twenty-five Village Sermons*, *Bewick's Birds*, Macaulay's *History*, *The Fair Maid of Perth*, *The Life and Works of Edwin Landseer*, Pope's *Homer*, *Coke upon Lyttleton*, Rogers's *Pleasures of Memory*, *Sir Charles Grandison*, *Robberies and Murders of the Most Notorious Pirates*, Bayle's *Dictionary*, *Ivo and Verena*, *The Pilgrim's Progress*, and *Gems of European Art;* a barometer in a case of walnut wood shaped like an anchor: the flukes of the anchor support the glass disk, in which is pictured Neptune riding a sea-horse within a circle of words (RAIN, FAIR, CHANGE, STORMY); a niche containing a marble Venus and Cupid: the winged, curly-haired boy reaches for his bow, which his seated mother holds away: her robe has slipped to her lap, and one breast is visible above his reaching arm; and a Gothic arch-topped set of small, glass-fronted shelves on which stand a barefoot porcelain girl holding a basket of flowers over one forearm, a pincushion set in a brass wheelbarrow and stuck with hat pins ornamented with china flowers, a playing-card box with a floral border and a center panel showing a castellated mansion in Tunbridge Wells, two small oval silhouettes framed in ivory and showing, respectively, a snub-nosed girl in a bonnet and a snub-nosed boy in a flat-brimmed hat, a red glass rose with green glass thorns, and a majolica snake devouring a toad.

Down, down, down. Would the fall *never* end? Alice has been falling for so long that she is beginning to grow uncertain. If the fall does end, then the vertical tunnel will be a connecting link, a transition, a bridge between the upper world and the unknown lower world; it will be unimportant in itself and, at the instant of ending, it will disappear. But if the fall never ends, then everything is changed: the fall itself becomes the adventure, and the tunnel through which she is falling becomes the unknown world, with its magic and mystery. Alice, looking about uncertainly, tries to decide whether she is on her way to an adventure or whether she is in the middle of one.

The shaft, well, or vertical tunnel down which Alice is falling has irregular walls of hard earth mixed with outcroppings of rock: granite, feldspar, and basalt. The hard earth is mostly dry, with occasional moist patches; here and there a trickle of dark water zigzags down, passing the edge of a map, slipping behind a cupboard's open door. Some of the cupboards have small dishes on top, placed back against the wall, as if to catch dripping water. The tunnel is a comfortable width for falling: Alice falls without fear of striking the walls, yet at any moment she can reach out and remove a jar from a shelf or adjust a tilted picture. Alice wonders how the shelves are reached from below. At first she imagines a very long ladder, but this presents difficulties even if the tunnel has a bottom, for how would such a long ladder get into such a narrow space? Next she imagines small openings in the walls, through which servants can enter the tunnel, but she sees no openings, no doors. Perhaps the answer is small birds who fly up from below, or from nests hidden in the darkness. It occurs to Alice that there may be another answer: the jars, the pictures, the maps, the lamps have always been here, unchanging. But how can that be? Alice, as she falls, feels a little frown creasing her forehead.

Falling, always falling, Alice closes her eyes and sees her sister on the bank under a tree, reading a book without pictures or conversations. The bank slopes down to a pool with reeds; the sun-shot shadow of the tree, a thick beech (*Fagus sylvatica*), trembles on the water. Circles of sun and shade move on her sister's hands. Deep in her book, Alice's sister scarcely hears the stir of leaves overhead, the distant cries of the shepherd boy, the lowing of the cattle, the rustle of Alice's dress. Gradually she becomes aware of a disturbance beside her; it is Alice, restless as always. It's difficult, thinks Alice's sister, to have a younger sister who won't ever sit still and let you read. Although Alice's sister is determined to keep her eyes fixed on the page, she feels that her attention has already been tugged away, it's as if she were being pulled out of a dream, the words are nothing but words now; irritably she places her finger at the end of a line. Raising her eyes, she is surprised to see Alice chasing a white rabbit across a field. With an impatient sigh, Alice's sister reaches into her pinafore pocket and removes a scrap of blue ribbon, which she places in her book before closing it. She rests the book carefully against a bare root. She then rises to her feet, brushing off her dress with sharp little flicks of the back of her fingers, and begins to walk quickly after Alice through the field of daisies. When she comes to the rabbit hole under the hedge she stops and crouches down, pushing away the hedge branches, careful not to kneel on the ground. "Alice!" she calls, looking down into the dark hole. "Alice, are you there?" There is no answer. The hole is just large enough for her to enter, but it is very dirty, and very dark. For a while she looks down thoughtfully into the dark. Then she raises her head; in the distance she hears the tinkle of sheep bells; the sun burns down on the tall grass; reeds stir at the edge of the pool; under the leaning beech, sun and shade tremble on the grass, on the closed book, on a purple wildflower beside the bare root.

Down, down, down: she can't really see too much, down there in the dark. She can see the hem of her dress outspread by the wind of her slow falling, and the dark earthen wall of the vertical tunnel, broken here and there by eruptions of rock. The upper view is better, but it makes Alice dizzy: raising her eyes, and bending back her head, she can see the ocher bottom of a cupboard, and higher up, on the other side of the wall, the shadowy underside of a bookshelf supported by two wooden brackets shaped like elephant heads with uplifted trunks. Still higher up she sees a dim glow passing into upper darkness; the glow is from a lamp concealed by the cupboard. When Alice looks down again, she sees the top of a new object rising into view: a strip of dark wood carved with wooden leaves and wooden bunches of grapes. Beneath the strip of carved wood a glimmering mirror appears. Alice sees, at the top of the glass, her shiny black shoes with their narrow black ankle-straps and the bottoms of her blue stockings. The large mirror in its heavy frame of carved mahogany is shaped like a shield. In the dim glass Alice sees, as she falls, the outspread hem of her yellow dress, and then the bottom of her white pinafore with its blue stripe along the bottom border, and then the two pinafore pockets, each with a blue stripe along the top: one pocket holds a white handkerchief. And as if she were standing at the side of a stairway, watching someone appear at the high landing and start to descend, Alice sees in slow succession the white cotton belt, the puffed-shoulder sleeves, the outspread yellow-brown hair, the dark, worried eyes under the dark eyebrows, the tense forehead; and already the shiny black shoes and blue stockings and pinafore pockets have disappeared, the bottom of the mirror is rising higher and higher, all at once the top of her head with its thick combed-back hair vanishes from view: and looking up she sees the bottom of the mirror rising higher and higher, floating away, slowly dissolving in the dark.

If only, Alice thinks to herself suddenly, I could let myself go! If only I could fall! For she feels, in her falling, a tension, as if she were holding herself taut against her fall. But a true fall, Alice thinks to herself, is nothing like this: it's a swoon, a release, it's like tugging at a drawer that suddenly comes unstuck. Alice, as she falls, is tense with alertness: she holds herself in readiness, although for what she isn't certain, she looks around eagerly, she takes everything in with sharpened awareness. Her fall is the opposite of a sleep: she has never been so awake. But if I were truly falling, Alice thinks to herself, then I would let myself go, myself go, myself go.

It occurs to Alice that she is of course dreaming. She has simply fallen asleep on the bank with her head in her sister's lap. Soon she will wake up, and the tunnel, the cupboards, the maps, the mirror, the jar of raspberry jam, all will vanish away, leaving only the bank of sun-patched shade, the sunny field, the distant farmyard. But suppose, Alice thinks to herself, the bank too is a dream? If the bank is a dream, then she will wake up somewhere else. But where will that be? Alice tries to think where she might wake up, if she doesn't wake up with her head in her sister's lap. Maybe she will wake up in Lapland, or China. But if she wakes up in Lapland, or China, will she still be Alice, or will she be someone else? Alice tries to imagine another Alice, dreaming: the other Alice has short brown hair, likes rice pudding, and has a cat called Arabella. But mightn't this Alice also be a dream? Who, then, is the dreamer? Alice imagines a series of Alices, each dreaming the other, stretching back and back, farther and farther, back and back and back and back and back.

On the afternoon of July 4, 1862, a boating party of five was to be seen on the Isis, heading upriver from Oxford to Godstow. It was a cloudless blue day. Heat-haze shimmered over the meadows on both sides of the water. Charles Lutwidge Dodgson, mathematical tutor at Christ Church, Oxford, and deacon of the Church of England, having changed from the black clergyman's clothes he always wore in Oxford to white flannel trousers, black boots, and a white straw boater, sat facing the back of his friend Robinson Duckworth, who rowed stroke to Dodgson's bow. In the stern, facing Duckworth, sat the three Liddell sisters, daughters of the dean of Christ Church: Edith, age eight; Alice, age ten; and Lorina, age thirteen. The girls, seated on cushions, wore white cotton frocks, white socks, black shoes, and hats with brims. In the boat stood a kettle and a large basket full of cakes; on river expeditions Dodgson liked to stop and take tea in the shadow of a haycock. "The story was actually composed and spoken *over my shoulder*," Duckworth recalled some years later, "for the benefit of Alice Liddell, who was acting as 'cox' of our gig. I remember turning round and saying, 'Dodgson, is this an extempore romance of yours?' And he replied: 'Yes, I'm inventing as we go along.' " Twenty-five years later Dodgson recalled: "I distinctly remember now, as I write, how, in a desperate attempt to strike out some new line of fairy-lore, I had sent my heroine straight down a rabbit-hole, to begin with, without the least idea what was to happen afterwards." He remembered the stillness of that afternoon: the cloudless blue sky, the watery mirror of the river, the tinkle of drops falling from the oars. Mrs. Hargreaves—as Dodgson always referred to Alice, after her marriage— also recalled the day sharply: the blazing summer afternoon, the heat-haze shimmering over the meadows, the shadow cast by the haycocks near Godstow.

Alice is growing thirsty, and as she falls slowly past a cupboard she opens the doors. She sees a bottle labeled GINGER BEER and grasps it as she falls, but the bottom of the bottle catches on the edge of the shelf and the bottle slips from her fingers. Alice covers her ears, widens her eyes, and opens her mouth to scream. But she sees the bottle of ginger beer falling lazily in front of her and not plunging down like a stone in a well. The bottle is tilted like the hand of a clock pointing to ten; at once Alice reaches out and seizes the bottle firmly. When she brings it close to her face she sees with disappointment that there is scarcely a swallow of ginger beer left. She wonders how long the bottle has been sitting on the shelf, for it simply won't do to drink from an old bottle, or one that has been used by someone else. She will have to speak to the housekeeper, if she ever finds one. How neat and clean the shelves are! The housekeeper must have a fine feather duster. But it must be a very long feather duster, to reach so high. Alice feels that her thoughts are growing confused, and without another moment's hesitation she raises the bottle to her lips and swallows the ginger beer. "Why," Alice says to herself in surprise, "this isn't ginger beer at all! It is nothing but soda water! I shall certainly have to speak to someone about this. Fancy if all labels meant something else, so that you never knew what you were going to eat. Please, Miss, would you care for more buttered toast? And out comes roast duck and dumplings. But that isn't what I mean, exactly." Alice is no longer certain what she means, exactly; when she looks up she can see the cupboard vanishing in the dark. As she falls past another cupboard, she manages to place the bottle inside. At the last moment she realizes that the label is still not right, since the bottle is now empty. But, Alice thinks to herself as the cupboard rises into the dark, it isn't as wrong as it was before.

It occurs to Alice that the shaft is a prison: she cannot climb out, she cannot escape. It may be that she can stop falling, by reaching out and grasping the top of a cupboard, the edge of a niche, or a protruding piece of stone; but even if the cupboard does not tear out of the wall, even if the edge of the niche does not crumble, and the stone not break, what possible use will it be to hang there like a coat on a peg, while her fingers and arms grow tireder and tireder? There are no doors or windows in the walls of her prison, no stairs or ladders: it seems more sensible to keep falling, and to hope for an end of falling, than to stop and think about regaining the upper world. Perhaps if she had stopped very early in her fall, it might not have been too late. Alice tries to imagine herself sitting on top of a cupboard as she looks up and cries for help: her legs dangle against the cupboard doors, she grasps the rim of the cupboard top, she raises her face and shouts for her sister. It occurs to Alice that she has never once cried out, in all her falling; until this moment, when it is too late, the idea has never come to her.

Down, down, down: something must be wrong, Alice thinks to herself, for the fall should surely be over by now. And a doubt steals over her, like a cloud-shadow over a pool on a summer's day. Did she do the right thing, when she jumped into the rabbit hole? Wasn't she guilty of a certain rashness? Shouldn't she have considered more carefully, before taking such a step? But the leap into the rabbit hole was the same as the leap to her feet beside her sister: it was the final motion of a single impulse, as if she had leaped from the bank directly into the rabbit hole. The mistake was to have jumped up in the first place. Alice tries to recall her feeling of restlessness on the bank, under the tree, beside her sister, but she recalls only the warm, drowsy shade, the sunny field of daisies, the blue, blue sky. Of course, it was the White Rabbit that made her jump up in excitement. But is a rabbit with a waistcoat and watch really so remarkable, when you stop to think about it? Was it really necessary for her to jump up without a moment's hesitation and run off so rashly, without considering anyone's feelings but her own? Her sister will be worried; when she looks up from her book, Alice will be gone; her day will be ruined. And is it possible, Alice thinks to herself, that the rabbit was only the usual sort of rabbit, after all? Is it possible that she had been daydreaming again, there on the bank beside her sister? Alice, doubting, feels a little burst of bitterness in her heart.

In the darkness, lit here and there by the dim glow of oil lamps, Alice feels a sudden revulsion: the tunnel walls oppress her, the cupboards bore her to death, she can't stand it for another second—and still she continues falling, past the always rising maps, the pictures, the cupboards, the bookshelves. She can hardly breathe in the dank, close air. It is like a long railway journey, without conversation and without any hope of taking tea. Above, the darkness pushes down on her like a column of stone; below, the darkness sweeps slowly upward, sticking to the dark above, increasing its height and weight. There is absolutely nothing to do. Do cats eat bats? Do bats eat cats? Do rats eat mats? Do blats eat clats? This can't go on much longer, Alice thinks to herself, and opens her mouth to scream, but does not scream.

There is no illustration of Alice falling, and so we must imagine the Tenniel drawing: Alice in black and white, falling against a dark background of minute cross-hatchings, upon which we can make out the bottom corner of a cupboard. Alice is wearing black shoes, white stockings with black shading, a white dress and white pinafore. Her long hair is lifted away from her face on both sides; her wide dress billows. Her elbows are held away from her sides and her forearms are held stiffly before her, at different heights; the fingers of the lower hand are spread tensely, the fingers of the upper hand are curved as if she were playing an invisible piano. Under her black eyebrows her black eyes are wide and brooding. The creases of her pinafore are indicated by several series of short parallel lines; the shadow of an arm across her pinafore shows as cross-hatching. In the lower right-hand corner is Tenniel's monogram: a large T crossed with a small J. The illustration is without a frame, and is fitted into the text in such a way that the words continue down the right-hand side of the drawing for most of the page before stretching across the entire width of the page for the last six lines. Alice is therefore falling alongside the text that describes her fall and at the same time is enclosed by the text; if she falls any farther, she will bump into words. Pictured in the act of falling, Alice remains motionless: she is fixed forever in her fall.

There are four dreams of falling. The first is dreamed by Alice, asleep on the bank with her head in her sister's lap: she dreams of falling down a long vertical tunnel or well. The second is the dream that Alice tells her sister, when falling leaves wake her on the bank: her tale includes the story of the long fall through the dark well. The third is the dream of Alice's sister, alone on the bank, in the setting sun: she dreams of Alice telling her dream, which includes the story of the fall through the dark tunnel. The fourth is Alice's sister's dream of Alice as a grown woman: she dreams of grown-up Alice telling the dream of Wonderland to little children gathered about her. Alice is therefore caught in a circle of dream-falls: no sooner does she wake than she begins to fall again down the dark tunnel, as she recounts her dream to her sister, and no sooner does she run off to tea than she begins to fall again, in her sister's dream; and even as a grown woman she is still falling through the dark, as the bright-eyed children look up at her with eager faces. It appears, then, that Alice can never escape from her dream: once she plunges into the rabbit hole, once she leaves the safe, predictable world of her sister, she can never return; once she starts to fall, she can never stop falling.

Down, down, down: Alice tries not to be unhappy, for what would be the use of *that*, but as she falls she bursts into sudden tears. "Come," Alice says to herself rather sharply, "there's no use in crying like that!" And no sooner has she spoken than she stops crying, for Alice always tries to listen to her own advice. She wipes her cheeks with the backs of her hands; a few tears drip from her chin, and Alice ignores them as she falls past a closed cupboard with six tiles over the doors. The tiles show rustic figures in sepia, blue, and black: a shepherd resting under a tree, a boy in a stream, a girl feeding tame rabbits, a woman and child resting from collecting sticks, a seated girl with goat and kid, and a young woman carrying a pail across a stream. The cupboard vanishes into the upper dark, and Alice, glancing down, sees a curious sight: in the air directly under her chin there are three tears, falling as she falls. For a while she watches the tears, pressing her chin against her neck and frowning down to see them; then she lifts out the handkerchief in her pinafore pocket and carefully wipes away the tears, as if erasing them.

If only, Alice thinks to herself, I weren't so tired! If only I could rest! For it's tiring to be always falling, falling down the rabbit hole. Alice wonders if it is possible to rest awhile. She doesn't want to catch hold of a cupboard or bookshelf, for fear of bringing it down; and in any case, to hang against a wall with your legs resting on air is hardly Alice's idea of a proper way to rest. Indeed, the act of falling requires no effort; Alice is puzzled why she should be tired of doing something that requires no effort. Is it possible that the fall itself is a rest? Alice tries to imagine what it would be like to sit on a chair as she falls. It would be very pleasant, she thinks, to curl up in a corner of a great armchair and close her eyes. But would there be room for an armchair in the narrow tunnel? Wouldn't it knock against the cupboard doors? And if she should fall asleep, and tumble out of the armchair, what then? But if she tumbled out of the armchair, wouldn't she simply fall through the air, as she is doing now? Again Alice feels that she is growing confused, and she decides to rest by raising her hands, interlocking her fingers, and leaning her cheek on her clasped hands. For a while she falls this way, with her eyes closed and her head resting lightly on her hands.

As in a dream, Alice remembers: she was sitting on the bank beside her sister. It was hot, even in the shade. Her legs hurt from sitting on the ground, her stockings itched, a gnat kept bumping against her hair. Her sister sat motionless over her book and refused to look up—even her fingers gripping the edges of the book were motionless, like table legs with claws gripping a ball, and her neck was bent in a tense, unnatural way, which meant that she didn't want to be disturbed in her reading.

The grass was tickly and sharp. Alice's skin itched, but she also felt an inner itching, as if all her bones needed to be scratched. Of course she loved her sister dearly, but just at that moment she would have liked to pick up a stone and crush her sister in the eyes. She was a wicked girl, to have thoughts like that. Her brain felt hot. Her ankles itched. Her blood itched. She felt that at any moment she was going to split open, like a seed pod. That was when, she remembers, she heard the noise in the grass.

Alice, raising her head abruptly, suddenly thinks of the White Rabbit: she had seen it pop down the rabbit hole and had gone down after it. He must therefore be under her, falling as she is falling. Of course, Alice reflects, it's possible that she alone has fallen down this endless well, while the White Rabbit has remained high above, in the tunnel-like part of the rabbit hole before the sudden drop. It's also possible that the White Rabbit has fallen much more swiftly than she and has long ago come to the bottom, if there *is* a bottom. But Alice doesn't recall any other opening in the tunnel-like part of the rabbit hole; and the maps, the cupboards, the bookshelves all suggest a familiar, much-frequented portion of the White Rabbit's home. And then, there is actually no reason to think that the White Rabbit should fall more quickly than she. It is therefore very likely that the White Rabbit is just below her, falling in the dark; and so certain does her reasoning strike her that, looking down into the dark, she seems to see a faint motion there, in the blackness through which she is already passing.

Why, of course, Alice thinks to herself: the White Rabbit lives here. I am falling through the White Rabbit's home. Why hadn't she thought of it just that way before? But what a curious sort of home it was—more like a chimney, really. Alice has never heard of a chimney with maps and cupboards on the walls; it would never do to start a fire here. Is it perhaps an entrance hall? But what sort of entrance hall can it be, with no place to leave your visiting card and no stand to put your umbrella in? Is it a stairway, then? Alice wonders whether a stairway must have stairs in it, in order to be a stairway. And as she continues falling she looks with sudden interest, as if searching for a clue, at the crowded walls, where she sees a glass-covered engraving of two dogs fighting over the nest of a heron; a wall bracket shaped like a swan with lifted wings, supporting a marble statuette of Whittington Listening to the Bells of London: he is seated on a block carved with the word WHITTINGTON, his right hand is raised, his forefinger is pointing up, his head is cocked to one side; and a marble shelf holding a clock: the round dial is set in a dark-blue porcelain vase surmounted by two white porcelain angels, and the vase rests on a pediment decorated with pink porcelain flowers. On the pediment, on each side of the vase, sits a naked child with flowers in his lap: one child holds up a butterfly, the other clutches an arrow. The hands are pointing to 2:05, and Alice wonders, as she falls past, whether the time is the same as the time on the bank, under the tree, where her sister sits reading, or whether it is some other time.

Falling through darkness, Alice imagines herself rising: past the clock, past the bottle of ginger beer, past the shield-shaped mirror, where she sees her hair pressed to the sides of her head, past the cupboard with the jar of raspberry jam, past so many shelves and maps and pictures that they begin to slide into each other like the dissolving views in the Polytechnic, higher and higher, until she reaches the place where the horizontal tunnel begins—and pulling herself onto the path, she makes her way through the dark toward a distant lightness, which reveals itself suddenly as the opening of the rabbit hole. Alice climbs out of the hole under the hedge into the brilliant day. Sunlight burns down on the field. The sky is the troubling blue of stained-glass windows or magic-lantern slides. Across a field of knee-high grass she sees her sister reading a book on a sloping bank in the shade of a beech tree. The beech, the bank, the sister are very still, as if they were made of porcelain. Alice runs across the field with her hair streaming out behind her and comes to the shady bank. All is still. Her sister does not move, does not raise her eyes from the book. Over the far fields the bright blue sky burns down. All is still.

On her sister's lap, Alice lies dreaming. Leaf-shadows move on her face and arms. She is far from the long grass bending in the wind, from the pool rippling to the waving of the reeds, from the sheep bells tinkling, the cries of the shepherd boy, the lowing of the cows in the distance. Alice's sister doesn't want to disturb her sleep and sits very still in the warm shade of the bank. It is a hot, drowsy day. When Alice fell asleep, Alice's sister continued reading for a while, but now she has laid the book aside on the grass, for she is feeling a little sleepy herself, and it's difficult to read for very long without changing the position of your arm and hands, which she doesn't wish to do for fear of waking Alice. She watches Alice breathing gently in and out. Strands of hair lie rippling over Alice's cheek and shoulder; a single hair, escaping from the rest, curves across her cheek and lies at the corner of her mouth. Her forehead is smooth, but a slight tension shows between the eyebrows, which are darker than her hair: Alice is closed deeply in sleep. In the warm shade her sister feels drowsy, but she knows she must not sleep: she must watch over Alice, here on the shady bank. Sleep is strange, Alice's sister thinks to herself: you are there and not there. Alice seems far away, like a princess in a tower. Alice's sister would like to pick up her book again, but her hand remains motionless; she would like to shift her position, for her left leg is beginning to tingle, but she does not move. It is very quiet. Are we mistaken to see in the brightness and stillness of this afternoon an echo of the afternoon on the Isis? In the brightness a darkness forms: the tunnel is a shadow cast by the sunny day. May we perhaps think of a story as an internal shadow, a leap into the dark? In a distant field, cows are lowing. Under a shady tree, Alice's sister keeps watch. Deeply Alice lies sleeping.

A long, low hall lit by a row of oil lamps hanging from the ceiling. A row of many doors, evenly spaced, all around the hall. In the middle of the hall a small three-legged table made of glass: a tiny gold key lies on top. On the right-hand wall, a dark-red curtain hanging to the floor. Behind the curtain, but not yet visible, a small door about fifteen inches high. Behind the small door, a garden of bright flowers and cool fountains. In the left-hand wall, rear, an opening: the entrance to a dark corridor or passage. The long passage leads to an unseen heap of sticks and dry leaves. Above the heap, a shaft, well, or vertical tunnel, stretching up into blackness.

Alice, falling, imagines that the tunnel comes to an end in a heap of sticks and dry leaves. In the instant that her foot touches the first stick, she realizes two things: that the tunnel does not exist, and that she is about to wake up with her head in her sister's lap. And indeed, already through the black wall she can see a shimmer of sun, the cupboards and maps are growing translucent, she can hear the tinkle of sheep bells in the fields. With a sharp, sudden motion of her mind she banishes the heap of sticks and dry leaves. And as when, in a darkened room, a heavy church or stone bridge becomes airy and impalpable, staining your hand with color as you pass your arm through the magic lantern's beam of dust-swirling light, so Alice's foot passes soundlessly through the heap of sticks and dry leaves, and she continues falling. Is it possible, Alice wonders, to resist the tug of the upper world, which even now, as she falls in darkness, entices her to wake? For should she wake, she would find herself on the bank, with itching bones, beside her sister, who will still be reading her book without pictures or conversations. Alice wonders whether it is possible to fall out of the bottom of a dream, into some deeper place. She would like to fall far, very far, so far that she will separate herself forever from the dreamer above, by whose waking she doesn't wish to be disturbed. Have they anything in common, really? Sooner or later the girl in her sister's lap will wake and rub her eyes. And in that moment she will sweep away the tunnel walls, the cupboards, the maps, the dark, replacing them with the tree, the book, the sun-dappled shade. But for dream-Alice the tree, the book, the sun-dappled shade are only a trembling and shimmering, a vanishing—for here there are only the hard walls of the tunnel, the solid shelves, the glistening glass jars, the lifted hair, the wind of her slow falling. And who's to say, Alice thinks to herself, that one's more a dream than the other? And is it possible, Alice wonders, that she will stop falling only when she releases herself utterly from the upper world, with its flickers of sunlight, its murmur of sheep bells, its green-blue shimmer of field and sky? Then in her toes she will feel the tingle of the end of falling. And with a sense of urgency, as if only now had she begun to fall, Alice bends her mind downward toward the upstreaming dark, looking expectantly at a map showing the Division of English Land by the Peace of A.D. 886 between King Alfred and the Danes, at a shelf on which sits a glass-domed arrangement of artificial leaves and flowers composed of knitting wool stitched over wire frames, at a painting in a carved gilt frame: in a parlor window-nook a woman with her hair parted in the middle is sitting in a maroon armchair with buttoned upholstery and an exposed frame of polished mahogany; in her lap she holds knitting needles and the beginning of a gray shawl, but her hands are idle, she is looking out the window; one gray strand leads to a ball of yarn on the floor, where a black kitten with green eyes and tilted head lifts one paw as if to strike the yarn-ball; the room is dark brown, but sunlight pours through the open window; in the yard stand blossoming apple trees; through the trees we see glimpses of a sun-flooded field; a brown stream, glinting with sunlight, winds like a path into the shimmering distance, vanishes into a dark wood.

JOYCE CAROL OATES

Friday Night

Yes it was a melancholy time but nobody'd have known it from looking at my face. I'm the kind of girl *I don't let hurt feelings show, ever.*

I'd had to come back home to Post, Michigan, after a year and three months in Traverse City. The mortgage interest rates went up and people stopped buying property and this real estate agency I worked for (not sales: I was a secretary in the office) went out of business, and with so many people out of work right then I couldn't find decent employment not even waitressing which I vowed I'd never do. So I came back home. Nineteen years old. Back to my old room in the old house, living with my mother. Same sad dumb job I'd had in high school, clerking in Norban's at the mall.

But I never complained, out loud. That isn't my nature. *A smile is easier than a frown* is a fact. Also when you're in sales, in the public eye, you're bound to be optimistic. You're not, people don't buy from you.

I loved my mother, and I'm sure my mother loved me, but we'd get on each other's nerves sometimes, just the two of us in the house. My father died when I was fifteen, my older brother Carly's married and living in Detroit, so it was just the two of us eating meals together and watching TV and she'd wait up for me sometimes when I went out which I resented—I was a grown-up in my own eyes and God knows my conscience was clear, going out to the movies mainly then for a few drinks with my old high school girlfriends, the ones not lucky enough to be married or engaged.

I am living proof of one of the mysteries of life: A girl can be pretty *but not pretty enough.*

But I wasn't lonely really, I'd gotten in the habit, a few nights a week, of dropping by Ryan's for a drink, and there was always somebody there. Ryan's is this neighborhood bar down by the lumberyard where my father worked for thirty years, he used to drop in at Ryan's too, he was what you'd call a regular, and his friends, older guys, are still there, but it was the younger crowd I mixed with, my age. Sometimes I'd play pool with the guys, I wasn't much good but now and then I'd get a lucky shot which made everybody laugh, and I'm the kind of girl loves to laugh, just throw my head back and laugh till tears squeeze out of my eyes. Ryan's was the kind of place that wouldn't get rough until later in the evening, past eleven, by then I'd be gone. I *wasn't* the kind of girl who hangs out too long.

And in Ryan's there was likely to be this boy I'd known in high school, Hillard Ludman was his name, two or three years older than me but I couldn't think of him as anything except a boy. He had a girlfriend named Stephenie but she wasn't always with him and we'd get to talking and if his buddies were there we'd all have a good time and back home in my room I'd lie in bed thinking about Hillard Ludman the way you do, *Why her and not me, why her and not me*, and it was a bittersweet kind of thing. I'd drop off to sleep thinking hoping I might dream about Hillard but most nights I never did.

My dreams are not much consolation, I'd say—like reflections in water and somebody tosses in a rock and everything is scattered, broken.

So there was this Friday night in summer, I'd been back from Traverse City for about six months, I drove over to Ryan's thinking I'd stay just an hour or so, no more. Helped Momma with the supper cleanup as always then felt I had to get out of the house or I'd be climbing the walls, so bored with TV and Momma's chatter which is like the parakeet's chatter, goes on all day whether anyone is listening or not. And when I came into Ryan's there was a good noisy crowd, I didn't have my glasses on so I couldn't see every face exactly, but somebody called my name and it turned out to be a guy named Polo, one of Hillard's pals from high school, and Hillard was there with him, and Hillard's girlfriend Stephenie in a bright maroon sweater, and these guys Jimmy Fenick and Mack Dancer I'd known since grade school, and they were sitting in a booth back a little from the bar toward the dining room, and it lit up my heart how they invited me to join them, just squeeze in beside Polo.

Polo was this shortish guy, pitted-looking skin but I don't think he ever had smallpox or anything, might have been acne scars, and a look around his nose like there's tiny bits of buckshot in his skin. I'd gone out with Polo a few times but we were more like friends than anything else, I mean to say there wasn't any bad feeling between us like there can be in situations of that kind, he was a nice guy, goodhearted. Saying, "Lemme buy you a beer, Toni," so I felt right at home.

Coming in Ryan's, Friday nights, you're taking a chance. You can wind up with the wrong people, or no one. You can be frozen out by your friends. You can leave in fifteen minutes or you can stay to closing time at two A.M. It depends. It's unpredictable. You must take your chances smiling and upbeat no matter in the smoky dim light you can't exactly see who's there or who isn't.

They asked me, "How's it going, Toni?" and I said, "Oh fine, can't complain," feeling my cheeks burn. Sometimes I'm relaxed and funny and able to be the center of attention but if another girl is there, especially a pretty girl like Stephenie Mueller, and she's there with Hillard Ludman's arm slung around her, I get tongue-tied and embarrassed. Also, with a girl like Stephenie who isn't my own friend (she was a year behind me in high school in fact), I'm aware this girl can freeze me out if she wants to, she's secure in the group and I'm not so I have to play up to her if I want to maintain my welcome.

Stephenie was one of those people in town who thought I'd worked in Traverse City selling real estate, that was a common misconception I'd stopped trying to correct, so she was asking me about that job, and other things, and I told her, and I was thinking that I did like her, I couldn't blame Hillard for being crazy in love with her as people said he was, she'd been a popular girl in high school, a cheerleader on the varsity squad, and very pretty, with marmalade-colored curly hair, and large wide-set brown eyes, and a dazzling smile. She'd learned that in high school and would never forget, that smile. And all her life if she lives here in Post, Michigan, people will think of her as a Post High School cheerleader strutting and leaping and arching her back and squealing and wriggling her cute little tight ass in the crimson jumper with the white long-sleeved blouse as if she's someone special and if enough people persist in believing a person is special she *is* special no matter how ordinary.

Such facts I know but they don't make me bitter.

That Friday night Hillard Ludman wasn't in a good mood, I knew the symptoms and Stephenie must have too. Hillard has a face that can look blood-heavy if he's sullen, and his mouth sort of slack, his gray eyes restless. And if he hasn't shaved for a day or two he can look mean. It was generally known that Hillard had a quick, hot temper like his older brothers (one of his brothers, Red, spent three months in prison for assaulting a guy in a bar in Traverse City) and some of us knew he had a sweet side to him too you could coax out if you went about it the right way.

Back in high school that one single year Hillard Ludman and I were both students at the same time we were assigned to the same study hall fifth period and I remember sitting in my desk staring at the back of his head . . . just staring. Straight lank straw-colored hair worn long, over his collar. I'd memorized the planes of his face, the bones, the bumps; his face in quarter profile, half profile, full profile. His left ear. The set of his shoulders. I knew every shirt that boy owned, every sweater. His sneakers, his boots. The way his legs were always restless under his desk, foot twitching, and his hands always moving, big-knuckled hands, long fingers and the nails edged with dirt. Hillard worked then after school for his uncle who owned one of the three gas stations in Post, then after graduating from school he started working full-time at the International Harvester plant in Sandusky about fifteen miles away where a lot of men in Post worked too. He'd joined up with the Michigan National Guard to keep from being drafted into the Army just like my brother Carly had.

Carly told tales about the Guard, though never to Momma. A lot of goofing off, he'd said. Drinking, dope-smoking, like that.

I'd never asked Hillard if he'd smoked dope at the camp: he was the kind of unpredictable boy, a question like that might be too personal and he'd squint his eyes and say something rude, or he'd maybe misunderstand, and say, *Why sure baby you wanna join me sometime?*—giving it all a sexual meaning.

Stephenie was entertaining the guys telling about her brother who got rammed in his car on the John Lodge Expressway in Detroit, and the black guy in the other car came out swinging his tire iron though his head was all bloody and it would turn out he'd broken an arm, and Stephenie's brother tried to take the tire iron away from him, and her sister-in-law got involved too: "Irene went right between those two trying to stop them, got cracked on the side of the head," Stephenie said, "—can you believe it? Crazy like that? I said to her, Jesus Irene why'd you do such a crazy thing and she said she didn't remember doing it actually, 'Maybe when I saw Larry going to get killed I went wild or something.' "

So Hillard said, "Sounds like a good woman," and the other guys agreed.

Stephenie was all breathless and vehement and wide-eyed, saying, "Oh but I think she was risking her life—coming between two big men and one of them's *black*."

Hillard said, "It's instinct. It's nature. Like a lioness or something protecting her cubs." He paused, and squeezed his arm around Stephenie's neck, and said, "It's love."

Stephenie said, "Irene got cracked hard on the head, it was a concussion. The doctor said it could've been a lot worse."

"Yeah," said Hillard, grinning at us. "Nature doesn't care shit for the individual."

So they talked. And drank beer. And I was thinking how in the booth like this just a few feet from Hillard Ludman I was as much in his company as Stephenie herself; how strange that was, and how precious. In high school I'd memorized so many things about him that when I saw him face to face, let alone talked with him, it was like a dream—he was the real thing and I was not.

So they got onto the subject of *What is the test of love*, and everybody had an opinion, including me.

Hillard gave Stephenie coins for the jukebox, Johnny Cash singing "She Died Young" and "Lyin' Eyes."

Every forty-five minutes or so Stephenie would excuse herself to go to the lavatory, it was the beer that did it. The next time she went I half wanted to follow her so we could talk a little, away from the guys, just the two of us, for I felt she would like me better if she knew me better. (I know I have certain mannerisms that put some people off, I get loud and excitable in a party situation, get carried away.) But also I wanted to stay with the guys, just me and not Stephenie for a few minutes, then when I finally got up to go Stephenie was coming back, we didn't have time for more than saying "Hi!" when we passed, and I complimented her on her earrings, beautiful wrought-silver hoops, and she said she really liked my hair in that new style, and I thanked her though it wasn't any new style exactly, I'd been wearing it like this for months.

In the rest room I was disgusted to see how flush-faced I looked. Like some middle-aged drunk. My nose was greasy where the powder wore off and one of my black bra straps was showing.

I used the toilet, and fixed myself up, taking my glasses out of my purse to check before I left: it's painful to see yourself with too much clarity, but sometimes it has to be done.

I was wearing a black V-neck cotton sweater, and black-and-white polka-dot slacks, and black textured stockings, and shoes with a little heel. I'm a tall girl, about five feet nine, and I could stand to lose maybe fifteen pounds, my bust is heavy, and my hips, but in nylon slacks like these, with the sweater pulled down, no one could tell. My face is moon-shaped, my eyes are dark gypsy-brown (a guy once said), my mouth is wider than I like but I try to correct that when I put on lipstick.

That night I thought I looked all right but who knows. Pink gloss on my lips, silvery-blue eye shadow on my eyelids, just by coincidence the same color Stephenie the cheerleader with the marmalade curls is wearing. I stared at myself through my glasses and saw hope shining in my eyes which is sometimes a shameful thing so I quickly took off my glasses and put them in my purse.

This is a fact: There are thoughts a girl will have only in lavatories like the one in Ryan's where there's an odor of drains and cigarette smoke overlaid with perfumy deodorant spray. And only when she's by herself. And not certain what is waiting for her when she returns to the party she's been with.

Once in Traverse City I came out of a rest room in a motel cocktail lounge and the dirty fuckers I'd been with, two guys and another girl, they'd played the cruelest trick on me . . . they'd left. Just walked out. Dropped some bills on the table and left and I'd been led to believe we were all having a good time. So I was standing there staring at the empty booth trying not to cry. Thinking, *Toni you deserve better than this, you're a decent-hearted person and you would never, never be so cruel to another human being.* For some reason I was thinking too of my father who died aged fifty-two, myocardial infarction of the heart they called it, he went to work at the lumberyard one morning like always and never came back home and none of us who loved him had the chance to say good-bye to him. It seemed to me the most terrible things happen to us with no warning, so how can we be prepared?

And after a terrible thing happens we have the idea another terrible thing won't happen again for a long time. That's a mistake, that idea.

But my friends were there, waiting for me.

I mean, not waiting for *me*, they'd hardly known I was gone I suppose. But they were there.

The night began to take a strange turn, I don't know why. They were still talking about the "tests of love," Hillard was teasing Stephenie but in a mean persistent way like she wasn't giving him the right answers in front of his buddies. There was a nervousness between Hillard and Stephenie like highly charged air before an electrical storm, like if you struck a match there'd be an explosion, I think because they were new with each other, not settled in, not certain of what was going to happen. I'd been told that Stephenie was crazy about Hillard too and hoped to get engaged but was afraid of him because of his quick temper and unpredictable ways and I thought, *That's because she isn't equal to him.*

Maybe I was getting drunk but it came so clear and lucid to me, that girl wasn't equal to him, just a pissy little girl, a dime a dozen.

Tests of love. They all had their opinions. Saving somebody from drowning . . . pulling somebody out of the fire . . . giving blood. Mack and Polo had stories of giving blood for relatives in the hospital. I said I'd given blood at the Red Cross in Traverse City, almost fainted when the needle went in but really it was no big deal. (Stephenie was making a face, fluttering her eyelids like she felt faint.) Hillard had one arm around Stephenie squeezing him against her and he flexed the muscles of his other arm to make the veins in his forearm bulge, a bluish ropy look to them, "*I'd* give a gallon of blood for somebody I loved, no questions asked," he said, grinning, holding his arm so tight it was quivering, and the veins stood out seemingly quivering too, "—hell *I* could give blood right here and now, anybody got a needle?—a *knife?*" and though he was joking it was a queer kind of joke, only the guys laughed, Stephenie pretended to hide her eyes. She had long nicely filed fingernails painted coral pink to match her lipstick.

That pretty maroon top of Stephenie's!—like nothing you'd buy in Norban's. When I'd come out of the rest room, blinking in the dim smoky air, trying to see, it was that bright dab of color I followed, leading me back to my friends.

Hillard and Jimmy weren't getting along too well. Beer made them both belligerent. Polo was talking to me, talking talking talking so I missed the point of what they were saying, just heard their voices, that sudden sharp edge. Hillard said, "This sergeant in the Guard, he told us the coward and the hero have exactly the same feelings of fear but the coward acts upon them, and runs away to save his ass, but the hero won't run which is why he's a *hero*," and Jimmy said, mocking, "Yeah— so the hero gets his ass blown off and the coward doesn't." Jimmy has some Indian blood—Iroquois—and he's a big guy, big shoulders like a weightlifter, he'd dropped out of high school to work at the lumberyard and I knew him a little, just to say hello, I knew his father was killed in the Korean War so there was logic to his words, and Hillard surely knew, but he said, disgusted, "Man, what a shithead you're getting to be, always taking the depressing side of things," and Stephenie tried to soothe him, and Mack and Polo joined in, and this went on for a while, it's a strange fact how, in places like this, when they've been drinking and getting along real well, or for instance playing pool all concentrated in the game and in one another's skill, suddenly something does it, some change in the air, my brother Carly's the same way, and my father had been that way too, quick-tempered ready to fight. And any woman who's a witness to this can't comprehend—*what happened? why?*

Hillard slammed off to the men's room and on his way back got into a disagreement, then a scuffle, with two guys from the Air Force base, slightly older guys we all knew, and Jimmy and Mack and Polo went to help, and the bartender shouted for them all to get out, just please get out, it was past midnight by now and Ryan's was jammed, a different atmosphere from the one I'm accustomed to, so the guys paid up and we left, Stephenie wide-eyed and breathless pretending to be scared, teetering in her high heels and leaning on Hillard's arm, and Polo's helping me walk—I'm surely not drunk but I *am* high, and in a great mood—so now we're in Ryan's parking lot trying to figure out which place to go next, this Italian place out in Frankfort, or this other bar, the Crescent Moon, in town, and we're laughing and I'm edging away from Polo 'cause I know he's going to ask me to ride with him in his car and maybe just maybe Hillard and Stephenie will ask me to ride in theirs, and Mack is teasing Hillard about blowing those Air Force fuckers away, lying in wait out here and letting them have it, it turns out Hillard has a rifle in the trunk of his Dodge Charger, a .22-caliber Winchester, and they get him to unlock the trunk and they're holding it and admiring it the way guys will do, they're all hunters, or would like to be, and Hillard says to Stephenie, "Bet you wouldn't trust me to shoot an apple off your head, would you?"—sort of sneering and smiling, and Stephenie says, "You crazy? Sure I wouldn't," and Jimmy says, "*That's* a test of love," and Hillard says, "Naw, that's a test of courage, and good marksmanship," and I hear myself say in this voice that's coming from somewhere not exactly me, "You know I'd trust you, Hillard," but it's like Hillard isn't listening 'cause the guys keep talking and Stephenie whispers to me, "Damn! I wish I'd used the rest room before we left, don't you!" and it's like a cruel reminder 'cause I feel my bladder sort of beginning to ache, just the suggestion, the very beginning, so I hope we get to wherever we're going soon so I can use the ladies' room, but the guys are talking, Polo's saying if you're a hunter you know what you're doing but these jerks with pistols and such in the house like in the bedroom and the kids can get to them, there was these little cousins of his, in Florida, the family'd gone down to live in a trailer park, and— but Hillard cuts him off, running his fingers through Stephenie's hair joking and sweet-talking her, saying, "You want to shoot an apple off *my* head?—I'd let you, honey," and Stephenie giggles sharply and says, "You know?—you're drunk. I'm not sure I like you drunk," and Hillard says, "I'm not sure I like you with your clothes on," which makes the guys howl with laughter and poor Stephenie just stand there stricken and ashamed and it's mean but I can't help laughing too, and Hillard turns to me, says, "Toni, baby, you're my old buddy—*you'd* trust me to shoot an apple off your head, wouldn't you?" and I just say, "Yes."

And everybody looks at me, and there's a silence. Hillard's looking at me. I know I need to say more, I need to modify it, turn the seriousness of it into a joke, but I can't think of a single word more.

Over and over like she's drunk or drugged Stephenie whispers, "You're crazy, you're all crazy. . . ."

But she comes with us, doesn't insist upon Hillard driving her home or even stopping to let her off on the road so she can walk, and we drive in three cars (I'm with Hillard and Stephenie in the back of the Dodge Charger) to this place down beyond the railroad yard, on the river. At first I can't figure out where we are 'cause my eyes are misted over from that damn smoky atmosphere in Ryan's, then I see, yes, sure, it's that secret kind of place where back in high school kids would come and park in their cars and make out, but everything looks different tonight, very still, no one around, trash scattered on the riverbank, smashed bottles and such, but the river is beautiful glittering in the moonlight, a romantic look to it so I'm humming a Johnny Cash song aloud that's been running through my head for hours.

At first Stephenie says she isn't going to come down with us, we're all crazy she says, and Toni's the craziest, too drunk to know what we're doing, but of course she comes along, wouldn't miss it for the world, scolding and half-sobbing stumbling in the gravel in her high-heeled shoes, her bare arms folded below her pointy little breasts as if she's cold.

The guys help me out to this flat wide rock that's like an opened hand, and I'm standing there trading wisecracks with them, feeling good, dear Christ I'm feeling the best I've felt in a long long time, breathing in the sweet night air, all the way up to the stars. The river along this stretch is shallow-looking even by day, and by night it looks flat like a surface only, but it's fast-moving, there are undertows and nobody's supposed to swim here but every summer they do, and every summer there's a drowning, or nearly.

I'm teasing Hillard like I tease the guys sometimes when we're playing pool, "You better be a good shot, son, or we're all in trouble," and the guys laugh, except Hillard who's nerved-up fussing over his rifle, checking the scope, aiming it at the tops of trees or at the moon . . . it's good strong steady moonlight here, almost clear as day.

Pissy little Stephenie calls over one more time, "Toni, y'know you're crazy, I'm gonna tell your mother about this. . . ."

Polo's dancing around edgy and nervous sucking his fingers.

Mark's nervous too, says in a weaker voice than I have ever heard from him, "Hillard? Hey? Maybe you hadn't ought . . . maybe just a regular target would be better. . . ."

Hillard says, hissing, "Shut *up*."

Jimmy is poking around on shore looking for something to use as a target, sure isn't going to be any apple, not down here, mainly rocks and trash but he comes up with this great idea: one of those tall Styrofoam cups, the kind a giant order of French fries comes in at McDonald's, he dumps some dirty water out and brings it over to me, it's a glaring kind of white, easy to pick it out in the shadows. Hillard says, excited, "Shit yeah that's perfect—man that's *it*."

He's standing bent-kneed on the riverbank maybe fifteen?—twenty?—feet from me, wriggling his shoulders inside his T-shirt like an athlete loosening his muscles, he raises the barrel and Jimmy giggles, "Lemme out of the way, fucker"—Jimmy has got the Styrofoam cup balanced on my head upside down and I take it from his fingers and press it down more firmly, my hair is springy from a perm so I have to press hard, and Jimmy scoots back out of range, and Hillard says, "Toni? You ready? Gonna count to five," and I say, "I'm ready," and I start to float breathing calm and trusting and in control, posture perfect as a drum majorette's, my eyes opened wide and it's as if I can see myself in all these boys' eyes but most of all in the rifle scope through Hillard Ludman's single opened eye as he counts, "One! Two! Three! . . ." in a hoarse whisper like he's counting to himself and it's the strangest sensation I have ever experienced in my life as if my spirit is floating free of my body like this rock is the hand of God I'm standing in, you know that gospel song the blacks sing sometimes Sunday mornings on the radio, *He's got the whole world in His hand* . . . except it isn't God but Hillard Ludman whose hand I am in *and the two of us will be bound together for all eternity*.

There's a deafening *crack!* like a firecracker thrown right at me, and every one of us, especially me, screams and ducks, and the Styrofoam cup goes flying into the shallow water, and there's a moment's shocked silence, then Jimmy says, breathing hard, "Jesus, asshole, you missed by three feet at least!—it went into those trees over there," and Hillard just wipes his face still and composed and says coolly, "I did it on purpose, fuckface, testing things out," and somebody giggles nervously, it sounds like Polo, and I'm shaking so bad now it's like a cold Arctic wind blowing over me, and I need to grit my teeth tight so they won't chatter, but we get ready a second time, I have the cup again, and again balance it on my head firm and steady, and this time I'm panting like a dog, my face frozen in a grin and I can feel my bladder pinching and the last clear thought I have before, this time, as Hillard goes down on one knee like an Army marksman, raises the barrel, begins his count again, "One! Two! Three! Four! . . ." is I hope dear God I do not pee my pants *that is all I hope Amen* 'cause I know this time Hillard Ludman isn't going to shoot into the trees.

". . . Bravest girl in this shithead town."

In the Crescent Moon where we end up Hillard buys me a special celebration drink, Hawaiian Bombshell it's called but I forget how it's made, comes with a big slice of pineapple hooked around the glass and the glass is frosted and he's toasting his buddy Toni, all of them are toasting Toni who's the center of attraction and I'm so high and frazzled I can't think of anything to say except "Thanks," and go off giggling like I'm being tickled. Hillard Ludman is kidding but he's serious too, he's the kind of guy sometimes most serious when he's kidding, touching his glass to mine, the two of us drinking together touching glasses and I'm chilly damp with sweat that's slow to dry, my sweater between my breasts, under my arms, my crotch and the nape of my neck, and everybody's calling me the bravest, craziest girl in Post, Michigan, that will go down in legend I think, and for a while Stephenie is cold and stiff and won't even drink then naturally she comes around, Stephenie Mueller is always going to come around, leaning her head on Hillard's shoulder sleepy and loving and I can see his hand under the table and she slaps at him and he baby-slaps at her, and she giggles.

EDNA O'BRIEN

Brother

Bad cess to him. Thinks I don't know, that I didn't smell a rat. All them
bachelors swaggering in here; calling him out to the haggart in case I
twigged. "Tutsy this and Tutsy that." A few readies in it for them; along
with drives and big feeds. They went the first Sunday to reconnoiter,
walk the land and so forth. The second Sunday they went in for refreshments. Three married sisters, all gawks. If they're not hitched up by now
there must be something wrong; harelip or a limp or fits. He's no oil
painting, of course. Me doing everything for him; making his porridge
and emptying his worshipful Po, for God knows how many years. Not
to mention his lumbago, and the liniment I rubbed in.

"I'll be good to you, Maisie," he says. Good! A bag of toffees on
a holy day. Takes me for granted. All them fly-boys at threshing time
trying to ogle me up into the loft for a fumble. Puckauns. I'd take a
pitchfork to any one of them; so would he if he knew. I scratched his
back many's the night and rubbed the liniment on it. Terrible aul smell.
Eucalyptus.

"Lower . . . lower," he'd say, "down there." Down to the puddingy
bits, the lupins. All to get to my Mary. He had a Mass said in the house
after. Said he saw his mother, our mother; something on her mind. I had
to have grapefruit for the Priest's breakfast, had to depip it. These Priests
are real gluttons. He ate in the breakfast room and kept admiring things
in the cabinet, the china bell and the bog-oak cabin and so forth.
Thought I'd part with them. I was running in and out with hot tea, hot
water, hot scones; he ate enough for three. Then the big handshake;
Matt giving him a tenner. I never had that amount in my whole life.
Ten bob on Fridays to get provisions, including sausages for his breakfast. Woeful the way he never consulted me. He began to get hoity-toity,
took off that awful trousers with the greasy backside from all the sweating and lathering on horseback, tractor and bike; threw it in the fire
cavalier-like. Had me airing a suit for three days. I had it on a clothes-
horse turning it round every quarter of an hour, for fear of it scorching.

Then the three bachelors come into the yard again, blabbing about buying silage off him. They had silage to burn. It stinks the countryside. He put on his cap and went out to talk to them. They all leant on the gate, cogitating. I knew 'twas fishy but it never dawned on me it could be a wife. I'd had gone out and sent them packing. Talking low they were and at the end they all shook hands. At the supper he said he was going to Galway Sunday.

"What's in Galway?" I said.

"A greyhound," he said.

First mention of a greyhound since our little Daisy died. The pride and joy of the Parish she was. Some scoundrels poisoned her. I found her in a fit outside in the shed, yelps coming out of her, and foam. It nearly killed him. He had a rope that he was ruminating with, for months. Now this bombshell. Galway.

"I'll come with you, I need a sea breeze," I said.

"It's all male, it's stag," he said, and grinned.

I might have guessed. Why were they egging him on, I'll never know except 'twas to spite me. Some of them have it in for me; I drove bullocks of theirs off our land, I don't give them any haults on bonfire night. He went up to the room then and wouldn't budge. I left a slice of griddle bread with golden syrup on it outside the door. He didn't touch it. At dawn I was raking the ashes and he called me, real soft-soapy, "Is that you, Maisie, is that you?" Who in blazes' name did he think it was—Bridget, or Mary of the Gods! "Come in for a minute," he said. "There's a flea or some goddamn thing itching me, maybe it's a tick, maybe they've nested." I strip the covers and in thou'll candle-light he's like one of those Saints that they boil, thin and raky. Up to then I only ventured in the dark, on windy nights when he'd say he heard a ghost, and I had to go to him. I reconnoiter his white body while he's muttering on about the itch, said, "Soldiers in the tropics minded itch more than combat." He read that in an almanac.

"Maisie," he says in a watery voice, and puts his hand on mine and steers me to his shorthorn. Pulled the stays off of me. Thinking I don't know what he was after. All pie. Raving about me being the best sister in the wide world and "I'd give my last shilling" and so forth. Talked about his young days when he hunted with a ferret. Babble, babble. His limbs were like jelly and then the grunts and him burying himself under the red flannel eiderdown, saying God would strike us.

The next Sunday he was off again. Not a word to me since the tick mutiny, except to order me to drive cattle or harness the horse. Got a new pullover, a most unfortunate color, like piccalilli. He didn't get home that Sunday until all hours. I heard the car door banging. He boiled himself milk, because the saucepan was on the range with the skin on it. I went up to the village to get meal for the hens and everyone was gassing about it. My brother had got engaged for the second time in two weeks. First it was a Dymphna and now it was a Tilly. It seemed he was in their parlor—pictures of cows and millstreams on the wall—sitting next to his intended, eating cold ox-tongue and beetroot when he leans across the table, points to Tilly and says, "I think I'd sooner her."

Uproar. They all dropped utensils and gaped at him, thinking it a joke. He sticks to his guns, so much so that her father and the bachelors drag him out into the garden for a heart-to-heart. Garden. It seems it's only high grass and an obelisk that wobbles. They said, "What the Christ, Matt?" He said, "I prefer Tilly, she's plumper." Tilly was called out and the two of them were told to walk down to the gate and back, to see what they had in common.

In a short time they return and announce that they understand one another and wish to be engaged. Gink. She doesn't know the catastrophe she's in for. She doesn't know about me and my status here. Dymphna had a fit, shouted, threw bits of beetroot and gizzard all about and said, "My sister is a witch." Had to be carried out and put in a box room, where she shrieked and banged with a set of fire irons that were stored there. Parents didn't care, at least they were getting one cissy off their hands. Father breeds French herds, useless at it. A name like Charlemagne. The bachelors said Matt was a brave man, drink was mooted. All the arrangements that had been settled on Dymphna were now transferred to Tilly. My brother drank port wine and got maudlin. Hence the staggers in the yard when he got home and the loud octavians. Never said a word at the breakfast. I had to hear it in the village. She has mousey hair and one of her eyes squints but instead of calling it a squint the family call it a "lazy eye." It is to be a quiet wedding. He hasn't asked me, he won't. Thinks I'm too much of a gawk with my gap teeth, and that I'd pass remarks and say, "I've eaten to my satisfaction and if I ate any more I'll go flippety-floppety," a thing he makes me say here to give him a rise in the wet evenings.

All he says is, "There'll be changes, Maisie, and it's for the best." Had the cheek to ask me to make an eiderdown for the bed, rose-colored satin. I'll probably do it, but it will only be a blind. He thinks I'm a softie. I'll be all pie to her at first, bringing her the tea in bed and asking her if she'd like her hair done with the curling tongs. We'll pick elder flowers to make jelly. She'll be in a shroud before the year is out. To think that she's all purty now, like a little peacock, preening herself. She won't even have the last rites. I've seen a photo of her. She sent it to him for under his pillow. I'll take a knife to her, or a hatchet. I've been in Our Lady's once before, it isn't that bad. Big teas on Sundays, and fags. I'll be out in a couple of years. He'll be so morose from being all alone, he'll welcome me back, with open arms. It's human nature. It stands to reason. The things I did for him, going to him in the dark, rubbing in that aul liniment, washing out at the rain barrel together, mother-naked, my bosoms slapping against him, often saw the stars fading and me bursting my sides with the things he said—"Dotey." Dotey no less. I might do for her out of doors. Lure her to the waterfall to look for eggs. There're swans up there and geese. He loves the big geese eggs. I'll get behind her when we're on that promontory and give her a shove. It's very slippy from the moss. I can just picture her going down, being swept away like a newspaper or an empty canister, yelling, then not yelling. I'll call the alarm. I'll shout for him. If they do smell a rat and tackle me I'll tell them that I could feel beads of moisture on my brother's poll without even touching it, I was that close to him. There's no other woman could say that, not her, not any woman. I'm all he has, I'm all he'll ever have. Roll on, nuptials. Daughter of death is she.

JOSEF ŠKVORECKÝ

TRANSLATED FROM THE CZECH BY KÁČA POLÁČKOVÁ-HENLEY

The Onset of My Literary Career

One evening Ulrych showed up on the terrace of our *pension*, where my blonde sister was soaking up the rays of the setting sun, and asked me, "Have you heard who's staying at the Miramare?"

"No, I haven't."

"Jim McKinley!"

"You're kidding!" I said, but it turned out he was right.

Less than two days later, he brought him over in person. Jim McKinley, alias Jiří Rychtr, looked a little like Hercule Poirot: he was slight, bald, and the tip of his nose bloomed fire-red. He sat down in an armchair in my room and his watery eyes flicked back and forth over the hotel furnishings.

"Mr. Rychtr wants us to help him. He doesn't feel well and he has to spend all his days in treatment," declared Ulrych eagerly. "And he needs to have a new novel finished by next Wednesday."

My breath caught in my throat. "Oh—well—" was the best I could do.

McKinley's fleeting glance settled on the glass front of the china cabinet. "Hmm," he said, "might I have a drink? The mud baths have dehydrated my mucous membranes."

I leaped toward the cabinet, poured a glass of Dad's Bonekamp liqueur, disguised as mineral water, and placed it in front of Jim.

"Hmm," said Jim McKinley, having moistened his mucous membranes. "I think you could do it for me. They aren't all that particular, and Mr. Ulrych says that you write the best Czech papers in all your school. You could see to the descriptions of the countryside, the depictions of the characters, and, say, the lyrical dialogues. I'll give you the plot outline, and we'll split fifty-fifty. I'll give it a quick look and put my name on it. Okay?"

I assured the Master that I would do just as he wished.

"The title is *The Rider from Sierra La Plata*. That's definite, because that's what they announced. The plot—" At that point, Jim fell silent. My blonde sister had walked into the room, and she rested a quizzical glance of her pale blue eyes on him. Just so you understand, my sister was a knockout. On account of her, and being jealous, our English prof attacked and beat up Dyntar, a senior who used to carry her leotard and her toe shoes to ballet class for her. The Reverend Father Meloun stared at her on the street so hard he fell down an open manhole and busted his rib.

Jim McKinley was in a similar frame of mind.

As a rule, I used to take careful note of such goings-on, because it occasionally generated an incidental income for me, but this time I never really noticed that in the next few days, Jim McKinley abandoned his treatment and instead started carrying my sister's tennis racquet. The reason I didn't notice was the fact that, along with Ulrych, I was devoting my time to literary creation.

First of all, I developed the scene depicting the appearance of the rider from Sierra La Plata, Bob Hopalong, against the blood-red horizon among the silhouettes of cactuses on the virgin prairie near the town of Cantaras City. He had muttonchop sideburns—which, incidentally, I boasted as well—and he wore an elegant western outfit: a broad-brimmed black sombrero trimmed in white; a black silk shirt with white seams and a black vest with white embellishments; black chaps with white fringes; and high-heeled boots with spurs of Mexican silver. Of course, his six-shot Colts hung confoundedly low in their black leather holsters trimmed with silver rivets.

Ulrych's specialty was the epic elements: he brought the fast-shooting Bob together with Jennifer, the rancher's daughter. The description of the raven-haired beauty was strikingly similar to that of Zorka Béhounková, national junior figure-skating champion, whose family had rooms in the neighboring *pension*, and who occasionally tolerated my bragging in her presence about one or another of my accomplishments. Like Zorka, Jennifer also had black, widely spaced eyes and a mole on her left cheek, and like her, she frequently peppered her conversation with the clever and delightful exclamation "Gee whillikers!"

When we had gotten to this point in our work, Jim McKinley paid us a surprise visit. He arrived cheery and freshly shaved, in a white tennis outfit and with a bouquet of carnations in his hand. While he waited for my sister to finish changing, he asked us amiably how far along we were. He listened absentmindedly to our report, declared that he was prepared to give us an advance, and passed each of us a fifty-crown note. My sister sailed out of her room in a white tennis skirt, and Jim McKinley leaped up to take her racquet.

Burning with the fever of creativity, we opened the window. Downstairs, Zorka Béhounková was waiting with an officer in red jodhpurs. I turned gloomy. When my sister came downstairs with Jim McKinley, the two couples introduced themselves and then set out toward the tennis courts.

Ulrych and I went back to work. Our first literary income charged us up, the view from the window brought me a malevolent inspiration, and we proceeded to outdo ourselves. Big Bill Haywood, cattle thief, painted from life after the model of the officer in the red jodhpurs, first spied on the rancher's daughter as she sunned herself on a rocky cliff in Horrible Canyon, in nothing but "the garb of Eve"; then he attacked her and finally carried her off. With true literary fervor, I paused for half a page to describe the charms of the girl's nude body. In the meantime, Ulrych had involved the Rider from Sierra La Plata in seventeen killings. Seven corpses bit the dust in the town saloon in Cantaras City, and ten more in the gorge behind Chichito Peak, where they made the mistake of attacking the fast-shooting Bob from behind.

Toward evening, we were tying it all together when my sister burst into the room, her cheeks flaming. I had considerable experience with her in this state, so I glanced out the window. The rays of the evening sun glinted off Jim McKinley's bald pate, but the red military jodhpurs glowed far more brightly. My sister reappeared in a chic turquoise cocktail dress, then vanished like the breeze. I looked out the window again. Receding into the dusking twilight was a blue cloud, flanked by two red blossoms. The larger one represented the red jodhpurs, the smaller was Jim's tonsure, its tint indicating that the author was extremely excited.

We returned to the fever of creativity and threw ourselves into our work without supper. This time we proceeded with the wild pursuit of Big Bill Haywood's gang in the nighttime landscape of the Rocky Mountains. Heading the posse was the boastful Fred Blowstone, sheriff of Cantaras City, dressed in pearl-gray trousers and a brown leather vest with a gold star. Beside him galloped Bob Hopalong, all in black, barely visible in the dark of night.

Ulrych recorded the last seven of the Rider's killings. They culminated, in an isolated cabin overlooking a rocky gulch, with a wild fracas in which Big Bill Haywood knocked out the boastful Sheriff Blowstone and tied him up, only to be beaten to a pulp and tossed into the gulch by the Rider from Sierra La Plata.

The conclusion of the book was up to me. In it, the pale moonlight glistened on the raven hair of Jennifer Rodriguez, safe in the black-clad arms of the sideburned Bob of La Plata.

It was midnight by the time we had the novel all tied up and had finished my father's Bonekamp. I heard rapid footsteps mounting the stairs, and then my sister dashed into the room. Her cheeks were more flushed than before, and she disappeared into her room without a word.

I opened the door a crack and spoke into the darkness: "What's up, sis?"

"Leave me alone!" came her voice from the darkness.

I turned back to Ulrych and tapped my forehead eloquently. Ulrych grinned, turned the Bonekamp bottle upside down and held it over his open mouth. When he was sure that not another drop would come out of it, he gathered the papers from the table and got ready to leave.

"I'll turn it in to him tomorrow," he said. "That should give him plenty of time to look it over. I don't expect he'll change a lot of our work."

Early the next day, the dragoon officer showed up and took my sister down to the mineral springs. He had a bandage on his nose with blood caked on it. In reply to my question about what happened, he said that he got hit by a golf ball.

I spent the morning bragging in the presence of Zorka Béhounková. She didn't seem to be in very good spirits; she wanted to know if the dragoon lieutenant had been at our place in the morning, and so I added to my usual boasts a remark that I had written a novel about her. That intrigued her. "What sort of novel?" she pressed me. "Will you let me read it!" "Not till it's published," I said quickly, realizing that it might not be prudent to disclose the whole ghostwriting interlude before the book came out, especially to a woman. "I'll let you read it as soon as it's published. It's easier to read in print. Of course, you appear in it as a rancher's daughter," I said, and Zorka was flattered. She promised to go to the beach with me that afternoon.

Around noon, Ulrych called my room. "Come on down to the railway station—it's urgent!"

So I hurried down to the railway station. In the restaurant sat Jim McKinley, nursing a double shot of potent plum brandy and looking nervous. The knuckles of his right hand were bandaged. He got his hand caught in a door, he said, but the novel was fine. "You did a great job, fellows, fifty-fifty still stands."

Then he asked me if I wouldn't deliver a letter to my sister. He said he had to leave in a hurry and didn't have time to say good-bye in person.

Still drunk with the atmosphere of literary greatness, I hurried down to the beach. My sister was there too, with an extremely hairy young man with a flattened nose. I gave her the letter; she read it, gave a contemptuous sniff and tossed it into a trashcan filled with crumpled paper bags. Later, on our way home, I realized that the hairy young man was in fact the dragoon officer. Without his jodhpurs he looked more like an ape man.

For the most part, it was a pleasant afternoon at the beach. Zorka, dressed in a white bathing suit, skipped around me and bounced a huge inflated rubber ball at me. I lay majestically on a towel, exulting in my literary prowess. I continued that evening in the outdoor movie theater; I even put my arm around Zorka's waist, and she left it there.

The outcome, however, was not so good. The novel was published within a week, but Jim McKinley had introduced several changes in the story that would have wiped me out in Zorka's eyes, so I had to pretend that the censors had banned the book. Naturally, Zorka didn't believe me. She pursed her lips scornfully and said, "I knew right away that you were just bragging!" She turned her back and left for the mud baths, where I'd heard they'd hired a new masseur who looked just like Robert Taylor.

And so all I had left to console myself with was the novel, *The Rider from Sierra La Plata*, published as the 723rd volume of the weekly Pocket Novel Series. I certainly expected that Jim McKinley would make some changes with his masterly hand, but his amendments didn't do much to improve the story. He transformed the raven-haired beauty Jennifer into a Nordic blonde with blue eyes, changed the mole on her left cheek to a coquettish dimple at the corner of her mouth. He seemed to have no objection to the exorbitant number of twenty-five corpses killed by the Rider of Sierra La Plata, whereas he totally devastated my closing scene, of which I was justifiably proud. In it, the fair Jennifer did not offer her raspberry lips to the Rider—McKinley had shaved off Bob's sideburns and given him a bald spot on the back of his head. Instead, she bent down to the dazed Sheriff Blowstone, the braggart, whose pearl-gray trousers McKinley had changed into blood-red ones.

So it is no wonder that the disappointed Bob finally rides off alone, among the silhouettes of the cactuses standing up against the blood-red evening sky, away from Cantaras City, away from the Circle M Ranch.

Jim McKinley sent one copy of the book, leather-bound, to my blonde sister. She was the wrong person to send it to, though. My sister never read Pocket Novels. She looked down her nose at trash. She subscribed only to Popular Romances.

GEORGE STAPLES

Gazelle

At the entrance to the stable Mustapha stopped, forked his hand over his hip, and stood surveying the yard. It was still early in the morning, and the iron gates were shut. Through the bars he could see a black motorcycle standing by the haystack, but besides a couple of hens pecking in the straw, there was no sign of life.

Situated at the end of a lane and separated from the neighbors by a rushing stream spanned by a narrow bridge, the stable seemed more distant from the house where Mustapha lived than the few hundred meters that separated them. The house, with its trim gardens and clipped hedges, intimidated him. The open stable yard was more like the country village where, until a month ago, he had lived all his life. For that reason alone he was glad to be coming to work there.

An orphan, Mustapha moved to Tangier to stay with his uncle when his sister married, for he had no other family in his village. For room and board he tended the garden and guarded the property when the old man was away. From the beginning he hated the atmosphere of the house. Weeding flower beds bored him, and at meals his uncle ate with a knife and fork and talked about Hadooj, a rich girl in his village whom the old man thought he should marry.

To escape the house Mustapha started taking walks in the neighborhood, and on one of these he discovered the stables. From the main road the barn was so well hidden that he would not have noticed it had he not heard a horse whinny as he passed. The lane that led to the place was thick with trees and bushes—you could see nothing until you reached the gate—but along one side of the exercise ring ran a footpath from which there was a view of the yard, the boxes, and the house of the Christian woman who seemed to be in charge. A large plane tree shaded the terrace in front of the house, and tall palms bordered the far side of the ring. In the middle was a green triangle where two horses, a bay and a chestnut, cropped at the grass, their eyes half closed, their noses almost touching. In particular, the chestnut, a light-boned mare, caught his eye, for she was the most beautiful animal he had ever seen.

Once he had discovered the stable, he came often to watch the woman work the horses in the ring. Soon he and the woman began to greet each other and, later, to converse. She said that her name was Basia and that she ran the stable for an Englishman who came only in the summer. From the start they got along, and one day, after she learned that he was not happy working in his uncle's garden, she told him she needed another groom and offered him the job.

Mustapha slipped his hand through the iron bars, slid back the bolt, and swung open the gate. Stepping into the yard, he paused to say *"Bismillah,"* for although he was expected, he was timid about entering strange places and would not do so without asking God's blessing. Halfway up the drive, a yellow dog appeared from around the back of the house, paused in mid-stride to sniff the air, then, catching his scent, snapped its head in his direction. As the dog glared at him, Mustapha waited, ready to reach for a stone or turn and run if he had to. Taking its cue from him, the dog stood motionless to wait for further developments.

Just then a door slammed and Mohamed, the head groom, appeared, fumbling with his belt as he rounded a corner of the barn. Mustapha had seen the black man often in the lane, but he had never been introduced. From across the yard he called a greeting, *"Salamu aleikum."*

The man's head jerked around, and his eyes narrowed. Then, when he recognized the boy, he scratched behind one ear and called back, *"Aleikum salam."*

As the dog slunk off, Mustapha crossed the yard, and the two shook hands.

"Basia is still asleep," said the man. His false teeth were chalk-white and clicked when he spoke. "You can start cleaning out the stalls. Do you know how?"

"Yes."

"Start over there," he said, indicating a line of boxes to his left. "Leave the mare in the first to me, and begin with the second."

The mare was the chestnut he had noticed before. He wondered why she was special, but not wanting to appear curious, he merely nodded and said, "Okay."

As the man turned to go, Mustapha went to the watering trough and drank from the short hose that was used to fill it up. The water swirled into the basin, through the drain, and down onto his shoes.

When Mohamed heard the splash, he turned and snapped, "Put the stopper in the drain next time. That way you won't get wet . . . and you won't waste the water."

It was nearly an hour before Basia appeared on the steps of her house. A short woman in her sixties, she had strong Slavic features and the trim figure of a much younger person.

"Mustapha, is that you?" she called, as she crossed the yard to the rail just above where he was standing. Her Arabic was stilted, and her dress, a faded red bathrobe stained with coffee, torn in several places, and much too big for her, contributed to the impression of a little girl in grown-up clothes.

"Good morning, Basia."

"Good morning." She continued to rub and blink her eyes, narrow slits of blue in a weathered face. "How long have you been here?"

"I came at eight."

"Have you met Mohamed?"

They both looked at the black man, who nodded.

"Good. What time is it?"

Mohamed interrupted the grooming of a bay gelding to look at his watch. "Ten."

Basia laughed. "No matter how I try, I can't wake up in the morning, Mustapha. My bed is so warm." Then she drew herself up, extended her hand, and added formally, "*Meerhaba*. Welcome to Basia's world."

"She wants to say '*Marhaba*,'" scoffed Mohamed as he corrected her pronunciation.

Ignoring him, Mustapha shook her hand and nodded. "Thank you, Basia."

The woman beamed. "I hope you will be as happy here as I am, Mustapha." With a sweep of her hand that took in the entire yard, she added, "This is my paradise, you know. I thank God for every day he gives me to live in it."

From the start Mustapha *was* happy in Basia's world, although as he had feared, he found Mohamed hard to work with. One day soon after his arrival he was watering the chestnut mare. He had been warned often that she was temperamental, so he took special care when he led her to the trough and attached her to the iron rail above it. Once she put back her ears when his arm rubbed her shoulder, but otherwise she behaved well. Pleased, he returned to muck out her stall and was just finishing when he heard Mohamed call his name. He leaned his pitchfork against the wall and went to the door. "What is it?"

"Come here."

Mustapha walked over to where the man stood scowling next to the mare.

"You are not in your village now. These are horses, not donkeys. When you tie them up, do it like this." He loosened the rope that attached the horse to the rail, and quickly refastened it with a different knot. "Next time remember."

As the rebuke was a just one, Mustapha accepted it, but he wondered how he was supposed to remember the new knot when the man had not shown him how to tie it.

With time there were more such incidents. When Mustapha put the wrong saddle on a horse, the man called him a jackass and said that from then on he would do all the saddling himself. At first he could not figure out why Mohamed was reluctant to teach him, but eventually it became clear to him that the black man saw him as a rival. And as he knew from the behavior of certain men in his village, the best way to put a rival in his place was to keep him in ignorance. Not wanting to trouble Basia with his problem, he consulted a woman who worked in his uncle's kitchen. Laughing, she suggested a powder to put in the black man's food which, she said, would make him more agreeable. But as he was never around when Mohamed's food was being prepared, he had to abandon the idea as impractical.

Basia, on the contrary, was very helpful. She knew that Mohamed was difficult, and she often intervened when he rebuked Mustapha unjustly. Patiently she taught Mustapha how to clean a hoof, brush out a mane, saddle and bridle a horse. With her he had a natural rapport, which surprised him, for although he had never known a Christian before, he had always heard that they were inscrutable. Although she seldom spoke about her past, he understood that she too had had a difficult life, first during the war with the Germans and Russians, later under the Polish communists, whom she had fled twenty years before. In choosing her new country she had had only two requirements: one, that it have a king; the other, a hot sun. Morocco was the nearest that satisfied both. Horses had always been her passion, and it had been easy enough to find work with them in Tangier.

As Mustapha's sympathy for Basia's world deepened, he began to delay as long as possible leaving at the end of the day. When bad weather came, he waited until the last cloud had left the sky. When it was fair, he found more chores to do. Basia noticed, and one day when he stayed a particularly long time, she asked him directly why he disliked going home.

"I'm not comfortable there," he began, but as usual when he had to explain his feelings, he faltered.

As he was cleaning a saddle at the time, it was easy for him to keep his back to her when she insisted, "Why?"

"I don't know."

"Do you get on with your uncle?"

He hesitated, not knowing how to answer. He did not quarrel with his uncle, because he was his father's brother, but he knew that was not what she meant by getting on. Still, he did not want to mention Hadooj.

"Does he treat you badly?"

"No."

"But you do not feel at home there."

"No."

"I see."

Did she? He doubted that she could see much when he had said so little, but he kept his thoughts to himself. As he continued to work, he noticed that she was scrutinizing him.

Finally after a time, she spoke again. "Tell me, Mustapha, how would you like to *live* in Basia's world?"

"Live?"

"To sleep as well as work here."

For a moment he was disconcerted. Then, as her words sank in, he began to understand. Basia was inviting him, a Moslem and a stranger, to share her home. He wondered that a Christian woman could have a heart so big. Suddenly he felt such joy that he clasped her hand in his and laid his cheek in her palm.

Embarrassed, she laughed. "The room next to the tack room would be perfect for you."

"Perfect," he echoed, for in his mind he saw himself already installed in the little room, with its crooked blue door and whitewashed walls.

"So you agree?"

"Oh, yes."

"What do you think your uncle will say?"

He thought and then began to smile. "He will run his fingers through his hair many times, and then because it did not come from him, he will say that he does not like the idea, but he will not oppose it."

She clasped his hand. "Good."

Then Mustapha frowned, for another thought had come to him. "I am more worried about Mohamed than my uncle."

"Why?"

"He will be jealous."

"No, no. He too will like the idea. It will mean that he will no longer have to work at night." There was some truth to what she said. Until then they had alternated staying at night when Basia was out, and Mohamed had always grumbled when it was his turn.

"Perhaps," he said. He was not completely convinced, but he wanted so badly for the plan to work that he refused to let his apprehension dampen his spirits.

As it turned out, both he and Basia had been too optimistic. His uncle and Mohamed opposed the move, essentially for the same reason. His uncle worried that the neighbors would think he had disowned a poor relation; eventually he relented, but only when Mustapha promised to continue to take his noon meal at his uncle's house. Mohamed gave his opinion the next day soon after he arrived for work. By then Mustapha was already installed in the little room. He gave Basia time to explain the new arrangement and then, as a gesture of goodwill, asked the other man to join him for a glass of tea during a break from their chores.

Mohamed accepted the tea but remained standing in the doorway. After a sip from the hot glass, he remarked, "Basia says that you will sleep here now."

"Yes."

"Alone?"

"Of course."

Mohamed shook his head. "A young man should not live alone. You have a family," he continued, gesturing in the direction of his uncle's house. "Why don't you live with them?"

Mustapha shrugged. He was puzzled and wary of Mohamed's sudden interest in his welfare. For a while they remained silent, each sipping his tea and staring at the floor.

Finally Mohamed lifted his eyes and spoke. "Is she paying you more money?"

"No."

Again Mohamed shook his head. "I thought not. You are stupid. You don't understand Christians. This woman wants a night watchman for nothing."

"Perhaps," he said, but he didn't believe it was so, and the suggestion angered him. "Anyway, why do you care?"

"I?"

"Yes."

"I don't care one way or the other. Only I don't like to see her take advantage of you."

Liar, he thought, but he said nothing.

Mohamed continued, "If she wants a night watchman, she should hire another man."

Finally Mustapha understood. He knew that Mohamed had a grown son who had been in trouble with the police and now was out of work. "Who?" he said. "Your son?"

Mohamed stared at him angrily, all the more resentful because the other had seen through his ploy.

Having made his point, Mustapha tried to soften the effect of his words by offering more tea, but the black man declined.

Although Mohamed's attitude did not improve in the weeks to come, Mustapha was so content otherwise that he paid him little attention. In fact, living at the stable suited him so well that soon he began to think of Basia's world as his own. The first one up, he unlocked the doors in the morning and greeted the horses as they thrust their heads out of the stalls. He watered and fed them and first heard them neigh. After lunch with his uncle he invariably returned before Mohamed did, and lay half awake on his cot, listening to the sounds of the stable—the munching of hay, the thud of a hoof, the occasional snort or sneeze. In the afternoon when Basia rode and he and Mohamed were left alone, he busied himself with chores that kept them apart. Often when the other man left, he loosed a couple of horses and stood watching in the twilight as they grazed on the patch of grass. In the evening he walked to the market in Dra Deb and bought what he needed to prepare a simple meal in his room. There he ate as he liked, Moroccan style with his hands, until there was nothing left but the bones, which he threw outside to Basia's dog.

His free time he spent getting to know the chestnut mare. When Mohamed had seen that Mustapha could work with her, he had left her to him. Her real name was a complicated French one, but Mustapha called her Gazelle. In the beginning she was hostile, but with time she came to tolerate him. Although she was still quick to flatten her ears if he startled her, her anger didn't last, and she often shook her head as if regretting her bad temper. In the evening he would linger in her box after feeding her. Standing near the door, he talked to her softly as she wolfed the grain and kicked out at the wall behind her. At first she resented his presence, shaking her head furiously, ears back, ready to attack should he attempt to come any closer. But eventually, as the sound of his voice began to calm her, her anger changed to curiosity, and if for any reason he went away before she had finished, she would leave her food and come to the door of the box, wondering where he had gone.

When they were alone, Mustapha observed her closely, marveling at the traces of silver and gold in her chestnut coat, the smooth curves of her nostrils, and the velvet planes of her cheeks. At such times she seemed to enjoy his admiration, for her eyes, so fierce when others were around, would soften and glow. He had heard that her English owner was afraid of her. He knew that Mohamed disliked her. And even Basia's love was qualified. But to him she was the jewel of Basia's world, all the more desirable for her flaws, for to his mind they made her exclusively his.

For a time he was able to hide his feelings, but one day it came out that Basia had noticed. He was holding the mare's bridle, as she was about to mount.

"She's your favorite, isn't she?" she asked, as she gathered the reins and accepted a leg up. When he made no reply, she went on. "I understand. She is very beautiful and very . . . special."

"You feel that too?"

"Well, sometimes," she answered, laughing, and he joined her, for he knew that she was alluding to the day she had tried to nuzzle the mare and suddenly found the lower part of her face locked in the horse's jaws. After stitches in both cheeks, she had never presumed to be affectionate again.

"But you do love her, don't you?" Mustapha went on.

"Of course I do, but there is a difference between my love and yours, and I think you love her . . . more." She finished lamely, for the distinction she had attempted was too subtle for her limited Arabic; and as she headed out on promenade, Mustapha was not sure that he understood what she had been trying to say.

One Monday Mustapha finished his chores early, for that night Basia had a lesson in classical Arabic at the cultural center, for which he had promised to help her prepare. In the late afternoon they took chairs out under the plane tree, and she opened her book to a story about a boy's visit to a zoo, with illustrations of the various animals he saw there. At their feet Basia's dog played with the stable cat and her litter of kittens as Mustapha tried to explain the word for "rat."

Basia was having trouble with her pronunciation. *"Fer?"*

"No, *far . . . ar.*"

"Are there rats in Moroccan zoos?"

He laughed. "Not in the cages . . . well, maybe sometimes. When the lions . . . *usud* . . . are asleep, the rats . . . *firan* . . . come out and eat their food."

"What do the lions . . . *usud* . . . eat?"

"Meat."

"Do *firan* eat meat too?"

"I think *firan* eat anything."

"What about—"

"Must you know the names of all these animals for tonight?" he interrupted.

"All of them."

"Difficult."

"At least I like animals. What if it were a story about a . . . space laboratory?"

"That would be easy. All the words would be in French."

She laughed. "When did you leave school, Mustapha?"

"Seven, maybe six years ago."

"Did you enjoy it?"

He shrugged. "It was a Koranic school. All we did was memorize the *suwar*."

"I would hate that."

"I wasn't unhappy when it ended."

"Why didn't you continue after the Koranic school?"

"There wasn't a higher school in our village. The nearest one was too far to travel to."

"It's a pity. You are quick. You could have learned."

He shrugged. "I could have. Now it's too late."

"No, it isn't. Look at me." Then she laughed. "Not that I learn very quickly."

"But I already know Arabic, and I don't care to know French."

"Then you could learn something else."

"What?"

"Anything. In fact, I have been thinking. You know I have been having trouble with the blacksmith."

He did indeed, especially as the trouble concerned Gazelle. The man could never shoe her without a struggle, and very often she had to be hobbled.

"He smokes kef, and his work is so slow," she went on. "What if you were to learn to shoe horses? Then you could replace him."

He looked at her, letting her words sink in. "Is there a school for shoeing horses?"

"No, but I might be able to arrange for you to go to Temara. If I can, would you agree to go?"

He hesitated. For the mare's sake he was tempted by her offer, but he hated the idea of leaving the stable, even for a short while. "Temara is a military base." In his mind he pictured officers in stiff gray jackets more rigid than his uncle's suit coats.

"Don't worry. You'll be a student, not a soldier. And you will learn quickly, so everyone will treat you well."

"Is it something you want very much?" he asked.

"Yes, for you."

"Then I will go, for you."

Since Basia had known the commandant at Temara for years, things were easy to arrange. Mustapha left a week later by train, the first he had ever traveled on, and to his surprise he enjoyed the trip. He shared a compartment with only one other passenger, a woman in a yellow djellaba who chewed bubble gum and listened to a Walkman until it put her to sleep.

Temara did not overwhelm him as he thought it might. When he saw the red earth, the royal palms, and the violet and purple bougainvillaea, it was merely as if the pretty pictures of the riding center he had seen in Basia's equestrian magazine had come to life. The taxi let him off at the entrance. From there he was escorted along a neat, graveled path near ivy-covered walls to the office of the commandant. After a short delay while his letter was examined by several clerks and finally the commandant himself, he was turned over to a noncommissioned officer and assigned to a barracks.

He got on well. At first the sergeants had wanted to treat him as a soldier, but when they understood his special status, they left him alone. The men followed suit. He worked hard and soon became the favorite of the teacher, a Frenchman. By the end of the second week Mustapha was allowed to cut a hoof, and soon afterward he shod his first horse.

Only a single incident marred his enjoyment of Temara. One day a soldier from the Rif, who was trying to strike up a friendship, invited him to see one of the stallions he tended cover a particularly fine mare. The breeding took place in a special area secluded from the stables by a line of cypresses. Mustapha, who until then had seen only the breeding of donkeys, was unprepared for the violence of the act. By the time the stallion dismounted, he was bathed in sweat. The soldier merely stroked his moustache and laughed, but the scene pressed on Mustapha's mind like a hot shoe on the bare sole of a hoof and repeated itself often in his dreams.

At the end of the month the commandant called him to his office and gave him a certificate stamped with a gold seal and signed by the Frenchman. To Mustapha it meant little, but he was glad to accept it, for he knew that it would please Basia.

He arrived back in Tangier on a Sunday evening after Mohamed had left for the day. Basia reacted to the certificate as Mustapha had expected she would. She took him by the shoulders, kissed him on both cheeks, and then stepped back and observed him with shining eyes.

"Now you are a *malim*," she said, with more pride in her voice than he would ever feel himself.

He saved his visit to Gazelle until they had drunk tea and Basia had retired for the night. He found the mare dozing, but the moment he whispered her name, her head came up, and her eyes blazed. "Gazelle," he repeated, as she came to the door. He stood facing her and lifted a hand to her neck. Her muscles tightened, and her ears went back, but she did not move away. Gently he caressed her shoulder until he felt the tension leave her body. Then, as he slid his hand back up her neck, she lowered her head until her mane fell on his shoulder.

It was raining hard in the morning, but Mustapha rose early and began his chores as usual. Mohamed was late, and by the time Mustapha heard his motorcycle coming up the lane, he had finished two horses. He waited until Mohamed had dismounted and taken off his helmet before greeting him.

"*Salamu aleikum.*"

"*Aleikum salam.*"

The greeting was a mere formality, and the black man moved away even before Mustapha had time to ask about his family. During the rest of the morning they kept out of each other's way.

In the afternoon Mustapha went to the tack room, where he cleaned saddles until he heard the motorcycle return. While Mohamed lunged the horses that Basia had been unable to ride in the morning, Mustapha mucked out their stalls and changed their water. At four-thirty he prepared tea and when it was ready called the other man to come. Mohamed took his time but finally joined him in his little room.

"So you're back," he said, taking the glass Mustapha offered him.

"I'm back."

"You saw the *cazerne* at Temara."

"I saw it."

"And you learned a trade."

Mustapha nodded, uncomfortable because of the resentment he sensed in the other's tone.

"And now you will replace the old *malim*."

"It was Basia's idea."

"Good," he said, smiling. "First she got a free watchman; now she has a free blacksmith."

Mustapha felt his neck begin to burn, but he said nothing.

They drank their tea in silence until finally Mohamed remarked, "The old *malim* has a family."

"Basia does not like his work."

"It was good enough before."

"He will find other work."

"Perhaps."

Mustapha could control himself no longer. "Is he your father or what?"

Pleased to have gotten this reaction, Mohamed smiled. In the dimly lit room his teeth were especially white. "No, but he is my friend."

"Look. Temara was Basia's idea. She wanted it, not I."

"Yes."

"Yes, what? I say your friend will find other work. That's all."

"If you say so, *malim*."

"I say so," said Mustapha, putting down his glass with such force that the noise rang through the room.

For the rest of the afternoon Mustapha was in a bad mood. He regretted that he had allowed Mohamed to unnerve him, and determined to avoid him until he had regained his usual detachment. Tomorrow, his day off, he would spend away from the stable and not return until Mohamed had left. By the day after, things should be better.

That night he went to Gazelle earlier than usual. Whispering her name as he entered her box, he let one hand move across her chest, while with the other he caressed her flank. Her muscles rippled, but her ears remained forward. His hand moved back, and he caressed her rump. Never before had he been able to do so, and the new intimacy thrilled him. For a while he remained at her side, stroking her chest and back, but eventually he returned to her head. With his fingers laced in her mane and his cheek pressed to her neck, he closed his eyes. Her warmth spread across his shoulders and flowed down his spine. "Gazelle," he murmured, oblivious of all except the presence of the beautiful mare.

In the morning he rose early and went directly to his uncle's house. Until lunchtime he helped the gardener, and when his uncle came home they sat down to eat. As there was nothing to do in the afternoon, he decided to waste it in a movie theater. He walked down the lane from his uncle's house to the bus stop; while he was waiting for the bus, Mohamed's motorcycle came up rue Vasco de Gama, passed him at the corner, and stopped under a tree opposite the house. At first Mustapha was perplexed, but then he remembered that Mohamed had been trying to persuade the *soussi* who lived there to give his son a job, and he thought no more about it.

In town he got off the bus and went along rue des Vignes until he came to a wall plastered with posters of current films. There he found a dozen young men discussing the pictures in voices loud enough to overhear, but he paid them no attention. He did not have any trouble making up his mind, for all the posters but one depicted scenes from films of violence. His choice showed two shadowy figures walking hand in hand across a field lit by a brilliant moon.

The film intrigued him. It was about a young couple who danced on ice. In the beginning the girl seemed to be the better skater, but with hard practice the boy overtook her. Mustapha enjoyed the skating, especially the practice sessions when there was nobody watching. When the boy lifted the girl, it looked as if she might disappear into the light above them. Off the ice they fought constantly, and the girl suffered, probably, Mustapha decided, because she was jealous of the boy's success; but finally, after a competition they lost, she changed and became so demonstrably affectionate that it was clear she had fallen in love. In the lobby he looked again at the poster and realized the field was actually an ice rink, and the full moon, a spotlight; but for all it mattered, it might have been a moonlit field.

It was still light when he came out of the theater, so he decided to kill time by walking back to the stable. From the center of town he went down boulevard de Paris to Dra Deb. Near the fruit market he left the main road and took a shortcut across a eucalyptus grove. Past a clearing where village boys played soccer, he chose a path that skirted the Oued Yahoodi and farther on came to a place where rocks had been pushed together to make a footbridge over the shallow river. He thanked God that he had arrived while it was still daylight, for he knew this was a well-known haunt of Aicha Kandisha, the she-devil who roamed at night and bewitched men who could not resist her power.

Mohamed had closed the gates after him when he left, so that when Mustapha arrived at the stable and peered through the bars, he had the same view he had had the day he first came to Basia's world. There was no motorcycle by the haystack, but as he walked into the yard, Basia's dog appeared and sniffed the air as she had done then. This time Mustapha did not have to wait. He spoke to her, and she trotted up to him, her tail wagging, ready to lick his hand if he would allow her. He crossed the yard with the dog at his heels and was about to enter his room when he heard Basia call his name. He went to her door and paused.

She stood just inside, wearing her red bathrobe, her hands folded in front of her. "Good evening, Mustapha."

"Good evening, Basia."

"Come in," she said, and led the way into her sitting room.

He hesitated, for he had never before gone beyond the threshold, but as she turned and beckoned to him, he followed.

One half of the small rectangular room contained a round table and three banquettes, enclosed by a red and green *haiti* which hung from the walls. The other was furnished with two armchairs and a bookcase, on top of which were several framed photographs of Basia's family and a collection of miniature horses in ceramic, wood, and glass. The floor was covered with overlapping Moroccan carpets.

Basia led him to one of the armchairs and told him to sit. She sat in the other. "Do you like my room?"

"Yes."

"It contains a little from your country and a little from mine. The chairs are from Poland. They are all that I brought with me. My parents used to sit in them in front of the fire in their house in the country." She paused and drew her bathrobe up around her neck. "Have I ever shown you a photograph of my parents?"

"No."

She got up and took from the shelf a silver-framed wedding portrait. "Here," she said, handing it to him.

The photograph showed a young couple in front of a mantelpiece with baskets of flowers on either side. The bride wore a long white dress; the groom, a dark uniform with gold braid and many medals on the jacket. The couple stared fixedly into one another's eyes.

Their expression made Mustapha uneasy, but he said, "Beautiful," as he handed it back.

After replacing it on the shelf, Basia took her seat again and put her hands in her lap. When she began to talk, Mustapha noticed that her fingers were playing with one end of the cord of her bathrobe.

"Dear Mustapha," she said, "have you never thought of getting married yourself?"

Mustapha, who had been smiling, felt his face muscles stiffen. "Never."

"You should, you know. You are a very young man. It is only right that you marry one day."

Suddenly he felt as if he were talking to a stranger. The Basia he knew had never married and had never, as far as he knew, wanted to marry. Puzzled, he let her go on.

"You saw my parents. They married young, and they were very happy."

And you, he wanted to say, *are you not happy?* but again he waited for her to continue.

"I realize that you are content in Basia's world. You like your work and . . . the horses."

He knew that she had been about to say Gazelle but had changed her mind when she saw his face redden.

"But," she continued, "in the end it is not good for a young man to be alone so much of the time."

Watching her fingers as they twisted the cord, he could contain himself no longer. "What makes you say all this?"

She sighed, and her discomfort was evident in her eyes. "Today your uncle came to see me."

"My uncle?"

"He came after lunch."

The motorcycle under the tree. So Mohamed had not been to see the *soussi* after all. "And?"

Her words had been rehearsed, and there was a tremor in her voice as she spoke.

"I am sure he is thinking of your welfare. He is convinced that it is time for you to take a wife. In fact, he has a girl in mind for you, a girl from your own village."

Hadooj. Fat and so ugly that no man would look at her, but rich enough so that no marriage payment would be required, and with a father who would give him a job tomorrow just for taking her off his hands. He had to speak. No matter what, she must know what he felt. "Oh, Basia, you know I can't . . ." he began, but she raised her eyes and looked at him, and instantly he realized that words were pointless, for it was clear from her expression that she already knew what he would say, perhaps had even tried his very words, but had been powerless to influence his uncle. Nevertheless, in desperation he went on: "Can't you speak with him? Can't you make him see?" Her silence confirmed what he already knew. How could he expect her to make the old man see that his nephew was better off as a groom in Basia's world than married to the daughter of the richest man in his village? As he looked into her eyes, so full of anguish, he saw the extent of her frustration and realized how useless it was to continue. He was silent until the words that had been on his lips went out of his mind, and then he said simply, "When?"

By her tears he saw that she was grateful. "Tomorrow he will take you to your village. Together you will see the girl's father."

He nodded and rose to go, but she stopped him with a hand on his arm. "Mustapha."

"What is it?"

From her shelf she took a ceramic horse, one of the most beautiful of her collection. Its coat was golden; its eyes, soft as a dove's. "Here," she said, and pressed it into his hand.

As his fingers closed over the ceramic figure, he smiled at her, then turned and left.

In his room he placed the horse on the windowsill, sat on the edge of his cot, and tried to think. At first his mind was a jumble of thoughts that would not come into order. But he considered for a long time, and eventually only two questions remained. Had it been Mohamed's idea to go to his uncle, or had Basia sent him? He tried but could come to no conclusion. At first he felt frustrated, but finally he realized the answer didn't matter. What did matter was that the image fixed in his mind was neither his uncle's nor Basia's, but Mohamed's. In his vision the black man's face persisted, its eyes bright and steely, its teeth chalky white. He knew he must drive that face from his mind. He thought some more, and at last he figured out how.

Quickly he rose from his cot and slipped out of the room. Basia's house was now dark, but even so he treaded softly so as not to wake her. At the end of the lane he cut down to the rue Vasco de Gama and followed the road to Dra Deb. It was dark, but the wind was still fresh, and high in the eucalyptus trees it tugged at the leaves and made the branches moan. On a narrow street near the public oven he soon found the house he was looking for, the house of a *fqi* renowned for his magic. Many boys he had cured of love for a girl; many men, of slavery to a wife. Mustapha knocked, and the man's woman appeared. At first she would not let him in, but when he showed her a handful of money, she opened the door. He found the *fqi* himself to be very attentive. He listened carefully to Mustapha's story and nodded often. It did not take him long to find a solution. As Mohamed was black, he said, it would take more black to defeat him. Then he gave his advice. When Mustapha heard it, he trembled, but he would not back down now. He had expected that the remedy would be drastic, and he was determined to do what had to be done.

Back at the stable he went straight to the empty box where Basia's female ratter slept with her litter of kittens, two of them black. Since the *fqi* had not specified a grown cat, he would use one of them. He found them sleeping in a pile of straw. To calm her, he stroked the mother's head. Then he picked up one of the black kittens and wrung its neck. Out in the back near the ring he removed the skin and flung it into a gully. The fire he prepared carefully. When it was ready, he roasted the carcass until the flesh was charred. Then slowly he ate it, thoroughly chewing each morsel before swallowing, as the *fqi* had directed.

In his room Mustapha lay down and savored his victory. The magic would work slowly, and before Mohamed began to feel its effect, Mustapha would be far away. One day he would return to see what it had done. Now he must think of his journey.

In the Rif mountains, not far from Chaouen, was a village where his father used to buy grain. A few years before, there had been an epidemic and the village had been quarantined. Since then, it was said, nobody, not even the gendarmes, ever entered it.

He waited until after midnight, when he knew that the neighbors would be asleep. In town he would have to choose his route carefully, but once in the country he would have no fear of detection. In the barn he got a halter and lead, and took them to Gazelle's box. When he opened the door, he found her standing, ears pricked, as if waiting for him. He fastened the strap of the halter and allowed his fingertips to play across the warm silky plane of her cheek. Then he led her out into the darkened yard. Beyond the gates the full moon rose above the cypresses at the end of the lane, and there were shadows everywhere, but tonight he had no fear of devils. As he passed his uncle's house, he saw that the windows were dark. Out in the lane the moon beckoned, and he recalled a proverb that the elders of his village often quoted. "If the full moon loves you, what does it matter if your stars decline?" His heart brimming, he walked into the night with Gazelle.

MELANIE RAE THON

Sisters

People still think my sister killed a man. At parties, women bend their heads together, nodding in my direction. Lies seem more true when they're whispered. Men I barely know watch me all night, searching for the flush of Grace's fever in my cheeks. Terrified and awed by the promise of our common blood, they almost love me. But fear is a beguiler, a mimic of lust. When one grows bold enough to ask to drive me home, he is inevitably disappointed. I can satisfy neither curiosity nor desire. The story of the night Grace stabbed a man in Boston's Combat Zone has power only if I don't tell it, and my sister's summer storms run cool in me, the drizzle of winter rain.

Even among our relatives, Grace inspires lies. My aunt Dee has claimed for years that she saw Grace spit in our father's grave the day he was buried. This is utterly false, although it is true that Gracie did not cry at the funeral.

My tears were few but real, despite Grace's accusation that I blinked until my eyes watered. Grace missed the actual funeral, and I didn't expect her at the burial either, but then she appeared, skinnier than I had ever seen her, wearing a black leather miniskirt and black fishnet stockings, a pillbox hat with mesh that fell over her eyes that she must have dug up in some ratty secondhand shop, a sleeveless black T-shirt, and no bra. Gracie, the bereaved in mourning clothes.

While the minister did his "ashes to ashes" speech, I felt Gracie fidgeting behind me; she kept stooping and I heard her bad knee crack. The familiar pop of my sister's bones gave me an odd sense of comfort. I imagined her twisting a handkerchief, dropping it again and again in silent distress. But when the preacher had had his say, I turned and saw Grace's true purpose: she had gathered up a whole fistful of dandelions, and now she clutched them as if she expected them to writhe away.

Mom glanced over her shoulder and shot Gracie a smile from the half of her face that still worked. "Glad you could make it, Grace," she said, and didn't wait for an answer.

"My sympathies to you too, Mother," Grace sputtered, close to my ear.

Mom threw a white rose into the open grave, and it slapped the box like a small, limp body. Uncle Eddie rolled Gran's wheelchair up to the edge and she tossed a handful of purple pansies from her own garden. But they fell short and Uncle Eddie had to get down on his hands and knees to gather them up and pitch them down the hole. His sluggishness irritated my grandmother; she would have kicked him if she'd had the strength. Her gnarled hands beat against fleshless thighs and her mouth was pulled tight, a wrinkled red *oh* of complete disgust. She was eighty-three, crippled by arthritis, with bones so porous they might wash away in a hard rain, but her mind was mercifully—or cruelly—as sharp as it had ever been. "I don't waste blood on my legs," she once said to me. "Who needs to walk at my age? Certainly not a woman with a forty-two-year-old son who never married. What good is such a boy if he can't take an old woman where she wants to go?" She said this right in front of Uncle Eddie; but he didn't protest, he only stared at his thick white toes wiggling in his sandals.

Aunt Dee, Daddy's older sister, cast a dozen lilies, one by one. "Show-off," Gracie hissed behind me. "I bet she's pissed he kicked in summer—can't wear your mink in July." But Aunt Dee didn't appear to be suffering without her furs. She had a new rock on her finger, a twenty-fifth anniversary present from my absent uncle Philip. "I guess Phil didn't want to mingle with the commoners," Grace said. "There's nothing worse than showing up at the wrong man's funeral." Aunt Dee's diamond caught a ray of sunlight and shot sparks of yellow fire.

The preacher was about to heave the first clod of dirt when Gracie stepped forward and flicked her dandelions into the shallow pit. I hope I was the only one near enough to hear her mutter, "Something sweet to smell, Daddy."

In the limousine, I sat between Grace and my mother. We hadn't made it to the bottom of the hill before Gracie dug a vial of white powder out of her purse. The top had a miniature spoon on a hinge. She scooped out the pale dust and held it to one nostril and then the other, snorting hard. Mom sobbed. "Don't you have any respect?" she said.

"Daddy doesn't care."

"I do."

"I'm grief-stricken, Mother, nearly paralyzed with pain. Let me comfort myself as I choose."

I put my arm around my mother. There was no sense in trying to keep Grace from doing or saying what she pleased, so I didn't try. But I thought she could have picked her words more carefully, and it made me sad to look at my mother's useless right arm, curled against her like a shrunken wing. I would have kissed her, but I was on the wrong side; I couldn't bear to press my lips against the sagging skin of her numb cheek.

"It's not fair," Mom said. "He's been so good."

"Two years on the wagon doesn't make up for twenty years in the gutter."

"Your father wasn't a bum."

"No, that's true," Grace said, her voice sharp as the flickering edge of a shattered windowpane. "No, he was no street slime, no sewer rat. He drank at home where we could all enjoy his fine company."

Mom said, "He's been an angel. You don't know."

"Can't live without a liver," Grace said, cold and exact.

I thought Grace was too hard on our father—even though he did force her to marry that pockmarked, sullen boy when she was only sixteen; even though he did forbid her to ever enter his house again after the night she made off with Mother's amethyst earrings and a strand of pearls we'd been told were real. They weren't, but they had belonged to Mother's mother, that much was true. Mom scoured Boston's pawnshops and paid fifty dollars for the string of beads, twice what they were worth. The earrings were forever lost.

"People shouldn't be so attached to things," Gracie said when I delivered the message that she was not to set foot in our parents' house again.

"People shouldn't steal," I said. "People should honor their father and mother."

"Oh, *please*," said Grace.

My sister has always lived by her own code; she even takes pride in her sense of honor. She would never read your mail. She would not use your last scoop of coffee or wear your clothes without asking. She would take punishment before she would name another as the guilty party. I know this because she bent over Daddy's knee for my whipping after I had set fire to the living room drapes and was too young and cowardly to confess.

The trouble between Grace and my father actually began long before she stole the pearls. Even as a child Grace seemed to delight in tormenting Dad, although she was always the one to suffer in the end. I do not know whether she considered annoyance an art or if she fell into her aggravating ways by accident. I do know she was fearless in the face of Dad's fury, and this gave her a strange power. His knuckles white with rage, his face red enough to pop, our 195-pound father would threaten to drive Grace's head through the wall if she uttered another word. Although she might have nothing left to say, my frail sister would never fail to speak that last word. And yet she lived. I considered this a miracle and regarded Grace with secret reverence.

Still, there were battles in which she spat out dangerous words and did not win. I remember the April day when Gracie was caught necking with Gordon Haddow, our seventeen-year-old neighbor. Gordon had slanted eyes and big feet that dragged when he walked as if they were a burden, too heavy for his legs. He mumbled three-word sentences and never went to school, but Grace didn't mind and had been his best friend since she was five and Gordon let her watch him pee.

The circumstances of their romantic explorations were peculiar. At the border of the Haddows' yard where juniper bushes grew thick against the high fence, Gordon and Grace dug a cave in the ground and crawled inside for an afternoon of delight. Hours later, when Mrs. Haddow found them and pulled them out of the hole, they both giggled and rolled on the grass, feeble from lack of oxygen.

Of course Grace was blamed, even though she was still a month shy of thirteen. Everyone understood that poor Gordon didn't know any better but that Grace certainly should have.

At dinner Mom was silent and Dad reminded my sister that she wasn't too old to have her pants pulled down and her fanny thrashed. "You could have died," he said.

Grace, cool and womanly even at twelve, asked: "What bothers you more, Daddy? That I could have died or that I spent all day smooching with Gordon Haddow?"

Dad stuttered. A vision of the hulking, clumsy boy wavered in front of him. He said, "One more word out of you . . ."

"You don't have such great taste yourself, Daddy."

Dad's ears blazed and I waited for steam.

Mom said, "What the hell is that supposed to mean?"

"Not you, Mom, I don't mean you. I mean that cow-eyed bimbo with the huge tits. What do you call her? Your *receptionist?*"

"She does a good job," Mom said.

Dad's right hand was raised, as if he'd reached for his glass of milk and turned to stone.

Grace stared at Mother. "Don't you know?" she said.

For thirty seconds no one moved or spoke. My father's hand still hung in the air and a ridiculous smirk twisted his mouth. Then my mother exploded, snatching plates half loaded with food off the table. She tossed them in the sink without scraping them, ran water, and squirted soap until peas and globs of mashed potatoes floated to the scummy surface. "Of course I know," she said at last, and my father's hand crashed against the table.

Grace was sixteen when she obeyed my father for the last time. She was pregnant, and my parents insisted on the decency of ritual. I loathed my brother-in-law, that scarred, stubby boy who always had the sand of sleep at the corners of his eyes. At thirteen, I was a heartless judge. But now I know something good came of this brief union, a daughter who makes me believe that Grace and I are not entirely alone in the world. No, somewhere there is a girl, the child of Grace's childhood. We do not even know her name, such are the rules that govern adoption, but I would recognize her anywhere. Like Grace, she has dimples in her knees instead of her cheeks, wispy hair that burns with gold fires at the end of summer. She never stands straight, and her mother, not the real one, constantly reminds her to stop slouching and to take her hands off her hips, until Little Grace (I call her that) sighs in exasperation and says "Oh, please" as she stomps out of the room, hands plunged deep in pockets, back defiantly curved.

My friends think I must resent my sister for all the trouble she's caused me. Even Claudia Reinhart, who is my oldest friend and claims to understand what's best for me, thinks I should move and get an unlisted number so Gracie can't call me in the middle of the night to rescue her from the police station in Tewksbury or some phone booth that she thinks is about ten miles south of Haverhill.

Claudia says she wants to spare me from the stress and expense of midnight missions with bail money. Perhaps her concern for me is genuine, but Claudia's quarrel with Grace is thirteen years old and goes back to the time Grace referred to her as "that pudgy midget."

Claudia is forever remaking herself, dyeing her hair or waxing her legs, plucking her brows or sanding her cheeks with pumice stones, eating nothing but grapefruit one week and nothing but tuna the next.

And Claudia is forever falling in love "for the first time." She says,

"I mean it, this is the first time I've *really* been in love." Then she disappears from my life, only to emerge two weeks later, eating chocolate and swearing she will never, never trust another man as long as she lives.

She maintains that Grace is responsible for destroying my "one chance for happiness with a man." Richard Egerton and I had finally moved in together after our senior year at Northeastern. This was three years after Grace stabbed a man in the Zone, and I hadn't seen her for fourteen months. Some friends of hers thought she'd gone out to San Francisco. I felt giddy, lightened by the knowledge of distance between us.

Richard and I had spent two years tossing in each other's arms without giving in to temptation. He had some archaic beliefs about sex sapping your strength and killing off brain cells. When things got dangerous, he rolled over on his belly and pounded the sheets with his fists.

I was tolerant. I let him keep his gaunt, pale body chaste. I watched him sweat over history papers instead of me. I believed in his future and his need to preserve his precious energy during exams. But on graduation day, with Richard safely accepted at Suffolk Law School, I gave him an ultimatum and we moved into a tiny two-room apartment in Cambridge, where I discovered that in some cases deprivation is preferable to fulfillment.

My degree was in psychology, but I took a job with a law firm downtown, pretending I had plans to go to law school. I wanted to justify my years of frustration with Richard; I wanted the two of us to fit together. Bigelow and Dropkin specialized in malpractice. My task was to dig through files for cases similar to the ones they were handling; I filtered out the best examples and arranged them in order of ascending importance to establish the power of precedent. This saved Bigelow and Dropkin from spending too much time toying with capricious juries; they did most of their work over lunch and martinis, using my research to bargain with the defendants' lawyers. I was good at this job because it all made so little difference to me.

The summer had almost ended when Gracie knocked at our door, blown in by a wind from the west, golden and glowing, her hair hennaed a brilliant red, her body slim and firm, not yet sunken in the chest or knobby at the joints.

I felt fat and white standing beside her, my hair colorless as stagnant water, my thighs loose with flesh. She was a goddess, my dark-eyed sister; the vast difference was not lost on Richard.

I could easily claim Grace seduced him, led him astray, transfixed him with her false beauty, but that would be a lie. I saw him follow her around the apartment, a dog on her heels. I saw him reach out and touch her hair, so lightly she could not feel his fingertips.

I didn't have to catch them together or anything so crude. I had only to come home one evening and find the apartment ransacked and Richard sitting in the middle of the floor, weeping into his hands. She had taken eighty-five dollars, two pounds of sugar, and Richard's diamond cuff links, a graduation gift from his mother. The mess was just for effect.

Telling Richard I would buy him another, identical pair of cuff links only made his wailing worse: they would not be *the* pair his mother had given him.

Claudia uses this as an example of one of the many ways Grace has tried to ruin my life. Of course I left a few details out of the version of the story I told my friend. She imagines Gracie stole the cuff links simply because they were the most valuable item in the apartment, and she could hock them for a hundred and score a gram of coke. Only I know Gracie's revenge was tribal, calculated to punish Richard for his unfaithfulness to me. Only I know this was Grace's way of saving me from years of misery with the wrong man.

I tell Claudia, "She's my sister," as if this explained everything.

Most times, Grace finds me when she wants company, but there was one occasion, one hot October in the flash of Indian summer, when I tracked her to a dive off Washington Street, a place called, cryptically, The End. On the sign, neon flashed: GIRLS GIRLS GIRLS. I would have let it lie when I heard what Grace was doing, but Mom had just had her first stroke, and I felt honor-bound to find my sister.

I cruised in at five; the joint was empty but already stale with smoke and thick with windowless gloom. I sat down at the bar and the tender said, "Let's see some ID, little lady." I was nineteen.

"I'm looking for my sister," I said.

"Aren't we all."

I pulled out a picture of Grace, an old one, when her tightly permed hair emphasized the unusual length of her skinny neck. The bartender studied it. He was thick in the chest and his head seemed to sink into his burly shoulders; his hair was shaved flat on top. He reminded me of an overdeveloped Marine. "No way," he said, chuckling.

"It's an old picture," I told him, "look again."

He shook his head. "That girl's an old maid somewhere in Ohio by now."

"I heard she was here."

"Trust me."

I asked him when the show started and thanked him for his help. "Bring some ID," he yelled as I swung through the door.

That night, I sat through two sets: through Golden Glory, a peroxide blonde decked out in yellow feathers and a sequined G-string. She twirled up and down the runway, feathers floating around her. She fell to her knees and then her back, body twitching, feathers fluttering like the wings of a wounded bird, a canary made hideous by its size. The final thrill came when she flung the G-string over her head and revealed a bleached triangle of frizzy curls. Something about pale hair in unexpected places drives men to hoot and growl. But their boredom surprised me; the sounds seemed gratuitous, and they didn't care when the yellow girl vanished.

A fleshy redhead dressed as a cowgirl peeled away a ruffled skirt and popped her corset. She pranced, cavorting in nothing but her garter, stockings, boots and spurs. The strip was fast, the tease nonexistent.

The entrance of the next girl—Domina—provoked a few lazy wolf-whistles. She strutted. She scowled. She spun on her three-inch spike heels. Her eyes were lined in black, made up to look long and slanted beneath the thick bangs of her dark wig. She wore a studded cat collar, a black leather bra with rhinestone nipples, leather shorts, and gloves that went past her elbows. Her whip cracked the air, and a man near the runway pretended he wanted to climb up and let her step on his head with those spiked boots. She sneered and would have been glad to accommodate him, I thought.

She stalked through a whole tune without shedding a stitch, but when the second song crackled through the speakers, men slapped the bar with their palms and chanted. The gloves rolled off first and a silky silver G-string fell last. As the girl scurried between the curtains to the final beats of the music, she'd lost the boldness of Domina and was just bare-assed Grace. Even the men must have sensed the fraud: in the long silent seconds before the next throb of drums, they sat still and numb, sipping their drinks, polite as church boys.

I made my way backstage fast enough to hear a man's low voice say, "She better develop some love for her work."

Gracie and Golden Glory were passing a joint between them when

I opened the dressing room door. "What the fuck?" the blonde said.

Gracie pulled the black wig off her head and ran her fingers through her flattened hair. It was cropped short and frosted. She had a red kimono wrapped around her, but it gaped open and I could see her naked breasts and white belly. "Shit," she said. "You shouldn't have come here."

"You know this baby face?" said the yellow woman.

"My sister."

"Looking for a job, baby sister?" The blonde gagged when she said it, choking on the weed.

"Get out of here," Gracie said. She glared at me, but I didn't budge. I had a mission; I could afford to be stubborn. "You heard me," she said, "move your ass." My feet were stuck to the floor, set in concrete, dragging me to the bottom of the river.

"Mind the lady," Blondie said, "before we get some *assistance*."

"I mean you, Marlene," Grace said, finally, looking at the peroxide princess. "Give us some space."

The blonde uncrossed her legs and snorted. "Yeah," she said, "glad to oblige, but the reefer's mine." She snatched the roach out of Grace's mouth. "Meet you on the funway," she said, brushing past me.

"Bitch," Grace muttered.

"Mom's sick," I said. I thought I'd spare us both the small talk.

"What else is new?"

"No, not like that—for real this time. You better see her." I told her about the stroke. If she was concerned, she didn't say so, and she didn't ask for many particulars. But she had one cigarette burning in the ashtray, one going on the edge of the counter, and another in her mouth by the time I was done with my story.

"I've got one more set," she said at last.

"More whips?"

"No, a little-girl routine, pigtails and all, Mary, Mary, quite contrary. Cheap joint. They pass me off as a fresh girl."

"Tomorrow?" I said.

"Sure," she said, "tomorrow."

But Gracie never made it to the hospital, because that was the night she put a paring knife through a man's hand and got sent to the women's prison in Framingham.

Our father wouldn't bail her out, and I had to go around to all our friends, scraping dollars and dimes, which is how the rumor got started that Grace killed a man.

It took me six days to get the money together; Grace was getting a bad rap—she'd severed a tendon in the man's hand and paralyzed two of his fingers. He had a story that she'd held the blade to his throat and threatened to slit him cheek to cheek before she coolly plunged the knife into his hand.

Grace denied this version of the story and claimed it was strictly an act of passion. Dudes could buy a dancer a drink for six bucks, and this guy, Mickey Moss, forty-five, married, father of four, was buying Grace her third gin-and-tonic when he started to think that eighteen dollars should be getting him more than conversation, especially since Gracie's half of the conversation consisted mainly of "yes" and "no," and came down heavily on the "no" side. She slapped his right hand away from her knee, knocked it away from her butt, told him flat-out she didn't mess with customers, but he wouldn't believe her. That's when he clutched her tit and wouldn't let go, and that's when she grabbed the paring knife that Al the bartender had left behind after he cut extra lime for her gin-and-tonic. She brought it down on the man's left hand and he pinched her breast so hard with his right that he made five fingerprints, deep purple bruises that were photographed in leering color and used as evidence.

Even so, the jury didn't have much regard for the virtue of a dancer called Domina who wore a cat collar and a leather bra. Her lawyer tried to make the ten women on the jury sympathize with her outrage, to remember being fondled at a party or tweaked at work. But the women resented the comparison; they had nothing in common with a trashy stripper from the Zone. The lawyer's tactics turned the women against Grace in the end. She never did have half a chance with the two men, who sat through the trial with their arms crossed over their chests, their hands tucked safely under their biceps.

Gracie got two years and served six months. The first time I saw her in prison she said, "Thank God Mom had her stroke *before* this happened. Otherwise she'd blame it on me." I nodded and didn't tell her that Mom blamed her anyway, holding Grace responsible for all the years she'd spent fretting over her wayward daughter.

I was the only one in the family to visit Grace at Framingham. I tried to make excuses for the others, but Grace covered her ears. We sat together in a bare room. A guard stood five feet away, hearing everything, responding to nothing. Grace wanted to talk about her lovers. It kept her sane to think about sex, she said, and besides, she knew how *deprived* I was. If she didn't tell me, how would I ever know anything? I told her I wasn't as deprived as she thought, but fortunately she didn't urge me to elaborate.

She liked variety and preferred men who couldn't speak much English. "It's easier," she said, "if you don't have to bother with conversation." She'd had two Arabs, an eighty-year-old Chinese grandfather, a Colombian dealer, and three Native Americans. "I like to do my part for the Indians," she said. "They got a bum deal from us."

But her most recent affair, one that hadn't quite ended before her bad luck in the Zone, was with a 352-pound man named Harry. "It's amazing," she said, "his *finger* barely fits in my mouth. I mean the man is *fat*."

"Aren't you afraid he'll crush you? Didn't Fatty Arbuckle kill some girl that way?"

"That's why it's so great. He's scared to death of hurting me and I always get to be on top. It's like making love to a whale, all that blubber, and me bouncing up and down; you never saw so much flesh. He'd die if he heard me say this, but I forget he's even there—it's not like being with a person—it's like fucking a giant jellyfish. I keep thinking he'll swallow me whole when we're done, that there's a huge mouth hidden in his belly, one gulp and I'll be gone."

"Sounds great," I said. She thought I meant it.

"There's only one problem."

"I can't imagine."

"He smells."

"Most of us do."

"Not like this. He can't get really clean, you know. All that fat. Sweats like a beast. He'd be lifting folds all day long to rinse everything away. So he doesn't bother—just a quick dip in the shower. I tried to get in with him once to give him a good soaping, but there wasn't room."

"Nobody's perfect," I said.

"Ever been with a dwarf?"

"Don't tell me." I meant it. I didn't want to hear this story.

"Neither have I," she said, "but I was with a guy with one leg once."

"Your time's up," the guard said.

"I'm almost through."

"Time's up." He wouldn't bargain. He was short and flabby; a gold band squeezed his thick finger. I wondered if he smelled. I wondered if his wife forgot he was a person when they made love.

When our father died, Grace had been out of prison for three years and banned from the house for eight, but she still knew our parents. She said, "Mom will be lucky to last a year without the old bugger to run her ragged. She lives to be his slave." Grace overestimated. It took our mother four months to give up and cut herself loose. Another stroke sent her reeling away from us for the last time.

She walked somewhere high and light without words, a world I could only imagine when I sat beside her and watched the first flurries of winter spin by the window. Her lids fluttered with dreams and secret visions. Sometimes I entered the room and her eyes were flung open, blue and brilliant, fearful or amazed. I'd hold her good hand, stroking the palm, uncurling the clamped claws of her fingers. I talked and talked but her look never changed; I could not share her joy or make her less afraid.

It took me three days and sixty-two phone calls to track Grace. When she finally stumbled into the hospital, I wished I hadn't tried so hard. She was bony and broke, strung out on speed because she didn't have the cash for cocaine. Ninety-nine pounds stretched over her five-seven frame. She smoked incessantly and answered no questions. She cussed at the nurses and told the doctor to eat shit when he said she could smoke only in the lounge.

The bags under her eyes were so black I thought she'd taken two punches. Her left eye twitched, her feet beat out a frenzied tap on the tile floor, she cracked her knuckles, chewed gum, and kept smoking.

In my head, I heard my mother's voice again and again, always the same words, the ones she had said to me just a week before the stroke: *Take care of Gracie when I'm gone. You're the only one who could ever make her listen.*

But that was a lie. Gracie never listened to anyone as far as I knew. Still, this was my mother's last request. I wanted to find some sense in it because she'd made it solemnly, as if she saw the closeness of her future, the future of this white room, with one tube pumping fluids into her and another sucking liquids out.

Before she died, there would be other tubes, first in her nostrils and then in her throat, finally one in her chest to drain the thick yellow pus that threatened to drown her. But Gracie would be long gone before she had to see any of that.

My father's relatives made their final obligatory visit two days before Thanksgiving. Gran insisted on being rolled to the very edge of the bed where she could poke at a balled-up fist or look inside Mother's open mouth. I thought of the time I had seen my grandmother use her wheelchair to back Mom into a corner of the kitchen. The old woman railed and spat on the floor, blaming my mother for her son's wasted life. "He never drank in my house," Gran said, inching her chair forward till her footrest pressed against Mom's shins. "I wouldn't allow it."

Gran also held my mother solely responsible for getting pregnant before Dad finished college. "He could have been a dentist," Gran said, although Dad had never shown any special interest or talent for such a profession. "And instead he sells life insurance, harbinger of death, making money off strangers' fear and swearing over their sorrows."

Aunt Dee brought tulips to the hospital. They sprang from the glass vase, their heads bright and furious, so red they seemed to excite the air. But even the assault of the delirious tulips could not stir my mother. Dee leaned over the bed and yelled, "You look fine today, honey, just fine, a regular beauty. You'll be dancing by next week."

"Yeah, on her own grave," Uncle Eddie murmured. Gran slapped his thigh and Mother blinked, hearing the mumbled truth more clearly than the compliments Dee shouted in her face.

On Thanksgiving, Mom said: *Gracie doesn't have anyone but you.* I snapped awake, cramped from sleeping in the chair, a bad taste in my mouth from the sticky potatoes and gravy I'd eaten in the hospital cafeteria. My mother had left the room. Only her body remained, that fragile sack of skin and bone shackled by tubes and bags. She was free at last and had stopped just long enough to whisper those words in my ear. They were true. My mother was an only child, and both her parents were dead. My father's family couldn't wait to forget their connection to me and Grace, the orphaned daughters.

I couldn't find my sister. It was seven months before she heard Mom was dead.

Perhaps I would have mourned more deeply for my mother if she hadn't left me such a mess of affairs. Everything was in my name: the house, the car, the costume jewelry. But as I dug through the yellowed papers of my parents' lives, I discovered they had bequeathed a startling array of hidden debts to me as well: there was a second mortgage on the house, unpaid hospital bills from when my father's health insurance was canceled, and a persistent pile of bills from a car accident after his car insurance was canceled. I found that notice too: "Termination due to seven claims and five speeding tickets in one year." He sold insurance but couldn't hang on to his own. He'd cashed in his life insurance policy six years before he died; Mom cashed in her policy to have him buried. I took a week off from work, and then an indefinite leave of absence, but I knew I could not go back to Bigelow and Dropkin, to the senseless job I found vaguely dishonorable. I had paid my dues for my wretched affair with Richard, and I finally admitted I had no intention of going to law school.

It took me six months to sort out the mess and sell the house; by the time the accounts were settled, I had less than $2,000, a crumpled Toyota riddled with rust, and a rhinestone brooch. Other children might have resented such a paltry legacy, but on the June morning when I paid the last bill and signed the final papers on the house, I felt weightless, a bag full of air, and I mistook this unexpected lightness for the pure joy of my new freedom.

With the two thousand in the bank and the brooch stuffed safely in the toe of a sock in my suitcase, I climbed into my beat-up blue Toyota and headed north for a week in a shack on the coast of Maine, where the weight returned. Like a body I dragged behind me, my burden bloated. Day by day it grew heavier and more foul. It tugged my legs through the dark, endless nights as the stars of the Milky Way swirled above me. I made up names for the constellations I saw: The Wild Boar, The Headless Horse, The Two Sisters.

I was grateful for the familiar smog of Boston, the strangely vacant night sky where only the brightest stars survived and did not spin into dizzy shapes. Claudia offered to let me stay with her until "I got myself together," but she fell in love. The walls of her cramped studio on Beacon Street seemed to bulge with so many bodies, the fresh body of Claudia's infatuation and the fetid corpses of my waking dreams. She gave me a week.

In the middle of Boston's worst heat wave of the summer, I found myself looking for a job and an apartment. The sticky July air made the thought of a real job, one that required stockings and a clean face, unbearable. When the days were crisp and brief, I'd be able to think; I'd get a job in my field and stop wasting my education. But now all I needed was money: fast, regular rolls of cash.

I landed a night shift in a fish house on the waterfront, a tourist joint with nets hanging on the walls and lobster traps dangling from the ceiling. I sublet a sweltering, roach-infested studio apartment on Park Drive, believing, I suppose, that the punishment of my surroundings at work and at home would be a constant reminder of the necessity of finding a real job in September.

I should have sensed that I was creating the perfect environment for Grace to resurface.

She was slumped in my entryway when I got home from work at two o'clock one Sunday morning. I spotted her as soon as I started up the walkway and had no doubts, no fleeting illusion that some street person had crashed in the foyer, although strangers occasionally drifted here from the Fenway and spent the night if no one hauled them out to the curb. But there was no mistake: the tilt of the head was undeniably my sister's.

"Shit," she said when I shook her shoulder. She rubbed her eyes and scrambled to her feet. "I thought you'd never get here."

She'd gained ten pounds but was still skinny. Her hair was shaved down to half an inch and bleached an icy blond. Her stockings were ripped, and she couldn't remember where she'd lost her shoes.

I spent a week trying to fatten her up, feeding her burgers and fried potatoes, the only foods she craved. Late at night when I came home smelling of clam juice and spilled beer, I'd find Grace sprawled on the couch, her half-eaten burger dropped on the floor beside her, dripping catsup onto the carpet.

She always woke, apologizing for the mess but making no effort to clean it up. We drank from jugs of cheap white wine and Grace told me stories.

The last night she was there, she told me about her German lover, an actor she had met in New York, a man who hadn't been home in twenty years, who never wrote his mother and father and had ceased to acknowledge his brother was his blood. He had left Kiel the summer his brother tried to drown him. For months he had begged to ride in the kayak, and at last, in the white blaze of afternoon, the older boy took him out on the Baltic. They paddled hard, skimming the choppy surface, noticing too late the clouds foaming in the western sky. The scud snuffed out the sun, turned the sea black and wild with rain. They fought the waves, beating their way back to shore. With safety in sight, the older boy began to rock and laugh, pitching left and right, harder and faster, until he swamped the kayak. He easily freed himself, but the younger boy panicked. Trapped in the dark, silent water where the wind stopped and the waves opened, he saw his brother's slow thighs, treading water above him. It was a lesson: *Now you don't have to be afraid of anything.* And he wasn't, but he never went home.

Grace said, "Can you imagine, trying to drown your own brother?" I shook my head as if it were unfathomable, but I have felt my own head go under, my lungs filling with water; I have beaten my way to the surface and seen my sister laughing on a distant shore.

"He was the best lover I ever had," Grace said, "but I had to give him up. He scared me. He didn't believe in anything."

We drank until the stagnant light before dawn filled the room. I downed far more than I usually did, or more than I ever should. Gracie seemed to match me glass for glass, but perhaps she fooled me, because as the room blurred and spun, I saw that her dark eyes glowed until they burned, two golden flames. When the streetlights dimmed, Grace's eyes were the only beacons in the world.

I dreamed of my sister holding my head underwater. Unlike the German boy, Grace did not tread water above me or swim toward shore. No, they found us together, facedown in the muck at the bottom of a shallow pond, arms and legs entwined, heads bent together, our hair tangled in the flowing reeds.

I woke in a heap on the floor, my skin imprinted by the scratchy tufts of the carpet, my tongue swollen and dry, my teeth fuzzy. Grace was gone. At least she was neat this time. She didn't tear the place apart to find my cash. She must have seen me stuff my tips in an envelope between the plastic liner and the cardboard box of the raisin bran. My week's earnings, $237, was the only thing she took.

This time I couldn't convince myself that it was for my own good. I hadn't seen Richard for two years, but I felt close to him now and knew at last why he wept so inconsolably over his stolen cuff links. I brushed my teeth, standing at the window instead of the mirror, tears rolling down my cheeks.

I know it's crazy, but I am hoping that when Grace's daughter is old enough to want to meet her mother, Grace will be impossible to find. That's not hard to imagine. I think of the little girl knocking at my door instead—of course she won't be little anymore, but halfway to woman-hood, her neck still too long for her to have learned to use it as Grace uses hers, stretching and arching so men dream of putting their hands around it, not too tightly, pressing their lips to her white skin. And I will tell a small lie, for all of us. I will say I changed my first name to hide from her abusive father. I will say I am her mother. I will live with Grace's name and take this child away, north, to Alaska, where Grace who hates the cold will never find us. I will be free at last, and not alone. Often, I curse our common name—Walker. That child will be a long time looking for us.

On New Year's Eve, Grace reappeared. "I wanted to celebrate with my sister," she said. She had forgotten the circumstances of her abrupt departure. She'd spent a month in detox and was straight for the first time since she'd been in prison. She had a job, she said, "sales," and then admitted, "selling muffins in Harvard Square." I told her I was going to a party at Claudia's, hoping she'd curl her lip in distaste. But she surprised me; she wanted to go. When she was off the dope, she didn't have any friends of her own. I thought of telling her that Claudia didn't trust her in her apartment, but Grace would have made me choose between them.

An hour before the party, my sister found me this way: sobbing my fool head off in the bathtub. She didn't ask why; she just put her arms around me—even though she was ruining the red silk blouse she planned to wear to the party. I would have considered this a great sacrifice, except that the shirt was mine.

She said, "I hope you aren't thinking of drowning yourself. I was thinking of that one day, just slipping down in the tub, letting myself go, you know, an accident. Then last week I was feeling fine; three weeks in detox and I'm a new person. I have a real life, you know, like anyone else. And I'm feeling so good that while I'm washing my hair, kneeling and leaning under the faucet, I get rambunctious and bring my head down so fast that I bash it against the end of the tub. I see constellations. I think, Oh great, I'm going to have a real accident and everyone will say I did it on purpose, that they expected it sooner or later. They'll find me facedown, ass up. God, I thought, I don't want to die with my bare ass in the air for the world to see."

The thought of her naked bum made us howl and shake, spouting giggles till I thought we'd burst, and Grace hugged me tighter and tighter until I was crying again and she had to say, "What is it, baby?"

But how could I explain? Mom had always told us, "Don't get married on a holiday. You get divorced and you can never forget the fourth of July, but May seventeenth—who remembers May seventeenth?" So wasn't it just like Mom to die on Thanksgiving, so I'd remember? Well, maybe she didn't choose the day, any more than a child chooses her day to be born. If Grace wasn't crying today, why should I remind her that this was her daughter's eleventh birthday, her daughter, our blood. Why should I tell her that I woke this morning and said to myself: *She'll never find us. And if she has any sense, she'll never even look.*

I should have been happy. Grace was straight and had a job. She was going to make it this time. So what whispering devil made me hide my rings; what demon of doubt drove me to make a special trip to the bank to deposit all my cash?

Claudia and I have kept our New Year's resolutions. It is spring in Boston and we both have new jobs. I've moved to Somerville, to a barren apartment where there is room to pace and no cockroaches to run after when you flick on the light in the bathroom in the middle of the night. Leaf buds have burst like green flames and the forsythia are painfully yellow.

I stop at Claudia's apartment on my way home. She is down on love this week. It's her day off and she's gone through a bag of chocolate cookies. She says that when she feels fat, the desire goes away. She's landed a job doing makeup for a local news show. One of the sportscasters has acne scars, and she tells me, "I have to cake him—I swear—a quarter of an inch." She holds up her thumb and forefinger to show me how thick his foundation has to be. In a hushed voice she reveals that the evening anchorwoman has down on her cheeks, "Like sideburns," she says. "I almost told her to shave the other day, but I want to keep this job. It's a piece of cake," she says, reaching for another cookie. "I can do it *fore*ver. I can be fat, pregnant, covered with warts—who cares? I just have to make other people look good. I'm sick of jobs where you have to take care of yourself. Even a waitress has to shave her legs and suck in her belly—and waitresses are the lowest of the low."

I nod but I don't agree. I'm "taking care of myself" this week, trying to avoid being fat and covered with warts. It has to do with my new job. I work with a psychologist at Boston University who's studying appearance and self-esteem. He has a thousand slides—kids with protruding brows and no chins, ears too low or no ears at all, kids with scabby growths that cover half their faces. Then there are the "normal" ones—children with crooked teeth and big noses, wide-spaced eyes or misaligned jaws.

I show these slides to college students and they rate the children for attractiveness. Then I photograph the students to see if there is any correlation between their appearance and the way they judge others. Later, I put on a white lab coat and take wax casts of their teeth. The psychologist thinks that the mouth and chin matter most. A kid can get by with a bumpy nose but not with buck teeth.

Sometimes the college boys flirt with me. They are cocky and long-legged, unintentionally seductive as they sprawl in the chair in front of me. They call me "Doctor" when I wear the lab coat, teasing me until I slip the soft wax in their mouths and say, "Bite down." This silences them, of course, and they do not recover. When I'm done, they sulk away, shoulders curved, thumbs hooked in belt loops. This is the closest I come to romance, these meaningless flirtations I must destroy.

At home I often stare into the mirror for an hour or more, but I never look at my whole face; I study it in parts. The eyes are gray and the lashes pale, unremarkable but the right distance apart and perfectly in line. I scan lips, skin, nose, looking for flaws or traces of beauty. There are none. Feature by feature, I realize I bear no resemblance to my sister, but sometimes, by accident, when I catch my reflection in a store window, there is a gesture, an angle of the head or the hips that is unmistakably Grace. I have decided my ears are my finest attribute. The lobes are pink and fleshy but not too large. Inside, the whorls are perfect as pale shells worn to a sheen by saltwater.

Claudia was supposed to cook me dinner, but she falls asleep, bloated and groggy from her overdose of sugar. Her hands rest on her belly, rising and falling with each snore. I crack open a window before I leave; she needs air.

Outside, the night is heavy with the musk of magnolia. I walk slowly toward Charles, where I can hop a train to Somerville. I stop in the Public Garden, in front of my favorite sculpture, the monument to the discovery of ether. A patient lies limp and free of pain in the doctor's arms, just as Christ lay across his mother's lap, head thrown back, arms dangling. The bearded doctor swabs the patient's chest with his cool, stone rag. ". . . inhaling ether causes insensibility to pain," I read. This is Boston's *Pietà*, a memorial to misery and redemption.

"I do not have a bad life." This is my exact thought as I walk down the quiet street in Somerville where nothing ever happens. I plan to live here a long time. Here there are no doormen or buzzers, no chains or double locks. "I am safe here," I think as I climb the stairs. That's when I realize my door is cracked open, the lock popped. What do I have left to steal? A rhinestone brooch, a black-and-white television, a photograph of my mother at thirty, a smiling girl full of hope.

I push the door with my fingertips, afraid to know what's gone. I can smell the intruder in my living room as if he had just stepped in front of me. I know he is still here. I resist the lights. Darkness is my friend, my advantage: this is my house. I have a crazy thought that the thief is one of the boys from the experiment, a kid who wants to pay me back for the humiliation he suffered when I shoved the wax between his teeth.

I slink along the wall to the kitchen, where I know the ironing board is still standing, where the cool iron sits, unplugged, another friend. I am watching myself, thinking: Run, run while there is still time, run before you kill the stranger in your house, but I want to kill him, to punish him for forcing his way through my door.

I have my hands on the iron when he moves, a shadow near the refrigerator; just a boy, I think, but no less dangerous for that. I am walking toward him, the iron raised, fear binding me to finish what I've begun.

Then I hear a wild peal, a cackle, and I know my sister. She bursts from her own shadow, falling into my arms, and I cry out, "I could have killed you. I could have fucking killed you."

She hugs me in the dark, her smell strong, unwashed but familiar. I cannot hug her back, not until the anger drains, a slow trickle of sweat down my spine, not until my rigid muscles go limp and I feel only the poison that panic leaves in the body. And I wonder: Did I sense all along that the shadow in my house was Grace? Even as I grabbed the iron, did the hot flame of recognition drive me toward her?

Grace grabs my face and kisses me on the mouth. She cares nothing for the moment we've just escaped, nothing for my rage or the knowledge of what I might have done.

I say it again, a murmur this time: "I almost killed you."

"But you didn't," she says. "You didn't."

WILLIAM TREVOR

A Bit of Business

On a warm Saturday morning the city was deserted. Its suburbs dozed, its streets had acquired a tranquillity that did not belong to the hour. Shops and cafés were unexpectedly closed. Where there were people, they sat in front of television sets, or listened to transistor radios.

In Westmoreland Street two youths hurried, their progress marked by a businesslike air. They did not speak, until they reached Stephen's Green. "No. On ahead," one said when his companion paused. "Off to the left in Harcourt Street." His companion did not argue.

They had been friends since childhood; and today, their purpose being what it was, they knew better than to argue. Argument wasted time and would distract them. The one who'd given the instruction, the older and taller of the two, was Mangan. The other was a pockmarked sallow youth known as Lout Gallagher, the sobriquet an expression of scorn on the part of a Christian Brother ten or so years before. Mangan had gelled short hair, nondescript as to color, and small eyes that squinted slightly, and a flat, broad nose. "Here," he commanded toward the end of Harcourt Street, and the two veered off in the direction he indicated.

A marmalade cat sauntered across the street they were in now; no one was about. "The blue Ford," Mangan said. Gallagher, within seconds, forced open the driver's door. As swiftly, the hood of the car was raised. Work was done with wire; the engine started easily.

In the suburb of Rathgar, in Cavendish Road, Mr. Livingston watched the red helicopter touch down behind the vesting tents in Phoenix Park. Earlier, at the airport, the Pope's right hand had been raised in blessing, lowered, and then raised again and again, a benign smile accompanying each gesture. In Phoenix Park the crowds knelt in their corrals, and sang "Holy God, We Praise Thy Name." Now and again the cameras caught the black dress of clergymen and nuns, but for the most part the crowds were composed of the kind of people Mr. Livingston met every day on the streets or noticed going to Mass on Sunday. The crowds were orderly, awed by the occasion. Yellow-and-white papal flags fluttered everywhere; occasionally a degree of shoving developed in an effort to gain a better view. Four times already the cameras had shown women fainting—from marveling, so Mr. Livingston was given to understand, rather than heat or congestion. Somewhere in Phoenix Park were the Herlihys, but so far Mr. Livingston had failed to identify them. "I'll wave," the Herlihy twins had promised, speaking in unison as they always did. Mr. Livingston knew they'd forget; in all the excitement they wouldn't even know that a camera had skimmed over them. It was Herlihy himself who would be noticeable, being so big, his red hair easy to pick out. Monica, of course, you could miss.

Mr. Livingston, attired now in a dark blue suit, was a thin man in his sixties, only just beginning to go gray. His lean features, handsome in youth, were affected by wrinkles now, his cheeks a little flushed. He had been a widower for a year.

Preceded by Cardinal O Fiaich and Archbishop Ryan, the Pope emerged from the papal vesting chamber under the podium. Cheering began in the corrals. Twice the Pope stopped and extended his arms. There was cheering then, such as Mr. Livingston had never in his life heard before. The Pope approached the altar.

Mangan and Gallagher worked quickly, although with no great skill. They pulled open drawers and scattered their contents. They rooted among clothes, and wrenched at the locks of cupboards. Jewelry was not examined, since its worth could not even roughly have been estimated. All they found they pocketed, with loose change and notes. A transistor radio was secreted beneath Gallagher's jacket.

"Nothing else," Mangan said. "Useless damn place."

They left the house they had entered, through a kitchen window, and strolled toward the parked blue Ford, Mangan shaking his head as though they had come to the house on legitimate business and had disappointedly failed to find anyone at home. Gallagher drove, slowly in the road where the house was, and then more rapidly. "Off to the left," Mangan said, and when the opportunity came Gallagher did as he was bidden. The car drew up again; the two remained seated, both their glances fixed on the rearview mirror. "Okay," Mangan said.

Mr. Livingston heard a noise and paid it no attention. Although his presence in the Herlihys' house was, officially, to keep an eye on it, he believed that the Herlihys had invited him because he had no television himself. It was their way to invent a reason; their way to want to thank him whenever it was possible for all the baby-sitting he did—not that there wasn't full and adequate payment at the time, the "going rate" as Monica called it. Earlier that morning, as he'd risen and dressed himself, it had not occurred to him that Herlihy might have been serious when he said that it was nice to have someone about the place on a day like this when the guards were all out at Phoenix Park. The sound of the television, Herlihy suggested, was as good as a dog.

"A new kind of confrontation," stated the Pope, "with values and trends which up to now have been unknown and alien to Irish society."

Mr. Livingston nodded in agreement. It would have been nice for Rosie, he thought; she'd have appreciated all this, the way she'd appreciated the royal weddings. When his wife was alive Mr. Livingston had rented a television set like everyone else, but later he'd ceased to do so because he found he never watched it on his own. It made him miss her more, sitting there with the same programs coming out, her voice not commenting anymore. They would certainly have watched the whole of the ceremony today, but naturally they wouldn't have attended it in person, being Protestants.

"The sacredness of life," urged the Pope, "the indissolubility of marriage, the true sense of human sexuality, the right attitude toward the material goods that progress has to offer." He advocated the sacraments, especially the sacrament of penance.

Applause broke out, and again Mr. Livingston nodded his agreement.

Gallagher had wanted to stop, but Mangan said one more house. So they went for the one at the end of the avenue, having noticed that no dog was kept there. "They've left that on," Mangan whispered in the kitchen when they heard the sound of the television. "Check it, though, while I'm up there."

In the Herlihys' main bedroom he slipped the drawers out softly and eased open anything that was locked. They'd been right to come. This place was the best yet.

Suddenly the sound of the television was louder, and Mangan knew that Gallagher had opened the door of the room it came from. He glanced toward the windows in case he should have to hurry away, but no sound of protest came from downstairs. They'd drive the car to Milltown and get on the first bus going out of the city. Later they'd pick up a bus to Bray. It was always worth making the journey to Bray because Cohen gave you better prices.

"Hey," Gallagher called, not loudly, not panicking in any way. At once Mangan knew there was a bit of trouble. He knew, by the sound of the television, that the door Gallagher had opened hadn't been closed again. Once, in a house at night, a young girl had walked across a landing with nothing on her except a sanitary thing. He and Gallagher had been in the shadows, alerted by the flush of a toilet. She hadn't seen them.

He stuffed a couple of ties into his pockets and closed the bedroom door behind him. On the way downstairs he heard Gallagher's voice before he saw him.

"There's an old fellow here," Gallagher said, making no effort to speak privately. "Watching His Holiness."

Gallagher was as cool as a cucumber. You had to admire that in him. The time Mangan had gone with Ossie Power it had been nerves that landed them in it. You couldn't do a job with shaking hands, he'd told Power before they began, but it hadn't been any use. He should have known, of course.

"He's staying quiet," Gallagher said in a low voice. "Like I told him, he's keeping his trap tight."

The youth in the doorway was wearing a crushed imitation-suede jacket and dark trousers. His white T-shirt was dirty; his chin and cheeks were pitted with the remains of acne. For an instant Mr. Livingston received an impression of a second face: a flat, wide nose between two beadlike eyes. Then both intruders stepped back into the hall. Whispering took place but Mr. Livingston couldn't hear what was said. On the screen the Popemobile moved slowly through the vast crowd. Hands reached out to touch it.

"Keep your eyes on your man," a voice commanded, and Mr. Livingston knew it belonged to the one he had seen less of, because it was gruffer than the other voice. "Keep company with His Holiness."

Mr. Livingston did not attempt to disobey. Something was placed over his eyes and knotted at the back of his head. The material was rough, like tweed. With something similar his wrists were tied in his lap.

Each ankle was tied to a leg of the chair he occupied. His wallet was slipped out of the inside pocket of his jacket.

He had failed the Herlihys; even though it was a pretense, he had agreed to perform a small and simple task; the family would return to disappointment. Mr. Livingston had been angry as soon as he realized what was happening, as soon as the first youth appeared. He'd wanted to get up, to look around for something to use as a weapon, but only just in time he'd understood it would be foolish to do that. Helpless in his chair, he felt ashamed.

On the television the cheering continued, and voices described what was happening. *"Ave! Ave!"* people sang.

"Pull up," Mangan said in the car. "Go down that road and pull up at the bottom."

Lout Gallagher did so, and halted the car at the opening to a half-built estate. They had driven farther than they'd intended, anxious to move swiftly from the neighborhood of their morning's work. "If there's ever a squawk out of you," Mangan had threatened before they parted from Mr. Livingston, "you'll rue the bloody day, mister." He had taken the third of the ties he'd picked up in the bedroom and placed it around the old man's neck. He crossed the two ends and pulled them tight, watching while Mr. Livingston's face and neck became flushed. He released them in good time in case anything went wrong.

"You never know with a geezer like that," he said now. He turned his head and glanced out of the back window of the car. They were both still edgy. It was the worst thing that could happen, being seen.

"Wouldn't we dump the wagon?" Gallagher said.

"Drive it in on the site."

They left the car behind the back wall of one of the new houses, and since the place was secluded they counted the money they'd trawled. "Forty-two pound fifty-four," Mangan said. There were various pieces of jewelry and the transistor radio as well. "You could be caught with that," Mangan advised, and the transistor was thrown into a cement mixer.

"He'll issue descriptions," Mangan said before they turned away from the car. "He'll squawk his bloody guts out."

They both knew that. In spite of the ugliness Mangan had injected into his voice, in spite of the old man's face going purple, he would recall the details of the occasion. In the glimpse Mangan had caught of him there was anger in his eyes and his forehead was puckered in a frown.

"I'm going back there," Mangan said.

"The car's hot."

Mangan didn't answer but swore instead, repeatedly and furiously; then they lit cigarettes and both felt calmer. Mangan led the way from the car, through the building site and onto a lane. Within five minutes they reached a main road and came eventually to a pub. High up on the wall above the bar a large television set continued to record the Pope's presence in Ireland. No one took any notice of the two youths who ordered glasses of Smithwick's and crisps.

The people who had been robbed returned to their houses and counted the cost of the Pope's personal blessing. The Herlihys returned and found Mr. Livingston bound with neckties, and the television still on. A doctor was summoned, although against Mr. Livingston's wishes. The police came later.

That afternoon in Bray, after they'd been to see Cohen, Mangan and Gallagher picked up two girls. "Jaysus, I could do with a mott," Lout Gallagher had said the night before, which was how the whole thing began, Mangan realizing he could do with one too. "Thirty," Cohen had offered that afternoon, and they pushed him up to thirty-five. They felt better after the few drinks. Today of all days a bit of fecking wouldn't interest the police, with the headaches they'd have when the crowds headed back to the city. "Why'd they be bothered with an old geezer like that?" Mangan said, and they felt better still.

In the Esplanade Ice-Cream Parlour the girls requested a peach melba and a sundae. One was called Carmel, the other Marie. They said they were nurses, but in fact they worked in a paper mill.

"Bray's quiet," Mangan said.

The girls agreed it was. They'd been intending to go to see the Pope themselves, but they'd slept it out. A quarter past twelve it was before Carmel opened her eyes, and Marie was even worse. She wouldn't like to tell them, she said.

"We seen it on the television," Mangan said. "Your man's in great form."

"What line are you in?" Carmel asked.

"Gangsters," said Mangan, and everyone laughed.

Gallagher wagged his head in admiration. Mangan always gave the same response when asked that question by girls. You might have thought he'd restrain himself today, but that was Mangan all over. Gallagher lit a cigarette, thinking he should have hit the old fellow before he had a chance to turn around. He should have rushed into the room and struck him a blow on the back of the skull, with whatever there was to hand, hell take the consequences.

"What's it mean, 'gangsters'?" Marie asked, still giggling, glancing at Carmel and giggling even more.

"Banks," Mangan said, "is our business."

The girls thought of Butch Cassidy and the Sundance Kid and Bonnie and Clyde, and laughed again. They knew that if they pressed their question it wouldn't be any good. They knew it was a kind of flirtation, their asking and Mangan's teasing with his replies. Mangan was a wag. Both girls were drawn to him.

"Are the ices to our ladyships' satisfaction?" he inquired, causing a further outbreak of giggling.

Gallagher had ordered a banana split. Years before, he used to think that if you filled a room with banana splits he could eat them all. He'd been about five then. He used to think the same thing about fruitcake.

"Are the flicks on today?" Mangan asked, and the girls said on account of the Pope they mightn't be. It might be like Christmas Day, they didn't know.

"We seen what's showing in Bray," Marie said. "In any case."

"We'll go dancing later on," Mangan promised. He winked at Gallagher, and Gallagher thought the day they made a killing you wouldn't see him for dust. The mail boat and Spain, posh Cockney girls who called you Mr. Big. Never lift a finger again.

"Will we sport ourselves on the prom?" Mangan suggested, and the girls laughed again. They said they didn't mind. Each wanted to be Mangan's. He sensed it, so he walked between them on the promenade, linking their arms. Gallagher walked on the outside, linking Carmel.

"Spot of the ozone," Mangan said. He pressed his forearm against Marie's breast. She was the one, he thought.

"D'you like the nursing?" Gallagher asked, and Carmel said it was all right. A sharp breeze was darting in from the sea, stinging their faces, blowing the girls' hair about. Gallagher saw himself stretched out by a blue swimming pool, smoking and sipping at a drink. There was a cherry in the drink, and a little stick with an umbrella on the end of it. A girl with one whole side of her bikini open was sharing it with him.

"Bray's a great place," Mangan said.

"The pits," Carmel corrected.

You could always tell by the feel of a girl on your arm, Mangan said to himself. Full of sauce the fat one was, no more a nurse than he was. Gallagher wondered if they had a flat, if there'd be anywhere to go when the moment came.

"We could go into the bar of the hotel," the other one was saying, the way girls did when they wanted to extract their due.

"What hotel's this?" he asked.

"The International."

"Oh, listen to Miss Ritzy!"

They turned and walked back along the promenade, guided by the girls to the bar in question. Gin-and-tonic the girls had. Gallagher and Mangan had Smithwick's.

"We could go into town later," Carmel casually suggested. "There'll be celebrations on."

"We'll give the matter thought," Mangan said.

Another couple of pulls of the tie, Mangan said to himself, and who'd have been the wiser? You get to that age, you'd had your life anyway. As it was, the old geezer had probably conked it on his own, tied up like that. Most likely he was stiffening already.

"Isn't there a disco on in Bray?" he suggested. "What's wrong with a slap-up meal and then the light fantastic?"

The girls were again amused at his way of putting it. Gallagher was glad to hear the proposal that they should stay where they were. If they went into town the whole opportunity could fall asunder. If you didn't end up near a mott's accommodation you were back where you started.

"You'd die of the pace of it in Bray," Marie said, and Mangan thought: A couple more gins and a dollop of barley wine with their grill and chips. He edged his knee against Marie's. She didn't take hers away.

"Have you a flat or rooms or something?" Gallagher asked, and the girls said they hadn't. They lived at home, they said. They'd give anything for a flat.

A few minutes later, engaged at the urinals in the bathroom, the two youths discussed the implications of that. Mangan had stood up immediately on hearing the news. He'd given a jerk of his head when the girls weren't looking.

"No bloody go," Gallagher said.

"The fat one's on for it."

"Where, though, man?"

Mangan reminded his companion of other occasions, in parking lots and derelict buildings, of the time they propped up the bar of the emergency exit of the Adelphi Cinema and went back in, of the time in the garden shed in Drumcondra.

Gallagher laughed, feeling more optimistic when he remembered all that. He winked to himself, the way he did when he was beginning to feel drunk. He spat into the urinal, another habit at this particular juncture. The seashore was the place; he'd forgotten about the seashore.

"Game ball," Mangan said.

The memory of the day that had passed seemed rosy now—the empty streets they had hurried through, the quiet houses where their business had been, the red blotchiness in the old man's face and neck, the processions on the television screen. Get a couple more gins into them, Mangan thought again, and then the barley wine. Stretch the fat one out on the soft bloody sand.

"Oh, lovely," the fat one said when more drinks were offered.

Gallagher imagined the wife of a businessman pleading on the telephone, reporting that her captors intended to slice off the tips of her little fingers unless the money was forthcoming. The money was in a package in a telephone booth, stashed under the seat. The pictures of Spain began again.

"Hi," Carmel said.

She'd been to put her lipstick on, but she didn't look any different.

"What d'you do really?" she asked on the promenade.

"Unemployed."

"You're loaded for an unemployed." Her tone was suspicious. He watched her trying to focus her eyes. Vaguely, he wondered if she liked him.

"A man's car needed an overhaul," he said.

Ahead of them, Mangan and Marie were laughing, the sound drifting lightly back above the swish of the sea.

"He's great sport, isn't he?" Carmel said.

"Oh, great all right."

Mangan turned around before they went down the steps to the shingle. Gallagher imagined his fancy talk and the fat one giggling at it. He wished he was good at talk like that.

"We had plans made to go into town," Carmel said. "There'll be great gas in town tonight."

When they began to cross the shingle she said it hurt her feet, so Gallagher led her back to the concrete wall of the promenade and they sat down with their backs to it. It wasn't quite dark. Cigarette packets and chocolate wrappings were scattered on the sand and pebbles. Gallagher put his arm around Carmel's shoulders. She let him kiss her. She didn't mind when he twisted her sideways so that she no longer had her back to the wall. She felt limp in his arms, and for a moment Gallagher thought she'd passed out, but then she kissed him back. She murmured something and her arms pulled him down on top of her. He realized it didn't matter about the fancy talk.

"When, then?" Marie whispered, pulling down her clothes. Five minutes before, he'd promised they would meet again; he'd sworn there was nothing he wanted more; the sooner the better, he said.

"Monday night," he added now. "Outside the railway station. Six." It was where they'd picked the two girls up. Mangan could think of nowhere else, and it didn't matter anyway since he had no intention of being anywhere near Bray on Monday night.

"Geez, you're great," Marie said.

On the bus to Dublin they did not say much. Carmel had spewed up a couple of mouthfuls, and in Gallagher's nostrils the sour odor persisted. Marie in the end had been a nag, going on about Monday evening, making sure Mangan wouldn't forget. What both of them were thinking was that Cohen, as usual, had done best out of the bit of business there'd been.

Then the lean features of Mr. Livingston were recalled by Mangan, the angry eyes, the frown. They'd made a mess of it, letting him see them, they'd bollixed the whole thing. That moment in the doorway when the old man's glance had lighted on his face, he had hardly been able to control his bowels. "I'm going back there," his own voice echoed from a later moment, but he'd known, even as he spoke, that if he returned he would do no more than he had done already.

Beside him, on the inside seat, Gallagher experienced similar recollections. He stared out into the summery night, thinking that if he'd hit the old man on the back of the skull he could have finished him. The thought of that had pleased him when they were with the girls. It made him shiver now.

"God, she was great," Mangan said, dragging out of himself a single snigger.

His bravado obscured a longing still to be ordering the girls gins at the bar, and talking fancy. He would have paid what remained in his pocket still to taste her lipstick on the seashore, or to hear her gasp as he touched her for the first time.

Gallagher tried for his dream of Mr. Big, but it would not come to him. "Yeah," he said, replying to his friend's observation.

The day was over; there was nowhere left to hide from the error that had been made. As they had at the time, they sensed the old man's shame and the hurt to his pride, as animals sense fear or resolution. Privately, each calculated how long it would be before the danger they'd left behind in the house caught up with them.

They stepped off the bus on the quays. The crowds that had celebrated in the city during their absence had dwindled, but people who were on the streets spoke with a continuing excitement about the Pope's presence in Ireland and the great Mass there had been in the sunshine. The two youths walked the way they'd come that morning, both of them wondering if the nerve to kill was something you acquired.

JEANNE WILMOT

The Company We Keep

Tonight David has brought a girl to our house—we are spending the summer in adjacent cottages with David—and we all are going to dinner. David is Harry's best friend, the man I live with. However, I do not know David very well; he moved to California the year Harry and I got together. And that year I was not really with Harry anyway, because I was getting divorced and not really with anything. Now David is getting over a divorce. He was married to someone named Sarah, and she and David and Harry were a real threesome. I never met Sarah, but I've heard a lot about her because, although she was David's wife, Harry carried a keen feeling for her around with him. David wishes it were a year from now. *Pain* is such a slight word. I don't want to tell him that a year is not long enough.

Anyway, here he is in our house with a girl half his age. He introduces her by saying their conversations duplicate those he has been having with his students. We cruise for an hour to a restaurant Harry knows will please David. David drives a big new silver Mercedes 450 SEL he bought just before the divorce became final. Sarah left him.

The girl's name is Marisa. David and Harry address her as they speak but they quickly travel beyond what she could know. They are old friends and their timing is impeccable. Their humor has been nurtured in such a way that its vibrancy is fed by its own insulation. David puts a country rock-and-roll tape into his AM/FM tape deck with a four-speaker sound system. Marisa has long slim legs, neither a crease nor a hair marring their symmetrical, sensual beauty. She knows this. There is a long slit up both sides of her dress, for maximum exposure. None of her self-awareness—of her bronze legs, her graceful arms, her small well-shaped breasts—is offensive to me.

I luxuriate in it. She is young in the way I was young. She looks a little like my childhood friend Barbara Chatfield, although Barbara was short. I am now my mother's age when I first knew Barbara, but I knew those things about myself that Marisa does, at her age. In fact, if the song happened to be a good one, each part of my body moved in its special way as if to join the music, accentuating whatever my magnetic appeal might have been, in the way Marisa is captivating us now. And at the same time I believed my nonchalance showed indifference to the attention I attracted, I wanted those eyes on me. I still do.

Harry pretends not to stare. He watches me watch, as if to say, You are betraying Sarah. Although I have been told that David's wife is lovely, one thing I can assume is that she does not have twenty-year-old legs that know the movement to each note of Rosanne Cash's last cut on the B side of her sixth album. I suspect that Sarah doesn't even know Johnny has a daughter named Rosanne who has put six albums out. David knows, even though he used to listen only to Bach and the stars of *fado*. But the thing is, I am certain Sarah's eyes would be drawn to Marisa too. There is something to share among the three of us—in the way Marisa extends her arm across the back of David's headrest, in the way she lays her hand to rest on David's thigh. Sarah would recognize the gesture—not as her own, but as one that might be tried out in the company of others when those others are strangers and you are the exotic yet uneasy outsider. There is something to share, too, in the way we, even Sarah and I, would always be outsiders here.

Marisa is smart. Not intelligent. Harry has told me that Sarah has intelligence. With her delicate fingers, Marisa grabs for bread and applies too much butter. I know that Sarah watches her weight, that she is diminutive, but for very different reasons would never put too much butter on her bread. She is a gourmand. David and Harry and Sarah have eaten all over the world together. And cooked. They cooked the way New Yorkers who know about food cook. Marisa twists her hand around so that the back of it faces me, on the other side of the table, when she eats. The style is not European. It is a simple case of bad form. David doesn't notice. He talks about his tan. Undoes the top buttons of his shirt for Marisa to touch the soft hairs of his chest. Marisa runs her slender fingers across the golden V David has created by opening his shirt. I imagine Sarah would have been compelled to do the same.

In part because of his physical beauty, David's life is metaphor. He is a painter. He mixes hues to paint a persimmon, using the color of his lips as that from which he distills tone. A kiwifruit in a blue bowl might be the result of his wearing an aquamarine shirt the evening before painting. He loves touch and poetry, wine and food, and attention. David had always needed attending to in such a way that while providing it Sarah must have neglected to discover what it was she needed in return, blaming finally the marriage instead of herself for the omission.

Why else could she have left in the way David told me she did. It was as if she had forgotten herself and, in forgetting, there came into being a palpable absence between them that David filled in other ways. He cared about his fruit.

Harry winces. I look over to see Marisa caressing David. It is not the same as being witness to someone else's indiscretion, someone's affair. I understand what Harry is feeling. It is raw. It is knowing that Sarah will never again be to Harry's right and David's left as they sit to eat in Da Silvano or Provence in New York, or Al Moro in Rome, or drink in the wine bar where they all gathered during the five years Harry saw his shrink across the street from where Sarah worked.

The girl stares at another table, feigning distraction. David and Harry are discussing the wine. It is a '79 Antinori Solaia they brought to the restaurant and they are comparing its nose to the '82 Sassicaia they had at a friend's farther down the coast the night before. The Sassicaia tested out fruitier, the Solaia fresher; not at all like Zinfandel fruit or the apricot highlights of late-harvest California wines. This is the dinner conversation, like so many others I have had with Harry, that follows the courses as smoothly as soft on suede. The girl knows California and Italian wines have come up in the world, or so she says, but after a bounty of Taylor and Almadén for so many school years, she'd prefer a good nine-dollar Pouilly-Fuissé. French is her second language—three years' worth. David and Harry exchange glances. Harry is a translator by trade, a poet and novelist by heart. As an upstart newcomer to the second-son literary world of an earlier Tangier, he wrote an original and very avant-garde novella in ancient Greek under the name Javert and then translated it for publication in *The Kenyon Review* under his name. He was criticized for the arrogance of his debut; but it acknowledged the arrival of a presence.

When the soup arrives, the girl has already consumed five pieces of bread. David and Harry move smoothly from wine to food. David starts:

"What's in this? There's something unusual here. It's not just halibut and eggplant. I think they put in walnuts and basil. Sarah would know."

"It's not walnuts. There aren't any nuts in this soup, David!"

Determined to be heard, Marisa knows that David's wife is a food person. Just as she has spoken, however, her teeth hit something hard.

"Could be eel eggs ground up a little." Harry's grin is grim. He feels uncomfortable. The conversation is both reminiscent and lacking.

I don't say anything. The hardest thing I have bitten into is a radish. But if Sarah were here, I am sure the conversation would go on for another five minutes until the chef was called from the kitchen and the mystery solved. I scrutinize Marisa. She is beginning to notice her lack of function here. Smart girl.

Marisa is full. She has had too much bread.

"I can't finish this soup. It's too rich and too much. They should have put it in smaller bowls." She takes an aggressive stance.

David agrees with her and slips his hand through her short-cropped hair. The Polaroids I have seen of Sarah show her off as a small, pretty woman with short hair. Marisa's hair is short like Sarah's, but thicker. I wonder as David touches the hair if he thinks for a moment he has recaptured the naturalness of brushing though his wife's hair. He lingers with Marisa. He listens to her.

Only this morning he said—simply, and without preface, as we three sat on the beach reading—"Sarah doesn't love me anymore." Harry put his book down and didn't speak. I didn't have to say anything. I had not been a part of their trio. Yet I hurt for David. I am touched by the fact that he still thinks in terms of love. Sarah hadn't even called to find out if he was doing all right, although the week before he arrived at our doorstep they had divided all their worldly possessions and said good-bye for the last time. An amicable divorce. That is what Sarah's guilt would call it, I suppose. I looked at the two men as I began to recall the ache David must feel, remembering the vivid physical quality of it. After a silence, it was David who spoke first. He asked me if I thought his legs were as tan as mine. I said we had different kinds of skin. He said his legs are always the last thing to tan on his body.

I am not sure how good Harry and I are. We have become pleasingly packaged. We Cuisinart our way through the weekends, trim city plants and window herb gardens, buy important California wines and still lifes, have chosen psychiatrists over psychologists and listen to jazz on a high-fidelity stereo system made by some computer whiz kids in L.A., instead of being there live in a club or after-hours jam joint like Said's or Mikell's. I used to hear about this kind of life; I even had contact with some old college friends who lived it. But I wasn't interested in circumscribed living back in the days when I'd hit Said's and boogie into the early-morning dancing hours, when the day would resolve itself in ecstasy, street fighting or horror. There is a terrifying undertow all around me now, but with great delicacy Harry and I trip around it, avoiding it with stories in translation and appetites for subtlety. I for reasons of survival, Harry for entirely logical reasons. He would rather smoke tuna in tinfoil over a wok filled with tea leaves than discuss why he walked out on me only to return two days later, the first month we were together. Perhaps it was because although my past wasn't easy for him to comprehend, I never hurt anybody. Impressed on my life there's a value which Harry intuited.

One morning before I left for work, Harry called me over to where he was sitting—at his desk, as every morning—with his books and his strong Italian brewed coffee. He keeps a journal of quotations and snippets, which includes everything from a picture of Calvino in the forties when he styled his hair after Dick Powell for a photo session, to cutouts of camels or favorite non sequiturs of former lovers. That particular morning it was a quotation from one of Updike's books. There was a woman who, when she stepped out onto a brisk New England coastal dock from the warmth of the cozy diner where she'd eaten lunch, was struck by the beauty and power of the winter as it changed the color of the water to a steelier blue and the clapboard houses to a more startlingly white white, "every nail hole vivid." Harry read to me what this woman thought at exactly that moment and how she "felt frightened that her own beauty and vitality would not always be part of it, that someday she would be gone like a lost odd-shaped piece from the center of a picture puzzle." I hadn't slept the night before, and Harry had tossed and turned with my absence from our bed. I said I lived every day like the woman lived that one moment, and Harry took the journal gingerly from my hands, gripped me tightly in his embrace and explained how it was not for the everyday—that feeling. Harry loves Morandi and irony and pleasure; I spent one year in prison after being caught for an act I believed was a call to duty, then some more time on the street with a "jones" as company, trying to find where I might fit, once the puzzle had changed and my husband had walked. Harry is with me for my passion, I with him for his constancy, not to me but to enthusiasm; and I must wait for one of his delicately circumscribed poems or stories to discover, in retrospect, his experience of me.

David is talking to Marisa and Harry about his life. His yearning is voracious. He wants everything, which is what?—everything, he says, as much as I can get of what there is. He will be fifty soon. He is making plans for the next year, the next month, the next week, and Marisa is wondering if she will be a part of any of these plans. However, what Marisa doesn't realize yet is that she has already vaporized for the moment. David and Harry are on a run now. Talking in that very intimate inside-chat language of artists speaking about great artists now past. Harry pushes David's ego. The crescendo is terrific. Their brilliance is breathtaking. When Wright was in Yugo at Lake Ohrid, he finally surrendered entirely to the dark-eyed beauty with the long knife-scar down the inside of her arm. Her mother was a gypsy from the Croatian lands. And it was the gypsy in her that made it possible for the mermaids of the lake to appear naturally later in the song. The song was unrhymed quatrains, predictably syllabic.

Marisa listens in rapt attention. Sarah probably would have as well, although I hear that sometimes she would quickly slip in a comment here or there if the boys stopped to catch their breath.

They discuss the poets—Lowell, Berryman and Schwartz—their lives and work, the summer they all spent congregating in Damariscotta, just up the coast from where we are now summering, and then their deaths. But mostly they speak intimately of how their favorite lines of each poet explain the stark insanity these men endured—pain similar to their own (but of course not their own, they'd never let those individual pains loose)—the torture of creation, not conceivable to the uninitiated. Harry quotes Berryman, who wrote about a night in Maine when he doffed his clothes and took off across the damp grass and nearby bluff that led to the water—that cold, turgid northern Atlantic water that he intended to walk beneath forever. Marisa has never heard of Berryman. She'd been an E-con major and the idea of some man walking underwater instead of imagining himself on the surface seems unproductive to her. She says so, but the boys don't notice.

I stand up and excuse myself. They don't notice. Neither David nor Harry has been jailed or institutionalized for madness, or jumped off a bridge into a frozen Mississippi River. It is unlikely they will enter the madness that was Schwartz's and be found dead in a welfare hotel. They've never had to smooth their moods with a palliative any stronger than Valium or wine. I believe these two know torment, but I believe they react to their fear of it in ways the initiated should not. If they are the analysts of human tumult, they should not flee from where shadows go in the dark. Yet the poems they speak of are self-referential, the discussion is indifferent to reality, aloof to its real horror and grandeur, and to the act of bearing witness to such as strange fruit. The conversation can only make people who are not a part of it feel uninitiated. And of course, that is part of its purpose—and for that reason more than any other I understand why Sarah finally left.

As I stand in front of the mirror in the ladies' room, I know that I would like to be Marisa tonight, expectant of new passion; my long legs, although ten years older, are able to move with a suppleness I feel can still compete with anyone. I will be forty in another year. At this age my mother was watching me grow into a twelve-year-old with dark-rimmed eyes and a friend with ratted hair—Barbara Chatfield. We used to tease our hair together in the bathroom that had built-in double sinks for me and my sister. Ratted hair, we called it. We would rat our hair into high peaks of fine flaxen hives. My mother used to try to add some class by calling the procedure back-combing, but finally she gave up and simply forbade me to wear my hair ratted. Marisa and my image of Sarah are reminding me of Barbara Chatfield.

One night Barbara and I were getting ready to go to the football game at North High School, which was not in our district. The bad kids were at North. The hoods. My mother had told me I couldn't go. I usually did what she said, but it seemed like such an unreasonable prohibition on her part that I told her I was going anyway. I was twelve and Barbara was twelve too and we were in junior high school together. I had just moved to Kansas City and was still in public school, where the girls put black eyeliner around their eyes, even on the inside lip of the rim of the eye. Both on the top and on the bottom. And that night, in total defiance of my mother, I stood with Barbara, each of us in front of a sink, and ratted first my hair and then Barbara's short hair. Hers was mostly on top of her head. The sides had been cut short. So with the ratting she had this big high head and little tiny body. Then we applied our eyeliner. My sister was already away at a girls' school studying music, and she had called me a slut the last time she had been home and seen my ratted hair. I had never done anything but put black eyeliner on my rims and rat my hair, and here I was a slut. When my mother joined in to call me a slut the night of the North football game, that did it. I was never to do anything girl-type naughty again, but I certainly did everything else, including bomb a building and end up on the lam for six months. But no slut stuff.

Something tugs my mind as I lean into the friendly bathroom lights while Harry waits at the table. Barbara had wide brown eyes, as if there could be a field of brown heather between the lashes. I wonder what she is going through now—now that we are about to become our mothers' age. Has she been divorced as I have. Is she without a child yet and therefore more of a child herself than our mothers before us at the same age. I still listen to Diana Ross and The Temptations, Eddie Kendricks singing about imagination more vividly than any bard. In front of the stereo, or with my headphones on, as loud as the ear can hear, I dance for hours in the dark, where fantasies come to life. I feel my strength when I dance, like the strength we had as children. That terrible hardness that promises us immortality. Even when we think we know about death, our conviction is that it is endless. That it is all possible. There is plenty of it all to go around. Time is what I'm thinking about—and friendships, as with Barbara. Relationships, like David and Sarah's. The big things. And now; now I don't feel that way. Does Barbara? Do her years have boundaries, specific memories associated with a unit of time, each one unique? I knew exactly when I had a particular thing. What it was and felt like. And which of those things I have already lost. Which are likely to be regained and which others are not. I feel my strength return when I dance. Always before, when there was the inevitability of change, no matter how sad, it was encompassed by the blind knowledge of youthfulness. For the first time that knowledge does not keep me company. I am a child at living without it, without the sureness of being young. All the hard child promises are leaving. On the other hand, neither are so many things irrevocable—abrupt—as they once seemed. Thoughts of return and certainty give an uneasy comfort as I dance now.

Youth is no loss to David tonight. I respect him for that. His energy has great resonance. He is the purist tonight. I leave the ladies' room revved.

I walk back to the table where Marisa is looking about angrily. Marisa, whose sensual antennae were so attuned to David only moments ago that the barest touch held an eroticism beyond any sexual act, rebukes David now when he reaches out to her as he continues speaking to Harry. The iridescence of David's jade-blue shirt is stunning as it hits his tanned skin. With his fascinating gift for articulating beauty, he carefully describes to Harry why he has placed the Italian peasant pitcher in the foreground of his new painting. Its whiteness will dominate, but there is a reason for that. I think that with his precise mind and own terrifying beauty, it is quite possible that David approaches that abstract notion of human perfection. Harry absently taps the fingers of my hand holding the stem of the red-wine glass. Marisa looks from one to the other of the men and slowly, individually grips each with an eye of contempt. She is supposed to be central to this evening. In the midst of David's explanation, Marisa interrupts. She says that she was not an E-con major for nothing. She emphasizes the word "nothing," and comprehends the effect of the words she has used to make the comment. She is interested not simply in the economy of lands and their finance, but of abuse, of feelings, of language. It is because of people like us she has found value in economizing. We who manufacture gratuitous pain, exert effort in undertakings such as walking underwater. We mourn too long and speak too much. We substitute talk for sex and food for eating. Marisa is playing her hole card, testing David, who finally turns to her. Harry leans back in his chair, bored with Marisa's outburst. He hates to see David interrupted.

I point to a man as he leaves the restaurant. Harry sees what I mean. The man is dressed in a suit, but bulging from every pocket, including the breast, are the articles of his daily commerce. Pencils, pads, a tool used for computers, handkerchiefs, stray strings, paper clips and rubber bands. Harry asks me first—Which is his? Outside the restaurant a line of cars is parked on the quaint little street. I point to a blue sedan, perfectly presentable at first glance but, upon inspection, filled with the odds and ends of a life, screwdrivers, a shirt, books, newspapers, even a bottle of wine. The man steps out of the restaurant and hesitates on the doorstep, looking up the street and down, enjoying the azure beginnings of sunset on the port, struck perhaps by the beauty and power of the summer sea, each docked fishing boat vivid against the darkening water. We wait until he leisurely strolls to the blue sedan. Then Harry and I touch pinkies as the entree is served and the tender pink meat of the fresh salmon in its intense green sorrel sauce becomes the topic of conversation.

The ocean, pinned alongside the road we travel back to our little vacation village, is stippled with moonbeams. It is as if the turbulence of the water lifts the waves up to the refulgent night light so that the sea will shimmer. Large shelves of driftwood become flotsam in the dark air and the slate and its rockweed appear as pirates of a modern sort, with long flowing hair and armbands and motorcycles as land gear. Harry tries to take my hand. I pull it away. His hair shapes a friendly halo around his face and I wish it could always look just as it does now. His father died when he was very young, so endings to him came early. Since then he has refused to start anything, until he met me.

Though there is, between us, a humor, we are tentative. Once when we were in Rome, where Harry says there are more priests than flies, I was suddenly petulant and quiet. I couldn't explain to him why. Well, he said, once I was quiet, but I went to see some people who lived on a soft carpet and I twirled into the middle of their favorite color and danced so well I was offered a Hollywood contract, which I turned down because of my impending ambassadorship to Jodrellia. And on and on he went.

The heat of the evening is waning and now I think of Harry and our summer bed, surrounded by windows which look out onto water and sky. Exactly where the elements meet is sometimes not at first apparent. There is no land, no shards of stone even, to break their contiguity. We float at night in the unseasonable chill of the strip of land that is so far from our city home. This morning when the sun did not come up over the sea and neither the night dampness nor the thick grayness out our window was broken, I looked to Harry's sleeping face for definition. I take his hand now in the backseat of David's silver Mercedes, tighten the grip of his fingers resting against the soft leather of the car's interior and so thank him for his company.

TOBIAS WOLFF

Migraine

It began while she was at work. At the first pang her breath caught and her eyes went wide open. Then it subsided, leaving a faint pressure at the back of her neck. Joyce put her hands on either side of the keyboard and waited. In the cubicles around her she heard the steady click of other keyboards. She knew what was happening to her, knew so well that when the next wave came she felt it not as pain but as dread for what was still to come. Joyce closed down the terminal.

She stopped in the doorway of her supervisor's office to say that she was leaving early. Her supervisor made a sympathetic face and offered to call a cab; she could pay for it out of casual cash if Joyce didn't feel up to the drive. "That's what it's there for," she said.

"I'll manage," Joyce told her. She added: "You don't have to whisper."

Joyce did not drive home. Instead she called a taxi from the lobby of the building, as she had meant to do all along. Her supervisor might think she was giving the money freely, but it wouldn't work out that way. Whatever people gave you from their overflowing hearts they remembered, and expected you to remember, forever. In Joyce's experience there was no such thing as casual cash.

When she got home she found two cardboard boxes in the living room, filled with her roommate's few belongings. Joyce and Dina had quarreled again, and now Dina was taking the final step in their agreement that she should move out. Joyce looked at the boxes. She considered searching through them but rejected the idea as beneath her. It was the kind of thing she used to do but had taught herself, with difficulty, to stop doing. She closed her eyes for a moment, swaying slightly from side to side, then crossed the room and turned the television on. A screaming host in a yellow blazer was trying to make himself heard over the delirium of his audience as a big clock ticked away the seconds. Joyce turned the volume off and went into the kitchen to boil water for tea.

The newspaper was strewn over the countertop, its edges fluttering in the breeze. Dina had left the window open again. Joyce kept after her, but she refused to take ordinary precautions, shrugging off her carelessness as the unimportant, even lovable consequence of being a free spirit with no material hangups. But Joyce saw through her; she saw that by playing this part Dina had forced the opposite part on her, the part of a grasping neurotic. Joyce caught herself acting like this sometimes. But not anymore. All that was over now.

Joyce started the water and went to the window. She put her elbows on the sill and rested her face in her hands, kneading her temples with her fingertips. She pressed harder and harder as the pulse quickened. At the worst moment she went suddenly deaf, as if someone had pushed her head underwater. Then it passed. Joyce heard her own ragged breathing. She heard the scrabble of pigeons' feet on the tile roof and children's voices from the playground of a nearby school. A jackhammer far enough away that its sound was bearable, even companionable, like the distant sound of marching bands in the college town where she had grown up.

Joyce let the breeze cool the sweat from her face. Then she closed the window and began to fill her brewing spoon with chamomile, tilia, and spearmint.

Joyce's eyes were scratchy. Her skin felt damp, and her blouse clung coldly where it had soaked through. She carried the tea to her bedroom and left it steeping on the nightstand while she undressed and sat on the edge of her bed. The room was a mess. Clothes everywhere, hanging from hooks and knobs and bunched on the floor. Newspapers. Suitcases still packed for a visit to Dina's parents which they'd never made because Joyce got sick. She bent to pick up a shoe, then dropped it again and rocked forward onto her feet. She wrapped herself in a terry bathrobe and went to the living room, where, propped up on the sofa, she sipped her tea and watched the silent television.

The tea helped. Not much, really, but it gave Joyce the only influence she had over what was happening to her. Except for Dina's massages nothing else worked at all. Joyce had taken medicinal baths. She'd gotten drunk and she'd gotten stoned. She had tried every remedy she'd ever heard of except obviously stupid ones like breathing through a scuba diver's tank. That suggestion appeared in a newsletter Dina had forced her to subscribe to until Joyce decided that reading about the problem all the time was making it worse instead of better. Also she despised the self-pitying tone of the newsletter, and its spurious implication that readers were not alone in their suffering.

Because they were alone. In fact everyone was alone all the time, but when you got sick you knew it, and that was a lot of what suffering was—knowing.

Joyce drank off the last of her tea. She set the mug down on the floor and looked at Dina's boxes. Almadén: Dina must have gotten them from the liquor store. The tops were open. A white mohair sweater lay on top of one box, a jumble of bottles and tubes on top of the other. Joyce leaned back. Even with her eyes closed she could sense the flickering of the television as the camera jumped from host to contestants, contestants to host. The apartment was profoundly quiet.

It was good to be alone. Really alone, without other people around to let you imagine that your life had mingled with theirs. It was never true. Even together, people were as solitary as cows in a field all facing off in different directions.

You couldn't enter the life of another person even when you wanted to. Back in August, Joyce and Dina had had a friend over for dinner, and in the course of the night she told a story about a couple they all knew who had recently been injured in a peculiar accident. A waterbed with a fat guy in it had crashed through their ceiling while they were watching TV and landed right on top of them. It was a miracle they weren't killed—not that this view of the episode could give much comfort to them, if you considered the hurts they did end up with: a broken collarbone for one, a sprained neck and concussion for the other. Joyce and Dina shook their heads when their friend came to the end of this story. They looked down at their plates. Joyce managed to keep her jaw clenched until Dina began snorting, and then all three of them let go. They howled. They couldn't stop howling. Joyce got so short of breath she had to push her chair back and lower her head between her knees.

And yet she had known these women. She had broken bread with them. Their pain should mean something to her. But even now, in pain herself, she could not feel theirs, nor come any closer than thinking she ought to feel it. And the same would be true if the waterbed had fallen on her and Dina instead of them. Even if it had killed her they would have laughed, then afterward regretted their laughter as she had regretted hers. They'd have gone on about their business, remembering her less and less often, and always with a sudden helpless smile like the one she felt on her own lips right now.

The effects of the tea were wearing off. Joyce raised her head from the pillows and slowly sat up. She put her hands on her knees. She blinked and was surprised to find that there were tears in her eyes. She stared at the boxes again, then looked at the television. A man in a booth was smiling steadfastly while the woman in the next booth emptied a bucket of white goo over his head.

Joyce pushed herself up. She went to the kitchen and filled the kettle with fresh water, then leaned against the counter with her head in her hands. The pulse was getting stronger again; each time it struck she dipped her head slightly as if she were nodding off. She entered another period of deafness. When she came out of it the kettle-top was rattling; beads of water rolled down the side of the kettle, hissing against the burner. Joyce refilled the brewing spoon, poured water into her cup, and carried it back to the sofa.

The man in the booth was now totally covered with gunk, some of it white, some satiny blue like motor oil. The woman in the next booth smiled at him while he leaned over and smashed eggs into her hair and against her forehead. The game seemed to have something to do with smiling. *Keep Smiling*—maybe that was the name of the show. Joyce set her tea down, knelt between Dina's boxes, and began searching through the one with the sweater on top.

Beneath the sweater were some photographs that Dina had kept in her vanity mirror, stuck between the glass and the frame. A whole series of her brother and his family, the two daughters getting taller from picture to picture, thinner, their sweet round faces growing narrow and sullen. A formal portrait of Dina's parents. Several snapshots of Joyce. Joyce glanced through these pictures and put them aside. She sat back on her heels. She drew a deep, purposeful breath and held her head erect, the very picture of a woman who has just managed to get the better of herself after a moment's weakness. The refrigerator motor kicked on. Bottles tinkled against each other. Joyce took another breath, then leaned forward again and continued to unpack the box.

Clothes. Shoes. A blow-dryer. Finally, at the bottom, Dina's books: *Chariots of the Gods, The Inner Game of Tennis, Many Mansions, In Search of Bigfoot, The No-Sweat Workout,* and *The Bhagavad-Gita.* Joyce opened *In Search of Bigfoot* and flipped through the illustrations. These included a voice-graph taken from a hidden microphone, the plaster cast of a large foot with surprisingly thin, fingerlike toes, and a blurry picture of the monster itself walking across a clearing with its arms swinging casually at its sides. Joyce repacked the box. No wonder her brain was going.

Dina had so much junk in her head that just having a conversation with her was like being sandblasted.

Once Dina moved out, Joyce was going to get her mind back in shape. She had a list of books she intended to read. She was going to keep a journal and take some night classes in philosophy. Joyce had done well in her philosophy survey course back in college, so well that when her professor returned the final paper he attached a note of thanks to Joyce for helping to make the class such a pleasure to teach.

Not that Joyce thought of becoming a professional philosopher. She knew that the chance for that, if it had ever really been there, was long gone. But she felt alive when she talked about ideas, and she still remembered the calm certainty with which her professor stalked the beliefs of his students down to their origins in superstition and hearsay and mere emotion. He was famous for making people cry. Joyce became adept at this kind of argument herself. She had moments of the purest clarity when she could feel herself striking closer and closer to the truth, while observing with detachment the panic of some classmate in danger of forfeiting an illusion. Joyce had not felt so clear about anything since then, because since then she had been involved with other people, and other people muddied the water. What with their needs and their demands and their feelings, their almighty anxieties to be tended to eight or nine times a day, you ended up telling so many lies that in time you forgot what the truth sounded like. But Joyce wasn't that far gone—not yet. Alone, she could begin to read again, to think, to see things as they were; to be as cold and hard as the truth demanded. No more false cheer. No more pretense of intimacy. No more lies.

Another thing. No more TV. Joyce had bought it only as a way of keeping Dina quiet, but that wouldn't be necessary anymore. She picked up the remote control, watched the rest of a commercial for shoes and another for pickup trucks, then turned the set off. The blank screen made her uncomfortable. Jumpy, almost as if it were watching her. Joyce put the remote control back on the coffee table and began to unpack the other box.

Halfway down, between two towels, she found what she was looking for. A pair of scissors, old German scissors that belonged to her. Joyce hadn't known she was looking for them but when her fingers touched the blades she almost laughed out loud. Dina had taken her scissors. Deliberately. There was no chance of a mistake, because these scissors were unique. They had cunning brass handles that formed the outline of a duck's head when closed, and the blades were engraved with German words that meant "For my dear Elise from her loving father." Joyce had found the scissors at an antique store on Post Street, and from the moment she brought them home Dina had been fascinated with them. She borrowed them so often that Joyce suspected her of inventing work just to have an excuse to use them. And now she had stolen them.

Joyce held the scissors above the box and snicked them open and shut several times. Wasn't this an eye-opener, though. Little Miss Free Spirit, Miss Unencumbered by Worldly Goods, Miss I Gots No Lock on de Door would rather steal than live without a pair of scissors. She was a thief—a hypocrite and a thief.

Joyce put the scissors down beside the remote control. She pushed the heel of her hand hard against her forehead. For the first time that day she felt tired. With luck she might even be able to sleep for a while.

Joyce slid the scissors back between the towels and repacked the box. Dina could have them. There was no point in saying anything to her because she would only pretend surprise and say it was an accident, and no way for Joyce to mention the scissors without revealing that she had searched the boxes. Dina could keep the scissors, and as time went by it would begin to dawn on her, so many months, so many years later, that Joyce must know she'd stolen them; but still Joyce would not mention them, not in her Christmas cards or the friendly calls she'd make on Dina's birthday or the postcards she'd send from the various countries she planned to visit. In the end Dina would know that Joyce had pardoned her and made a gift of the scissors, and then, for the first time, she would begin to understand the kind of person Joyce really was, and how wrong she had been about her—how blind and unfeeling. At last she would know what she had lost.

When Joyce woke up, Dina was standing beside the sofa looking down at her. A few bars of pale light lay across the rug and the wall; the rest of the room was in shadow. Joyce blinked and tried to raise her head. It felt like a stone. She gave up and settled back again.

"I knew it," Dina said.

Joyce waited. When Dina just kept looking at her, she asked, "Knew what?"

"Guess." Dina turned away and went into the kitchen; Joyce heard her running water into the kettle. Joyce called, "Are you referring to the fact that I'm sick?" Dina did not answer.

"It doesn't concern you," Joyce said.

Dina came to the kitchen door. "Don't do this, Joyce. At least be honest about what's happening, okay?"

"Pretend I'm not here," Joyce said. "This has nothing to do with you."

Dina shook her head. "I just can't believe you're doing this." She went back in the kitchen.

"Doing *what*?" Joyce asked. "I'm lying here on the couch. Is that what I'm doing?"

"You know," Dina said. She leaned into the doorway again and said, "Let's not play head games."

"Head games," Joyce repeated. "Jesus Mary and Joseph."

Dina took a step into the living room. "It isn't fair, Joyce."

Joyce turned onto her side. She lay motionless, listening to Dina bang around in the kitchen. "I'm not stupid!" Dina yelled.

"Nobody said you were."

Dina came into the living room carrying two cups. She set one down on the coffee table where Joyce could reach it and carried the other to the easy chair. "Thanks," Joyce said. She sat up slowly, nodding with dizziness. She picked up the tea and held it against her chest, letting the fragrant steam warm her face. Dina leaned forward and blew into her cup. "I have to admit," she said, "you look horrible."

Joyce smiled.

The two of them drank their tea, watching each other over the cups. "I'm going crazy," Dina said. "I can't plan a trip to the beach without you pulling this stuff."

"Ignore me," Joyce told her.

"That's what you always say. I'm leaving, Joyce. Maybe not now, but someday."

"Leave now," Joyce said.

"Do you really want me to?"

"If you're going to leave, leave now."

"You look just awful. It really hurts, doesn't it?"

"Pretend I'm not here," Joyce said.

"But I *can't*. You know I can't. That's what's so unfair."

"Dina."

"What?"

Joyce shook her head. "Nothing. Nothing."

Dina said, "Damn you, Joyce."

"You should leave," Joyce said.

"I'm going to. That's a promise. Don't ever say you didn't have fair warning."

Joyce nodded.

Dina stood and picked up one of the boxes. "I heard a great Polack joke today."

"Not now," Joyce said. "It would kill me."

Dina carried the box to her bedroom and came back for the other one, the one with the scissors. It was bulkier than the first and she had trouble getting a grip on it. "Damn you," she said to Joyce. "I can't believe I'm doing this."

Joyce finished her tea. She crossed her arms and leaned forward until her head was almost touching her knees. From Dina's bedroom she could hear the sound of drawers being yanked open and slammed shut. Then there was silence, and when Joyce raised her head Dina was standing over her again. "Poor old Joyce," she said.

Joyce shrugged.

"Move over," Dina said. She arranged herself at the end of the sofa and said, "Okay." Joyce lay down again, her head in Dina's lap. Dina looked down at her. She brushed back a lock of Joyce's hair. "Head games," Joyce said, and laughed.

"Shut up," Dina said.

Dina shifted a little to one side. She laid one hand on each side of Joyce's face, fingers along her cheeks, and began to push her thumbs against Joyce's temples. She moved her thumbs back and forth in tight rhythmic circles, steadily increasing the pressure. At first the rhythm was fluid and almost imperceptible, but as it grew more definite Dina began humming to herself. Joyce closed her eyes. She felt her eyelids flutter nervously, then grow still. She heard the newspaper rustle in the kitchen. She felt Dina purring her song. She felt the softness of Dina's thighs, and the warmth they gave off. Dina's hands were warm against her cheeks. Joyce reached up and covered them with her own hands as if to keep them there.

RAINER MARIA RILKE

TRANSLATED FROM THE FRENCH BY WILLIAM KULIK

Preface to Mitsou:
Forty Images by Balthus

Accompanied by Seven Images

Who understands cats? Do you think you do? As far as I'm concerned, their existence has never struck me as more than a fairly risky hypothesis.

If animals are going to belong to our world, they have to come partway into it, agreeing to tolerate to some extent our way of life; if not, whether it's out of hostility or fear, their way of relating will be to measure the distance between us and them.

Think of dogs: their relationship to us is so confidential and full of admiration that some of them seem to have abandoned their most ancient canine traditions to worship our customs and even our mistakes. And that's what makes them tragic and noble. Their decision to let us in forces them to live, so to speak, at the boundaries of their nature, constantly overstepping them with their humanized expressions and sentimental snouts.

But what attitude do cats have?—Cats are cats, and theirs is a cat world from one end to the other. They watch us, you say? But does anyone know if they condescend to hold even for a second our meaningless images at the backs of their eyes? Is their staring simply a kind of opposition, a magic refusal of eyes that have no room for us?—It's true that some of us let ourselves be moved by their cuddly, electrical caress. But they only need to recall how their favorite animal's strange, abrupt loss of attention often put an end to expressions of emotion they thought were reciprocated. And it's those same ones, privileged to be allowed near, who have been denied and rejected many times and, even as they pressed the mysteriously indifferent creature to their bodies, felt themselves stopped at the entrance to that world inhabited exclusively by cats, where they live in the midst of events none of us can even guess at.

Was man ever a contemporary?—I doubt it. And I assure you that sometimes at dusk the neighbor's cat leaps across my path, either unconscious of me or proving to the astonished world of things that I don't even exist.

Do you think I'm wrong to involve you in these reflections, all in the name of leading you up to the story my dear friend Balthus is going to tell you? Granted, he drew it without using words, but by and large his pictures should tell you what you need to know. So why should I repeat them in another form? I'd rather add what has not been said. Let me summarize the story:

Balthus (I think he was ten years old at the time) finds a cat at the Château de Nyon, which you are no doubt familiar with. He is allowed

to take him, and off he goes on a trip with his trembling little find. By
boat to Geneva, by streetcar to Molard. He introduces his new companion to home life, domesticating, spoiling and treasuring him. "Mitsou"
joyfully goes along with the rules and regulations, sometimes breaking
the monotony of the house with a playful, ingenious trick. Do you think
the fact that his master attaches an annoying leash when he walks him
is overdoing it? He does it because he's wary of all the fantasies lurking
in the heart of his loving but unknown and adventurous tomcat. However, he's wrong. Even a dangerous move is made without a problem,
and the unpredictable little creature adapts to his new surroundings with
amused obedience. Then suddenly he disappears. The house is in an
uproar; but, thank God, this time it's not serious: they find Mitsou out
on the lawn and Balthus, far from scolding the deserter, installs him on
the kindly radiator. I guess you can savor, as I do, the rich feeling that

follows such anguish. Alas! it's no more than a respite. Sometimes
Christmas is too seductive. You eat cake without counting the cost. You
get sick, and you go to bed. Mitsou, bothered by your overly-long sleep,
runs away instead of waking you up. What commotion! Fortunately,
Balthus has recovered enough to get right into the search for the run-
away. He begins by crawling under his bed: nothing there. Doesn't he
look really brave all alone in the cellar with his candle, a symbol of the
search that he takes everywhere, into the garden, out in the street:
nothing! Look at his solitary little figure: who abandoned him? A cat?—
Will his father's recent sketch of Mitsou comfort him? No, there was a
sense of foreboding in it, and the loss, permanent and inevitable, began
God only knows when! He comes back inside. He cries, showing you his
tears with both hands:

Look carefully at them.

That's the whole story. The artist told it better than I could. So what's left for me to say? Very little.

Finding a thing is always fun, because a moment before it didn't exist. But finding a cat: that's incredible! Because, let's admit it, that cat does not enter your life completely as, for example, one plaything or another would. While it's yours now, it's still somewhat apart, and that will always add up to:

$$\text{life} + \text{a cat},$$

which, I assure you, is a huge total.

To lose a thing is very sad. You need to imagine it's in poor condition, that wherever it is it's broken or has ended up rotting away.

But to lose a cat: No! that's not allowed. No one ever has. How can you lose a cat, a living thing, a live creature, a life? But you can lose a life: that's death!

> Right, that's death.

Finding. Losing. Have you considered carefully what loss involves? It's not simply the negation of that generous moment that fulfilled an expectation you yourself weren't aware you had. For between that moment and the loss there is always what we call—awkwardly enough, I admit—possession.

Now loss, as cruel as it is, has no effect on possession. If you like, it ends it or affirms it. But at bottom it's just a second acquisition, this time completely internal, with a different intensity.

Rainer Maria Rilke / *351*

And you experienced this, Balthus. No longer seeing Mitsou, you began to see him more.

Is he still alive? He lives on in you who, having delighted in his carefree kittenish gaiety, were obliged to express it through the labors of your sorrow.

And thus, a year later I found you grown and comforted.

But for those who will always see you only at the end of your book, I wrote the first—somewhat fanciful—part of this preface. So I could tell them at the end: "Don't worry: I'm here. So is Balthus. Our world is still intact.

There are no cats."

Château de Berg-am-Irchel
November 1920

ROY BLOUNT, JR.

A Man's Got to Read

*If there's one thing New York women share, it's a deep
lack of affection for Saul Bellow. . . . "Like Updike,
he's part of that generation of men that doesn't like
anybody." . . . But—and here's the poignant
part—they blame themselves and pathetically persist in
trying to read him. . . .*

    *And while we're on the subject of literary peeves,
we'd like to point out another absurdity—lying about
the books one has read. It's a very silly pretension, and
it implies grave intellectual insecurity. . . . And worse:
"I just reread Dead Souls!" Fat chance.*

—NEW YORK WOMAN

*If a single generalization can be made about
contemporary American literature . . . it would be that
it is the province of middle- and upper-class women.*

—JONATHAN YARDLEY, *The Washington Post*

It happens I am a guy who is all male, the ladies and I have no problems
my friend, yet it just so happens I read everything from the Virago Press
before the ink is dry, and take it from me *The Well of Loneliness* is eleven
hundred pages long about same-sex love among women which I am not
threatened by in the least, don't start with me.

    I got news for you, I dip back into *The Well of Loneliness* every night
of this world, unless we're talking Women's Poetry Collective night,
which I am there for, pallie, and you can bet the rent I have reread all
the poems myself, first, aloud, because that's the only way to catch all
the allusions.

    I catch all the allusions, my friend, you can take that to the bank,
and why? For one reason and one reason alone: I so desire.

    I read all the women's books and their reviews as they come out,
not to check my responses against the reviews because nothing could be

further from my thoughts, I could care less, and you're damn shootin' they pile up but I also never miss a panel discussion among women novelists who have never even been invited to appear in a panel discussion before, which is a special area of interest of mine which I wouldn't read too much into if I were you because it's been tried.

Ask around, I've got sealed postmarked letters mailed to myself registered mail containing my signed responses dated weeks before any of these old girl critics start telling you what response you're supposed to have—I know that game—so nobody has any valid basis for telling me my response is not my response, my friend.

The Bellows, the Updikes of this world, their men are as if they're in constant problems with women, being threatened by women, being sued by women, and it makes you want to go: Wait a minute, don't these men *read*? So don't start with me, my friend, reading's not a popularity contest, you want to start with me? Edith Wharton? I could show you candid shots of myself reading Wharton, printed in my high school yearbook junior year. No big deal, I was well-rounded, I dated all the majorettes, they had no complaints. But I'm just saying, in ninth grade I had to weather criticism (and not just from the boys, *compadre*) that I was favored by Mrs. Bissonette.

Put me through the fire, is what Mrs. Bissonette did, and I read and reread every woman she gave me, thank you. And you're hearing this from somebody who didn't go to Vassar Prep, my friend, where I went, unless you had a rep for not reading any men even, you had to fight your way into the rest room and out of it.

That's why, I don't have to tell you, I can handle myself—you're looking at a guy who knew he had to go out for baseball year after year because you'd better not get caught voluntarily reading anything by a woman in my high school without a bat in your hands, my friend. I read all of Carson McCullers in the on-deck circle.

Where I come from? Read a book by a woman? Out of the sheer desire to? If you couldn't handle yourself? Don't be in a dream world.

Dorothy Richardson—I've read over all of Richardson so many times I've lost track.

Wollstonecraft, all the commentary, all the letters.

Millet, Dworkin, Charlotte Yonge.

Ms. Lou Andreas-Salomé? You don't know her, except in the original.

Danielle Steel—that surprises you. I'm not the kind of guy you would think, to look at me, to hear my manner of speaking, that I would read quote romance fiction end quote, but the thing you don't understand about me is, I've got nothing to prove. The heroine's bodice ripped by swashbucklers and it's cool because they're there for her—*I* got no problem with that, believe me, it's what women have instead of porn, which I don't read. That is I do read the classic porn but only once and that's the one thing I don't read out of the sheer desire to, I read it because I want to be able to keep certain women intellectually honest, my friend.

You can write this down: The main market for porn is women, certain women, I'm not saying all women, I'm saying certain women, who read it to find out what they think men really think about women so they can keep certain men defensive.

That's their problem, that's their nose out of joint, they wouldn't believe you if you're standing right there in front of them with *The Golden Notebook* in your hand with your finger holding your place where you've been rereading it for the fifth or sixth time with obviously well-thumbed pages and frequent underlining. Or a Sarah Orne Jewett or a Djuna Barnes, or any of the many neglected early accounts by pioneer women who were abducted by Indians in which they constantly go out of their way to allude to people being stripped naked, men and women alike being stripped naked by Indians for all to see their shame, but I don't read them for that reason, *I* know I don't, it doesn't matter what anybody else thinks because *I* know *I* don't.

That's all. Enough said. I got to go read.

EDWARD KOREN

The Lust for Revenge

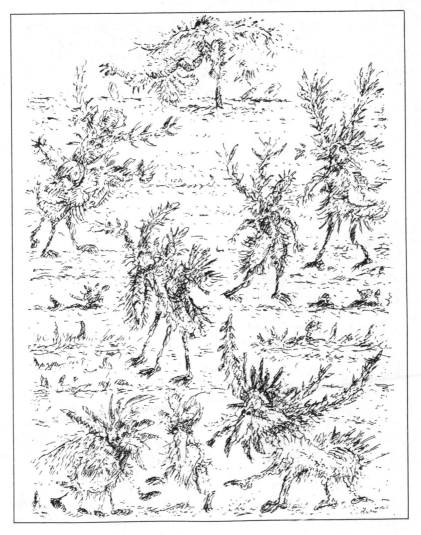

GRETEL EHRLICH

This Autumn Morning

When did all this happen, this rain and snow bending green branches, this turning of light to shadow in my throat, these bird-notes going flat, and how did these sawtooth willow leaves unscrew themselves from the twig, and the hard, bright paths trampled into the hills loosen themselves to mud? When did the wind begin churning inside trees, and why did the sixty-million-year-old mountains start looking like two uplifted hands holding and releasing the gargled, whistling, echoing grunts of bull elk, and when did the loose fires inside me begin *not* to burn?

Wasn't it only last week, in August, that I saw the stained glass of a monarch butterfly clasping a purple thistle flower, then rising as if a whole cathedral had taken flight?

Now what looks like smoke is only mare's tails—clouds streaming—and as the season changes, my young dog and I wonder if raindrops might not be shattered lightning.

It's September. At this time of year light is on the wane. There is no fresh green breast of earth to embrace. None of that. Just to breathe is a kind of violence against death. To long for love, to have experienced passion's deep pleasure, even once, is to understand the mercilessness of having a human body whose memory rides desire's back unanchored from season to season.

Last night while driving to town I hit a deer. She jumped into my path from behind bushes so close I could not stop. A piece of red flesh flew up and hit the windshield. I watched as she ran off limping. There was nothing I could do. Much later, on the way home, I looked for her again. I could see where a deer had bedded down beside a tree, but there was no sign of a wounded animal, so I continued on.

Halfway up our mountain road a falling star burned a red line across the sky—a meteorite, a pristine piece of galactic debris that came into existence billions of years before our solar system was made. The tail stretched out gold and slid. I stopped the truck, then realized I was at the exact place where, years ago, I declared love to a friend as a meteor shower burst over us. At dawn, a belted kingfisher peered down into water as if reading a message to us about how to live, about what would suffice.

Tonight on the same road in a different year I see only the zigzagging of foxes whose red tails are long floats that give their small bodies buoyancy. No friends meet me to view the stars. The nights have turned cold. The crickets' summer mating songs have hardened into drumbeats and dark rays of light pole out from under clouds as if steadying the flapping tent of the sky.

Even when the air is still I keep hearing a breeze, the way it shinnies up the bones of things, up the bark of trees. A hard frost pales the hayfields. Tucked into the flickering universe of a cottonwood tree, yellow leaves shaped like gloved hands reach across the green umbrella for autumn.

It's said that after fruition nothing will suffice, there is no more, but who can know the answer? I've decided to begin at the end, where the earth is black and barren. I want to see how death is mixed in, how the final plurals are taken back to single things—if they are; how and where life stirs out of ash.

On May 5, the first day the roads opened, my husband and I drove to Yellowstone Park. Twenty miles before the east entrance, we were greeted by buffalo: four mother cows, one yearling, and a newly born calf. At Sylvan Pass a young couple were skiing down a precipitous snow-covered landslide, then trudging up the nearly vertical slope carrying their skis. Just before we reached Yellowstone Lake, a pair of blue grouse, in the midst of a courting display, could not be moved from the center of the road. Neck and tail feathers plumed and fanned out; we waited. The lake was all ice. Far out, a logjam—upended, splintered, frozen in place—was the eye's only resting place in all that white.

Around the next bend I came on a primordial scene: north of Mary's Bay, wide, ice-covered meadows were full of dead buffalo, and searching for grass in among the carcasses were the barely live bison who had survived a rigorous winter, so thin they looked like cardboard cutouts, a deep hollow between their withers and ribs.

We drove on. More dead bison, and dead elk. The Park biologists were saying that roughly twenty-eight percent of both herds wintered-killed this year, not only because the fires diminished some of their forage but also because the drought had brought us five years of mild winters, thus allowing the old and sick animals to survive.

Between Madison Junction and the Firehold River we stood in the charred ruins of a lodgepole pine forest. The hollow trunks of burned-out trees looked as if they had been picked up and dropped, coming to rest at every possible angle. The ground was black. Where the fire had burned underground, smoldering root systems upended trees; where there had once been a pond or a bog with ducks and swans was now a waterless depression. Way back in the trees, a geyser hissed, its plume of white steam a ghost of last year's hundred-mile-long streamer of smoke.

Later we returned to the lake and sat on the end of a long spit of land that angles out into water. From there it's difficult to tell there was a fire. Lodgepole pines fringe the shore. A cloud that had moved off Mount Sheridan to the south rolled toward us, its front edge buffeted by a north wind. In ancient Greece it's said that Boreas, god of the north wind, became jealous of his lover, Pitys, who had been flirting with Pan, and threw her against a rocky ledge. In that moment she turned into a pine tree. The amber drops of sap at the breaks of limbs are her tears.

Boreas shattered the cloud above me and blew it over the lake, and the trees at the edge took on wild shapes. The Buriats in eastern Siberia considered groves of pines sacred and always rode through them in silence. A trumpeter swan glided by, then a tribe of golden-eye ducks headed for a sheltered inlet.

Pines are such ancient trees—first appearing 170 million years ago. But what does Boreas care? He cut through the cloud and sent a bulbous chunk toward me until it broke off that fragile tail of land as if it had been a tree.

That was May, and now it's September and already frost is breaking down the green in leaves, then clotting like blood as tannin, anthocyanin, carotene, and xanthophyll. If pines represent continuance, then cottonwood leaves show me how the illusion of time punctuates space, how we fill those dusty, gaseous voids with escapades of life and death, dropping the tiny spans of human days into them.

This morning I found a yearling heifer, bred by a fence-jumping bull out of season, trying to calve. I saw her high up on a sage-covered slope, lying down, flicking her tail, and thought she must have colic. But I was wrong. The calf's front feet and head had already pushed out, who knows how many hours before, and it was dead.

I walked her down the mountain to the calving shed, where a

friend, Ben, and I winched the dead calf out. We doctored the heifer for uterine infections, and I made a bed of straw, brought fresh creekwater and hay. The heifer ate and rested. By evening she had revived, but by the next morning she seemed to have contracted pneumonia. Immediately I gave her a huge shot of penicillin. She worsened. The antibiotics didn't kick in.

That night she lay on her straw bed emitting grunts and high-pitched squeals. The vet came at midnight. We considered every possibility—infection, pneumonia, poisoning—what else could it be? Another day and her condition worsened. Not any one symptom, but a steady decline. I emptied more medicine into her, knowing it was doing no good, but my conscience forbade me to do less. The vet came again and left. He suggested it might be "hardware disease"—a euphemism for an ingested piece of metal, a nail or barbed wire, cutting into her throat or stomach or heart. I put a magnet down her throat. Strange as it seems, it sometimes picks up the metal, taking it all the way through the digestive tract. No response. I sat with her. I played music—Merle Haggard and Mozart—wondering if my presence consoled or irritated her. This was not a cow we had raised, and she seemed unsure of me. Could a calf-puller, a shot-giver *not* mean harm?

In the morning I found she had not eaten or taken any water. Her breathing was worse. I lay on the straw beside her and slept. Before coming to the barn I had smelled something acrid—an old, familiar smell of death's presence, although she was still alive. Yet the sounds she made now had changed from grunting to a low moan, the kind of sound one makes when giving in to something. By nightfall she was dead.

Today yellow is combed all through the trees, and the heart-shaped cottonwood leaves spin downward to nothingness. I know how death is made—not why—but where in the body it begins, its lurking presence before the fact, its strangled music as if the neck of a violin were being choked; I know how breathing begins to catch on each rib, how the look of the eye flattens, gives up its depth, no longer sees past itself; I know how easily existence is squandered, how noiselessly love is dropped to the ground.

When I go to town I notice the feed store calendar: a cornucopia bursting with the produce of the season—nuts, apples, wheat, corn, pumpkins, beans. I've seen death eat away at the edges of plenty. Now I want to watch life fill in the fractal geometries of what exists no more.

Now I walk to the ranch graveyard. On a ranch, death is as much a constant as birth. The heifer is there with her calf, legs stretched out straight, belly bloated . . . but the white droppings of ravens—who are making a meal of her—cascade down her rib cage like a waterfall.

I wander through the scattered bones of other animals who have died. Two carcasses are still intact: Blue and Lawyer, saddle horses who put in many good years. Manes, tails, hair gone, their skin has hardened to rawhide, dried to a tautness, peeling back just slightly from ribs, noses, and hooves, revealing a hollow interior as if letting me see that the souls are really gone.

After fruition, after death, after black ash, perhaps there is something more, even if it is only the droppings of a scavenger, or bones pointing every which way as if to say, "Touch here, touch here," and the velocity of the abyss when a loved one goes his way, and the way wind stirs hard over fresh graves, and the emptying out of souls into rooms and the mischief they get into, flipping switches, opening windows, knocking candles out of silver holders, and after, shimmering on water like leaked gas ready to explode.

Mid-September. Afternoons I paddle my blue canoe across our nine-acre lake, letting water take me where it will. The canoe was a gift: eight dollars at the local thrift store.

As I drift aimlessly, ducks move out from the reeds, all mallards. Adaptable, omnivorous, and hardy, they nest here every year on the two tiny islands in the lake. After communal courtship and mating, the extra male ducks are chased away, but this year one stayed behind. Perhaps he fathered a clutch on the sly or was too young to know where else to go. When the ducklings hatched and began swimming, he often tagged along, keeping them loosely together until the official father sent him away. Then he'd swim the whole circumference of the lake alone, too bewildered and dignified to show defeat.

A green net of aquatic weeds knots the water, holding and releasing me as if I were weightless, as if I were loose change. Raised on the Pacific, I can row a boat, but I hardly know how to paddle. The water is either ink or a clear, bloodless liquid, and the black watersnakes that writhe as I plunge my paddle are trying to write words.

Evening. In Kyoto I was taken to a moon-viewing room atop an ancient house on temple grounds. The room was square and the windows on four sides were rice-paper cutouts framed by bamboo, rounds split down the center, allowing the viewer to re-create the moon's phase. To view the moon, one had to look through the moon of the window.

Tonight the lake is a mirror. The moon swims across. Every now and then I slide my paddle into its face. Last week I saw the moon rise twice in one night: once, heavy and orange—a harvest moon—heaving over the valley, and later, in the mountains, it rose small, tight, and bright. But in August the moon went blind. I sat outside with a bottle of wine and watched a shade pull across its difficult, cratered solitude. Earlier, while thumbing through a book of late Tang poets, I came on this: "But this night, the fifteenth of the eighth month, was not like other nights; for now we saw a strange thing: the rim was as though a strong man hacked off pieces with an axe," and "Darkness smeared the whole sky like soot, and then it seemed for thousands of ages the sky would never open." That was 810. Over a thousand years later, a lunar eclipse happened again: same day, same month.

Now a half-moon slants down light, and shadows move desolation all over the place. At dawn a flicker knocks. The hollow sound of his labor makes leaves drop in yellow skirts around the trunks of trees. Water bends daylight. Thoughts shift like whitecaps, wild and bitter. My gut is a harp. Its strings get plucked in advance of any two-way communication by people I love, so that I know when attentions wane or bloom, when someone dear goes from me. From the same battered book I read this by Meng Chiao: "The danger of the road is not in the distance, ten yards is far enough to break a wheel. The peril of love is not in loving too often. A single evening can leave its wound in the soul."

Tonight thin spines of boreal light pin down thoughts as if skewered on the ends of thrown quills. I'm trying to understand how an empty tube behind a flower swells to fruit, how leaves twisting from trees are pieces of last year's fire spoiling to humus. Now trees are orange globes, their brightness billowing into cumulus clouds. As the sun rises, the barometer drops. Wind swings around, blasting me from the east, and every tin roof shudders to a new tune.

Stripped of leaves, stripped of love, I run my hands over my single wound and remember how one man was like a light going up inside me, not flesh. Wind comes like horn blasts: the whole mountain range is gathered in one sucking breath. Leaves keep coming off trees as if circulating through a fountain; aspens growing in steep groves glow.

I search for the possible in the impossible. Nothing. Then I try for the opposite, but the yellow leaves in trees—shaped like mouths—just laugh. Tell me, how can I shut out the longing to comprehend?

Wind slices off pondswells, laying them sharp and flat. I paddle and paddle. Rain fires into the water all around me, denting the mirror. The pond goes colorless. It is blue or gray or black. Where the warm spring feeds in, a narrow lane has been cut through aquatic flowers to the deep end. I slide my canoe into the channel. Tendrils of duckweed wave green arms. Are they saying hello or good-bye?

Willows, clouds, and mountains lie in the lake's mirror, although they look as if they're standing. I dip my paddle and glide—I think I'm getting the hang of it now—and slide over great folds of time, through lapping depositions of memory, over Precambrian rock, then move inward, up a narrow gorge where a hidden waterfall gleams. After fruition, water mirrors water.

The canoe slides to shore and I get out. The way a cloud tears, letting sun through, then closes again, I know that every truth flies. I get down on my hands and knees and touch my tongue to water: the lake divides. Its body is only chasm after chasm. Like water I have no skin, only surface tension. How exposed I feel. Where a duck tips down to feed, one small ripple causes random turbidity, ceaseless chaos, and the lake won't stop breaking. . . . I can punch my finger through anything. . . .

Much later, in the night, in the dark, I shine a flashlight down: my single wound is a bright scar that gives off hooked light like a new moon.

I try to cut things out of my heart, but the pack rat who has invaded my study won't let me. He has made himself the curator of my effects, my despair, my questioning, my memory. Every day a new show is installed. As if courting, he brings me bouquets of purple aster and sage gone to seed, cottonwood twigs whose leaves are the color of pumpkins. His scat is scattered like black rain: books, photographs, manuscripts are covered. The small offering I set out years ago when I began using this room—a fistful of magpie feathers and the orange husks of two tangerines—have been gnawed into. Only the carved stone figure of a monk my mother gave me during tumultuous teenage years stands solid. The top of the narrow French desk where I write is strewn with torn-off cactus paddles—all lined up end to end—as if to remind me of how prickly the practice of vandalizing one's consciousness can be, how what seems inexpressible is like a thorn torn off under the skin.

The pack rat keeps me honest and this is how: He reminds me that I've left something out. Last August I returned to Yellowstone Park. I wanted to begin again in barrenness, I wanted to understand ash. This time the carcasses were gone—some eaten by bears, coyotes, eagles, and ravens; others taken away by the Park. Those charnel grounds where only a green haze of vegetation showed had become tall stands of grass. And the bison—those who survived—were fat.

In a grassland at the northern end of the Park I stood in fairy-rings of ash where sagebrush had burned hot, and saw how mauve lupine seeds had been thrown by twisted pods into those bare spots. At the edges were thumbnail-size sage seedlings. Under a stand of charred Douglas firs was a carpet of purple asters and knee-high pine grass in bloom for the first time in two hundred years—its inflorescence had been stimulated by fire. I saw a low-lying wild geranium that appears only after a fire, then goes into dormancy again, exhibiting a kind of patience I know nothing of. In another blackened stand of trees it was possible to follow the exact course of the fire by stepping only where pine grass was in flower; I could see how groundfire had moved like rivulets of water. In places where the fire burned hottest there was no grass, because the organic matter in the soil had burned away, but there were hundreds of lodgepole pine seedlings; the black hills were covered with dark pink fireweed.

Just when all is black ash, something new happens. Ash, of course, is a natural fertilizer, and it's now thought to have a water-holding capacity: black ground is self-irrigating in a self-regulating universe. How quickly "barrenness becomes a thousand things and so exists no more."

Now it's October. I'm on the pond again, that dumping ground for thought. Water clanks against the patched hull. It is my favorite music, like that made by halyards against aluminum masts. It is the music emptiness would compose if emptiness could change into something. The seat of my pants is wet because the broken seat in the canoe is a sponge holding last week's rainwater. All around me sun-parched meadows are green again.

In the evening the face of the mountain looks like a ruined city. Branches stripped bare of leaves are skeletons hung from a gray sky and next to them are tall buildings of trees still on fire. Bands and bars of color are like layers of thought, moving the way stream water does, bending at point bars, eroding cutbanks. I lay my paddle down, letting the canoe drift. I can't help wondering how many ways water shapes the body, how the body shapes desire, how desire moves water, how water stirs color, how thought rises from land, how wind polishes thought, how spirit shapes matter, how a stream that carves through rock is shaped by rock.

Now the lake is flat but the boat's wake—such as it is—pushes water into a confusion of changing patterns, new creations: black ink shifting to silver, and tiny riptides breaking forward-moving swells.

I glide across rolling clouds and ponder what my astronomer friend told me: that in those mysterious moments before the big bang there was no beginning, no tuning up of the orchestra, only a featureless simplicity, a stretch of emptiness more vast than a hundred billion Wyoming skies. By chance this quantum vacuum blipped or burped as if a bar towel had been snapped, and resulted in a cosmic plasma that fluctuated into and out of existence, finally moving in the direction of life.

"But where did the bar towel come from?" I asked my friend in a small voice. No answer. Somehow life proceeded from artlessness and instability, burping into a wild diversity that follows no linear rules. Yet, in all this indeterminacy, life keeps opting for life. Galactic clouds show a propensity to become organic not inorganic matter; carbon-rich meteorites have seeded our earthly oasis with rich carbon-based compounds; sea vents let out juvenile water warm enough to make things grow, and sea meadows brew up a marine plasma—matter that is a thousandth of a millimeter wide—and thus give rise to all plant life and the fish, insects, and animals with which it coevolved.

I dip my paddle. The canoe pivots around. Somewhere out there in the cosmos, shock waves collapsed gas and dust into a swirl of matter made of star-grains so delicate as to resemble smoke, slowly aggregating, gradually sweeping up and colliding with enough material to become a planet like ours.

Dusk. A bubble of cloud rises over the mountain. It looks like the moon, then a rock tooth pierces it and wind burnishes the pieces into soft puffs of mist. Forms dissolve into other forms: a horsehead becomes a frog; the frog becomes stick figures scrawled across the sky. I watch our single sun drop. Beyond the water, a tree's yellow leaves are hung like butterlamps high up near the trunk. As the sun sinks, the tree appears to be lit from the inside.

Another day. Listen, it's nothing fancy. Just a manmade pond in the center of the ranch, which is at the northern, mountainous edge of a desolate state. And it's fall, not too much different from the last fourteen autumns I've lived through here, maybe warmer at times, maybe windier, maybe rainier. I've always wondered why people sit at the edge of water and throw rocks. Better to toss stones at the car that brought you, then sit quietly.

This lake is a knowing eye that keeps tabs on me. I try to behave. Last summer I swam in its stream of white blossoms contemplating "the floating life." Now I lie on its undulant surface. For a moment the lake is a boat sliding hard to the bottom of a deep trough, then it is a lover's body reshaping me. Whenever I try to splice discipline into my heart, the lake throws diamonds at me, but I persist, staring into its dangerous light as if into the sun. On its silvered surface I finally locate desire deep in the eye, to use Wallace Stevens's words, "behind all actual seeing."

Now wind pinches water into peaked roofs as if this were a distant city at my feet. I slide my canoe onto one of the tiny, humpbacked islands. The rind of earth at water's edge shows me where deer have come to drink and ducks have found shelter. It's not shelter I seek but a way of going to the end of thought.

I sit the way a monk taught me: legs crossed, hands cupped, thumbs touching, palms upward. The posture has a purpose—it helps transform breathing into energy, but the pose, as it must appear to the onlooker, is a ruse. There is no such thing as stillness, of course, since life progresses by vibration—the constant flexing and releasing of muscles, the liquid pulse, the chemical storms in the brain. I use this island only to make my body stop, this posture to lower the mind's high-decibel racket.

The ground is cold. All week blasts of Arctic air have braided into lingering warmth. Sometimes a lip of ice grows outward from shore, but afternoon sun burns it back. Water rubs against earth as if trying to make a spark. Nothing. The fountain of leaves in trees has stopped. But how weightless everything appears without the burden of leaves.

At last light my friend the bachelor duck makes a last spin around the lake's perimeter. When the breeze that sweeps up from the south turns on itself, he swims against the current, dipping out of sight behind a gold-tinged swell. Fruition comes to this, then: not barrenness but lambency.

November 1. The ducks are gone. A lip of ice grew grotesquely fast during the night and now stretches across the water. I *can't* sit. Even the desire to be still, to take refuge from despair in the extremes of diversity, to bow down to light is a mockery. Nothing moves. Looking out across the lake is like viewing a corpse: no resemblance to the living body. I go to the house despondent. When news of the California earthquake came I thought about stillness and movement, how their juxtaposition creates an equilibrium, how their constant rubbing sparks life and imposes death. But now I don't know. Now the island is like a wobbly tooth, hung by a fine thread to the earth's mantle, and the lake is a solid thing, a pane of glass that falls vertically, cutting autumn off.

A week later. It has snowed and I'm sitting on the white hump of the island. My thrift-store canoe is hopelessly locked in ice. Today the frozen lake is the color of my mother's eyes—slate blue, but without the sparkle. Snow under me, ice at my feet, no mesmerizing continuum of ripples forwarding memory, no moving lines in which to write music. And yet . . .

I put my nose to ice. It's the only way I'll know what I'm facing. At first it looks flat and featureless, like an unborn cosmos, but closer I see its surface is dented and pocked, and across the middle, where the water is deepest, there are white splotches radiating arms like starfish. It's like looking up the spiral arm of a galaxy.

At midday the barometer drops and the radio carries stockman's warnings: high winds, snow and blowing snow in the northern mountains. That's us. Sure enough the wind comes, but it's a warm chinook. Instead of snow, rain undulates across the face of the mountains. Then the storm blows east.

In the morning I go to the lake. Drifts of snow dapple the white surface like sand dunes, and between, dead leaves scud across the ones trapped under ice. But at the north end, where the warm spring feeds in, there is open water—a tiny oval cut like a gem. Something catches my eye: a duck swims out from the reeds, all alone. Is it my bachelor duck? Around and around he goes, then climbs onto the lip of ice and faces the warm sun.

How fragile death is, how easily it opens back into life. Inside the oval, water ripples, then lies flat. The mirror it creates is so small I can see only a strip of mountains and the duck's fat chest bulging. I want to call out to him: "Look this way, I'm here too this autumn morning," but I'm afraid I'll scare him.

He goes anyway, first sliding into the water, then swimming anxious laps. When he takes off, his head is like a green flame. He circles so close I can hear the wing-creak and rasp of feathers. Over the lake he flies, crossing the spillway and dam bank, then up through a snowy saddle, not south as I would have expected, but northwest, in the direction of oncoming storms.

September–November 1989

JIM HARRISON

Poetry as Survival

There have been quite enough exquisite apologias for poetry written over the centuries, from Aristotle to Catullus and Vergil, Wang Wei, Dante, Shakespeare and Dryden, down to Whitman, Yeats, Pound and García Lorca. But then, unlike the sciences, such knowledge is not easily transmittable or cumulative, and an art so seemingly fragile to the masses has its value in continual question by even apparently educated men.

Frankly, this is not my fault, and I have long since given up concerning myself with the matter. As a poet I am the bird, not the ornithologist, and I am not going to spend my increasingly precious days stuffing leaks in an educational system as perverse and sodden as the mercantile society for which it supplies faithful and ignorant fodder. If you wished to draw attention to poetry in a country where anything not at least peripherally attached to greed is considered nonsense, you would have to immolate a volunteer poet in a 751 BMW. In a Giorgio Armani suit. Wearing a gold Rolex. With the first infant porpoise to wear eye shadow on his lap. That sort of thing.

In other words, if you have to ask what poetry is good for, it's never going to be any good for you. Poetry came into being before the first club was swapped for an attractive antler, and about the same time Orc traded a lady a wild melon for raising her otter-skin skirt. Poetry, like the grizzly bear, is good for its own magnificent selfness and is not a utilitarian cog to improve someone's life-style. Poetry may very well help you get behind. Your legs might grow downward into the ground in certain locations. You will also turn inside out without warning.

The most ubiquitous misunderstanding of poetry is that it is heightened and energized daily speech. Martin Heidegger said, "Poetry proper is never merely a higher mode of everyday language. It is rather the reverse: everyday language is a forgotten and therefore used-up poem, from which there hardly resounds a call any longer." Poetry at its best is the language your soul would speak if you could teach your soul to speak. Poets are folks who know they are going to die someday and feel called upon to make up songs about this death and the indefinite reprieve they are traveling through. Rarely a philosopher, the poet hopes to celebrate life on life's terms, even though he works within the skeleton of a myth to which there is no longer a public celebration. As Gerald Vizenor (the astounding Native American author of *Griever: An American Monkey King in China*) would have it, "He holds cold reason on a lunge line while he imagines the world."

Of course, such temperaments are capable of grand absurdities, and the presumption of the comic is a more graceful modus operandi than a longish face, or waving your heart around by its bloody strings; like the ministry, poetry is thought to be a calling, but unlike specifically religious vocations, poetry can't cut off the horse's legs to get him into a stall. In order for Shakespeare to create the character of Hamlet he must also be capable of creating Falstaff, and *A Midsummer Night's Dream*.

But to return to earth: Americans seem to wish to live within situation comedies and unquestionably elect their officials on this basis. Yet there is a wild spiritual longing in the landscape that surfaces in dozens of odd forms: Jimmy Swaggart, est, channeling and other New Age nostrums, body-Nazi fitness mystics, drug obsessives, music goofies, even the nether forms of the ecological movement where Smokey the Bear seems to want to mate Saint Teresa.

You particularly notice this on long first-class expense-account flights when your seatmate invariably asks, "What do you do?" When you say "Poet" you get either a quiet ride or the sort of weirdly fascinating conversation I imagine you might receive if you admitted you were a psychiatrist. What emerges, à la those fictive Russian train rides of the nineteenth century, is the secret life, the unlived life, the immense weight of longing, the puzzlement of mortality, the concealed idiosyncratic religion everyone carries around like a bulletproof (one hopes) vest. It is important to keep the conversation visceral, so you insist that a poet is only "the pulse of a wound that probes to the opposite side" (García Lorca). You tell your seatmate that when he looks in the mirror he might say, "Jeezo-peezo, I'm getting old," while Shakespeare said, "Devouring time, blunt thou thy lion's paws," and the latter scans better. You tell him that when he sees a lovely naked woman on a bed he might say "Wow," while García Lorca said:

> Your belly is a battle of roots,
> your lips a blurred dawn,
> under the tepid roses of the bed
> the dead moan, waiting their turn.

If my fellow passenger is involved with computers or becomes irritable, I like to use Vizenor to remind him that "we remember dreams, not data, at the wild end." Of course it is important to remain light, loose and friendly through all of this. The average highly placed executive is more macho than a Mexican assassin, what with the executive's insistence on playing hardball around the clock. In return for my modest bon mots I receive insider stock tips, although I am too mistrustful to indulge myself in these.

"Who shall revoke jubilance?" Rilke asked, rather innocently, to which we could answer, "Everyone and everything." Joseph Campbell pointed out that in mythological terms the "rejection of the call" walls the Hero up in boredom and dread. A poet is supposed to be a hero of consciousness, and the most destructive force in his or her life is liable to be the unwritten poem. There is a touch of the schizoid to the practice of any art, and the poet becomes an outsider to maintain the integrity of what he writes. During not infrequent depressions (an occupational hazard) I wonder how black and Native American poets survive at all, for they are enveloped in a double schizoid bind, the Indians perhaps more than the blacks because they are our most thoroughly ignored minority.

Perhaps I've rejected too loudly certain utilitarian aspects of poetry, if only because we are capable of turning everything—from a simple rock to a guitar to violent death—into a nostrum, another of those self-help missions we use to hammer ourselves as if we were tract houses. D. H. Lawrence insisted that the only aristocracy was consciousness, if we consider all the other limitations within and without our lives. If this notion is valid, and I suspect it is, then poetry could be the primary aid if you wish to be more conscious, a somewhat singular ambition when you take a sideward glance at popular culture.

The flip side comes from that grandiose, rather romantic philosopher Friedrich Nietzsche, who once said, "I'd rather be a satyr than a saint," when he, in fact, was a tertiary-syphilitic hunchback. But he also said, "Stare into the abyss long enough, and it will stare back into thee." It has become apparent to many that the ultimate disease, the abyss of postmodernism in art and literature, is subjectivity, and that the disease is both sociopathic and terminal. In other words, if the poet or aficionado of consciousness does not own a coequal passion for life herself, the social contract, he better be wary about the abyss he chooses. The obvious traps are the two halves of the brain in incestuous embrace, neurotic noodling, and ordinary spiritual adventurism of the most claustrophobic sort.

I remember that in my weakest moments I have regretted the problems I've caused my family and myself for refusing to be a poet-teacher: the shuddering economic elevator of the self-employed to whom the words *boom* and *bust* are euphemisms; the writer as farm laborer, block-layer, journalist, novelist, screenwriter, but still thinking of himself as a poet. At times when I actually needed a battery of psychiatrists the alternatives were fishing, bird hunting, and drinking. I suspect this intimacy with the natural world has been a substitute for religion, or a religion of another sort. I remember as a young bohemian discovering garlic in New York City in 1957 when a Barnard girl made me listen to Richard Tucker sing something from Jewish liturgy. I was swept away by beauty, also jealousy, as the music was so powerful and unlike the sodden Protestant hymns of my youth. I felt the same thing years later in St. Basil's Cathedral in Leningrad, where I was told that in the Russian Orthodox Church one does not talk to God, one sings.

I am reaching toward something here by a circuitous route. At the very least the life I have chosen, although it always lacked a safety net, made up for the lack with pure oxygen. I remember a single year when I went to Europe, the Soviet Union, Africa and South America. I kept recalling Allen Ginsberg's line about "the incredible music of the streets." Cultures less economically sophisticated than our own began to fascinate me. Gabriel García Márquez's "magical realism" doesn't seem unrealistic in South America, but you don't have to go that far to discover a different way of looking at things.

Up until half a dozen years ago I had collected a large library on the Native American, but was unremarkably short on firsthand knowl-edge—unremarkably and typically, as it is far easier to read about a people than to encounter them. I had been to the Blackfoot reservation in Browning, Montana, on a prolonged drunk with Tom McGuane; we were actually kicked out of a local bar, and that takes some doing in Browning. I had also attended the Crow Fair, a massive gathering and celebration in Crow Agency, Montana, with five to seven thousand Native Americans in attendance. This was more than a decade ago, and there were only a few whites present. I watched the dancing for two days and nights, sleeping sporadically on the Custer Battlefield. It was a *spellbinding* experience, one of the few of my life, and there was a deep sense of melancholy that there was nothing in my life that owned this cultural validity except, in a minimal sense, my poetry. Thousands of people in traditional costumes dancing together! What the hell's going on here? My bubble of reality had temporarily burst; it was as if I were stoked on peyote on the planet Jupiter.

The power of the experience passed, although it nagged until a few years ago when I worked on an abortive film project about Edward Curtis, the photographer of Indians. There was research money so I left my books at home and wandered around Indian reservations for several months. I was a quiet observer, quite shy in fact, because I didn't want to be confused with the anthropologists and spiritual shoppers who drive these people crazy.

On the Navajo reservation up Canyon de Chelly, on the branch called Canyon del Muerto, two very disturbing things happened. A man, ragged and plainly insane, rushed out of a thicket, skipping across the shallow river, and began beating our truck with a club. His head appeared to turn nearly all the way around in the manner of an owl's head. Our Navajo guide, who was Christian, yelled, "Get out of here, you demon, in the name of Jesus," explaining as the lunatic fled back into the thicket that what he yelled was the only thing that "worked." A little later I spent hours helping get a truck loaded with crab apples unstuck from the river. There was a young Navajo man, his wife, and two children, and the children were terribly frightened of me. I found this embarrassing and sorrowful as I worked away half under the truck, glancing up at the Anasazi petroglyphs. If you're from northern Michigan you know how to get a pickup unstuck. I tried everything to charm the children, and the parents attempted to help, but I was plainly a "demon" to them. Later I was told that the terror might have come from my blind left eye, which is foggy and wobbles around with a life of its own.

What actually began that day was an obsession, fueled less by guilt than by a curiosity that was imperceptibly connected to my poetry. Charles Olson said that a poet "must not traffick in any but his own sign," but I thought these people might clarify why I had spent over forty years wandering around in the natural world. I hoped the two cultures had more to offer each other than their respective demons.

This little essay, in fact, was occasioned by absolute exhaustion after a book tour; a retreat to my cabin in Michigan's Upper Peninsula; and the reading of the novel *Love Medicine* by the Native American Louise Erdrich, and then *A Yellow Raft in Blue Water* by her husband, Michael Dorris, somehow equal and absolutely first-rate books, which restored my equilibrium and energies, and an intense and nagging curiosity. Then I reread *Survival This Way*, a series of interviews with American Indian poets by Joseph Bruchac, published by the University of Arizona Press (whose Sun Tracks series seems to lead in the publishing of American Indian writers); *Songs from This Earth on Turtle's Back,* an anthology edited by Bruchac and published by Greenfield Review Press; and the new and comprehensive *Harper's Anthology of 20th Century Native American Poetry* edited by Duane Niatum.

After I had read through a sequence of fine prefaces and introductions (especially that by Brian Swann in the Niatum volume), there seemed to me to be a vacuum or missing chord. Over the years I had read the work of James Welch, Simon Ortiz, Leslie Marmon Silko, and Scott Momaday, whose wonderful novel *House Made of Dawn* was a ground-breaker for other Native American writers. These four poets are known, but not widely, and certainly not in proportion to their talents. Of late, Louise Erdrich has achieved a measure of fame but there ought to be room for more than one, not to speak of a dozen other specific talents in the anthologies. Why are these poets so rarely reviewed or represented in "white anthologies"? I mulled over this problem for a couple of months as if it were a raw and abrasive Zen koan. Then, on a recent driving trip through Nebraska, the Dakotas, and eastern Montana, I revisited the site of the murder of Crazy Horse and the small church graveyard that overlooks the site of the Wounded Knee massacre, and a possible answer occurred to me.

First you must try to imagine a map of the United States covered with white linen as if it were a recently (true, in the sweep of history) murdered corpse. Carefully note where the blood is soaking through, from right to left, beginning with the splotches on the black slave ports of the East and South. Make a point of ignoring Civil War battle sites, as they constitute something we did to ourselves out of a mixture of necessity and vainglory. You will now notice that the rest of our linen map is riddled with the blood of over two hundred Native American civilizations we virtually destroyed from Massachusetts to California. This is an unpleasant map and is not readily available for purchase or publication, especially not in history books or in what is blithely referred to as the "American conscience." Our nation has a soul history, not as immediately verifiable as the artifacts of the Smithsonian, whose presence we sense in public affairs right down to the former president's use of the word "preservation," or his cinema-tainted reference to oil-rich Indians. In any event, schoolchildren who we think need a comprehension of apartheid could be given the gist of this social disease by field trips to Indian reservations in big yellow buses.

A logical assumption, then, is that Native American writers are largely ignored by readers because they represent a ghost that is too utterly painful to be encountered. Actual readers of literature are people of conscience (I am discarding the sort of literacy that never gets beyond the Sports and Modern Living pages and is ignorant of the locations of Nicaragua and Iran), but conscience can be delayed by malice, stereotypes, a natural aversion to the unpleasant. I'm old enough to remember when Langston Hughes and Richard Wright were considered the only black writers of interest. Publishers come largely from the East and anything between our two Dream Coasts tends to be considered an oblique imposition. There is also the notion that the predominantly white literary establishment idealizes a misty, ruined past when life held unity and grace. The late (and great) Richard Hugo pointed out that for Native American poets the past isn't misty, that the civilization that was destroyed was a living memory for their grandparents, and thus the Indian poet is a living paradigm of the modern condition.

Oddly, when you study the anthologies, or separate volumes by individual poets, you find very little romantic preciousness and almost no self-pity (certainly the most destructive emotion). And there are none of the set pieces of current "white anthologies": the workshop musings, campus melancholy, the old-style *New Yorker* poem in which the city poet sees his first seagull of summer, then nuzzles the wainscot of a clapboard cottage and reflects on the delicacy of Aunt Claudia's doilies; none of the Guggenheim or National Endowment year poems about fountains in Italy, the flowers of Provence, English weather, the buttocks of bullfighters in Madrid. There is a natural and understandable sorrow over losing a vast cathedral and being given an outhouse in return. Even the renowned Indian killer General Philip Sheridan admitted that "an Indian reservation is usually a worthless piece of land surrounded by swindlers." Quite naturally, Native Americans don't agree with Robert Frost's drivel about the land being ours "before we were the land's."

I suspect I am attracted to these Native American poets because there is a specific immediacy, urgency, a grittiness to the work. Of the thirty-six poets in the *Harper's Anthology*, fifteen are women; such a proportion is unthinkable in current, broadly based anthologies. The women are, if anything, more stridently energetic, natural and instinctive feminists, and I was reminded of the Sioux woman who drove an awl in dead Custer's ear in hopes that he would hear warnings better in the afterlife. Another oddity is that some of the best poets are also equally fine novelists: Momaday, Welch, Silko, Erdrich, and Vizenor. This is less frequently true among white poets.

An additional urgency is found in mixed-blood poets such as Erdrich, Vizenor, or Linda Hogan, an extraordinary Chickasaw writer:

> Girl, I say,
> it is dangerous to be a woman of two countries
> You've got your hands in the dark
> of two empty pockets.

Louise Erdrich's poem, "A Love Medicine," a miniature tale of doom,
almost an English ballad, will bring you near to weeping, or you are not
human. It begins with a novelist's sense of detail, almost as if she were
fitting a noose around your neck. You can find out how it ends by buying
the book (in *Jacklight*, published by Henry Holt or in the *Harper's
Anthology*).

> Still it is raining lightly
> in Wahpeton. The pickup trucks
> sizzle beneath the blue neon
> bug traps of the dairy bar.
>
> Theresa goes out in green halter and chains
> that glitter at her throat.
> This dragonfly, my sister,
> she belongs more than I
> to this night of rising water.

When the poetry is political it assumes a quiet hardness, all the more
effective because of the simplicity and control. James Welch, the Blackfoot author of the striking novel *Fools' Crow*, writes in "The Man from
Washington":

> The end came easy for most of us.
> Packed away in our crude beginnings
> in some far corner of a flat world,
> we didn't expect much more
> than firewood and buffalo robes
> to keep us warm. The man came down
> a slouching dwarf with rainwater eyes,
> and spoke to us. He promised
> that life would go on as usual,
> that treaties would be signed, and everyone—
> man, woman, and child—would be inoculated
> against a world in which we had no part,
> a world of money, promise and disease.

I am drawn to the way Ray A. Young Bear and Lance Henson treat nature, as if they, in fact, were part of the natural world rather than observers shouting the presumptive "I" of postmodernism. Young Bear writes in long powerful forms difficult to quote. In "north" Lance Henson finishes with:

> in the house my daughter
> has disappeared into dream
>
> her small trembling hands
> flower into a cold wind that smells
> of the moon.

It is equally true of the work of Duane Niatum, Peter Blue Cloud, and Joseph Bruchac, in whose work nature is treated in terms of familiarity, love and a little fear, as if they were speaking in another mode of their parents.

Joy Harjo is an engaging wild woman of a poet. She has seen de Soto

> having a drink on Bourbon Street,
> mad and crazy
> dancing with a woman as gold
> as the river bottom.

Harjo's style is somewhat incantatory; there is an urge to hear her read aloud. Her "Anchorage" is one of the strongest single poems in the *Harper's* volume; it ends:

> And I think of the 6th Avenue jail, of mostly Native
> and Black men, where Henry told about being shot at
> eight times outside a liquor store in L.A., but when
> the car sped away he was surprised he was alive,
> no bullet holes, man, and eight cartridges strewn
> on the sidewalk
>   all around him.
>
> Everyone laughed at the impossibility of it,
> but also the truth. Because who would believe
> the fantastic and terrible story of all of our survival
> those who were never meant
>   to survive.

There is a rich comic spirit, perhaps the quality that whites are most ignorant of in Native Americans. In *Survival This Way* there is a splendid comic poem, too long to quote here, "Hills Brothers Coffee" by Luci Tapehenso. For reasons never clear to me, the very richest core of humor is found in oppressed people, whether blacks, Jews or Native Americans. At the few pow-wows I've attended, I've noticed the wild, delightful humor of people to whom "dirt poor" would serve as a euphemism.

What I've offered here is a rather slight sampling in an attempt to whet some appetites, not necessarily the best material but certainly representative; this I think typifies a renaissance in Native American literature similar to that of black writers in the sixties.

I have saved the most difficult of Native American poets for last, perhaps out of aversion to entering the often painful labyrinth of his work, which I have followed carefully for over twenty years. Simon Ortiz is an Acoma Pueblo Indian and for some time now I have thought of him as a major poet: this is an unstable category but the range is there, as is the depth, volume, and grace. It is a matter of absolute emotional credibility married to craft. Among others he had written, "Going for the Rain," "From Sand Creek," "Fight Back," "A Good Journey," the latter just recently reissued by the University of Arizona Press. Ortiz has said that he writes poems because writing is, finally, an "act that defies oppression." In a curious way Ortiz reminds me of that great contemporary Russian, Vosnesensky. It is a peculiarity of genius that no concessions are made, and in Ortiz there is a quiet omniscience expressed only by talents of the first order. I understand he is a modest though difficult man, given to disappearing. I would hope that his selected or collected poems might appear so the work might reach a larger audience, whether we deserve it or not. It is the kind of poetry that reaffirms your decision to stay alive.

Almost as an afterthought, but really a cruel whim, a wish to rub our collective noses into the beauty and horror of the situation, I conclude with the rest of Louise Erdrich's poem, "A Love Medicine":

> The Red River swells to take the bridge.
> She laughs and leaves her man in his Dodge.
> He shoves off to search her out.
> He wears a long rut in the fog.
>
> And later, at the crest of the flood,
> when the pilings are jarred from their sockets

and pitch into the current,
she steps against the fistwork of a man.
She goes down in wet grass
and his boot plants its grin
among the arches of her face.

Now she feels her way home in the dark.
The white-violet bulbs of the streetlamps
are seething with insects,
and the trees lean down aching and empty.
The river slaps at the dike works, insistent.

I find her curled up in the roots of a cottonwood.
I find her stretched out in the park, where all night
the animals are turning in their cages.
I find her in a burned-over ditch, in a field
that is gagging on rain,
sheets of rain sweep up down
to the river held tight against the bridge.

We see that now the moon is leavened and the water,
as deep as it will go,
stops rising. Where we wait for the night to take us
the rain ceases. Sister, there is nothing
I would not do.

In a curious way Native American poetry is written in our language but
not in our voice. Perhaps it's because the tap root of ritual poetry is closer
to the surface, and the traditions of Shaman and Trickster are often right
out there in the dark looking in the window of the poem. This is partially
true, but there is an even more dominant factor. Chief Seattle once told
us in specific terms how his people were going to haunt us. He also said
that the earth does not belong to man, man belongs to the earth. This
simple notion offers a schism larger than that between Jew and Muslim,
or Christian and Jew. We have always believed we owned the earth and
could do what we please, and our current and frontier theocracies never
hesitated in their pillage for a moment. In *American Indian Holocaust*
Russell Thornton points that in 1492 there were at least 5 million Native
Americans and in 1890 there were only 250,000, the decline resulting
from introduced diseases and sheer firepower. It is indeed ironic that
those whom we crushed could help us survive.

LOUISE ERDRICH AND
MICHAEL DORRIS

Manitoulin Island

The name of the village of Kagawong on Manitoulin Island, Ontario, translates roughly in the Anishinabec language as "the place of mists." And in fact, to drive down the single street at dawn, wisps of fog silhouetting lone cedars and ghostly gnarled oaks, is to be reminded that the Grand Isle is named for its most ancient purported dwellers, the manitous, supernatural beings that traditionally guide the lives of the Anishinabec people—native Odawa, Ojibwe (Chippewa), and Potawatomi groups who today inhabit the island's five reserves.

As one version of the story goes, the Kitche Manitou created a perfect retreat for his own pleasure and cast it adrift like a giant birchbark canoe on the clear waters of the Great Lakes. Through endless time it meandered here and there, collecting the choice flora and fauna from wherever it docked, until finally it encountered the ideal shore for mooring on the north coast of Lake Huron and came to permanent rest just across a narrow channel.

And so it remains, the largest island anywhere in fresh water, an expanse of rolling hills and deep azure lakes, suffused with highly differentiated vegetation, animal life, and geological oddities. You can travel for more than a hundred kilometers in an east-west direction, from Meldrum Bay and Cockburn Island, within sight of the eastern extremity of Michigan's arching northern peninsula, to Cape Smith on Georgian Bay. Or you can drive south from Little Current, with its swinging bridge, to the high trees and almost balmy ambience of South Baymouth, where a two-hour ferry, the *Chi-Chi-maun*, runs to Tobormory.

Last September, when three of our older children had begun school and five months before our youngest baby, Aza, was born, the remaining four of us—our daughters (ages four and three) in their car seats and we alternating the driving—made the quick trek from our farm in New Hampshire. We travel to Manitoulin often, drawn back by friends, by the dazzling renaissance of traditional Native American arts, by the peace and beauty of the landscape, the remarkable skies, and so the route brought to mind previous journeys. We compared the smooth highways, now bordered with their full growth of hay rolled and baled, with their snow-packed, January incarnations when the daylight is short, when ice forms a second shore around the island and Bridal Falls is frozen into a milky sculpture, and when automobiles are often the least practical of the possible means of transportation.

The passage is easier in early spring. Then tufts of new grass push through patchy frost, and gray deer with hides stretched around stark ribs stray to the roadsides, where they graze ravenously, intently, unconcerned for the people who idle to watch from only feet away. At the height of midsummer we have even occasionally encountered traffic, Manitoulin style, en route to the enormous multiday powwow near Manitowaning, or when going to the annual tribal elders' conference.

The masonry "jailhouse" at Gore Bay, the graceful Victorian brick farmhouses, or the still-in-use stone church with its ruin of the Jesuit enclave on the unceded reserve of Wikwemikong, all testify to a nineteenth-century Euro-Canadian presence. But nature, on Manitoulin, is as much a reminder of the past as are the signs of relatively recent human habitations. Seated on a driftwood log at the southern coast near Providence Bay, watching the brilliant waves of Huron roll against the dark and gentle swell of forested bluffs where Indians from around the Great Lakes used to bury their most important dead, we imagine the even earlier arrival, via barge, canoe, bateau, and dory, of a determined succession of French missionaries, secular priests, and British Protestant parsons who set down the earliest written accounts of the island's history.

One of the first of these visitors, Father Louis André, endured an arduous 1671. So scarce were fish and game that year, he reports in his journals, that he nearly starved along with his potential converts, and managed to save himself only by devouring his moccasins and the embossed bindings of his books. Fortunately for the future of his flock, Father André's flute was not edible, and he eventually attracted both the devout and the curious by accompanying his spiritual canticles with music.

Not long afterward, however, something devastating happened on Manitoulin, although its cause is now forgotten. Perhaps the ability of the soil to sustain life became less reliable because of drought or flood; perhaps, and more likely, widespread European infections decimated and terrified the indigenous population. At any rate, the island was completely abandoned by human beings. The only indisputable fact known about the place for over a century (1700–1825) is that a great fire raged across the land. Some speculate that it was set intentionally in order to eradicate both evil spirits and disease. Contemporary residents, hunting or gathering medicinal plants in the deepest brush, have discovered the charred remains of cedars more broad in their trunks than any that now exist. It is said that at one time thousands of acres were forested with this fragrant tree, the bark of which is still burned for purification in traditional religious ceremonies.

Officials of the Canadian Department of Indian Affairs spearheaded a resettlement in 1838, armed with a plan to attract a new immigrant population of Natives. Manitoulin was to become a kind of Oklahoma of the north, a segregated pan-Indian reservation where members of many tribes could be confined and "improved" under close Christian supervision. "Soon the Indians came about us, seeking instruction, and the first two who desired to be baptized were an old man and his squaw," writes "Miss Anderson," one of the main chroniclers of the venture. "They were called Adam and Eve, and were lawfully married at the same time. Two of their sons, grown men, were also baptized. One of them was called Abel."

The ubiquitous Miss Anderson headed a team of "females . . . highly educated, refined and delicate, heretofore shielded from every storm," who claimed success mainly for teaching young boys to knit and sing hymns, and also for introducing some Odawa, farmers already, to farming. But when large numbers of Natives did not adopt vocations as smiths, tailors, coopers, mechanics, or carpenters, the establishment was dismantled. Much like the United States Indian Territory, the government's theoretical intent yielded to the push of European westward migration, and in 1866, over the grief and objections of both Wikwemikong Anishinabec and their missionaries, Manitoulin land was surveyed and sold to Canadian settlers at fifty cents an acre.

Since that time, Manitoulin has remained more a collection of small distinct communities than a melting pot of peoples. To the tourist, it appears that Indians and non-Indians meet primarily where different ethnic groups have always interacted: in the marketplace, which these days means the mainland shopping malls of Sudbury or Espanola. The large supermarket in Espanola's modern arcade was our first stop as well, as we headed toward our rented cabin with cooking facilities.

Even on a sunny weekday afternoon, whole families make a constant promenade around and around the tiled indoor avenues, dropping off a member here or there to browse, to make some essential purchase, or to compare prices. Present are the full spectrum of Manitoulin's current inhabitants—from an Ojibwe grandmother with a deeply lined face framed by a flowered scarf, patiently rocking a tiny infant in a stroller, to sandy-haired, thick-calved descendants of the English men and women who arrived from eastern Ontario in the late nineteenth century, cleared land, sold the chopped lumber to passing steamboats.

In the center of the active concourse, a series of blue veiled partitions housed a mini-convention of part-time psychics. Our four-year-old daughter walked straight up to the presiding medium and asked in a surprisingly deep voice, "Where will you sleep tonight?" The woman, dressed casually in jeans and a tie-dyed T-shirt, answered with weary insouciance: "Anywhere I can hang my hat, honey." She hailed from Toronto, she told us, and according to her publicity handout she had made more than one appearance on a syndicated TV program called *Psychic World*. Behind the curtains, beneath the cardboard cutout of a white unicorn, we could at considerable expense have had our palms, auras, and/or cards read. For an extra couple of dollars the whole session could be taped on videocassette and preserved "forever." The gnawing temptation to look into our futures was countered, however, by a six-P.M. reservation deadline for our cabin in Gore Bay, so we departed Espanola laden not with prescience and foreboding, but only with twelve peanut butter jars of locally preserved gooseberry jam.

For many, tourism has replaced lumbering and commercial fishing as a way to make a living on Manitoulin, and we waited in a line of cars just north of Little Current until a progression of boats passed through the channel and the two-lane swing bridge revolved back to its moorings. Our fellow travelers drove station wagons laden with fishing gear and wore hats festooned with colorful lures and flies. According to their license plates they came mostly from Hamilton or Toronto, but there were some from as far away as Alberta and Kansas.

West through the Birch Island and Sucker Creek Indian reserves, the coastal vistas were sparkling, the trees dense and rich, the rock shores a subtle blend of pink and tan. Away from water, the land was illuminated with an end-of-summer, late-afternoon glow, and the thick breeze from inland was scented by pollen and hay. Farms that we passed seemed, in many cases, to be struggling for survival, although the split-rail cedar fences, some a hundred years old, were maintained in top condition. Beyond their boundaries, in the undeveloped areas, woods and tangled stretches of bush harbor a profusion of wild plants.

Non-Natives who were born on Manitoulin refer to themselves as

Haw-eaters, after the same hips and fruit that grew in the hedgerows of Adam Bede's British countryside and, transplanted, yet make a favorite jam on Manitoulin. And each June, the fields abound with people bent over patches of the tiny, piercingly sweet and fragrant wild strawberries called *odaemin*, or "heart berries" in Anishinabec language. Little wonder that in Ojibwe mythology, a deserving newcomer to the next world must first resist the lotuslike lure of a gigantic strawberry, so huge that it can be nibbled at forever, before he or she attains spiritual paradise. *Odaemin* is, not uncoincidentally, also the name of the legendary first medicine man instructed by the trickster Nanabush in the uses of botany.

Home-remedy healing is still a popular way of treating malady. In the Ojibwa Cultural Center, located at the West Bay town crossroads, we met a delegation of Native women from an interior Ontario reserve who journeyed to this legendary home of their tribe in search of the snakeroot they use for poultices. To their delight, they found the plant quickly and in great profusion not twenty feet from a paved road, and collected several bagfuls. The director of the Center, Mary Lou Fox, led us to a second-floor closet crammed with small plastic containers of the roots, leaves, and bark essential to traditional Anishinabec curing. This ethnobotanical treasure-trove is located adjacent to videotape and photography libraries meticulously recording for future study the words and events of today's elder generation. On the ground floor, a music-keyed slide show extolling "Manitoulin, Land Where the Eagle Flies," runs continuously and is both a civic point of pride and the first thing each off-islander is expected to view.

A reliance on folk pharmacopoeia is not confined to the island's Ojibwe community. Beulah Oil for sore feet can be mail-ordered through want-ads in the biweekly *Manitoulin Recorder*. Even the drugstore on Main Street in Gore Bay carries, in addition to the usual over-the-counter anodynes, bottles of a provincially manufactured "Extract of Wild Strawberry," which is proclaimed to counteract "sudden changes in diet or water, as well as over-indulgence."

We managed without a dose that night at the Gordon's Lodge smorgasbord, but—after the extravaganza that offered homemade Polish pirogi, cabbage rolls, sweet-and-sour beef ribs, rice and shrimp salad, and desserts of every hue and density, from trifle to carrot cake—it was a struggle.

Another evening soon after our arrival, we were welcomed into the comfortable home of William and Helen Trudeau, a long-married couple much renowned in the town of Wikwemikong for their knowledge of tribal culture and mores. Mr. Trudeau, wiry, thin, with a narrow face and an ironic manner, explained how he cured a winter of what must translate from Anishinabec into English as "the blahs" with locally gathered elixirs. He went on to tell us how, while chopping wood, he had discovered a tumbled-in old dwelling and within it, a rolled woven straw mat of exquisite design. He had spread it out and studied the pattern until he understood it well enough to reproduce it, then carefully replaced the artifact where he had found it. It would be impolite, he explained, to take more than the idea of a thing that did not belong to him.

In typical Anishinabec fashion, more people gathered at the Trudeaus' house as the evening went on: Mary Lou Fox and her witty, caustic cousin Honorine; Mary Lou's brother and sister-in-law, Al and Mary Lou Shawana, recently retired to the island after jobs in the oil industry in Edinburgh, Bombay, and Calgary. The custom of hospitality proscribes any stinting, and Honorine produced urns of coffee, tea, store-bought doughnuts, and a big platter of doughy "Indian bread," or *pikwayzigun*. Helen searched a private cache in her room and found fruit-punch powders for our children, then shared with us her collection of clippings and pamphlets documenting local Native history. We all admired the extraordinary work that she had just completed, a large oval bark-and-quill box decorated with graceful strawberry designs. Al noted that Anishinabec children are cautioned not to kill crickets, who are responsible for painting the berries red.

Before the advent of traders' glass beads, the quills of porcupines were dyed and used for all manner of adornment. Recently museums, collectors, and tourists have rediscovered the beauty and intricacy of the art form. Manitoulin stores and cooperatives, such as the Ojibwa Cultural Foundation, have provided support and outlets, and Native quill-workers have been encouraged to develop and experiment with their craft.

Quilling requires dexterity, imagination, a large supply of porcupines, and abounding patience on the part of the practitioner. Some of the more ambitious works, for instance a "tufted" box, in which only the very tiniest, hairlike, quills are sewn in bundles of six onto bark, then trimmed with a razor to form a thick mat, consume extraordinary amounts of time. A masterpiece might take as long as a year to complete; in one day, working six to eight hours, even an experienced artist can cover only a thumbnail's width of birchbark.

The technology for creating basic quill boxes demands skill and a great deal of practice. Each individual spine must be sorted, washed, softened with brine or saliva, and if desired, dyed—either with crushed plants or berries, the old-fashioned way, or with a marker. Then, with an awl, one by one they are inserted into freehand-cut birchbark. Their articulation, which makes full use of their natural shadings, builds complicated designs, borders, and weavings, often highlighted by strips of pale-green sweetgrass. The aesthetics are rigorous and very old, but each artist is free to innovate within certain conventions. A connoisseur can easily identify the work of a particular woman or man, and value is assigned by the finesse of the execution, the seamlessness of the construction, the originality of the conception.

Some artisans use designs that have cosmological significance; a woman named Maime Migwans, for example, is famous for her natural quill boxes inspired by pictographs of Misshepeshu, the horned underwater serpent. Inspiration may come from illustrations clipped from wildlife magazines, or from other sources: as Helen Trudeau modestly admits of her pattern, "I was looking at my tablecloth and thought I could try the flowers on the border." She carefully trimmed her model from the margins of the material. She has sketches, kept in a neat succession of candy tins, ranging from birchbark cutouts of moose and red foxes, to lilies or roses snipped off the side of a cardboard Kleenex container. The modern and the ancient, the spiritual and the gently humorous are incorporated into this art form as into so much of Native life.

With this flowering of interest, the sine qua non ingredients for boxes have grown scarce on Manitoulin Island. William Trudeau, who regrets not having started a porcupine farm several decades ago with a tiny motherless litter he carried home in his hat, now deplores the quality of quills he must trade for or buy from mainland dealers. Delia Beboning, whose masterworks now attract knowledgeable buyers from around the world, gathers her own bark—and sweetgrass too—and leaves a pinch of tobacco at the roots as her grandmother taught her. She has been known, when she runs out of material at a crucial juncture, to take her children in the car and drive the roads of Manitoulin after midnight, hoping to come across a porcupine casualty whose remains she can convert into a unique belt buckle or container.

Delia is a perfectionist. As a child making her first box, she was so dissatisfied that she repeatedly pulled out the quills. "When I was finally finished, how I wanted to keep that box!" she recalls. But her family needed money, so she passed the object to her grandmother, who sold it for $2.50. Nowadays Delia's creations command far greater prices, and much of her work is displayed in museums.

The evening before our departure we visited with Delia while she cut out a pair of moosehide gauntlets and planned her next trip to the bingo games at Elliot Lake. It had been a full day for us, commencing with a dawn visit to Dreamer's Rock, a dramatic promontory jutting high above Birch Island. From this aerie slopes a gentle terrain, divided by low oaks and young cedars, decorated with blue chicory, cattails, clumps of goldenrod. For lunch Mary Lou Fox had served us corn-and-bean soup at her house in Kagawong, and we passed the sunny afternoon at the Lake Mindemoya cottage of Chief Jim Debassige, where our daughters curled together for their nap in a blue net hammock, rocked by the breeze from the waves.

We shared with Delia the story of our dinner with Honorine at the band-run Tee-Pee Restaurant in West Bay, when our waitress matter-of-factly answered our query about the sliced beef "special" with, "We're out of beef." Cheese sandwich? "We're out of cheese." How about a chef salad? "No lettuce." So we ate fresh tomatoes in abundance, and home-made french fries ("hot spuds"), and too many fresh butter tarts, so irresistible that we were later glad for our souvenir bottle of Fowler's Extract of Wild Strawberry.

The story goes that the Odawa—"the people who sell things"—originated on Manitoulin Island and eventually return there, lured and enchanted by the unique interplay of past and present, of earth and sky . . . like Honorine, absent in Vancouver from the island of her birth for some twenty-five years, who recently came back, driving alone straight through the western plains in a tightly packed camper.

"It wasn't five A.M., just before dawn, when I crossed the bridge at Little Current," she told us. "As I got closer to Wikwemikong, I heard a crackling sound, lowered my window, and looked up. It was the northern lights, rolling across the sky in bands of green and gold, snapping with electricity. I sat there and watched, glad to be here, glad to be finally home."

There is a reason why painting, sculpture, and ceramics thrive along with quillwork and beadwork on the Reserves of Manitoulin, and it has to do with the sense of the place. You feel it at Blake and Shirley Chechoo Debassige's gallery in the village of West Bay. It imbues Ms. Chechoo's quietly lyrical views of childhood and Mr. Debassige's darker visions, rendered in emphatic colors, of Ojibwe mythology and redemption through personal communion with the spiritual world. It fuels

Leland Bell, from Wikwemikong, who like most Native graphic artists works in his house, surrounded by extended family; at any time his studio may be invaded by children in the midst of their games, calling out to each other in the old language. Accordingly, his oils are concerned with community, with custom, with the ceremonies of sharing and exchange.

It's a sense that permeates most of the work by Manitoulin artists. Informed by ancient pictographs and influenced by Norval Morrissey, one of the first Ojibwe painters to gain an international reputation, many follow the Woodlands conceit of depicting a subject's interior being in an expressive, decorative core, and a subject's thoughts, words, or manitou in radiating lines of symbolic form and length. Within the body of a human or an animal there might appear a stylized esophagus, a stomach, a delicate suggestion of skeleton, a fragile viscera at counterpoint to the dynamic exterior power.

The high proportion of professional artists and skilled craftspersons in a Native population of only 3,000 (out of the island's total 11,000) corroborates what many people on Manitoulin believe about themselves and the sacred island where they live: There is something special here, a spiritual blessing, a palpable, primal energy. Mary Lou Fox recounts an old belief, a prophecy of seven parts, in which Manitoulin figures as a haven where Anishinabec language and custom are forever cherished and revitalized, where a new spirit of optimism and delight is constantly re-formed. Even in myth, it is a place where people come to gain a glimpse of a world in balance, a world as it could be, a world of beauty governed and reflected by art.

The Mourning Fan: or, Meanwhile and Elsewhere

In her window Flora sitting,
  Heraclitus on her knees,
Spied a black-clad figure knitting
  Something vague among the trees.

At the edge of Lower Truddle
  Uncle Odo, lost in thought,
Ruined, stepping in a puddle,
  The new shoes he just had bought.

Major Hacksaw, cycling slowly,
  Breathing in great gulps of air,
Found himself among some lowly
  Cottages in disrepair.

Lupin at the topiary
  With a pair of rusted shears,
Though he kept his manner airy,
  Was a prey to niggling fears.

As the flaming sunset ended
  To the left of Truddle Spur,
From the 5.12 train descended
  Several strangers wrapped in fur.

No one saw them leave the station,
  But it came out in a while
They'd obtained accommodation
  At The Weeping Crocodile.

Lady Elspeth, having dithered
  Half the morning quite away,
Saw the roses all had withered
  She had cut for a bouquet.

Heraclitus, vainly stalking
  Pigeons on the parapet,
Heard beneath some person talking,
  Saying it would not be yet.

Miss O'Guernsey, hemming ruffles
  For a set of pillow shams,
Was disturbed by distant scuffles,
  Incoherent squeaks, and slams.

Maud, without the servants knowing,
  Crept down to the shore and hid;
Then across the lake went rowing,
  Humming Handel while she did.

Uncle Odo in his slippers,
  Hearing goings-on below,
Saw a group of muffled trippers
  Munching biscuits in the snow.

On a bench outside The Weeping
  Crocodile a dog lay stretched,
Till, not dead but only sleeping,
  By another it was fetched.

Lupin in the pantry rinsing
  Plates that had been used at tea,
Felt his story unconvincing
  How he came to graze his knee.

Major Hacksaw, at the juncture
  Of two Mortshire cattle tracks,
Underwent a triple puncture,
  Caused by scattered carpet tacks.

In the twilight Flora playing
  On the lawn of Frogmarch Hall,
Bumped into the Vicar straying
  Up the drive to pay a call.

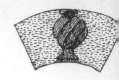

Afternoons the strangers wandered
  Aimlessly, with frequent stops
During which they squandered freely
  Largesse in the village shops.

On the stairway Maud returning
  For a mislaid glacé glove,
Thought she scented something burning
  On the landing just above.

Miss Irene Figg was shaken:
  While her shop was oddly full,
Wantonly someone had taken
  All her skeins of lilac wool.

Lady Elspeth, hard of hearing
  And the conversation brisk,
Did not catch her diamond earring
  Fall into the lobster bisque.

Stilton was disposed to linger,
  Though the sun had long gone down;
Then he found he'd bruised his finger
  Since he had come out from town.

Flora glancing in the mirror,
  Saw a figure on the lawn;
It was gliding slowly nearer,
  But she turned, and it was gone.

Uncle Odo in the study
  Was surprised, to say the least:
On the blotter were the bloody
  Footprints of an unknown beast.

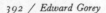

Lupin sensed disaster looming,
  And took up the telephone,
Quite mistakenly assuming
  He was in the hall alone.

Waiting for the glaze to harden
  On a cauliflower mousse,
Cook strolled in the kitchen garden,
  Wondering what was the use.

In the ha-ha Heraclitus,
  Fiercely leaping after mice,
Found among the heaped detritus
  Something that was not quite nice.

With no warning something furry
  Ran between the Major's wheels,
And then in a tearing hurry
  Vanished with unearthly squeals.

Read twelve times, a message limply
  Slipped from Lady Elspeth's hand;
What it meant to say she simply
  Could not seem to understand.

In St Aftermath's the Vicar
  Did not see (as was his wont)
Someone in a yellow slicker
  Pouring liquid in the font.

Soon the strangers, thus ensuring
  Their well-being, swallowed pills,
And at once climbed in a touring
  Car and drove off towards the hills.

Something intricately knitted
  Was fished up out of the lake:
Whom or what could it have fitted?
  Was it all a sad mistake?

SUSAN SONTAG

In Memoriam: Donald Barthelme

He was unremittingly vivacious, fastidious, acute—in his writing and in his conversation. His brilliance was inimitable. But so was his charm, which had a distinctly western flavor. The big frame, the wire-rimmed glasses, the mildly patriarchal beard, the cowboy boots and measured walk they sponsored, the artful pauses in his eloquence, the quizzical look and the intimidating silences when he just listened—all these never let you forget that he hailed from Houston, and had been just visiting us in New York all these years. I find something more western than not in the good-natured, exuberant use he made of all that cosmopolitan modernist erudition that was his and in the sheer appetitiveness with which he evoked the phantasmagoria and oddments of the contemporary. How all-American the reach of his wit was! He was at least as much the heir of Mark Twain as he was the disciple of Joyce and of Max Ernst and of Borges.

His beginnings were dazzling; he never seemed to have had an apprenticeship. From the start he had enormous luster and authority as a writer, and the influence on other American writers of his mordant, ecstatically inventive tales—with their amazing velocity, their distinctive undertow of heartbreak—was immediate and profound. The resourcefulness of his short fiction over more than three decades, much of it variations on the story in dialogue form pioneered by Sterne and Diderot, somewhat overshadowed the accomplishment of the longer fiction, most unfairly in the case of the incomparable *Dead Father*. His work constitutes one of the few unrivaled summits of accomplishment of American literature in the second half of the twentieth century.

Donald Barthelme was a writer from whom one could continually learn about one's craft. No American writer had a better ear, a livelier vocabulary, a more alert take on what commas and periods (and their omission) could do to the rendering of voice in prose. No American writer read fiction aloud in public as well, as winningly as he did. He was also a superb line editor of fiction and the most gifted teacher of fiction I've observed—if we are to believe that fiction *can* be taught. (And if anyone could make you believe that, it was Donald.) His fellow writers also knew him as an exemplary citizen of the republic of letters. I am thinking of the lavish gifts of time, energy, responsiveness, patience he bestowed on magazines such as *Fiction;* on the writing programs at the City College of New York and, in recent years, at the University of Houston, which he largely animated; and on writers' organizations, principally PEN American Center, of which he was virtually a shadow president for the last decade.

He gave us so much. It is hard to accept that he has gone, suddenly at fifty-eight; that there will not be more.

JOHN CLARE

EDITED BY ERIC ROBINSON

Selections from the Northborough Poems

This handful of poems comes from a much larger group written at Northborough, near Peterborough, England, in the years 1832-7. They are written on letter-wrappings and other scraps of waste paper, some of which have almost disintegrated because of the homemade ink that Clare used. Its corrosiveness has eaten into the paper so deeply that, until recently when they were repaired by paper-conservators, bits of manuscript could have wafted away with the wave of a hand, like the scraps of a debt-collector's letter thrown into the fire. The poems are memorials of Clare's life after he had "flitted" from his parents' cottage at Helpston to a new cottage provided for him by the great Fitzwilliam family in a village only four miles away as the crow flies. In his new home Clare began to feel out of touch with his roots and became disorientated and isolated, but his eye was as sharp as ever for the details of country life, each impression following fast upon the other, like a series of vignettes wood-engraved by his contemporary, Thomas Bewick. The comparison is not mine but Timothy Brownlow's. It has been recognized as so just that it has become a commonplace of Clare criticism. Each line of "The sparrow chirps the spring begun" is wonderfully precise both to ear and eye but the recorded impressions are filled with cinematic movement and bound together in a consistent mood. Yet it is not true to say that these poems derive from a camera rather than a mind. It should be noted that, in many of the poems, "the stranger" or "the passer-by" appears, the ghost of Clare who no longer feels he truly belongs to this landscape reflecting upon a world in which he has become an intruder.

In "Our common fields the journey lay," Clare recreates his own boyhood as he watches other children idling in the fields, for Clare's boyhood is a vision of innocence before the Fall of Manhood. The ancient flowers that recall Clare's Eden are not garden flowers, the roses and pinks of seventeenth-century poetry, but the common thistle or the white potato-flower of the villager's backyard. The flat lands of the

Fenland fringe seem crazy with striving motion: the boy stretching for the bird's nest, the snake slithering down the gullet of the pike, the cattle switching their tails, and the frog plopping along the water. Overhead, the kite, or puddock, swings in lazy circles watching for his prey. This is the English countryside but it is not the comfortable countryside of the contemplative landowner. It is full of sweat and the driving urgency of the clock.

Yet it is the country air that Clare must breathe, not the fumes of the city. Here, at Northborough, he finds peace and though he knows, as an agricultural laborer, that weeds mean trouble he can yet rejoice in the flowers the weeds sport. There is a fine irony in the "green wealth" that Spring brings him when we recall the insistent knock of the debt-collector on the cottage's front door—while Clare escapes through the back door to the "hospitality" of the Fens. But however depressed and humiliated he might be, Clare always had an eye for a pretty woman and a sympathy for every girl bombarded with the rude proposals of the laboring men. His way was gentler, more perceptive, more apprecia-tive, as:

> She sees the hedges full of flowers & song
> & breaks a blossom as she goes along

—ERIC ROBINSON

O fortune keep me in the country air

O fortune keep me in the country air
Let woods lanes fields my spirits still repair
They who for wealth to crowded citys stray
But little know what wealth they throw away
For springs green wealth & hospitality
Gives pleasures more then any wealth can buy
Aye let the wide unheeding world go bye
Pleasures too low & humble for its eye
Peace cannot bear the bustle of the crowd
& lowness shrinks from notice of the proud
Living at ease in calm unnoticed ways
Unruffled by its notice or its ways
Weeds only come as troubles to the soil
& they bring flowers to reccompense the toil

The sparrow chirps the spring begun

The sparrow chirps the spring begun
The schoolboy cracks the pellet gun
The cow is noising on the moor
The nettle springs agen the door
& stings the maiden when she stoops
To pick the noisey chicken up
The ploughman bawls the robin sings
The idle boy makes marble rings
& lays his taws & knuckles down
The maiden stops & tucks her gown
& laughs & looks before she stoops
To pick the fallen pocket up
The boy pulls nettles in his play
& pats her gown & runs away

The old hen thrusts & trys agen
To get the corn about the pen
The maiden runs to twirl her mop
The stranger makes a sudden stop
& whipes his cloaths she stays her toil
& pays the forfeit with a smile
The piegons flop to peck the ricks
The boy goes out & gathers sticks
& often lays the bottle down
To play at marbles in the town
The ploughman throws his jacket down
The ploughboys hat without a crown
He throws away & goes without
The cabbage tops begin to sprout

Fair & affraid of men though always kind

Fair & affraid of men though always kind
She fears the rude embraces of the wind
For insult follows beauty in her walks
& always hurts her ear with vulgar talk
She sees the hedges full of flowers & song
& breaks a blossom as she goes along
The posey offered she will seldom take
& vulgar fellows feel their hearts can ache
She never talks with men in any place
& never stands or looks them in the face
Yet she has favours which she never tells
& well can fancy where her sweetheart dwells
Who never talks so forward as the rest
& in her presence never cares to jest

The farmer sees what time the day alows

The farmer sees what time the day alows
& takes his stick & coat to seek the cows
The little dog goes trotting on before
& drives the hens & chickens to the door
He bustles on an idle working pace
The swallows almost meet him in the face
& rests on bench by oak & hazle tree
Where the old broke down hovel used to be
The cows look up & hear the farmers song
& snatch the wet grass as they toss along
The shower is gone the sun is going down
& seems to stop & rest behind the town
The evening sky is stooping down to rest
With all the rainbows beauties on his breast

Oer common fields the journey lay

Oer common fields the journey lay
& awthorn hedges all the way
The gaps where broke the cattle out
The linnets nest was thrown about
The tending boy was half undrest
& could not reach the sparrows nest
The snake runned down the greedy pike
Plunged sudden down the weedy dyke
The cattle switched their tails & stopt
The frog along the water plopt
They drank & sunk among the clay
Half mired before they turned away
Then crop the thistle top & lye
To look at every passer bye

& better places where they wait
To rub & watch the open gate
The lazy boy will lead the way
& leave undone the broken tray
Or half shut gate they rub about
& find a better pasture out
The boy will pull his knife & laugh
& cut the wounding prickles off
The only choice of idle hours
& fill his hat with thistle flowers
The only flowers that care to bloom
Where crowds of hungry cattle come
& gardens void of pleasant bowers
Keep nothing but potatoe flowers

The geese are out the spring is come
& yellow gosslings leave their home

& by the green & by the wood
& every puddle owns a brood
& on the pond in open sky
Like yellow water lillies lie
The puddock & the noisey crow
Go sailing oer the brood below
The old ones hiss the pelting boys
The horses wonder at the noise
The gander sits & guards the brink
The dog starts back that comes to drink
The maidens watering cloaths the day
Bring sticks to drive the noise away

The noisey oath to drive the hogs
The maidens bawl & barking dogs
The noise to make the waggon stop
The falling wood & frequent chop
The noisey cart the clanking pump
The weary frails incessant thump
The broken pots in corner tost
The bucket tumbled from the post
By jumping cat that sprung to see
The linnet on the eldern tree

The noisey hen & louder cock
The frequent ring of urging clock
& many more are daily heard
The noises of the farmers yard

PAUL BOWLES

Journal, Tangier

[Part II]

May 16

The one enjoyable attribute of Ramadan was the *rhaïta* solo played in the minaret of each mosque at the times of the call to prayer. This year they have done away with music. I suppose someone came up with the idea that it was anachronistic or unorthodox. "People don't want to listen to somebody blowing a *rhaïta*, anyway," says Abdelouahaid. "They have music on the television." In 1977 I recorded the oboe concerts nightly for the entire month of Ramadan. Unconsciously I must have suspected that sooner or later they would dispense with them. Good things do not continue.

June 20

Very little to write about. I've been receiving clippings in various languages, all of them announcing Bertolucci's intention of filming *The Sheltering Sky*. But in the cinema world any statement can be construed as propaganda, so I still have no idea as to whether or not he'll make the movie. People find it hard to believe that Helen Strauss included no time-limit clause in the contract when she sold the film rights back in the fifties. So if Bertolucci has acquired them, I don't know from whom.

June 26

The hernia has been giving me too much pain too unremittingly for me to go on with it. Dr. Rawa agrees to remove it if I'll let him do it with a local anesthetic, and if I'll leave the hospital immediately afterward. This seems to me the ideal way of handling it. The Hôspital Kortobi has a very unsavory reputation. The less time one spends in it, the safer one is.

July 3

A dark day. Phillip Ramey volunteered to go to the hospital with me and wait during the operation. Abdelouahaid was in the car outside. He hadn't believed that I'd be able to walk from the front entrance to the gate, but I made it without trouble. The anesthetic began to wear off as we drove home, and the rain came pouring down. The deluge managed to cut off the electricity, so that when we got to Itesa the lift was not running. By this time I was not very clear in the head. Someone came upstairs and fetched a chair from the flat. I was seated in it, and Phillip, Mrabet and Abdelouahaid carried the chair and me all the way to the top floor. That part of the day is unreal. I was in bed; the ceiling suddenly sprang a leak and the cold rain began to drip onto my feet. The pain was bearable. But then Regina Weinreich, just in from New York, arrived to talk about the film she proposes to make for American television. It was not the right time to get into that, and I was not very happy. There are few things as unpleasant to look forward to as a prolonged bout with a television crew. In principle I agreed to it, but since it won't take place until October, I was thinking: Perhaps she or I will die first. That's one way of making the future a little more acceptable.

July 23
I think of how nowadays I never go near the beach. Fifty years ago it was where I spent my summer days. The days when for one reason or another I did not go, I felt were nonexistent, wasted. The Moroccans said I was crazy. Not even the men sunbathed in those days. They believed the sun was poisonous. After the war the younger men played football on the beach, and now and then you saw a female walking into the waves, heavily dressed, of course. The Moroccan girl who lived next door to us in Calle Maimouni got into the habit of taking the women of the neighborhood down to the beach in the afternoon. They would return before sunset in great spirits. Of the girl, Jane said: "She's a revolutionary. She's got the only pair of water wings in Tangier."

August 7
A delight to be able to walk as far as I please along the waterfront without hernia pain. An inexplicable official decree now provides the beach with two dozen special police whose job it is to keep people not wearing bathing suits from walking on the sand. Those who are dressed must remain on the sidewalk. This apparently senseless new law works to the advantage of no one except the owners of the cafés and restaurants that provide cabins where bathers can undress. Said proprietors must discourage the traditional maneuver of undressing on the beach and leaving one's clothing behind during the swim. There is a good deal of thieving by a squad of young men who never cease to move among the

piles of garments, removing watches, wallets, sweaters—whatever seems easy to carry. The additional police fail to deter these troublemakers, naturally. They all work toward a common end, and one wonders if perhaps the restaurant owners don't hire the hooligans along with the police to help enforce the new *dahir*.

August 11

Yesterday an unfortunate day. Gavin Lambert and Phillip hatched a plan whereby we would go in two cars to Xauen, the two of them, Rodrigo, Krazy Kat, Abdelouahaid and I. Before we started out, Gavin remarked facetiously: "Happy August the Tenth" (the title of the first story Tennessee published in *Antæus* back in 1971). It was the wrong thing to say; in the story the tenth of August was not a happy one for the protagonists. This August tenth was hellishly hot. We in the Mustang were trying to keep up with Gavin, who hurried ahead of us at an unnecessarily high speed. At one point we saw his car slow down and stop. We all got out and stood uncomfortably in the strong sun. "It needs water," said Gavin. Abdelouahaid ran down to a river below and brought up some water. This did no good. Everyone got into the Mustang, sat one on top of the other, and went to Tetuan, where we drove from street to street in search of a garage which might still be open. Since it was midday everything was in the act of shutting. Gavin had to stay behind and find a *remorqueur* to tow him back to Tangier. The rest of us continued to Xauen. When we arrived it was just a little too late to get lunch at the Parador. We had to satisfy ourselves with omelettes and beer. It was even hotter up there than in Tangier, for the lack of any wind. After lunch we climbed up to Ras el-Ma and ordered tea. The bees were plentiful and insistent, and insisted on covering the rims of the glasses and sliding into the tea. Honey bees don't ordinarily sting, but there were so many here that there was nowhere one could touch one's lips to the glass in order to drink. Phillip took countless pictures and Krazy Kat made friends with everyone in sight. I wanted to get back to Tangier before dark, so we set out early. But with the extra people in the backseat, the car began to make agonized groans at each curve and pothole, so loud that it was hard to talk. The heat continued, because we were driving directly against the sun. Made Tangier just at dusk. End of Happy August the Tenth.

August 12

I was in bed last night having my supper, when Patricia Highsmith was ushered in. She'd been invited down from Switzerland to visit Buffie, but

Buffie had forgotten she was arriving, and gone out. I asked her to sit down, then told her where she could find some scotch and a glass, and we talked. After an hour or so she wanted to go down to Buffie's flat and unpack. I gave her a set of keys. Buffie returned as she was trying to unlock the door, and said: "I didn't realize you were coming," quickly adding, "today."

August 19
Robert Briatte says he intends to write my biography, and that Plon will publish it. He seems to believe that he needs no documents, which pleases me, since I have none to give him. He intends to give a certain amount of importance to the music, which also pleases me.

August 23
Drove Pat Highsmith and Rodrigo to Achaqar. We drank beer in the café they've built over the caves. Highsmith very agreeable company. Too bad she's leaving, although I'm afraid she hasn't had a very good time in Tangier. Buffie was ill most of the time and shut herself into her room, so that her guest was left to her own devices.

August 25
When Jerez came back from America she had her mother with her. She'd already rented a fairly large three-story house in Dar el-Baroud with fine views over the harbor, so they both moved in. Her mother seemed delighted with Tangier, and everything went well until Jerez (who had carefully refrained from admitting to her mother that the house in Mraierh was finished, but that she was not going to be able to have it) confessed that Mrabet was not going to give it to her. This news provoked a violent reaction. Jerez went off to Jajouka for a rest. When she returned with Bachir el-Attar, her mother refused to allow either of them to sleep in the house. It seems she confused Bachir with Mrabet, and thought it abject of Jerez to remain friendly with a man who had swindled her. Jerez has begun a campaign among those Americans interested in the Master Musicians of Jajouka to help Bachir get an American visa. I wrote a letter of recommendation to the consul in Rabat.

September 9
Jerez successful. Bachir given visa. They've left for New York. Will they marry? The mother stays on alone in the big house.

September 10
William Betsch arrived this afternoon from Paris, bringing a particularly handsome (but heavy) art book, *Cites d'Islam*. Why it's called *Cites* instead of *Cités* I don't understand, nor can I find the word in any dictionary. Betsch supplied many of the Moroccan photographs for the book. He wants me to write a preface for his own book *The Hakima*. I agreed. A very strange amalgam of photos and text, recounting what was probably the murder of a girl, but could have been suicide or a simple accident. A disturbing atmosphere suffuses the book. The lack of agreement among members of the family and those close to the girl makes all attempts to pierce the mystery impossible. It will be published by Aperture, which guarantees quality.

October 7
Quai Voltaire has been trying to persuade me to go to Paris and appear on the television program *Apostrophes*. So far I've resisted successfully. But yesterday Daniel Rondeau flew down from Paris to try to make me see how overwhelmingly important such a broadcast would be for my "career." They would pay all expenses, yes, but the problem was in getting there. I didn't want to fly (when have I ever in the past forty years?); I could take the boat to Sète, and a car and chauffeur would pick me up there and speed me to Paris. Statistically, however, the autoroutes in France are more lethal than the airways. And why more television? Especially when no payment is offered? Rondeau said that it was the duty of a writer to let his public see him, not to speak of the stimulus such an appearance gave to sales. I promised nothing, and he went back to Paris, after first commissioning an essay on the winter fifty-eight years ago when I lived on the Quai Voltaire. Can I manage even that?

October 10
Lunch with Gavin Young, who advises me to go to Paris. He's on his way to Indonesia.

October 17
Decided it would do no harm to have a French visa in my passport, whether or not I make the trip. Called the always helpful Monsieur Bousquet, who offered to take me to the French Consulate and see that I was given a visa immediately.

November 2

Wrote Rondeau today that I'd fly to Paris. He'll send me a return-trip ticket.

November 11

Knowing I've got to go is very depressing. Hard to think of anything else. I leave on Thursday, and am determined to return here Saturday.

November 20

Got back last night. Acute euphoria going through the customs at the airport. Abdelouahaid had the Mustang outside, and Abdelwahab was inside to meet me. Getting to Paris was nerve-racking. Had to sit for five hours waiting for the plane to come in from Casablanca. Each time I asked for information I was told that it still hadn't left the Casa airport. Never found out why. The flight was easy. It was nearly dusk when we hit Orly. Rondeau and Claude Thomas were waiting, and had been waiting all afternoon. There were great complications in the Paris streets. Strikers had built bonfires in the middle of the avenues, there were police swarming like ants everywhere, and traffic barely moved. Finally we got out and walked, leaving my luggage in the car for the chauffeur to deposit at the hotel when he got there. John Hopkins had come over from Oxfordshire to see me, and Claude, John and I had dinner in my room. A fine dinner—the first good steak I've had in twenty years.

Next day very busy. Bibka (Madame Merle d'Aubigné) gave a huge complex lunch for publishers and critics. I was treated like a star, and enjoyed it. The afternoon was crowded with people who came to the hotel and asked questions and took photos. Rondeau and I dined alone, and were driven to the studio. Program longer than I'd expected, but it went off easily. Pivot obviously clever; how seriously devoted to literature I don't know. He was a bit hard on Miss Siegel, although if you bill yourself as Sartre's secret mistress you can't object to a little rough treatment.

Saturday I went shopping with Claude, hoping to find a good bathrobe. The first shop we hit had one, but it cost nearly five thousand francs, which I had no intention of spending. Finally got one of cashmere for something over three hundred dollars, which still seems rather high for a garment no one but me will ever see. But I was glad to have a trophy to bring back to Tangier. It was already night when Claude, Rondeau and Sylvaine Pasquier said good-bye at Orly. Paris more splendid than in 1938, but I wanted to escape from it before I began to remember it.

November 22

A telegram from Regina Weinreich says she is arriving with TV crew. I'd more or less decided that the whole idea of the film had been abandoned, since October had gone by without any word from her.

December 1

In an early missive Weinreich mentioned an honorarium of ten thousand dollars. But on arriving she announced that there would be no money. The crew was here for a week. Catherine Warnow, the *metteuse-en-scène*, kept me and the crew working overtime. Scenes outdoors in the wind at the Café Hafa, in the Fez Market, in my bedroom showing me eating in bed. Hard to imagine anyone being interested in such material.

December 20

The TV crew rented Buffie's apartment downstairs for a week, where they stored their equipment. But according to Fatima they left it in a bad state. (They also neglected to give her any money for cleaning it up, so she is complaining to Steve Diamond, who's now occupying the place, in the hope that he'll tell Buffie on his return to New York.) Steve has the flat for a month or six weeks. Each morning he calls for me and we take the walk, necessary for my leg, either into town or toward the country.

December 31

Last night Mrabet gave the annual birthday party for me at his house. No orchestra, but a group of girls who sang and beat drums. Abdelwahab hesitated about going because he knows that Mrabet dislikes him. But Mrabet dislikes everyone who comes to see me, so I encouraged him to accept. Great quantities of delicious food.

January 8

Steve had it in his head that he wanted to give me a parrot. When we spied an African gray opposite the Spanish cathedral, he went into the shop to inquire the price, and was told it was two thousand dirhams. Then yesterday we went again to look at the bird, I all the time objecting that it was much too expensive. The owner now wanted three thousand dirhams, which made it possible to leave without further conversation. Steve later remarked to Abdelwahab that he thought I would rather see things go badly than well, because I seemed so relieved after we'd left the shop.

February 5
Three elderly people now living in Buffie's flat. Very quiet. It must be frigid down there with no heating apparatus. They brought me a copy of Buffie's book, *Lady of the Beasts*. Very impressive production.

February 25
Books arrive practically every day from one place or another, and Abdelouahaid is indispensable in getting them through the censors and the customs, and to the postal authorities. But yesterday he came out to the car where I was waiting and in great excitement began to upbraid me. "A book that is killing people all over the world, and you want it. It's very bad. They're angry in the post office." I had no idea what was the matter. "What book? Where is it?" I got out of the car and went into the building, where I saw them all fixing me with baleful stares. One of the employees came to me and explained. "You have a book here that's forbidden." I asked him if I could see it, but he said it had already been repacked, and no one could see it. "Can't you show me the parcel so I'll know where it came from?" He went behind a counter and held up a package in the dark by its string, not wanting to touch it with his hands. By this time I'd guessed that the book was the one that was making all the trouble, thanks to the dictator of Iran. Still I had no idea who had sent it. Another official came up frowning. "This is contraband goods. You cannot have it." "I don't want it," I told him.

February 26
Today at the post office the clerks wanted to know if the police had been to see me. I said they had not. "They came here and wanted your name and address, and they took away the book to deliver it to the government in Rabat."

March 1
The police haven't bothered me yet, so I suppose they won't. But now my incoming books are held up for an extra day while they're given a more thorough examination than they were previously.

March 10
Another French TV show wants to send a crew next week. This one called *Ex Libris*. I've been worrying that Claude Thomas may not be translating *The Spider's House*. If she isn't by now, does that mean they'll get someone to make as bad a translation of it as they have just made of *Without Stopping*?

March 18
French TV crew here today. Interviewer, intelligent and pleasant, seemed shocked by the humble aspect of the flat, saying he'd expected me to be living on the Mountain in a big house with a fine garden. Very earnestly he said: "Do you *like* living this way?" Then he decided that the interview should be conducted in the wine bar at the Minzah, a decor more in keeping with the expectations of his public.

March 19
Interview not too lengthy, so now it's finished. To be broadcast April 5.

March 27
Young man from *Le Quotidien* came from Paris to ask questions. Couldn't give him much time.

March 28
Claude Thomas arrived from Paris for a few days. She is not working on *The Spider's House*. This is the worst news yet. She's justified in insisting on having a contract with Quai Voltaire. It's something of a mystery why they keep promising the document and then fail to send it. I naturally assume that they've already given the work to someone else who will do it more quickly, since Claude is conscientious and takes her time, as indeed she should.

March 31
Went to dinner last night at Claude's, taking along Bergil Howell, who was enchanted by the beauty of the estate. The forest was dark, and the half-moon lighted the scallops of foam as the waves broke almost without sound against the rocks. The interviewer has been coming every day. It seems he's also writing a piece for the *Globe*.

April 3
Two photographers from Rome. They had an idea that there were picturesque cafés along the waterfront. After letting them drive all around the town without finding anything suitable, I suggested the Café Hafa. It delighted them. One of them had been in Moscow last week, and he talked about the city while the other took picture after picture, always saying, "Look at me" between snaps.

April 4
Suomi Lavalle came this morning and made his own hundred or so photos, taking me up to the garden of the Shaikha Fatima F.S. al-Sabah.

(I never know what to call her; I only know she's the daughter of the Emir of Kuwait.) I like her very much.

April 20
Annoyed with post office. New record with eleven of my songs, just issued, had been put on a cassette and sent me from New York, but some employee ripped the envelope across and removed the tape, pasting it up again with official stickers. So no songs. I suppose this is connected with the Salman Rushdie book having been sent me—by Carol Ardman, who ought to have known better, and who probably did know better. (She wrote me last week, admitting that it was she who was responsible.)

April 23
Ramadan makes everything difficult. Once again Mrabet has shown the inflaming effect it has on him. I knew he disliked Abdelwahab from the beginning, but until Ramadan he found it possible to behave in a normal fashion. Then, seeing that Abdelwahab was eating and smoking instead of fasting, his dislike turned to fury. This afternoon he came in and found A. sitting on a hassock drinking a cup of tea. He lifted the table and flung it, tea and all, upon A., accompanying this action with a stream of invective in both Arabic and Spanish. *"Zamel! Yehudi! Maricón de mierda!"* His small daughter (to be five next week) stood by in a state of bewilderment. There will probably be more such scenes before the end of the fast, since Abdelwahab comes each noon and prepares my lunch for me, and Mrabet can't abide the thought that he should refuse to observe Ramadan and fast along with everyone else.

April 24
I thought I was finished with entertaining TV crews. They've come from Milan, Amsterdam, London, Paris and New York. But there's another crew coming, this time from Geneva. I had a German couple here yesterday and today, recording for a Berlin radio station. The woman had a penchant for beginning her questions with the word "why." I told her that questions starting with "why" couldn't be answered intelligently or truthfully. Of course her question then was "Why not?" I recanted and said that my remark had to do only with me. This didn't help, because she countered by saying: "But we're talking only about you."

April 25
Two disreputable-looking Moroccans rang my bell at about two-thirty in the afternoon. They didn't seem to know how to begin talking. Then

the lift arrived and Abdelouahaid got out of it, standing behind them. "Your daughter wants to see you," said one. When I objected that I had no daughter, he only laughed. The other said: "Yes, you have, and she's here. The one named Catherine, from Germany. She's never seen you, and she wants to come and meet you." "I don't want to meet her," I told him. Abdelouahaid spoke up, assuring them that there was a mistake, but they carefully paid him no attention. "Shall we bring her here at five?" "No, no, no! I have no daughter. Thank you, but I don't want to see her."

They left. Abdelouahaid came in, warning me that they were criminals, and not to let them in if they came back. I felt fairly sure they wouldn't return. But after I got back from the market and post office and Abdelouahaid had gone home, the bell rang again. The two were there, looking as though they were supporting a woman between them. She wore a wide hat and kept her head down, so I could not see her face. "This is your daughter," they told me. "She comes from Essen." By this time it was all so unlikely and ridiculous that I yielded to temptation and decided to let her in, but I made the Moroccans stay outside. As if to introduce herself she pulled from her pocket a paperback copy of *So Mag Er Fallen*. Then she said in heavily accented English: "I have shame, but I go tomorrow to Germany." Apparently she could think of no way to meet me during her one afternoon in Tangier, save by going to the Zoco Chico and begging everyone who would listen to take her to her father, named Paul Bowles. The two outside the door, after arranging a price in the Zoco, had taken pity on her and claimed to know me, although surely they had never seen me.

Her conversation went in various directions and was hard to follow. I began to wonder how I could get rid of her. During the rambling she declared that she wanted to die. This made me even more eager to get her out. I gave her a cup of tea. As she drank it she explained that she had hoped to die in Merzouka on top of a big sand dune, but hadn't managed it. I said it was a pity, and she agreed. Finally she corrected herself. "I don't want to die. I want to change." Her glance was coy as she painted her lips.

I gave her a copy of *Gesang der Insekten* and signed it. She seemed disappointed to see that the locale was Latin America. It was clear that she had an obsession: she wanted to read only about North Africa. By the time I eased her out, her two friends were gone. I hope they hadn't already been paid, and were waiting downstairs, for she'd told me she had no idea of how to get back to her *pension*.

April 26

A house down the street has a large stork's nest on top of its chimney. Each spring a family of birds arrives, stays two months or so, and then goes on. Last year there were two young ones. They moved around the nest constantly and practiced flying by jumping up and down and flapping their wings. The male, apparently annoyed by all the hubbub, built himself another nest on the top of an electrical pylon about a hundred feet from the first. During the winter workmen came and pulled down the nest. Yesterday I noticed that the storks were in residence. Once again a big nest has been built atop the tower. Is it the same couple each year, and do the young birds return with their parents?

I haven't seen storks migrating for many years—thirty at least. I used to go down to Merkala and see hundreds of them moving past in perfect V-formations, so low that I could hear the regular beat of their wings. In the spring they flew out across the strait toward Spain, and in the autumn they came back. Storks strike me as particularly beautiful in flight, in spite of the two sticklike legs that dangle beneath. The long neck and the great wings slowly beating are what one notices.

April 28

Scarcely an afternoon passes without a visit from someone I never saw before and probably shall never see again. Giving all this time makes life seem a static thing, as though an infinite number of years lay ahead. It's become a serious problem only during the past year or two. Not having a telephone makes it worse: people come all the way out here and knock on the door. This makes it difficult to refuse to see them. Someone has come every afternoon this week.

May 10

Sometimes I wonder how long this routine is going to continue, the eating of all meals in bed. After the sympathectomy the doctor thought it a good idea. Now, after nearly three years, I go right on. At noon Abdelwahab comes and makes my lunch. In the afternoon Mrabet brings food and prepares dinner. Breakfast is the most important of the three meals, but Mrabet doesn't seem to understand this, since recently he fails to appear in the morning, so that I have to invent my own breakfast and eat it at the kitchen table. I consider myself lucky to have friends willing to serve me in bed. But Abdelouahaid says: "You're not sick. Why do you have to eat in bed?" Of course, Moroccans have a horror of staying in bed, even if they're running a fever. Anyone who takes to his bed with an illness is presumed ready to die.

Paul Bowles / 415

Someone came from New York and presented me with a copy of that biography Sawyer-Lauçanno insisted on writing, even though I begged him not to. His annoyance with me for refusing to cooperate shows clearly, so that it becomes, whether or not he wishes it to, a defamatory work. In order to produce it he was obliged to use my autobiography. The difference between mine and his lies in his decision to doubt the veracity of my account and substitute his own version. Doubtless he thought his own more piquant since it makes me out to be a liar. There's an endless list of false statements based purely on assumptions and hearsay, but with obvious malevolence.

For one thing, Sawyer-Lauçanno was much too ready to listen to certain mischievous gossips, and to include their scurrilous nonsense in his text, without bothering to verify. That's annoying, but at least the so-called information is credited to those who proffered it. What is infuriating is his tendency to imagine that I gave what I knew were false versions of events. The truth is too tame for his kind of journalism. I'm angered by his portrait of me as an accomplished moocher in the thirties. It's enraging to read his personal story about why Jane left Portugal in 1958. She and I went every day for two weeks to the American Embassy in Lisbon to procure a new passport, hers having expired while we were in Madeira. "No," they said. "We must get in touch with the FBI first." We continued to go to the embassy, in the hope of a quick reply from Washington. It was not quick, and when it came, it was negative. "Mrs. Bowles will have to return to the United States immediately. We'll give her a paper in place of her passport." Jane left a day or two later. Mr. S.-L. says that the State Department assured him that such proceedings were quite impossible, and so he assumes that my story is fictitious and that I used it as a "ruse" in order to get Jane off my hands. The book is defamatory, but unfortunately not actionable.

May 12

Many letters from Jerez in New York. Bachir is with her. She speaks of arranging jobs for him. One of these was the La Mama production of *The Night Before Thinking*, the play that Ahmed Yacoubi had hoped to see produced several years ago, and which I'd vetoed because his collaborator had excised the baby with eyes everywhere on its body. The baby seemed to me the most important character in the story. Now the piece was presented (without baby, of course) and Bachir played *rhaïta* and *liara* and even *guinbri*, but he was annoyed by La Mama; finally Jerez decided that La Mama was crazy.

In one letter Jerez said that she and Bachir had been married "at the mosque around the corner." This will make it easier for him to extend his stay in the U.S., important because he hopes to go on tour with various groups, including The Rolling Stones.

May 25
Instead of an American tour, Jerez managed to arrange a Moroccan trip during which Mick Jagger would visit Jajouka with a BBC crew, to perform with Bachir in his native village. Jerez and Bachir will arrive here June 4, and the Stones a few days later.

June 2
Phillip and Krazy Kat just in from New York, Phillip laden with gifts. All that was lacking here in the flat was a Christmas tree. Krazy Kat is pleased that he'll be meeting Jagger. I of course am pessimistic about the whole project, suspecting that the BBC won't have had time to prepare the necessary formalities for getting equipment into the country. I remember how the Dutch had to make three trips here from Holland before they were able to persuade the officials to allow their recording equipment through customs.

Some of Phillip's most important gifts were the new records, one of *Music for a Farce* (Reference Recordings, Chicago Pro Musica) and the other of songs sung by William Sharp, who gives what I'd call definitive performances of eleven of my old songs. The *Farce* pieces sound very fresh and immediate, after years of hearing the old Columbia and MGM recordings.

June 3
I wrote Sawyer-Lauçanno, giving my outraged reaction to the voicing of all his suspicions. Then he replies: "At the urging of my editor, I made an inquiry to the State Department. They categorically, even emphatically, denied that they would have done such a thing. . . . In retrospect I can see how I created the impression that I did not entirely believe your account. All I was trying to do was give another version of the story." He should have displayed his inventive virtuosity by giving three or four more versions.

June 5
Jerez and Bachir are here in Tangier. Both are excited about the Stones' arrival, and I don't dare voice my pessimism. They have to be careful to come to see me only when they're reasonably sure that Mrabet won't be here.

Now that Bachir is Jerez's husband, he naturally feels that the house built with her money belongs partly to him. I think he knows that there's virtually no chance of his ever getting it, since it's registered in the name of Zohra and not of Mrabet.

June 7
Some advance crewmen from the BBC arrived with a view to shooting Jagger when he comes. *If* he comes, I thought. Their chief seemed pretty sure he would.

June 8
Today everyone is much less certain. Customs refuses to let any of the BBC equipment into the country. Great *Geschrei*, and much telephoning to London. Ultimatum from Stones' manager: If equipment is not through customs by nine o'clock tomorrow morning he will cancel the engagement. Jerez arrived this evening, panting with anxiety. "You've got to call the king," she told me, although she knows I've never met him and wouldn't call him even if I had. Then she mentioned that she'd been to see Lalla Fatima Zohra during the day and had been told to call her by telephone later. Her eyes lighted on me. "*You* know Lalla Fatima Zohra. You call her. Tell her how important it is for Morocco to have BBC make this film." I was in my bathrobe, downstairs with the others, in Buffie's bedroom. Everyone seemed to be of the opinion that the least I could do was to call Lalla Fatima Zohra and explain the situation, which I think Jerez had found it difficult to do because of language obstacles. (I had forgotten that Lalla Fatima Zohra speaks perfect English.) "But I can't speak Arabic well enough to talk to her," I objected. Abdelwahab made a suggestion that I call her and give my name, then pass the telephone to him. This we did, and she asked Abdelwahab to call back in a half hour. When he made the connection later, she seemed to be speaking into two telephones at once. There were very long waits, while everyone looked at Abdelwahab to see by his facial reactions what words were coming through from the palace of Moulay Abdelaziz. He merely said, "*Naam, lalla,*" from time to time. The conversation, if that's what it was, went on for ten minutes. At the end Abdelwahab hung up, saying that she had promised to call customs and ask that the television equipment be let in. By that time it looked as if The Rolling Stones would not be coming to Tangier. I said that I doubted Lalla Fatima Zohra had the power to force the airport officials to do anything, one way or the other. Both Bachir and Abdelwahab hotly disputed this. "Her

word is law in Tangier," Abdelwahab cried. I said I certainly hoped so, and came upstairs to sleep.

June 8
Abdelwahab, who is almost as interested as Bachir in seeing that the film gets shot, came by at noon to tell me that Jagger and Keith Richards had gone to the Intercontinental and refused the suites reserved for them by Jerez. (Abdelwahab is getting married next month and is trying to have as good a time as possible before the wedding.)

So permission was given and the Stones came from London. All day yesterday and today Jerez, never once doubting that all would be well, has been rushing from one place to another, trying to find a likely place where the film could be shot. She has no time to eat, can't sleep at all, and will be ill in another day or two. She got a go-ahead from Malcolm Forbes for equipment to be set up in his garden, but the TV people turned it down in favor of the courtyard of the Akaboun house, which I suggested because it provides a more authentic background. About five o'clock Jagger arrived, accompanied by so many others that the room was archicomplete. Keith Richards was among them. He paid his respects to me and left, saying he was going to bed. Jagger sat down beside me, and we started to talk. It was a while before I noticed that our conversation was being filmed. After a quarter of an hour the filming stopped. "I'm tired," he said. "My kids woke me up at daybreak today. You see, Sunday's Father's Day, and they had to give me their presents today before I left. See you tomorrow at the show."

June 10
Sat for two hours this afternoon in the Akaboun courtyard. There were sixteen men from Jajouka with their *rhaïtas* and *benadir*, all wearing heavy brown djellabas. Much too hot for all that wool. They were impressive and sounded magnificent. How they sounded on film God knows, but it probably doesn't matter. Bachir did a lot of solo work with and without drums. The only sounds made by Mick Jagger were made on drums. He may have sung after I left, but I doubt it. In the adjacent room, whenever there was no music, I could hear a kind of pedal point that went on without respite, a constant tonic, very low in pitch, and not quite a quarter-tone higher than the tonic of the key in which the *rhaïtas* and the *liara* played.

June 12
Had lunch on the Mountain with Gloria Kirby. Her guests from Madrid knew all about Pedro Almodóvar, who seems to specialize in comic films.

It's hard to understand, if that's the case, why he chose to take an option on *The Time of Friendship*, a story in which there's not a suggestion of a humorous situation. Unless he does the whole thing tongue-in-cheek. It wouldn't be difficult to satirize the crèche scene. Or making Slimane three or four years older could provide a different sort of liaison between him and Fraülein Windling. But humor? The guests at lunch suggested that Almodóvar felt he had exhausted his comic vein, and intended to add a serious dimension to his work.

June 16
Yesterday the American ambassador to Rabat set up an appointment with me at the Minzah bar. Seemed pleasant enough, but I had no idea why he wanted to see me, and still have none.

June 20
After lunch Rodrigo, as he often does on fine days, went to Merkala in order to swim out at the Sindouq. Before my artery got blocked I used to go almost every day, following the coast, climbing among the boulders, jumping from one to the other. It was my favorite activity, imitating a chamois, sure of my feet. If someone mentioned that I was like a goat, I joked about my zodiacal sign. "Of course. Capricorn." I can hardly get along the shore now even if I have someone pulling and pushing. Pointless to pretend that time makes no difference.

June 24
Last night Bertolucci sent a car for me, to take me to the Minzah for dinner. At the beginning of the meal he said: "At last, it's happening." "Yes. For two years I've been wondering whether it would," I told him. Everyone connected with the making of the film was there, including the producer, whom I'd met a few years ago when Bill Burroughs was here with him from London. Conversation was difficult. A very noisy floor show was going on for the benefit of a huge group of shrieking tourists. Bertolucci brought up the subject of music. He was still thinking of using David Byrne, although he mentioned Richard Horowitz as well and at one point said he'd like me to provide some of it. We didn't discuss it. I suspect he'd like electronic material rather than symphonic. Much easier, much cheaper. No parts or rehearsals needed. Scarfiotti had mentioned that he'd like to use Agadèz as the setting for final city in the south. I hope this can be managed, and that they don't try to shoot everything in Morocco. I can appreciate their not wanting to get involved with the Algerians, but Morocco is no substitute for Algeria or Niger.

June 30
Yesterday a French TV crew came to interview. Nothing memorable. We repaired to the belvedere at Sidi Amar, and they shot a long scene there against the sea. Occasionally I can view these things on video afterward, but not usually. They're disappointing for always coming out in black-and-white.

July 5
Yesterday lunch at Gavin Young's, taking along Abdelwahab. We had mint tea in the garden afterward. When I picked up one of the pillows off the lawn, I found a very excited centipede on it. Abdelwahab: "Don't kill it! Please!" Gavin, later: "Have you become a Buddhist?"

At noon today I had a visit from Riki Suzuki, who presented me with a copy of my new story collection from Shinchosha in Tokyo. As usual, I was a little ill-at-ease, as I always am with the Japanese. It's so hard to know what they're thinking, and to know how awkward I'm being, according to their standards. Are they in the act of approving, or disapproving?

July 17
A Moroccan sent from Holland by Robert Briatte arrived this morning. I can't quite make out what he wants from me. I know he hopes to make a film, but since he's leaving for the U.S. shortly, it doesn't seem likely that he'll do it very soon. We went, at his insistence, to Café Hafa. On the way Abdelwahab, with his brother-in-law, overtook us in a car, and drove us the rest of the way to the café.

Another Moroccan came in the afternoon—a professor at the University of Limoges. He was quite frank about his intentions, and pulled out a tape recorder immediately.

July 19
Today Gavin asked Abdelwahab and me to lunch. He's about to leave for England, but will be back here in October, when he'll tell me more about being designated as a chief in British Samoa, a function he expects to assume this coming winter. He suggested I go out there and see him in regalia, knowing I shan't.

July 21
There are three Moroccans coming regularly to ask me questions: Mohand, Rais and Fqih Aouami. When Rais arrived the first time he

brought roses and a sugar loaf. As he handed the loaf to me he said: "You know the tradition." I agreed that I did, which was untrue. I still don't know, because no one seems to be able to explain it. Fqih Aouami is a professor at the University of Limoges, and has many questions prepared.

July 25
Last night Phillip, Krazy Kat, Rodrigo and Lidia Breda were with me at Abdelwahab's wedding. Chaotic and noisy. More than a hundred guests. The music was *raï*, deafening. It made conversation almost impossible, and dancing almost obligatory. Only the men and boys danced, moving in violent gyrations hour after hour without appearing to tire. The girls sat in long rows, watching.

July 27
Abdelwahab tells me that the family of his bride came and demanded of his parents that they give them the nuptial sheet stained with blood. The bridal couple, after forty-eight hours of celebration with no sleep, had merely collapsed on the bed and lain inert for a two-hour respite before being called to continue the festivities. Thus there was no blood. Abdelwahab's parents were outraged. "Such backward people!" they commented, but they did agree to let the bride's family have the sheet once it was marked with blood, which presumably will be tomorrow.

July 28
Last night Fatima es Sabah sent a car for me, and I was able to attend her garden party, where Bachir and a group of Jajouka musicians performed sitting in a line atop a big boulder above the pool. As the guests went down the path to the garden, they passed a row of ten servants in livery standing side by side, to greet them. The princess, however, was not in evidence, and David Herbert took great exception to her absence, exclaiming: "This . . . is not *my* way." Previously, up at the house, she had brought out a handsome camel's-hair garment, a Kuwaiti variation on a djellaba, for me to wear, because she knew I was *frileux*, and the garden, being at the edge of a high cliff over the ocean, is subject to sudden bouts of chilly wind. The cape was welcome. I spent a certain amount of time being photographed by Suomi Lavalle lying on the rock at the feet of the musicians, and without my covering of camel's hair I'd have been cold. When I left, Fatima insisted that I keep it because, according to her, it suited me perfectly.

July 30
The Yarmolinskys gave a Jilala party last night at Villa Julie. There was dancing, especially by women, some of whom seemed to be in a state of trance, although I don't believe they were. (Mejdoubi's widow was particularly pleasing.) The couscous was excellent. I was fortunate to be eating inside, for there were mosquitoes in the garden. Abdelouahaid amused us by calling for us in a huge bus that held seventy passengers. He played the clown, driving us up the mountain and then down again, ostensibly without brakes. Phillip was worried that he'd go over the edge of the road, but of course he knew what he was doing and got us all home without a mishap.

August 1
Dinner last night at Abdelwahab's, with his bride. Phillip, Krazy Kat, Rodrigo, Lidia and I watched two video clips of life with P.B. One was Gary Conklin's old film which was recently shown on French TV, and the other was a part of *Ex Libris*—the least interesting part. We were also entertained by endless sequences of last week's wedding. Dinner was good, and we left after Abdelouahaid had agreed to come into the house and sit, despite his feud with Abdelwahab. Farewells were lengthy and emotional. The bridal couple leave this morning for the Netherlands. I'll miss Abdelwahab.

August 2
Went tonight to the Marquis for dinner with Goldstone. Food not as good as usual. He wants Mrabet to consult his cardiologist for a checkup and insists on paying for the consultation.

August 7
Went last night to the annual Callaway dinner at the Marquis. Roast beef a little tough, but better than one would expect to get in Tangier, where beef is invariably awful.

August 12
Now I must take back what I said on Monday about beef in this city. Last night Phillip gave a dinner at a restaurant where I'd never eaten, called Osso Buco. I had a filet that was perfect, which I'd have considered perfect in Paris or New York. Why that restaurant should be able to get good beef while all the rest is nearly inedible, I don't understand. Jerez was there. Bachir came in unexpectedly while we were eating and sat down with us to drink beer. He and Jerez were not on speaking terms.

August 15

The Moroccans keep coming every day. Sometimes it's hard to keep track of what each one wants. Fqih Aouami is the most difficult one to satisfy; he always has a new set of questions. Last night I heard drums— not the *darboukas* of Aachor, but in a variety of timbres. I had the impression that an *ahouache* was in progress. Never having witnessed an *ahouache* save in the High or Anti-Atlas, I decided that my hearing was deficient. When I opened my bedroom window and heard the chanting above the drums I was no longer in any doubt. An *ahouache* was going on, up the street in the vicinity of the school. I ran out and found thirty men in traditional white robes, each with his dagger, dancing in a long line. Eight drummers crouched in front of them. I might have been in Tafraout. I stood motionless for about an hour, mystified and delighted, until they filed out of the courtyard. Then I asked a policeman sitting at the gate how it happened that such a group found itself here in Tangier. "They were brought by the American chief," he told me. "You mean the government?" "You know, the chief with the palace on the Marshan." That could mean only Malcolm Forbes. I have an invitation to a dinner he is giving on the nineteenth. A great idea, I thought, to bring performers from the deep south all the way here. There were nine very large buses parked outside the entrance to the school, which means that several hundred dancers and singers have come.

August 16

I went again last night to watch the performers, but arrived too late to see anything but a few youths dancing. They were good, but I don't think professional.

August 17

Jerez and Bachir came last night with the idea of going to the school with me. This time there was a crowd of two or three hundred men dancing, and perhaps fifty women. A great performance, including an astounding group of Haouara and even Bechara with her girls, dancing to the *guedra*. Bachir, who used to work in Goulimine and knew Bechara from that time, spoke with her after the rehearsal. She asked us to have tea with her upstairs in a room devoted to the *guedra* dancers. When she saw me she claimed to remember me, although I don't quite see how she could. The last time I saw her was in 1962 backstage in New York. (Katherine Dunham had imported her and three dozen other Moroccans to appear in her ill-fated musical; it lasted two nights.) I'd recorded her in Goulimine in 1959, but she wouldn't have been likely to have recalled that one evening. In any case, we were received with the traditional Moroccan hospitality. Some of the dancers reached into their bosoms and pulled out bundles of silver trinkets, which Jerez and Bachir bought. When we left, Bachir told me she had said to him: "If that American lives in Tangier he must have a lot of money. Is he married?" We agreed to go back tonight and see her.

August 19

Last night we did go back, but everyone was out at the airport to welcome the planes arriving with Forbes's guests from New York. It must have been an impressive scene, with all those members of the Royal Guard on their black horses, and the long lines of dancers in white robes and turbans. On the airstrip there would have been ample space for everything, whereas later in the street it would necessarily be crowded. I'd like to have seen it, but security was so tight that no one could have gotten into the airport to see anything.

August 20

The party must be over by now. I'm told that it went on all night. By midnight I'd had enough. There remained only the birthday cake and the fireworks to look forward to, and I saw the pyrotechnical display from my bedroom window after I got home. A tiring evening. First, the police refused to let us anywhere within a quarter of a mile of the entrance, so that we had to park in the *plazuela* behind the Café Hafa. The crowd in the street was so dense that Abdelouahaid had to push people aside roughly to make it possible for me to make any headway. When we got within sight of the Palais Mendoub he wished me good luck and went back. There was a long queue of guests waiting outside in the street. As we moved slowly forward we were pelted with rose petals by girls standing on each side of the queue. Beyond were the ranks of the dancers and drummers, and in the background, along the wall of the garden of the Palais du Marshan, stood the horses with their uniformed mounts, still as statues. I could think only of how fortunate it was that the weather was fine. Even a few drops of rain would have ruined a hundred evening dresses. It didn't seem an ideal manner of welcoming guests, to force them to stand in the street for a half-hour waiting to get to the bottleneck just outside the gate. There we exhibited our invitations, had our names checked on lists, and were admitted one at a time. The line continued through the courtyard, until we were given maps of the terrain and assigned to our tents. I counted nine of these objects, once I had passed through the receiving area, where our host stood grinning, flanked by his sons, and with Elizabeth Taylor seated by his side. "Wait till you see how fat she's grown!" people had warned me. To me she didn't look fat; she looked solid and luscious. She must have been tired; it's not easy to be introduced to nine hundred people one after the other. I refused the champagne and set out in search of the tent I'd been assigned to, pushing my way through the crowd until I'd found it. There were no placecards. I sat down at an empty table until a waiter asked me to choose another, also empty. No one seemed to be in a hurry to eat. My table did eventually fill up—with, among others, the governor, the chief of police and a military man decked with medals. At the next table sat Malcolm Forbes and his family. Miss Taylor was on his left, her back to me. The crown prince sat on his right. For three hours as I ate I watched their table. The French woman next to me made repeated comments in a whisper about Elizabeth Taylor's shoulders and the crown prince's face, which she characterized as "frightening" and "almost Japanese." All I could reply was that he never altered his poker-face expression and spoke very little. I myself thought he was unutterably bored; if that is so, it was understandable.

August 22

People who did not attend the Forbes dinner ask: "What was it like, really? Was it a ghastly farce?" Nothing so frankly commercial can properly be called a farce. It was what sixty years ago would have been called "spectacular and colossal," the difference being that in this case the adjectives are apposite.

August 26

A man named Jancovici who runs Les Éditions de la Différence in Paris has been bringing me art books (very well produced) in the hope that I'll provide a text for a book of reproductions of paintings by a *Mallorquín* named Barceló. I'm still busy on the piece for the Munich magazine, and trying to prepare the third part of this *Journal Tangérois* for Briatte and Librairie Plon. It occurred to me that it might be possible to do the Barceló book as fiction rather than as exposition. The paintings are pale gouaches, mainly monochromatic. If I were to illustrate them with a story of some sort, the welding of the two elements might stick.

August 27

Bertolucci now thinks I should appear in certain scenes of the film. I don't understand exactly why, and therefore suspect this to be a whim which he'll possibly think better of sooner or later. Richard Horowitz is busy gathering material to use in his soundtrack; I hope he doesn't decide that Moroccan music will make a satisfactory auditory backdrop for the Algerian Sahara.

September 1

Buffie left today for New York. We had lunch yesterday in the garden at Güitta's, after which she said: "She's lost a customer," referring to Mercedes, who runs the place singlehanded. The sole was far from fresh, and for it she charged exactly double the price quoted on the menu: one hundred forty dirhams instead of seventy. That sort of behavior would drive anyone away. There was too much insect life around: flies by the dozen, ants hurrying along the tablecloth, and an insistent hornet which crawled on my fish and nibbled on it voraciously throughout that entire course. In the afternoon went with Umberto Pasti (of the Italian *Vogue* piece) and his associates to the Avenida de España for a lot of photographs.

September 4

The king's ship was due to arrive back from Tripoli today, so everything was shut, the market padlocked, the streets barricaded, so that in order to get to the Almohades, Abdelouahaid and I had to walk in various directions through mud and piles of gravel. (The city is a mess, with big apartment houses going up everywhere.) At the Almohades, where the Sahara Company's office is located, I was measured for the film's costume designer, who is in London at the moment. What sort of clothes is he going to make for me, and in which scenes will I wear them?

September 5

The thousands of people waiting along the waterfront to see the king's ship come in waited in vain throughout the day. Last night, during a very loud and protracted thunderstorm, the vessel arrived, and the king was spirited aboard his train for Rabat. Neither he nor anyone in the government trusts the people of Tangier, and so he makes a point of not ever coming here if he can help it. I've never understood the official antipathy for Tangier and Tetuan, but doubtless those who feel it have their reasons. I returned to the Almohades this afternoon with a message for Bertolucci; while I was there he called from the Tafilelt, where he said the heat was intense. He told me he was en route to Algeria tomorrow: Béni-Abbès. It will be hotter there.

(This is the second part of a two-part journal. Part I appeared in Antæus 61.)

We must not expect all the virtues. We should even be satisfied if there is something odd enough to be interesting.

—ALFRED NORTH WHITEHEAD

POPULAR LAWS

According to a health ordinance in Riverside, California, kissing on the lips is against the law unless both parties first wipe their lips with carbolized rose water.

A Louisiana law upholds your right to grow as tall as you like.

A New York judge ruled that if two women behind you in a movie house are discussing the probable outcome of a film, you can give them a Bronx cheer.

It is against the law to drive camels along Nevada's main highways.

In Hawaii, it is illegal to insert pennies in your ears.

You are not permitted to swim on dry land in Santa Ana, California.

In Idaho, you cannot fish for trout from the back of a giraffe.

A kiss can last no longer than one second in Halethorpe, Maryland.

In Baltimore, Maryland, it is against the law to mistreat an oyster.

In Indiana a mustache is illegal on anyone who "habitually kisses human beings."

In Michigan you may not hitch a crocodile to a fire hydrant.

It is unlawful for goldfish to ride on a Seattle, Washington, bus unless they lie still.

In Utah, the law requires that daylight be seen between two dancing partners.

Teaching your household pet to smoke a cigar is unlawful in the state of Illinois.

In Macon, Georgia, for a man to put his arm around a woman, he must have a legal excuse or reason.

In any place in Montana where liquor is sold, a fan dancer's costume must weigh at least three pounds, three ounces.

José Manuel Miguel Xavier Gonzales, in a few short weeks, it will be spring. The snows of winter will flee away, the ice will vanish, and the air will become soft and balmy. In short, José Manuel Miguel Xavier Gonzales, the annual miracle of the years will awaken and come to pass, but you won't be there.

The rivulet will run its soaring course to the sea, the timid desert flowers will put forth their tender shoots, the glorious valleys of this imperial domain will blossom as the rose. Still, you won't be here to see.

From every tree top some wild woods songster will carol his mating song, butterflies will sport in the sunshine, the busy bee will hum happy as it pursues its accustomed vocation. The gentle breeze will tease the tassels of the wild grasses, and all nature, José Manuel Miguel Xavier Gonzales, will be glad but you. You won't be here to enjoy it because I command the sheriff or some other officer of this country to lead you out to some remote spot, swing you by the neck from a knotting bough of a sturdy oak, and let you hang until you are dead.

And then, José Manuel Miguel Xavier Gonzales, I further command that such officer or officers retire quickly from your dangling corpse, that vultures may descend from the heavens upon your filthy body until nothing shall remain but bare, bleached bones of a cold-blooded, copper-colored, blood-thirsty, throat-cutting, chili-eating, sheep-herding, murdering son-of-a-bitch.

—UNITED STATES OF AMERICA V. GONZALES
United States District Court, New Mexico Territory Sessions

You are about to begin reading . . . Relax. Concentrate. Dispel every other thought. Let the world around you fade. Best to close the door; the TV is always on in the next room. Tell the others right away, "No, I don't want to watch TV!" Raise your voice—they won't hear you otherwise—"I'm reading! I don't want to be disturbed!" Maybe they haven't heard you, with all that racket; speak louder, yell: "I'm beginning to read!"   —ITALO CALVINO

The flow of talk goes forward. Words or no words we must make a sound of voices to each other and we will; but it will be better if we can launch a thought now and then on the stream of words.   —ROBERT FROST

To find my home in one sentence, concise, as if hammered in metal. Not to enchant anybody. Not to earn a lasting name in posterity. An unnamed need for order, for rhythm, for form, which three words are opposed to chaos and nothingness. —CZESLAW MILOSZ

One demands two things of a poem. Firstly, it must be a well-made verbal object that does honor to the language in which it is written. Secondly, it must say something significant about a reality common to us all, but perceived from a unique perspective. What the poet says has never been said before, but, once he has said it, his readers recognize its validity for themselves. —W. H. AUDEN

The best short fiction, contrary to popular belief, is not to be found in the literary quarterlies. It is to be found in the great big slick magazines, where it belongs. This demonstrates, incidentally, either that money talks or that the literary quarterlies are all edited by poets.

—GORDON LISH

The tree was down and cut to lengths, the sections spread and jumbled over the grass. There was a stocky man with three fingers bound up in a dirty bandage with a splint. With him were a Negro and a young man, the three of them gathered about the butt of the tree. The stocky man laid aside the saw and he and the Negro took hold of the piece of fence and strained and grunted until they got the log turned over. The man got to one knee and peered into the cut. We best come in this way, he said. The Negro picked up the crosscut and he and the man began sawing again. They sawed for a time and then the man said, Hold it. Goddamn, that's it again. They stopped and lifted the blade from the cut and peered down into the tree. Uh-huh, said the Negro. It sho is now, ain't it?

The young man came over to see. Here, said the man, look sideways here. See? He looked. All the way up here? he said. Yep, the man said. He took hold of the twisted wrought-iron, the mangled fragment of the fence, and shook it. It didn't shake. It's growed all through the tree, the man said. We cain't cut no more on it. Damned old elum's bad enough on a saw.

The Negro was nodding his head. Yessa, he said. It most sholy has. Growed all up in that tree. —CORMAC McCARTHY

First came birds, covered with green sauce, served in red clay dishes embellished with black designs; then all species of shell-fish caught on the Punic coast, followed by broths of barley, wheat, and beans; and snails dressed with cumin, on plates of yellow amber. Later the tables were covered with every variety of meats: roasted antelopes, with their horns—peacocks in their plumage—whole sheep cooked in sweet wine—legs of camels and buffaloes—hedgehogs, with garum sauce—fried grass-hoppers, and candied dormice. In bowls of Tamrapanni wood large pieces of fat floated in the midst of saffron—every dish overflowed with pickles, truffles, and assafoetida; pyramids of fruit rolled over honey-cakes; nor had there been forgotten some of those red-haired, plump little dogs fattened on olive-lees: a Carthaginian dainty held in abomination by all other peoples.   —GUSTAVE FLAUBERT

Immediately when you arrive in the Sahara, for the first or the tenth time, you notice the stillness. An incredible, absolute silence prevails outside the towns; and within, even in busy places like the markets, there is a hushed quality in the air, as if the quiet were a conscious force which, resenting the intrusion of sound, minimizes and disperses sound straight-way. Then there is the sky, compared to which all other skies seem faint-hearted efforts. Solid and luminous, it is always the focal point of the landscape. At sunset, the precise, curved shadow of the earth rises into it swiftly from the horizon, cutting it into light section and dark section. When all daylight is gone, and the space is thick with stars, it is still of an intense and burning blue, darkest directly overhead and paling toward the earth, so that the night never really grows dark.

You leave the gate of the fort or the town behind, pass the camels lying outside, go up into the dunes, or out onto the hard, stony plain and stand awhile, alone. Presently, you will either shiver and hurry back inside the walls, or you will go on standing there and let something very peculiar happen to you, something that everyone who lives there has undergone and which the French call *le baptême de la solitude*. It is a unique sensation, and it has nothing to do with loneliness, for loneliness presupposes memory. Here, in this wholly mineral landscape lighted by stars like flares, even memory disappears; nothing is left but your own breathing and the sound of your heart beating. A strange, and by no means pleasant, process of reintegration begins inside you, and you have the choice of fighting against it, and insisting on remaining the person you have always been, or letting it take its course. For no one who has stayed in the Sahara for a while is quite the same as when he came.

—PAUL BOWLES
Their Heads Are Green and
Their Hands Are Blue

When I was nine they started to bind my feet again and they hurt so much that for two years I had to crawl on my hands and knees. Sometimes at night I could not sleep. I stuck my feet under my mother and she lay on them so they hurt less and I could sleep. But by the time I was eleven my feet did not hurt and by the time I was thirteen they were finished. My feet were very small indeed. —NING LAO

Then I think of my father, of Papa, and wonder what it would be like to be married to such a man, to see him coming out of the shower, to sit at dinner at six o'clock, turn off the lights at nine, embrace, make love frequently in honor of his long day of working, get up at five, visit with the relations on Sunday, never leave town. I wonder about this and of course I know. I know what the men are like, but I do not know what she is like. . . . —ELIZABETH HARDWICK

From March 25 till April 10 I was laid up in Ostroumov's clinic. Hæmorrhage. Creaking, moisture in the apices of both my lungs; congestion in the apex of the right. On March 28 L. N. Tolstoi came to see me. We spoke of immortality. I told him the gist of Nossilov's story "The Theatre of the Voguls," and he evidently listened with great pleasure.

—ANTON CHEKHOV

I was distressed when she seemed to question the love which was so necessary to her; I was no less distressed when she seemed to believe in it. I felt she was better than I; I despised myself for not being worthy of her. It is a fearful misfortune not to be loved when you love; but it is a much greater misfortune to be loved passionately when you love no longer. —BENJAMIN CONSTANT

Laughter makes the universe tremble, deranges it, reveals its vitals. Tremendous laughter is a divine manifestation. Like sacrifice, laughter is a denial of work. And not only because it is an interruption of labor, but also because it casts doubt on its seriousness. Laughter is a suspension, and in certain instances, a loss of reason. Thus it robs work, and consequently the world, of all meaning. In fact, work is what gives meaning to nature: it transforms its indifference or its hostility into fruitfulness, it makes it productive. Work humanizes the world, and this humanization is what gives it meaning. Laughter restores the universe to its original state of indifference and strangeness: if it has a meaning, it is a divine one, not a human one. —OCTAVIO PAZ

Anyone, provided that he can be amusing, has the right to talk of himself. —BAUDELAIRE

He could not be allowed to say Mass, to take part in processions or even to sit at meals, for at any moment he was apt to rise into the air and remain suspended for a long time. Amongst his other peculiarities, he had the habit of uttering a shrill cry like a bird on taking flight.

—THE LIFE OF ST. JOSEPH OF CUPERTINO

If there's one thing less pleasing than another,
It's a brisk and nimble antic man,
Who, to prove himself both young and able,
Leaps over hedge and ditch, clashing his castors.
I am a grave and proper woman.

—DJUNA BARNES

If I don't ask for money, I don't get any. I love you.

—DR. C. W. BURPO
Preacher

Son, let me tell you something. Do you know when you can tell a revival meeting is over? Do you know when God's saying to move on to the next town? When you can turn people on their head and shake them and no money falls out, then you know God's saying, "Move on, son."

—A. A. ALLEN
to Brother Marjoe

The glanis, an Aristophanic fish, consulted the wizard Bacis and learned not to bite the hook, then he consulted Glanis, the older brother of Bacis, an even greater wizard, and to satisfy nominalist problems, Glanis the wizard, the equal of Glanis the astute fish, taught him not only to bite the hook, but how to eat the fleshy worm. Once mature, Glanis the fish ceased to consult his namesake and learned to sleep in the curve of the hook, making his dream parallel that of the fisherman wizard.

—JOSE LEZAMA LIMA

A traveller, who has lost his way, should not ask, Where am I? What he really wants to know is, Where are the other places? He has got his own body, but he has lost them. —LORD ALFRED WHITEHEAD

Oscar Wilde: I wish I'd said that.
James McNeill Whistler: You will, Oscar, you will.

—JAMES McNEILL WHISTLER

As for borrowing Mr. Whistler's ideas about art, the only thoroughly original ideas I have ever heard him express have had reference to his own superiority as a painter over painters greater than himself.

—OSCAR WILDE

I have never admired being human, I must say. I want to be like God. But I haven't begun yet. First I have to go to Massachusetts and be alone.   —JANE BOWLES

If they cut my bald head open, they will find one big boxing glove. That's all I am. I live it.   —MARVELOUS MARVIN HAGLER

The Nobel Prize has become an international lizard hunt.

—GABRIEL GARCIA MARQUEZ

CONTRIBUTORS

WALTER ABISH's most recent book is *99: The New Meaning*. His books are published in Britain by Faber and Faber and include *How German is it?* (1983). *In the Future Perfect* (1984) and *Destiny: Tomorrow's Truth*, which will be published in 1991.

JORGE AMADO is Brazil's most widely translated novelist. His latest novel to appear in English is *Showdown* (Bantam, 1988). "The Leather Strap" is adapted from a translation-in-progress of *The War of the Saints*, translated by Gregory Rabassa. Copyright © 1990 by Jorge Amado and Gregory Rabassa. Reprinted by permission of Bantam Books, a division of Bantam Doubleday Dell Publishing Group, Inc. All rights reserved. *The Violent Land*, *The Tent of Miracles*, *Shepherds of the Night* and *Home is the Sailor* are available as Harvill Paperbacks.

WILLIAM ARROWSMITH, a renowned classics scholar, teaches at Boston University. Well known as a translator of Eugenio Montale, Professor Arrowsmith is a coeditor of *The Greek Tragedy in New Translation*, thirty-three volumes currently in publication by Oxford University Press.

JOHN ASHBERY's most recent collection of poems is *April Galleons* (Carcanet, 1988). *Selected Poems* and a volume of his art criticism, *Reported Sightings*, were published by Carcanet in 1986 and 1989 respectively.

MARGARET ATWOOD's latest novel is *Cat's Eye*, published in hardback by Bloomsbury in 1989 and in paperback by Virago in 1990. *Poems 1965–1975* is forthcoming from Virago. She lives and works in Toronto.

BALTHUS is a world-renowned French painter who lives in Paris. Guy Davenport's recent study *A Balthus Notebook* is available in the USA from Ecco. Excerpts from *Mistou* appear by permission of Librairie Seguier, Paris © 1988.

RUSSEL BANK's latest book is *Affliction* (Picador, 1990). He is currently at work on a new novel.

ANN BEATTIE's most recent novel, *Picturing Will* is forthcoming from Cape.

MARVIN BELL lives in Iowa City, Iowa, and Port Townsend, Washington. His many books include seven volumes of poetry from Atheneum, which issued his *New and Selected Poems* in 1987, and essays about writing, *Old Snow Just Melting*, available from the University of Michigan Press.

ROY BLOUNT JR's tenth book and first novel, *First Hubby*, was published in the USA by Villard. He is a contributing editor to *The Atlantic*, and his "UnBritish Crossword" appears every month in *Spy*.

EVAN BOLAND's poetry is published in Britain by Carcanet and includes *Outside History* (1990) and *Selected Poems* (1989). She lives in Dublin with her husband and two daughters.

PAUL BOWLES's new selected stories, *A Distant Episode*, was published in the USA by The Ecco Press in 1988. In Britain his books are published by Peter Owen, Paladin and Abacus. His classic novel *The Sheltering Sky* is being filmed by Bernardo Bertolucci in and around Tangier. His autobiography, *Without Stopping*, is available from Peter Owen.

BOGDANA CARPENTER teaches in the Slavic department at the University of Michigan. She recently published a bilingual anthology entitled *Monumenta Polonica: The First Centuries of Polish Poetry* (Michigan Slavic Publications).

JOHN CARPENTER is a writer and translator who lives in Ann Arbor, Michigan. Last year he was a fellow in literature of the National Endowment for the Arts.

JANE COOPER's most recent book is *Scaffolding: New and Selected Poems* (Anvil, 1984). She has new work in *The American Poetry Review*, *The American Voice*, *The Iowa Review*, and *Ploughshares*.

ROBERT COOVER's most recent book is *Gerald's Party*. His novels published in Britain include *A Night at the Movies: Or, You Must Remember This* (Paladin, 1989), *Whatever Happened to Gloomy Gus of the Chicago Bears?* (Minerva, 1989) and *Spanking the Maid* (Paladin, 1988). He teaches at Brown University.

GUY DAVENPORT, short story writer and essayist, is most recently the author of *A Balthus Notebook* and *The Drummer of the Eleventh North Devonshire Fusiliers* published in the USA by Ecco and North Point respectively. *Thasos and Ohio (Poems and Translations 1950–1980)* was published by Carcanet in 1985, and *Every Force Evolves a Form* appeared from Secker & Warburg in 1989.

NUALA Ń DHOMHNAILL is widely regarded as the best Irish-language poet of her generation. Her *Selected Poems*, translated by Michael Hartnett, is published by Raven Arts Press, Dublin.

DEBORAH DIGGES has written two books of poetry: *Vesper Sparrows*, which won the Delmore Schwartz Memorial Prize from New York University, and *Late in the Millennium*, recently published in the USA by Knopf. A book of nonfiction, *Fugitive Spring*, is forthcoming from Knopf.

ANNIE DILLARD is the author of eight books, most recently *The Writing Life*. In 1975 her novel *Pilgrim at Tinder Creek* won a Pulitzer Prize. In Britain her books are published by Picador. She lives in Middletown, Connecticut.

STEPHEN DOBYNS's poetry collections include *Black Dog, Red Dog* (Holt Reinhart), *Cemetery Nights* and *Body Traffic* (both Viking Penguin,

USA). His most recent novel is *The Two Deaths of Signora Puccini* (Penguin, 1989) and his latest Charlie Bradshaw thriller is *Saratoga Hexameter* (Century, 1990). He teaches at Syracuse University and in the MFA programme at Warren Wilson College.

MICHAEL DORRIS has written three books of nonfiction, the most recent being *The Broken Cord: A Father's Story* (Collins, 1990), and a novel, *A Yellow Raft in Blue Water* (Pan Books, 1989). He is completing a collection of short stories entitled *Working Men*.

STEPHEN DUNN's most recent collection of poetry is *Between Angels*, published in the USA by Norton. He teaches at Stockton State College.

GRETEL EHRLICH books include *The Solace of Open Spaces* and *Wyoming Stories*. Her novel, *Heart Mountain* was published by Heinemann in 1989 and by Mandarin in 1990. She lives with her husband on a cattle ranch in northern Wyoming.

LOUISE ERDRICH's latest poetry collection, *Baptism of the Desire*, was published in the USA in 1990. Her first collection of poems, *Jacklight*, is published in paperback in Britain by Abacus, and her three novels *Love Medicine* (Abacus), *Beet Queen* (Picador) and *Tracks* (Picador) are also available in paperback.

CAROLYN FORCHÉ teaches at George Mason university. "Recording Angel" is excerpted from *The Angel of History*, a book of poetry in progress. Forché is a cotranslator of *The Selected Poems of Robert Desnos*. Her book of poetry, *Country Between Us*, was published by Cape in 1983.

RENATA GORCZYNSKI, author of *Conversations with Czeslaw Milosz* and editor of the selected prose of Zygmun Haupt, translated Adam Zagajewski's *Tremor* from the Polish and contributed to the translation of *The Collected Poems* of Czeslaw Milosz.

MARY GORDON's most recent novel is *The Other Side* (Bloomsbury, 1990). She teaches at Barnard College and lives with her husband and two children in New Paltz, New York.

EDWARD GOREY has written-and-drawn a large number of small books. *Amphigorey* was published in 1989 by Penguin.

JORIE GRAHAM will publish a new volume of poetry in 1991. She recently edited *The Best American Poetry of 1990*.

EAMON GRENNAN comes from Dublin and teaches at Vassar College. *What Light There Is and Other Poems* was published in the USA by North Point. He is published in Ireland by Gallery.

PETER HANDKE was born in Griffen, Austria, in 1942; he is a playwright and screenwriter as well as an acclaimed novelist. His fiction is published in Britain by Methuen. "The Companions" is excerpted from *Absence*, translated by Ralph Manheim. Translation copyright © 1990 by Farrar, Straus & Giroux. All rights reserved. Originally published in German © Suhrkamp Verlag, Frankfurt Am Main,

1987. *Afternoon of a Writer* (Methuen, 1990) is Handke's latest novel to be published in Britain.

JIM HARRISON's new collection of novellas, *The Woman Lit by Fireflies*, was published by Houghton Mifflin (June 1990). *Dalva* was published in hardback by Cape in 1989 and in paperback by Picador in 1990.

ROBERT HASS's latest book of poems is *Human Wishes*, published in the USA by Ecco. He lives in Berkeley, California.

SEAMUS HEANEY's latest book is *New Selected Poems 1966–1887*, published by Faber and Faber in 1990. He was elected Professor of Poetry at Oxford University in 1989.

ZBIGNIEW HERBERT's *Selected Poems* was published by Carcanet in 1985. *Report from the Besieged City and Other Poems* was published by Oxford University Press in 1987. He has a collection of apocrypha based on Dutch pantings forthcoming in the USA from Ecco. He lives in Paris.

BRENDA HILLMAN's most recent book is *Fortress* (Wesleyan University Press, 1989). She teaches at St. Mary's College.

JOHN HOLLANDER recently edited *The Essential Rossetti*, the latest volume in Ecco's Essential Poet series. He has written children's books and many books of criticism, and has collaborated with composers on operatic and lyric works. His most recent books of poems is *Harp Lake*, published in the USA by Knopf in 1988.

RICHARD HOWARD is the Ropes Professor of Comparative Literature at the University of Cincinnati.

BENJAMIN IVRY is a poet whose verse has appeared in *Ambit, Encounter, The New Republic*, and *The Spectator*. Translations by him have been published in *The New Yorker* and the *Times Literary Supplement* (London).

DONALD JUSTICE lives in Florida. His most recent book is *The Sunset Maker*, published in 1987 by Anvil Press.

EDMUND KEELEY's latest book is *The Salonika Bay Murder: Cold War Politics and the Polk Affair* (Princeton University Press). His new collection of Ritsos translations, *Yannis Ritsos: Repetitions, Testimonies, Parentheses*, were published by Princeton in 1990.

GALWAY KINNELL's latest collection of poems is *When One Has Lived a Long Time Alone*. He teaches in the graduate creative-writing programme at New York University.

KARL KIRCHWEY's collection, *A Wandering Island*, appeared in the USA in the Princeton Series of Contemporary Poets in 1990. Kirchway is director of the Poetry Centre of the 92nd Street YM-YWHA in New York City.

CAROLYN KIZER's most recent book is *Carrying Over*, a book of translations published in the USA by Copper Canyon Press.

EDWARD KOREN is a well-known cartoonist for *The New Yorker*.

WILLIAM KULIK is a cotranslator of *The Selected Poems of Robert Desnos*, which will be released in the USA by Ecco in January 1991.

PHILIP LEVINE is working on a new book of poems for publication by Knopf in the spring of 1991, and his sequel to *Don't Ask*, a book of essays and interviews entitled *Don't Ever Ask Again*, will be published by the University of Michigan Press. His most recent book of poems, *A Walk with Tom Jefferson* (Knopf, 1988), won the Bay Area Book Reviewers' Award.

LARRY LEVIS was awarded a National Endowment for the Arts fellowship in creative writing in 1989. In 1988 he was a Fulbright lecturer in Yugoslavia. His most recent collection of poems is *Winter Stars* (University of Pittsburgh Press, 1985).

CAMPBELL MCGRATH lives in Chicago. His first book, *Capitalism*, was published in the USA in 1990 as part of the Wesleyan New Poets series.

RALPH MANHEIM has translated works by Peter Handke, Louis-Ferdinand Céline, Günter Grass, Elias Canetti, and others. His many awards include a 1983 MacArthur Foundation Lifetime Fellowship, the first such award to a literary translator.

WILLIAM MATTHEWS's most recent book of poems is entitled *Blues If You Want* (Houghton Mifflin, 1990). His book of essays *Curiosities* was published by the University of Michigan Press in 1989, as part of the Poets on Poetry series.

WILLIAM MAXWELL has published six novels, two collections of short fiction, a family memoir, and a volume of essays and reviews. *So Long, See You Tomorrow* was published by Secker and Warburg in 1989. Maxwell was fiction editor at *The New Yorker* for forty years.

JAMES MERRILL's most recent collection of poems, *The Inner Room*, was published in the USA by Knopf in 1988.

W. S. MERWIN's most recent books are *The Rain in the Trees* (Knopf) and *Selected Poems* (Atheneum). *Vertical Poetry*, a book of his translations of the Argentine poet Roberto Juarroz, was also recently published (North Point).

STEVEN MILLHAUSER is the author of *Edwin Mullhouse: The Life and Death of an American Writer* and *In the Penny Arcade*.

CZESLAW MILOSZ received the Nobel Prize for Literature in 1980. His *Collected Poems 1931–1987* is available from Penguin.

PAUL MULDOON is the author of *Selected Poems 1968–1986* (1986), *Meeting the British* (1987) and *Madoc: A Mystery* (1990), published by Faber and Faber.

JOYCE CAROL OATES's latest novel is *Because It Is Bitter, and Because It Is My Heart* (Dutton). Her books published in Britain include *Marya: A Life* (Pan, 1987), *On Boxing* (Bloomsbury, 1987; Pan, 1988), *You Must Remember This* (Macmillan, 1988; Pan, 1989) and *American Appetites* (Macmillan, 1989). She lives in Princeton, New Jersey, where she edits *The Ontario Review*, and teaches at Princeton University.

EDNA O'BRIEN's latest books are a collection of short stories, *Lantern Slides* (Weidenfeld, 1990) and a novel, *The High Road* (Weidenfeld, 1988; Penguin, 1989).

ERIC PANKEY, author of two books of poems, *For the New Year* and *Heartwood*, is completing a new manuscript, *Apocrypha*. He directs the writing programme at Washington University in St. Louis.

LINDA PASTAN's seventh book. *The Imperfect Paradise*, was published in the USA by Norton in 1988 and was a nominee for the Los Angeles Times Book Award. She is on the staff of the Bread Loaf Writers' Conference.

ROBERT PINSKY's new book of poems, *The Want Bone*, was published in the USA in 1990. *Explanation of America* was published by Carcanet in 1979.

STANLEY PLUMLY's most recent book is *Boy on the Step*. He is working on a book of essays, tentatively titled *Sentimental Forms*.

KÁČA POLÁČKOVÁ-HENLEY has translated many Czech writers, including Pavel Kohout and Ivan Klima. She is the translator of *The Bass Saxophone* by Josef Škvorecký (Chatto & Windus and Picador).

SUSAN PROSPERE has published poetry in *Field* and *The New Yorker*. She recently held an Ingram Merrill grant.

GREGORY RABASSA teaches at Queens College. His latest translation is *Sado Alexandrino* by Antonio Lobo Atunes, published in the USA by Grove Weidenfeld in 1990.

YANNIS RITSOS is considered one of the major living Greek poets. Much honoured in Europe, he is the most prolific Greek writer of this century, having published over 100 volumes of poetry, prose, drama, and translation.

ERIC ROBINSON is professor of Modern History at the University of Massachusetts at Boston. He is currently editing a collection of John Clare's poems for the Clarendon Press, Oxford.

IRA SADOFF's most recent book of poems, *Emotional Traffic*, was published in the USA by Godine in 1989.

DAVID ST JOHN is the author of *Hush, The Shore*, and *No Heaven*. His new collection is entitled *Terraces of Rain*. He is professor of English at the University of Southern California and poetry editor of *The Antioch Review*.

JAMES SEAY's new collection of poems is *The Light As They Found It* (William Morrow). In 1988 he received an award in literature from the American Academy and Institute of Arts and Letters.

CHARLES SIMIC is the author of many collections of poetry including *Unending Blues* (1986) and a sequence of prose poems, *The World Doesn't End* (1989), both published in the USA by Harcourt Brace Jovanovich. His *Selected Poems 1963–83* was published by Secker & Warburg in 1985. His most recent book of poems, *The Book of Gods and*

Devils (1990), is published in the USA by Harcourt Brace Jovanovich.

JOSEF ŠKVORECKÝ left Czechoslovakia in 1945 and now lives in Toronto where he writes, translates and teaches. His many novels include *The Bass Saxophone* (1978), *The Swell Season* (1983) and *The Engineer of Human Souls* (1985), all published in Britain in hardback by Chatto & Windus and in paperback by Picador. *Dvorak in Love: A Light-hearted Dream* was published by Hogarth in 1989. In 1990, Faber and Faber published *The End of Lieutenant Boruvka*, *The Return of Lieutenant Boruvka* and *The Sins of Father Knox*.

SUSAN SONTAG is the author of *On Photography* and *Salvador*. Her most recent book to be published in Britain is *AIDS and Its Metaphors* (Penguin, 1990). She is currently writing a novel.

GEORGE STAPLES lives in Tangier. "Gazelle" is the fourth in a series of stories inspired in that city.

GERALD STERN's new book is *Leaving Another Kingdom: Selected Poems*, published in the USA by Harper & Row. He teaches at the Writer's Workshop at the University of Iowa.

MARK STRAND's new book of poems, *Figure in a Landscape*, was published in the USA by Knopf (1990), together with a new edition of his *Selected Poems*.

MELANIE RAE THON is originally from Montana. Her first novel, *Meteors in August*, was published by Viking in 1990.

WILLIAM TREVOR was born in Cork, Ireland, in 1928. *The Silence in the Garden* (Bodley Head, 1988) won a Sunday Independent (Ireland) Arts Award and was the *Yorkshire Post*'s Book of the Year for 1988. His latest book is *Family Sins and Other Stories* (Bodley Head, 1990).

CHASE TWITCHELL teaches in the creative-writing programme at Princeton. She received a fellowship from the New Jersey State Council on the Arts.

DEREK WALCOTT's books published by Faber and Faber include *The Arkansas Testament* (1988), *Omeros* (1990) and *Collected Poems* (1990).

WILLIAM WEAVER has lived in Italy for many years. He is the Italian arts correspondent for the *Financial Times*. He has written several books on Italian opera and a biography of the actress Eleonora Duse. *Golden Century of Italian Opera from Rossini to Puccini* was published by Thames and Hudson in 1988.

JEANNE WILMOT has been published in numerous literary magazines in the USA and was included in the O. Henry Stories of 1986. She is an attorney in New York and a cofounder of AIDS Helping Hand.

TOBIAS WOLFF's most recent book is *This Boy's Life* (Picador, 1990). *The Stories of Tobias Wolff* (1990), which includes *The Barracks Thief*, is also available in Picador. His other books published in Britain include *Back in the World* (1986) and *The Barracks Thief* (1987), both published by Cape.

CHARLES WRIGHT lives in Charlottesville, Virginia. He is the author of *Lone Journals*. His next book, *The World of the 10,000 Things*, is forthcoming.

ADAM ZAGAJEWSKI is one of Poland's finest young poets. A book of his poetry, *Tremor*, was published by Collins Harvill in 1988. His collection of essays, *Solidarity, Solitude*, is available in the USA from Ecco.

ANTÆUS
JOURNALS, NOTEBOOKS AND DIARIES

Since 1970 *Antæus* has established itself as one of the most successful and distinguished international literary magazines in the world. Now, special issues of the magazine will be published as substantial paperbacks. The first of these celebrates the journal as prose genre: V.S. Naipaul's "Congo River Journal" gets its first British publication; Paul Bowles sends despatches from Tangier; Tess Gallagher and Raymond Carver meet Edmund White in Paris; Oliver Sacks blows the dust off his youth; Edna O'Brien goes to a cockfight in Mexico; and Edward Hoagland learns to eat soup. Other contributors include Annie Dillard, Mary Gordon, M.F.K. Fisher, Jim Harrison, Ursula Le Guin, Norman Mailer, Stephen J. Pyne, Mordecai Richler, Charles Simic and Stephen Spender.

"A gallery for the best imaginative writers in the USA and abroad"
TOBIAS WOLFF

"The touchstone of the highest standard in new literature"
NADINE GORDIMER

ANTÆUS
LITERATURE AS PLEASURE

Twenty writers whose own work has given enormous enjoyment revel in the pleasure of reading.

"The big time came after lights out! Cuddled in my bed, I covered myself, head inclusive, with a blanket, from under the mattress I fished out an electric torch, and then indulged in the pleasures of reading, reading, reading. . ." JOSEF ŠKVORECKÝ

"I learned to read – I mean learned to read carefully – in 1969, when I was twenty-five years old. I was in graduate school then and trying to figure out if I should begin to write short stories. . ." RICHARD FORD

"It might be argued that reading constitutes the keenest, because most secret, sort of pleasure. And that it's a pleasure best savoured by night: by way of an ideal insomnia" JOYCE CAROL OATES

"I like to read. Reading, say, the latest Elmore Leonard gives me pleasure. Reading Dostoevsky gives me pleasure too. Is there a qualitative difference between these two experiences?"
MADISON SMARTT BELL

ANTÆUS
ON NATURE

"We shall never fully understand nature (or ourselves), and certainly never respect it, until we dissociate the wild from the notion of usability"
                                                                                    JOHN FOWLES

The thirty writers who here discuss man's relationship with the natural world in all its aspects, from the study of nature in the past, through fieldwork, to Western man's sense of alienation from nature, include: Italo Calvino on Pliny's *Natural History*; Edward Hoagland on the great naturalist, John Muir; Annie Dillard on experiencing a total eclipse; Edward O. Wilson on an electrical storm over the Amazon; John Rodman on dolphins; Keith Basso on the Western Apaches; and John Fowles on the myth of the Green Man of the Woods

"Confirms that today's most exciting work is not being done in fiction but in essays, memoirs and travel writings. *On Nature* presents a feast in four courses . . . and landmark collection of splendid writing" *New York Times Book Review*

"A magnificent omnibus of nature writing from Pliny to Annie Dillard"
                                                                                    Kirkus

"A host of fine nature writers, many of whom do double service as scientists, poets, and novelists, participate in this . . . outstanding topical reader"   *Booklist*

Peter Matthiessen

NONFICTION

THE SNOW LEOPARD

**Winner of the US National Book Award
and the American Book Award**

Peter Matthiessen went in search of the elusive and beautiful snow leopard and returned with one of the most celebrated accounts in our time of the bonds between man and nature.

"Matthiessen's triumph is a book that will outlive him. It is a masterpiece"   JOHN HILLABY

"An enchantment, and an extraordinarily rich book . . . powerful in its descriptions and arresting in its spiritual content"   *Horizon*

THE CLOUD FOREST
A Chronicle of the South American Wilderness

"His book deserves as long a life as the records of such earlier naturalists as Darwin, Bates and Hudson"   *New York Herald Tribune*

"Beautifully told . . . Anyone who reads this book is almost certain to be infected with jungle fever and a desire to explore the wild, neglected continent to the south"   ROGER TORY PETERSON

"A completely delightful book. Beneath the clean, dry, straightforward prose, there is an extraordinary perception"   *New York Times*

UNDER THE MOUNTAIN WALL
A Chronicle of Two Seasons in Stone Age New Guinea

"*The Cloud Forest* and *Under the Mountain Wall* depict man and nature with unusual perceptiveness and with dramatic power, in a prose notable for vividness and control"   ROBERT PEN WARREN

"A superb writer . . . a classic"   *Harper's*

"One thinks of Darwin's *Voyage of the HMS Beagle*. But Matthiessen is a better writer than Darwin and infinitely more imaginative"
Atlanta Journal

Peter Matthiessen

FICTION

AT PLAY IN THE FIELDS
OF THE LORD

"Expertly crafted and sometimes deeply affecting . . . an entertainment full of glittering colour, nose-to-nose conflict and heroic gestures"
Washington Post

"This is naturalistic reporting of incredibly moving and disturbing dimensions . . . A remarkable performance"   *San Francisco Chronicle*

"A large and powerful novel that is simultaneously a tale of violent adventure and a parable"   *Time*

FAR TORTUGA

"Beautiful and original . . . a resonaant and symbolical story of nine doomed men who dream of an earthly paradise as the world winds down around them"   *Newsweek*

"*Far Tortuga* is a singular experience, a series of moments captured whole and rendered with a clarity that quickens the blood . . From its opening moment, the reader senses that the narrative itself is the recapitulation of a cosmic process, as though the author had sought to link his storytelling with the eye of creation"   *New York Times*

"This novel is Matthiessen at his best – a masterfully spun yarn, a little other-worldly, a dreamlike momentum . . . Like everything of his, it is also a deep declaration of love for the planet"   THOMAS PYNCHON

ON THE RIVER STYX
& OTHER STORIES

"These compelling tales of elemental fear and ever-pressing silence culminate in the great, dark and desperate final story, a masterful piece of work by one of our best writers"   DON DELILLO

"Peter Matthiessen is an original and powerful artist who has produced as impressive a body of work as that of any writer of our time"
WILLIAM STYRON

"A wonderful collection by one of our few genuine masters"
THOMAS McGUANE

"Matthiessen spins these yarns with hard luminosity and edgy clarity. The reader is at once disturbed, enchanted and enlightened"   *Blitz*

Harvill Paperbacks are published by Harvill,
an Imprint of HarperCollins *Publishers*

1. Giuseppe Tomasi di Lampedusa *The Leopard*
 2. Boris Pasternak *Doctor Zhivago*
 3. Alexander Solzhenitsyn *The Gulag Archipelago 1918-1956*
 4. Jonathan Raban *Soft City*
 5. Alan Ross *Blindfold Games*
 6. Joy Adamson *Queen of Shaba*
 7. Vasily Grossman *Forever Flowing*
 8. Peter Levi *The Frontiers of Paradise*
 9. Ernst Pawel *The Nightmare of Reason*
10. Patrick O'Brian *Joseph Banks*
11. Mikhail Bulgakov *The Master and Margarita*
12. Leonid Borodin *Partings*
13. Salvator Satta *The Day of Judgement*
14. Peter Matthiessen *At Play in the Fields of the Lord*
15. Alexander Solzhenitsyn *The First Circle*
16. Homer, translated by Robert Fitzgerald *The Odyssey*
17. George MacDonald Fraser *The Steel Bonnets*
18. Peter Matthiessen *The Cloud Forest*
19. Theodore Zeldin *The French*
20. Georges Perec *Life A User's Manual*
21. Nicholas Gage *Eleni*
22. Eugenia Ginzburg *Into the Whirlwind*
23. Eugenia Ginzburg *Within the Whirlwind*
24. Mikhail Bulgakov *The Heart of a Dog*
25. Vincent Cronin *Louis and Antoinette*
26. Alan Ross *The Bandit on the Billiard Table*
27. Fyodor Dostoyevsky *The Double*
28. Alan Ross *Time Was Away*
29. Peter Matthiessen *Under the Mountain Wall*
30. Peter Matthiessen *The Snow Leopard*
31. Peter Matthiessen *Far Tortuga*
32. Jorge Amado *Shepherds of the Night*
33. Jorge Amado *The Violent Land*
34. Jorge Amado *Tent of Miracles*
35. Torgny Lindgren *Bathsheba*
36. Antæus *Journals, Notebooks & Diaries*
37. Edmonde Charles-Roux *Chanel*
38. Nadezhda Mandelstam *Hope Against Hope*
39. Nadezhda Mandelstam *Hope Abandoned*
40. Raymond Carver *Elephant and Other Stories*
41. Vincent Cronin *Catherine, Empress of All the Russias*
42. Federico de Roberto *The Viceroys*